Encyclopedia of
WORLD COOKERY

Encyclopedia of

WORLD COOKERY

ELIZABETH CAMPBELL

SPRING BOOKS

First published 1958; Tenth impression 1968
© Paul Hamlyn Ltd. 1968
Published by
SPRING BOOKS

Hamlyn House · The Centre · Feltham · Middlesex
Printed in Czechoslovakia by Tisk, Brno
T 1945

Contents

Introduction

For years I have collected foreign recipes, some from my own travels, some drawing on the experience of friends. The simplicity and variety of foreign cooking, as well as its excellence, seemed something I would like to share with a wider audience than my own circle of friends, and consequently I thought of enlarging my collection sufficiently to justify a new book of international recipes. It wasn't hard to do this — the difficulty, where so much is good, is deciding what to leave out.

The thing about good cooking is that it is creative and imaginative, but not difficult technically — so that with a little guidance and encouragement any ordinary person with a liking for food can become an excellent, instead of an ordinary, cook. I haven't included chefs' recipes, triumphs of decoration and elaboration which would be out of place in an ordinary home. They are a different kind of thing altogether, requiring years of training and practice. I have concentrated on dishes which can be made by anyone with a minimum knowledge of the basic techniques of the kitchen. And I have included a few hints about these techniques which I have gained by experience, and which do not always appear in the books.

The meals I have eaten abroad and which have left the most abiding memory fall into this same category. They are not the grand hotel meals which are much the same the world over, but the meals served deliciously in station buffets or unexpectedly in student restaurants. Coming back from the Engadine once, where we had been staying in a hotel which was a gastronome's paradise of *truite au bleu* and *profiteroles* in creamy chocolate sauce, we stopped in Zürich before catching the night train for England. One of our party had been a student there and remembered a students' restaurant in a back street which he thought had been good. He suggested that we should try to find it. After a search we reached the place, in the corner of a tiny square, up a steep hill. We had an excellent soup and then *Wiener Schnitzel* fried to such a nicety and with such a perfectly right coating of egg and breadcrumbs that it fulfilled the demands of the exacting Viennese in this matter. A *Schnitzel* to be satisfactory, they say, should be so dry that you could sit on it and rise without a grease stain on your trousers. With the *Schnitzel* we had a green salad with French dressing. Doubtless we had cheese afterwards, but the perfection of the *Schnitzel* effaced the memory of the rest of the meal. The best meals are often the simplest: good ingredients perfectly cooked and perfectly accompanied can more than hold their own with all the pink sauces coating indifferent fillets of sole and hiding under a fancy foreign name.

I once ate a dinner at a friend's flat in Paris of similar simple excellence — this time it was a *tournedos*, grilled, and topped with a pat of very fresh butter. The trick that transformed this from any ordinary steak, my friend told me, was that it was rubbed with butter not only before it was cooked, but once during its grilling as well. A lemon cream of the most melting kind ended this meal — a lemon cream made with whipped cream, lemon juice, sugar and egg yolks, ingredients not difficult to come by, but exquisitely blended on this occasion.

One of the most vivid food memories of my life comes from a holiday spent when I was ten with friends in Normandy. We were camping and usually we ate miraculously well considering the torrential downpour that memory tells me prevailed throughout my stay. We had a potato soup, the taste of which I can still recall with pleasure. But the vivid memory is not of the good soup, but of the apprehensive excitement with which we all got ready to dine with the owner of the farm, whose wife was going to give us octopus for dinner. Alas, the apprehension was justified; octopus on this occasion turned out to be just the hard rubbery lumps of flesh we had expected. But the tables were turned twenty years later when spending another holiday with the same hosts, but this time in the South of France. Cooking facilities were primitive in the tiny peasant's cottage near Marseilles which we shared, but the food was uniformly excellent and particularly memorable were the baby octopus or *poulpes* cooked with rice which we had one day for lunch.

Similar memories come flooding back from Greece where the food is not uniformly good — the Western stomach finds some difficulty in accommodating itself to an endless diet of warm fat mutton (the Greeks, being often too poor to own ovens of their own, have their food cooked in the baker's oven, and this accounts for their food never being really hot). But sometimes the staple *mousaka* becomes more than minced mutton with tomato sauce. And in Greece, as indeed in all Mediterranean countries, all the fruit is of a quality unknown in harsher northern climates. I have eaten melons, from which the inside has been scooped and which have been stuffed with any other fruit in season, which seemed the most exquisite food man could expect to eat.

Food, as everything else, depends so much not only on being perfect of its kind, but also on being of a kind suitable to the time and place. I remember reading a description in a book of two bachelors meeting in the war and sharing a meal of fresh boiled eggs, fresh bread with farmhouse butter and strawberry jam. There was no doubt in their minds that, eaten in those circumstances, this simple meal was better than a banquet. Much of the food in this book has been devised for other climates than our own. Provided, however, that one does not make the mistake of eating the rather heavy kind of food devised by the Dutch and Germans for their cold winters, during a heat wave, or a light and appetising Mediterranean salad meal on a cold winter's night, other people's food is surprisingly adaptable.

Most of the ingredients mentioned are easily available at home. We can learn to make the best use of the cheap staple foods of other lands. Italian *pasta* — spaghetti, ravioli, tagliatelli — with suitable sauces provide splendid, satisfying and most inexpensive meals. Similarly Italian *risotto*, rice cooked with fish, meat or vegetables, if properly cooked is simple and delicious. French *cassoulet* — haricot beans, cooked with boiling sausage, onion and tomato — is most nourishing and very tasty. I could elaborate the list considerably, but I hope readers will experiment at my suggestion and find out for themselves.

The space given to each country represented has been allotted according to two principles. I have considered firstly the availability of the necessary ingredients and suitability for home cooking. These two necessarily very often coincide; we cannot easily get whale blubber and undoubtedly would not like it if we could. Secondly I have been influenced by the variety and genius in the culinary arts of each country. For various historical reasons the Austrians outclass the Germans in this field despite similar geographical and climatic conditions, and therefore I have included more recipes from Austria. For similar reasons I have included more recipes from France than from any other single country. There can be no question that French cooking is the subtlest, the most imaginative and the most varied in the world, and consequently it is from the French that we can learn most.

There is a widely held popular view that French cooking is elaborate and difficult. This is a misconception arising partly from a confusion between *haute cuisine* and the cooking of the ordinary French housewife. 'French cooking' is restaurant cooking, showy and sometimes grandiose. The cooking of the French housewife is like that of the housewife anywhere else, except that she is more attentive and imaginative, so that what might be a commonplace dish in other lands is transformed by the loving care with which it is seasoned and flavoured. There is no difficulty about making a sauce flavoured with cider, capers, and rosemary to serve with pork chops, but it lifts the dish from the realms of ordinary food to something worthy of our guests. This raises the question of time and trouble. There is no doubt that good cooking demands both, but since even an indifferent meal cannot be achieved without spending a certain amount of time and energy — even a tin opener has to be washed up — one might as well spend a little bit more to achieve really good results. Very often, however, the demands made are on imagination and thought rather than on time. It takes no longer to make the kind of pastry needed for French apple tart than English; it takes only the imagination and energy to try a new recipe rather than use one already well known.

Many, probably most, of the recipes in this book do not require any ingredients other than those generally at hand in every kitchen supplemented by a few less usual spices. The most frequent exception to this rule is wine. Almost all foreign cookery demands the use of wine with many meat dishes, even such comparatively simple ones as *spaghetti bolognaise*. This is not really a great difficulty: cooking wine is quite inexpensive and a little goes a long way. If you keep two bottles of cheap wine, one white and one red, and cork them carefully after use, they will last a long time as the amount used in each dish is very little. And you will be amply rewarded by the results.

Olive oil is another ingredient which may not be in the average store cupboard. This is one of the things which it pays to buy in large quantities — a gallon at a time is ideal. It does not deteriorate in any way and the financial saving compared with buying small quantities at a time is enormous.

Cooking with cream presents rather greater difficulties, and I think can only be seriously considered for special occasions. Some dishes can be made with the top of the milk instead, but there is no substitute for the real thing. Evaporated milk and synthetic creams are worse than useless: the first has a strong taste of its own which is discernible through the strongest flavourings, and the second has a texture quite different from natural cream. The only exception to this rule is where a recipe calls for sour cream. Here I have used yoghourt and smetana with a fair degree of success, but again they have perceptible individual flavours. Apart from cream, however, none of the ingredients is prohibitively expensive. Wine, olive oil, nuts, olives, spices can all be added to a dish for a fraction of the cost of the basic meat or fish, and make all the difference to the quality of the dish.

If, for any reason, you are forced to use substitutes for the original ingedients, do not use the classic name for the dish. An approximation to *boeuf stroganoff* can be made with yoghourt, but it must be recognized that it is not the real thing. Failure to accept this rule leads to the debasement of such great classic dishes as *sole véronique* or *crêpes suzette* and a consequent diminution of standards.

It always pays to buy the best possible basic ingredients you can afford and to use them suitably. However good the sauce, nothing will disguise poor meat or fish. If, as so often happens nowadays, one cannot afford fillet steak, it is best to abandon the idea of fried meat and make a dish of braised meat or a risotto.

In planning a meal for guests there are two things to be borne in mind. The first, and I think the more difficult to observe, is not to allow yourself to become over-enthusiastic and ambitious. Never try out more than one new dish in one meal. Never have more than one dish which needs last-minute preparation. No one can enjoy a meal at which the hostess appears hot and exhausted from the efforts of creation. Secondly, make sure that the meal is properly balanced. If the sweet is to be rich let the main course be simple. If your main dish is ambitious let it be preceded by grapefruit or a simple hors-d'oeuvre and followed by fruit and cheese. But if there is no sweet, serve plain chocolate with the coffee, so as to round off the meal properly.

Almost all the recipes give quantities for four people. Obviously the amounts will vary a bit according to the size of the appetites and what other dishes are to make part of the meal.

The essential quality in a good cook is a taste for good food. If you like good food, and are prepared to take a little trouble in preparing it, you will be sure of an appreciative audience for these recipes when you try them out.

Some useful facts and figures

COMPARISON OF ENGLISH AND AMERICAN
WEIGHTS AND MEASURES

English weights and measures have been used throughout this book. 3 teaspoonfuls equal 1 tablespoon. The average English teacup is ¼ pint or 1 gill. The average English breakfast cup is ½ pint or 2 gills.

When cups are mentioned in recipes they refer to a B. S. I. measuring cup which holds ½ pint or 10 fluid ounces. The B. S. I. standard tablespoon measures 1 fluid ounce.

In case it is wished to translate any of the weights and measures into their American, Canadian or French counterparts, the following tables give a comparison.

Liquid Measure

The most important difference to be noted is that the American pint is 16 fluid ounces, as opposed to the British Imperial pint and Canadian pint which are 20 fluid ounces. The American ½-pint measuring cup is therefore actually equivalent to two-fifths of a British pint.

Solid Measure

ENGLISH		AMERICAN
1 lb. Butter or other fat		2 cups
1 lb. Flour		4 cups
1 lb. Granulated or Castor Sugar		2 cups
1 lb. Icing or Confectioners' Sugar		3 cups
1 lb. Brown (moist) Sugar		2½ cups
1 lb. Golden Syrup or Treacle		1 cup
1 lb. Rice		2 cups
1 lb. Dried Fruit		2 cups
1 lb. Chopped Meat (finely packed)		2 cups
1 lb. Lentils or Split Peas		2 cups
1 lb. Coffee (unground)		2½ cups
1 lb. Soft breadcrumbs		4 cups
½ oz. Flour	1 level tablespoon*	
1 oz. Flour	1 heaped tablespoon	
1 oz. Sugar	1 level tablespoon	
½ oz. Butter	1 level tablespoon	
1 oz. Golden Syrup or Treacle	1 level tablespoon	
1 oz. Jam or Jelly	1 level tablespoon	

* must be standard measuring tablespoon

FRENCH WEIGHTS AND MEASURES

·It is difficult to convert to French measures with absolute accuracy, but 1 oz. is equal to approximately 30 grammes, 2 lb. 3 oz. to 1 kilogramme. For liquid measure, approximately $1\frac{3}{4}$ English pints may be regarded as equal to 1 litre; 1 demilitre is half a litre, and 1 décilitre is one-tenth of a litre.

OVEN TEMPERATURES

	Electricity °F.	Gas Regulo	°C.
COOL oven	225 to 250	O to $\frac{1}{2}$	104 to 121
VERY SLOW oven	250 to 275	$\frac{1}{2}$ to 1	121 to 135
SLOW oven	275 to 300	1 to 2	135 to 149
VERY MODERATE oven	300 to 350	2 to 3	149 to 177
MODERATE oven	375	4	190
MODERATELY HOT oven	400	5	204
HOT oven	425 to 450	6 to 7	218 to 233
VERY HOT oven	475 to 500	8 to 9	246 to 260

Note. This table is an approximate guide only. Different makes of cooker vary and if you are in any doubt about the setting it is as well to refer to the manufacturer's temperature chart.

To convert °F. to °C., subtract 32° and multiply by $\frac{5}{9}$.
To convert °C. to °F., multiply by $\frac{9}{5}$ and add 32°.

The Tools of the Trade

Knives: Good, very sharp knives are essential and save both time and temper. The size and type of these is largely a matter of personal choice, but it is a good idea to keep one special one for vegetable peeling and one for cutting up meat. If you have a dual-purpose knife for these, it has to be constantly washed between operations. It is also as well to keep a separate knife for cutting garlic, so that there is no danger of inadvertently cutting butter with the same knife. A palette knife is also essential.

Spoons. A large number of wooden spoons of different shapes and sizes must be kept for different purposes. Small ones with one flattened edge are invaluable for sauces as they can get into the edges of the pan. A perforated metal draining spoon is useful for poaching eggs, removing dumplings when cooked, etc.

Boards: Pastry-board, bread-board, chopping-board are all essential. It is most unwise to try to make one do the work of another.

Mechanical Aids: I have found the Mouli range of food mills invaluable. The *passe-vite*, provided with three different-sized sieves, saves endless time in sieving soups, etc. The mouli-grater, a small and most inexpensive tool, saves hours when grating cheese and the *parsmint* halves the time taken chopping parsley, lemon-peel and so on. A mincer and an egg whisk are the only other mechanical aids which I regard as essential, but I have no doubt that the electric mixer with its infinite variety of attachments will within measurable time come to be regarded as equally essential. It can save both time and trouble and bring certain dishes which are arduous to prepare within the range of the shorthanded housewife.

Storage Jars: Get small glass jars with screw tops in which to keep spices and dried herbs, and bigger ones for fresh herbs. Fresh herbs, like fresh salad, will keep very well for some time in an airtight jar.

Cooking Vessels: At least one heavy saucepan, which can be quite small, is essential for sauces, otherwise they stick to the pan. A fairly small pan with rounded sides kept specially for omelettes and pancakes is a great help.

Invest in an enamelled cast-iron cooking pot with a lid. This makes it possible to fry onions and meat for stews in a pan which can be transferred to the oven and saves dirtying two receptacles.

Kitchen Scales: I find the Tala measuring cup, which is very inexpensive and universally obtainable, far more convenient than scales for all but large-scale jam making operations.

Australia
and
New Zealand

COOKING IN AUSTRALIA
AND NEW ZEALAND

Both these countries are lands of sunshine and open air life, of wide open spaces with rich natural resources. The people are friendly and hospitable, fond of sport and outdoor life and consequently good hearty eaters.

Basically their culinary traditions are based on their mother country England, and the national kitchen is very similar to that of England. The great difference is that they eat much more meat and less starchy foods. Wouldn't anybody forgo all the potatoes and pies if they had freshly killed New Zealand lamb or prime Australian beef offered to them instead? Butter and all kinds of tropical fruits like avocado and pineapples are all used generously in the Australian kitchen. Added to the agricultural richness of these countries you also have the fact that they are both relatively sparsely populated by European standards and therefore home entertaining forms an important part of the life of most people. You must offer a huge meal to your guests when they come to see you from a long distance. All these factors result in a wholesome, countrified and rich cookery.

When we think of canapés, most of us imagine tiny tit-bits, really just enough to make your drink go down more easily. Not so the Australians. Come-again Canapés are king-sized and satisfying — so good that everybody will want to come again! You will find the same hospitable opulence in many of these dishes, especially the Carpet-bag Steak and the Wahgunyah Steak Casserole.

Australian puddings and cakes too are made with a large hungry family or party in view. Apple Honey Sponge is slightly reminiscent of the American upside-down cake, and the lovely mixture of apples and honey makes it a most warming dessert. Boomerang Chocolate Cake has many virtues apart from its delightful name: it is a rich homely cake, very economical to make and easy to prepare.

There are so many households in both Australia and New Zealand where one cannot just rush out and buy a family block of ice cream, that inevitably they have mastered the art of making really fine home-made ice creams. The two recipes in this section are well worth following.

VEGETABLE DUMPLING SOUP

2 *carrots*
1 *onion*
1 *turnip*
1 *potato*
3 *sticks celery*
1½ *pints meat stock*
2 *teaspoons salt*
1 *teaspoon meat extract*

For soup, dice vegetables and simmer with stock, salt, meat and meat extract for 1 hour. Then add dumplings, which are made by rubbing cooking fat into sifted flour, salt and baking powder adding minced vegetables and mixing to a stiff dough with the milk. Roll into small balls, place in boiling soup and cook for 20 minutes with the lid on.

DUMPLINGS:

6 *oz. flour*
2 *teaspoons baking powder*
2 *oz. cooking fat*
pinch salt
2 *oz. finely minced carrot, onion*
   and celery mixed
¼ *pint milk*

FRIED EGGPLANT

2 *eggplants (aubergines)*
2 *cloves garlic*
3 *oz. breadcrumbs*
1 *egg*
2 *tablespoons milk*
1 *oz. butter*
salt and pepper

Cut eggplant into half-inch slices. Crush garlic and mix with breadcrumbs, salt and pepper. Dip slices of eggplant in beaten egg and milk and coat with the breadcrumb mixture. Melt butter in a pan and fry the eggplant until golden brown on both sides.

COME-AGAIN CANAPÉS

10 *slices bread*
2 *oz. butter*
2 *egg whites*
6 *oz. cheese*
2 *oz. finely chopped green pepper*
salt and pepper
1 *teaspoon chopped parsley*
3 *slices bacon*

Using a 2-inch cutter, cut bread into 20 rounds. Toast on one side only and brush the untoasted side with melted butter. Beat the egg whites stiffly, and fold in grated cheese, chopped parsley, chopped pepper and salt and pepper. Sprinkle with finely chopped bacon and cook under a hot grill for about 10 minutes until the bacon cooks and the cheese melts. Serve at once, garnished with parsley sprigs.

TOM UGLY'S RICE

1 16-oz. can stewed steak
1 can tomatoes
3 oz. seeded raisins
1 packet cashew nuts
6 oz. rice
3 tablespoons olive oil
1 onion
1 clove garlic
1 pint stock
salt and cayenne pepper

Heat oil, add rice and cook slowly in a heavy saucepan, stirring occasionally until lightly browned. Add chopped onion and garlic, cook for a few more minutes then add stock, steak, tomatoes, raisins, salt and pepper. Mix well and turn into a covered casserole. Cook in a moderately hot oven for 15 minutes. Remove lid, scatter with cashew nuts and cook for a further 10 minutes without lid.

CARPET-BAG STEAK

4 lb. piece of topside beef

STUFFING:
12 oz. butter
12—18 oysters
1 lb. mushrooms
1 tablespoon chopped parsley
6 oz. breadcrumbs
grated rind of ½ lemon
salt and paprika pepper
1 egg

Heat butter and toss oysters and roughly chopped mushrooms in it. Cook for 5 minutes. Transfer to a bowl and mix in breadcrumbs, parsley, lemon rind and seasoning. Add beaten egg, then press mixture into pocket in steak and sew or skewer edges together. Roast in a slow oven for 2 hours. Serve with roast potatoes and pumpkin.

WAHGUNYAH STEAK CASSEROLE

1 16-oz. can stewed steak
2 tablespoons tomato purée
1 apple
1 large onion
3 stalks celery
1 tablespoon Worcester Sauce
½ pint stock
8 oz. mashed potato
onion salt
2 oz. butter
1 oz. cooking fat

Peel, core and slice apple, onion and celery. Heat fat in a pan and sauté vegetables until golden brown. Add steak, tomato purée, Worcester sauce and stock and allow to simmer for 15 minutes. Beat mashed potato with butter and onion salt, and pipe round the edge of a shallow fireproof dish. Pile meat mixture into centre and bake in a moderate oven until potato is golden brown.

LAMB CHOPS IN PAPILLOTE

4 *loin chops lamb*
2 *hard-boiled eggs*
1½ *oz. fresh breadcrumbs*
1 *small clove garlic*
½ *teaspoon salt*
pinch pepper
1 *tablespoon chopped parsley*
1½ *oz. melted butter*

Chop the hard-boiled eggs finely, and mix with the breadcrumbs, chopped garlic, seasoning, parsley and melted butter. Coat each chop with this, then wrap in a piece of foil or greaseproof paper. Bake in a hot oven for 25—30 minutes. Open the foil, place the chops in grill pan and grill until golden brown.

BANANA BEEF STEAK

1½ *lb. fillet steak*
1½ *oz. butter*
1 *egg yolk*
3 *bananas*
1 *onion*
1 *gill cream*
1 *tablespoon flour*
salt and pepper
egg and breadcrumbs to coat
½ *teaspoon horseradish sauce*
parsley for garnish

Cut the meat into thin flat pieces about 3 inches long. Fry in butter for 6—8 minutes until cooked. Keep hot while you prepare sauce and fried bananas. Stir in the cream and horseradish, then the egg yolk. Cook gently, stirring all the time. Cut the bananas in half lengthways, dip in flour, salt and pepper, egg and breadcrumbs and fry in butter. Pour the hot sauce over the steak, and garnish with the fried bananas and parsley.

GUARD OF HONOUR

2 *best end necks lamb*
   (6 cutlets on each)
orange for garnish

ORANGE STUFFING:

2 *oz. butter*
1 *small onion*
8 *oz. breadcrumbs*
2 *egg yolks*
1 *dessertspoon chopped parsley*
2 *oranges*
salt and pepper

Trim the meat, leaving 1½ inches of clean bone at the end of each cutlet. Interlace the bones and skewer the meat to form an arch. Fill the centre with orange stuffing. Roast in a moderately hot oven allowing 25 minutes to the lb. and 25 extra minutes. Put cutlet frills on top of the bones, and garnish with slices of orange. To make stuffing melt the butter and fry the finely chopped onion in it until soft but not brown. Add to the breadcrumbs with other ingredients and mix to a soft consistency.

SAVOURY RABBIT

1 rabbit, jointed
4 oz. breadcrumbs
1 onion, chopped
parsley
thyme
8 rashers streaky bacon
½ pint milk
salt
pepper

Blanch the rabbit in boiling water with 1 tablespoon salt for 30 minutes. Cut the flesh from the bones. Mix the breadcrumbs with the onion and chopped herbs, season with salt and pepper. Line a pie dish with the breadcrumb mixture and then fill it with alternate layers of rabbit and breadcrumbs. Cover with the bacon rashers, pour in the milk. Put a lid on the dish and bake in a moderate oven for 2 hours, adding more milk if necessary.

HERRING CHOWDER

1 large onion, chopped
1 oz. butter
2 medium potatoes, thinly sliced
¼ pint milk
4 cream crackers, crushed
4 cooked herrings, filleted
salt
pepper

Cook the onion in the butter until transparent. Add the potatoes and ¼ pint of boiling water. Simmer until the potatoes are tender. Add the milk, biscuit crumbs and seasoning. Simmer for 5 minutes. Stir in the herrings. Serve very hot.

AUSTRALIAN SUMMER SALAD

1 cup each diced celery, apple,
    cucumber
2 tablespoons orange juice
8 slices cooked ham
4 tomatoes
lettuce
mayonnaise

Roll up the ham slices. Mix together diced celery, apple, cucumber and orange juice. Pile in the centre of a large dish and surround with lettuce leaves, sliced tomato and rolled ham. Serve with plenty of mayonnaise.

ORANGE AND CUCUMBER JELLY

½ pint orange juice
1 tomato
1 medium-sized cucumber
1 orange
1 tablespoon gelatine

Dissolve gelatine in ¼ pint hot water. Add orange juice. Slice the orange, cucumber and tomato thinly, and arrange in a small mould, covering the bottom and sides. Pour in the orange gelatine mixture and chill. Turn out carefully onto a bed of lettuce leaves.

ORANGE MERINGUE PIE

1 *cooked flan case*
  (use pastry in Passion Fruit
  Flan recipe, page 20)
¾ *pint orange juice*
grated rind of 1 orange
2 *tablespoons cornflour*
8 *oz. sugar*
3 *eggs*

Heat 4 oz. sugar in top of a double saucepan. Mix in the cornflour, then add orange juice, grated rind and finally the beaten egg yolks. Heat without boiling, stirring continually. When really thick remove from heat and cool. Turn into the flan case. Top with meringue made by beating the egg whites until very stiff, then beating in the remaining 4 oz. sugar. Pile meringue all over the pie and place in a hot oven until golden brown.

PASSION FRUIT CREAM

½ *pint passion fruit pulp*
1 *lemon*
¼ *pint milk*
½ *pint cream*
½ *oz. gelatine*
2 *oz. sugar*

Dissolve gelatine in a little hot water. Sieve the fruit pulp. Whip the cream, then add milk and whip again. Blend in gelatine, passion fruit and lemon juice. Pour into a mould to set.

FRUIT SALAD PAVLOVA

4 *egg whites*
8 *oz. castor sugar*
vanilla
fruit salad with liqueur to taste
ice cream
¼ *pint double cream*
8 *oz. raspberries*

Beat the egg whites very stiffly, fold in the sugar, flavour with vanilla pod or essence. Line the base and sides of a tart tin with greased greaseproof paper. Put the meringue mixture in the tin, making a depresssion in the centre. Bake in a slow oven for about 2 hours. Turn out of the tin carefully when cold. Fill the depression with drained fruit salad just before serving, top with ice cream, whipped cream and raspberries.

BLACKBERRY PANCAKES

6 *oz. blackberries*
4 *oz. flour*
2 *oz. sugar*
¼ *pint milk*
1 *egg*
2 *oz. butter*

Mix the egg yolk and sugar together, beat in the sifted flour, milk and the blackberries. Add 1 oz. melted butter and fold in the stiffly beaten egg white. Melt a little butter or fat in a frying pan, cook spoonfuls of the mixture on both sides.

PASSION FRUIT FLAN

PASTRY:
2 oz. butter
4 oz. flour
3 oz. sugar
1 egg yolk
½ teaspoon baking powder

FILLING:
½ oz. gelatine
4 oz. sugar
6 oz. cooked passion fruit
fruit and cream to decorate

Rub the butter into the flour, mix to a stiff dough with all the other ingredients and a little milk if necessary. Roll out and cook in a greased pastry tin for 15 minutes in a moderate oven. Fill with the following mixture: dissolve the gelatine in a little water. Sieve the passion fruit, add the sugar to the pulp, stir it into the gelatine. When nearly set pour into the pastry shell, decorate with pieces of passion fruit and whipped cream.

BLACKBERRY FLUFF

1 lb. blackberries
4 oz. sugar
rind and juice of ½ lemon
½ oz. gelatine
3 egg whites

Stew the blackberries with the sugar, a strip of lemon peel and a little water until tender. Pass through a sieve. Dissolve the gelatine in a little water. Pour the fruit purée into it, add the lemon juice and enough water to make 1 pint. Leave in a cold place. When nearly set fold in the stiffly beaten egg whites.

FRUIT CAKE

8 oz. self-raising flour
4 oz. sugar
12 oz. mixed raisins, sultanas
   and currants
2 beaten eggs
4 oz. softened butter
¾ teaspoon mixed spice
scant ¼ pint milk

pinch of nutmeg
pinch of salt

Mix the flour with the sugar and dried fruits. Stir in the eggs and the butter. Add the milk and the spices. Beat all together until thoroughly mixed. Turn into a cake tin lined with greased greaseproof paper. Bake in a slow oven for 2 hours.

PAVLOVA CAKES

2 egg whites
4 oz. sugar
1 oz. cornflour
1 dessertspoon coffee essence
2 oz. chopped nuts

Beat the egg whites stiffly. Fold in the sugar and then the other ingredients. Arrange in small mounds on a lightly greased baking sheet. Cook in a cool oven for 45 minutes.

KIRRIBILLI RAISIN PLAIT

1 *lb. self-raising flour*
pinch salt
4 *oz. butter*
4 *oz. stoned raisins*
2 *oz. glacé cherries*
1 *egg*
½ *pint milk*
1 *tablespoon brown sugar*

Sift flour and salt, and rub in butter with the finger-tips. Add chopped raisins and cherries. Beat egg and milk together and keep 1 tablespoon separate for glazing. Add egg and milk to dry ingredients (except sugar) and mix to a soft dough. Roll out on a floured board to a sausage shape, then cut into three strips and plait. Place on a greased tin, brush with egg and milk and sprinkle with brown sugar. Bake in a hot oven for 20—25 minutes. Cool and split and spread with butter.

BUSTERS

8 *oz. flour*
6 *oz. grated cheese*
2 *oz. butter*
cayenne pepper

Rub the butter into the flour, add the grated cheese and a pinch of cayenne pepper. Add a little water and roll out to ¼ inch thick on a floured board. Cut into rounds, prick with a fork, bake on a greased baking sheet for 15 minutes in a hot oven.

ORANGE NUT BREAD

2 *eggs*
8 *oz. sugar*
¼ *pint milk*
12 *oz. flour*
1 *teaspoon salt*
4 *teaspoons baking powder*
1 *oz. butter*

2 *oz. chopped nuts*
peel of 1 orange, chopped

Beat the eggs with the sugar. Sift the flour, salt and baking powder and add them to the eggs and sugar alternately with the milk. Mix in the nuts and orange. Leave to stand for 15 minutes in a greased pan. Bake in a moderate oven for 45 minutes.

CHEESE APPLES

cream cheese
paprika
cloves

Shape the cheese into small balls, roll them in paprika until red all over. Stick a whole clove into one side of the ball and a clove stalk into the other.

WALNUT AND CHEESE TARTLETS

puff pastry made with 8 oz. flour
  (see p. 205)
4 oz. grated cheese
1 egg yolk
salt
pepper
dry mustard
½ oz. butter

2 oz. chopped walnuts
2 egg whites

Blend the grated cheese with the egg yolk. Season with salt, pepper and mustard. Beat in the butter and chopped walnuts. Fold in the stiffly beaten egg whites. Cut the pastry into rounds, put in small greased tart tins, fill with the cheese mixture. Bake in a medium hot oven for 20 minutes.

AUSTRALIAN GEMS

6 oz. flour
1 oz. butter
2 oz. sugar
1 egg
¼ — ½ pint milk

Cream butter and sugar, then beat in egg, milk and sifted flour. Put into greased gem irons (patty tins) and bake for 15 minutes in a hot oven. Serve like scones with butter.

MELON JAM

melon
12 oz. sugar to every lb. prepared
  fruit
lemon juice or ginger

Peel melon and remove seeds. Dice, then place in a large bowl with half the sugar and leave for 12 hours. Add lemon juice or ginger to taste and boil together with the rest of the sugar until the jam is clear and sets immediately. This will take about 4 hours.

ANZACS

4 oz. flour
4 oz. rolled oats
4 oz. desiccated coconut
4 oz. sugar
½ teaspoon baking powder
1 tablespoon golden syrup
4 oz. butter

Mix all the dry ingredients together, stir in the syrup and the melted butter. Roll into small balls and then flatten onto a greased baking tin. Bake in a cool oven for 15 minutes.

APPLE CHUTNEY

3 lb. apples
1 lb. seeded raisins
8 oz. onions
1 lb. tomatoes
2½ lb. brown sugar
4 oz. currants
1 teaspoon cloves
1 oz. chopped preserved ginger
1 dessertspoon made mustard

salt and cayenne pepper
1½ pints vinegar

Peel and core the apples and stew gently in very little water until tender. Chop raisins and onions and skin tomatoes by plunging into boiling water, after which the skin can easily be removed. Put all the ingredients into a saucepan and simmer gently for 1½ hours. Place in sterilized jars and cover.

APPLE HONEY SPONGE

2 lb. apples
4 level tablespoons honey
4 oz. butter
2 oz. sugar
2 eggs
¼ pint milk
8 oz. self-raising flour
pinch salt

Peel and core apples and stew gently with 2 tablespoons honey. When cooked place in a buttered pie dish. Beat butter, sugar and remaining 2 tablespoons honey to a cream, then beat in the eggs one at a time. Add milk, and lastly sifted flour and salt. Cover apples with this sponge mixture and bake in a moderate oven for 20—30 minutes until cooked.

COFFEE FRUIT CAROUSEL

2 eggs
1 pint milk
2 tablespoons coffee essence
2 oz. sugar
2 level tablespoons gelatine
¼ teaspoon vanilla essence
2 oz. chopped blanched almonds
1 16-oz. can pears
1 lb. fresh ripe apricots

Beat egg yolks lightly and add to milk. Heat gently in a double boiler until the mixture coats a spoon. Remove from heat and stir in sugar and coffee essence. Dissolve the gelatine in a little hot water and add to the mixture. Stir well and allow to cool. Then beat egg whites stiffly and fold into the custard with the chopped almonds and vanilla essence. Pour into a ring mould and set in a refrigerator. Turn out mould on serving dish and fill the centre with sliced pears and peeled and stoned apricots. Garnish the outside with more fruit.

BOOMERANG CHOCOLATE CAKE

5 oz. self-raising flour
4 oz. butter
2 level tablespoons coconut
2 level tablespoons cocoa
8 oz. sugar
2 eggs
pinch salt
3 tablespoons milk
few drops vanilla essence

ICING:
6 oz. icing sugar
1 level tablespoon cocoa
3 oz. butter

1 teaspoon coffee essence
few drops vanilla essence
1 tablespoon coconut

Cream together butter, coconut, cocoa and sugar, then add the eggs gradually, beating well. Sieve the flour and salt and beat it in alternately with the milk and vanilla essence. Line the bottom of a greased 7-inch cake tin, pour in the mixture and bake for 40—45 minutes in a moderate oven. To make icing, sift icing sugar and combine with cocoa, melt the butter and add to the sugar with the coffee and vanilla essences. Beat until the icing is smooth. Spread on the cake when cold, and pull the top into peaks. Sprinkle with coconut.

LAMINGTONS

5 oz. butter
7 oz. sugar
½ teaspoon vanilla essence
3 eggs
10 oz. self-raising flour
pinch salt
4 tablespoons milk
raspberry jam

ICING:
7 oz. icing sugar
1 oz. cocoa
3 tablespoons boiling water
6 oz. desiccated coconut

Cream butter, sugar and vanilla essence. Add eggs one by one and beat well. Fold in sifted flour and salt alternately with the milk. Pour mixture into a greased 8-inch square cake tin and bake in a moderate oven for 50—60 minutes. Cool and store in an airtight tin. Next day slit cake through centre and spread with jam. Sandwich together and cut the cake into 2-inch squares. To make icing, blend sifted icing sugar and cocoa and pour over the boiling water. Work together with a wooden spoon, adding more water if necessary. Stand the icing over hot water to keep it thin, then dip the squares of cake in it, using a fork to hold the cake. Toss in coconut, then stand on a wire cake tray to set.

HOME-MADE ICE CREAM (1)

2 egg whites
8 oz. sugar
1 small tin cream
¼ pint fruit juice, liquid
  chocolate or coffee

Beat the egg whites until stiff, slowly adding the sugar. Next beat in the unwhipped cream, and finally the liquid. Pour into trays and place in freezing chamber, with the refrigerator turned to cold.

HOME-MADE ICE CREAM (2)

1 *tin unsweetened condensed milk*
2 *tablespoons sugar*
juice of 1 lemon
2 *teaspoons gelatine*
a little hot water
flavouring

Have the tinned milk already iced. Beat until over twice the original volume. Beat in the sugar, lemon juice and flavouring. Dissolve the gelatine in hot water and stir in last. Pour into trays and place in freezing chamber.

APPLE AND ORANGE JAM

1 *lemon*
4 *navel oranges*
10 *breakfast cups water*
4 *Granny Smith apples*
6 *lb. sugar*

Remove pips from lemon and oranges and slice them. Pour on water and allow to stand overnight. In the morning peel and core apples. Slice them thinly and add to oranges and lemon. Boil 1 hour. Add heated sugar. Put skins and cores into a little water and boil to a jelly; strain and add to jam and cook till it jells. Bottle and seal.

FROZEN PLUM PUDDING

3 *dessertspoons powdered gelatine*
3 *tablespoons cocoa*
1 *lb. mixed dried fruit*
2 *oz. dates*
2 *oz. dried figs*
4 *oz. mixed chopped nuts*
8 *oz. sugar*
1½ *pints milk*
1 *tablespoon rum*
pinch salt

Mix cocoa and 1 pint milk to a smooth consistency. Mix fruit, nuts, dates, figs, sugar and salt together and add these. Boil gently for 5 minutes then allow to cool. Meanwhile soak gelatine in cold water. When ready to use, melt in a very little boiling water. Add to cooled mixture, stirring well, and finally add the rum. Put into a wet mould and set in refrigerator. Turn out when set and decorate with cream and holly.

AVOCADO PEAR SANDWICHES

buttered bread
avocado pears
little vinegar, olive oil, salt,
  pepper, mustard

Avocado pears make a delicious and unusual sandwich filling. Mash the flesh with a fork and mix with just a little of each of the ingredients listed.

PINEAPPLE MINT JULEP

1½ pints pineapple juice
6 oz. sugar
¼ pint lemon juice
1½ pints ginger ale
6 sprigs mint

Bruise the washed mint leaves, then cover with sugar and lemon juice. Leave for 15—20 minutes. Add the chilled pineapple juice and ginger ale and serve with ice in tall glasses. Garnish with more springs of mint.

BANANA FROTH

4 ripe bananas
2 pints chilled milk
2 tablespoons sugar
nutmeg

Mash the bananas with sugar. Gradually add the milk and beat with a rotary whisk until frothy. Pour into tall glasses, add ice and sprinkle with nutmeg. Serve at once.

SWAGS

PASTRY:
1 lb. flour
10 oz. butter
4 tablespoons water
½ teaspoon lemon juice
pinch salt

FILLING:

1 12-oz. can Australian spiced ham
2 rashers bacon
2 oz. raisins
1 red apple
1 tablespoon chopped chives
1 clove garlic (finely chopped)

2 tablespoons red wine
1 egg
salt and cayenne pepper

A good picnic pastry. Sift flour and salt and rub in butter. Mix to a firm dough with water and lemon juice. Roll out and cut into 6-inch squares. Chop bacon, seeded raisins, apple and garlic and combine together all the ingredients for the filling. Place a good tablespoon of filling in the centre of each square of pastry. Gather up the four corners of pastry and twist together in the centre. Wrap round this a ¾-inch strip of pastry moistened with milk to keep in place. Place swags on a baking tray and bake in a moderate oven for 20—25 minutes. Cool on a wire tray. Serve with tomato sauce.

Austria

COOKING IN AUSTRIA

Looking through the recipes of Austria one could almost reconstruct history. There are the basic German dishes, recalling Teutonic domination. Then inevitably the Austro-Hungarian Empire with all its nationalities shows an influence. But they are all interpreted in the light-hearted gay Austrian manner. The Hotel Sacher, famous for its old-world atmosphere, reigns supreme over the gastronomic world of Austria, and radiates its influence over the cookery of the whole country. The various recipes in this chapter may have been originally German like Sauerkraut, or Italian like Ravioli, or Hungarian like Chicken Paprika. It is the interpretation, the light touch which welds them into part of the Austrian heritage.

Soup is an important dish in Austria, sometimes a meal by itself. What could be more cosy than a rich home-made soup on a cold winter's night or as a finale to a late night party? Again, you see the light Austrian touch in the featherweight little garnishings they add to their soups. Any packet-soup will immediately acquire glamour and glitter with a few Austrian Batter Drops or Liver Dumplings. They do not take long to make and they are not expensive. It is the nuances which count in good cooking — such as the salting down of the cucumber before you make a cucumber salad — you'll be amazed at the difference it makes. You could try serving hare prepared the Austrian way next time you have guests to dinner — it has a wonderfully rich game flavour and is so easy to prepare. To say nothing of Wiener Schnitzel, the classic Viennese creation, and a firm favourite with everybody who ever tasted it.

Vienna has always been associated with music, waltzes and gracious living. Also with Apple Strudel, Wiener Schnitzel, Gugelhupf and Sacher Torte. If you have ever travelled in Austria, you can recall the delicious smell of the little cake shops of Vienna and Salzburg, where, under glass cases, dozens of different cakes and pastries fascinate you. With the help of these recipes you can make them all in your own kitchen. It is well worth following the advice of Austrian cooks in using very little flour in cakes. Their chocolate cake, made with more eggs than you feel you ought to use, and replacing flour with ground almonds and breadcrumbs, will win you many praises. Once you overcome the deep-seated fear of working with yeast, you can create the most economical Croissants and Gugelhupf and ask your friends in for a genuine Coffee-klatch.

CABBAGE SOUP

1 *large cabbage*
1 *oz. flour*
1 *oz. dripping*
2 *pints stock*
salt
pepper
8 *small frankfurters*

Remove the hard stalks from the cabbage and shred it. Brown it and the flour in the dripping, pour in the stock, season with salt and pepper. Simmer for 1 hour. Boil the sausages separately, cut them into slices and add to the soup just before serving.

BEEF BROTH

2 *lb. topside*
1 *lb. beef bones or chicken bones and giblets*
4 *onions*
2 *leeks*
4 *celery stalks, including the leaves*
1 *turnip*
1 *cauliflower broken into flowerets*
3 *tomatoes, peeled and quartered*
2 *oz. dripping*
8 *peppercorns*
salt

pepper
parsley

Cut the onions, leeks, celery and turnip into large pieces. Brown them in the dripping, sear the meat in the fat. Add the cauliflower, the tomatoes and the bones. Pour in enough water to cover the contents of the pan. Add salt, peppercorns and parsley. Put a lid on the pan and simmer until the meat is tender (about 3 hours). Remove the meat and the bones, pass the vegetables through a fine sieve. The meat can be served as a separate dish accompanied by freshly cooked vegetables and horseradish sauce.

GOULASH SOUP

8 *oz. shin of beef, cut up very small*
3 *cooked potatoes, diced small*
3 *or 4 onions, sliced*
2 *tablespoons tomato purée*
1½ *oz. dripping*
1 *tablespoon paprika*
½ *tablespoon caraway seeds*

salt
2 *cloves garlic, well crushed*

Brown the onion in the dripping, add the meat and brown it. Add all the other ingredients except the potato. Stir, cover with water and bring to the boil. Simmer the meat until it is tender. Five minutes before serving add the potatoes.

KALTSCHALE (Fruit soup)

1 *lb. berries (raspberries, straw-berries or red or black currants)*
4—6 *oz. sugar*
1½ *pints scalded and chilled milk*

Cook the berries until they are just tender. Pass them through a sieve. Whisk up this fruit purée with the sugar until it is frothy and light. Mix into it the milk. Put it into the refrigerator and serve it very cold.

BREAD SOUP

4 *slices or crusts of stale bread*
2 *pints veal stock*
2 *smoked sausages or large*
  frankfurters
1 *egg yolk*
salt
black pepper
2 *tablespoons parsley fried in butter*
2 *hard-boiled eggs for garnishing*
2 *oz. butter*

Bake the bread crisp. Break it up and put it into a saucepan with the warm stock. Leave it to steep for 15 minutes, season with salt and pepper and simmer for 1 hour. Then sieve it. Beat the egg yolk and mix it quickly with 2 or 3 tablespoons of the hot soup. Add it to the soup, taking care not to let the mixture boil again. Five minutes before serving add the chopped sausages, and add the parsley when serving.

BATTER DROPS

1 *egg*
2—3 *tablespoons milk*
2 *oz. flour*
deep fat for frying
salt

Stir the egg, milk and salt carefully into the flour, keeping the mixture smooth. Beat thoroughly. Adjust milk and flour to make a thick batter. Drip the batter into smoking fat through a coarse grater or perforated spoon. Cook till golden, drain and serve as a garnish for clear soup.

NOODLES

6 *oz. flour*
1 *egg*
1—2 *tablespoons water*
salt

Put the flour and salt in a bowl. Make a well in the centre, break in the egg and mix with a knife, adding the water as required so as to make a stiff dough.
  The resulting dough can be treated in two ways:
1. Press the dough through a coarse sieve or perforated spoon into boiling soup and simmer for
   5 minutes.
2. Roll out very thinly, leave it to dry for 30 minutes. Cut it into narrow strips or squares, leave
   it to dry again for 30 minutes and simmer for
   10 or 15 minutes in soup as required.

LIVER DUMPLINGS

8 *oz. liver, coarsely minced or*
  chopped
4 *oz. stale bread, soaked and*
  squeezed
2 *oz. butter*
1 *small onion, sliced*
salt
black pepper
1 *teaspoon chopped marjoram*
1 *tablespoon chopped parsley*

Gently fry the onions and parsley in the butter. Add the other ingredients and beat well. Leave the mixture to cool. Shape into small round dumplings, adding more breadcrumbs if the mixture is too wet. Drop these into boiling soup and simmer for about 20 minutes.
These dumplings may be varied by pressing the mixture through a very coarse sieve or perforated spoon into the boiling soup and cooking for 3 or 4 minutes.

EEL

1 *medium-sized eel*
½ *pint white wine or cider*
2 *oz. parsley*
salt
pepper

SAUCE:

1 *oz. butter*
2 *mashed hard-boiled egg yolks*
¼ *pint stock*
1 *tablespoon vinegar*
2 *tablespoons chopped parsley*

1 *tablespoon made mustard*
salt
1 *teaspoon sugar*
black pepper

Cut the eel into pieces, salt them well, and stand them in a cold place for 4 hours. Drain off the water, then pack them tightly in a saucepan and add the wine or cider, parsley and the seasoning. Simmer for about 45 minutes or until tender. For the sauce, melt the butter and mix with the other ingredients. Season with salt and pepper. Serve the fish accompanied by the sauce and slices of lemon.

PAPRIKA FISH

2 *lb. fish, preferably carp, but fresh haddock, bass and mackerel are also suitable*
1 *lb. onions, sliced*
4 *oz. butter*
salt

¾ *pint cream*
2 *teaspoons paprika*

Fry the onions lightly in the butter. Put the fish on the onions and add the cream mixed with the paprika, salt and pepper. Bake till tender. Strain the sauce over the fish.

FISH STEW

2 *lb. fish, freshwater if possible*
light stock or water
6 *onions*
2 *teaspoons paprika*
salt
black pepper

2 *oz. butter*
¾ *pint sour cream*

Brown the onions in the butter. Add the fish cut into pieces and the seasoning. Just cover with stock or water and simmer for 1½ hours, stirring carefully to keep the fish pieces whole. Just before serving add the sour cream.

AUSTRIAN CABBAGE

1 *small head of cabbage*
butter or bacon fat
½ *teaspoon salt*
1 *teaspoon paprika*
1 *tablespoon minced onion or crushed clove garlic*
½ *pint sour or sweet cream*

Shred and wash the cabbage. Sauté it lightly in the butter or bacon fat. Add the salt, paprika and onion or garlic. Put it into a baking dish and pour the cream over. Bake in a moderate oven for about 20 minutes.

SAUERKRAUT (How to make it)

12 *firm cabbages*
2 *lb. salt*
peppercorns
juniper berries

Remove all the discoloured outer leaves from hard white cabbages. Quarter them, take out the hard centre stalks and shred. Press a layer of shredded cabbage into a crock and sprinkle with salt, a few juniper berries and peppercorns. Continue filling the crock with alternate layers of cabbage and salt, peppercorns and juniper berries until it is three-quarters full. Press the cabbage down but take care not to break it. Cover it with several thicknesses of butter muslin. Place a lid or plate over it and put a heavy weight on this. After a while fermentation will start and the weighted lid will sink under the salt water. Remove some of the brine but leave enough to cover the lid. The sauerkraut will be ready for use after a month.

When sauerkraut is taken out of the crock, wash the lid and the cloth before replacing them and pour a little fresh water on the cover. Wash the sauerkraut before cooking it so as to get rid of the smell of the fermentation.

SAUERKRAUT (How to cook it)

1 *quart sauerkraut*
1 *oz. butter or bacon fat*
2 *small or 1 large onion, sliced*
1 *medium-sized potato or 1 large tart apple*
enough stock to cover the sauerkraut
1—2 *tablespoons brown sugar (optional)*
1 *teaspoon caraway seed (optional)*

Melt the butter in a large frying pan and sauté the sliced onion in it until transparent. Rinse the sauerkraut and drain it. Add it to the onion and butter and sauté it for 5 minutes. Peel and grate the potato or apple and add it to the sauerkraut. Cover it with the stock. Cook it without a lid for 30 minutes, then cover it and cook it in a moderate oven for a further 30 minutes. Season it with the brown sugar and caraway seeds if desired.

POTATO SALAD

2 *lb. waxy potatoes boiled in their jackets*
1 *tablespoon finely chopped onion*
1 *clove crushed garlic*
2 *tablespoons olive oil*
3 *tablespoons wine vinegar*
salt
pepper

$\frac{3}{4}$ *teaspoon French mustard*
1 *tablespoon parsley to garnish*

Peel and slice the potatoes while still warm. Put them in a salad bowl with the onions, garlic and seasoning. Bring the oil, vinegar and mustard slowly to the boil, pour over the potatoes. Mix carefully. Serve cold, garnished with parsley.

CUCUMBER SALAD

1 *large cucumber*
salt
black pepper
2 *tablespoons chopped parsley*
French dressing (see p. 161)

Peel and slice the cucumber thinly. Sprinkle with salt and leave for 30 minutes. Squeeze gently in a clean cloth to remove the moisture. 15 minutes before serving pour French dressing over it and sprinkle with chopped parsley and black pepper.

LENTIL SALAD

½ *pint stock*
½ *pint lentils*
2 *tablespoons chopped parsley*
1 *tablespoon chopped onions or chives*
French or sour cream dressing (see pp. 36, 161)

Soak the lentils for 2 hours. Cook them gently in the stock until tender. Mix them with the parsley, onions and dressing. Serve cold or warm with sour cream dressing.

CABBAGE SALAD

DRESSING:
1½ *tablespoons wine vinegar*
salt
black pepper
1 *dessertspoon sugar*
few caraway seeds

1 *medium cabbage, raw, cooked or blanched*
12 *oz. chopped fried bacon*

Shred the cabbage finely and pour it over the well-mixed dressing ingredients. Garnish with the bacon.

DUMPLINGS (Nockerl)

8 *oz. flour*
2 *eggs*
3 *oz. melted butter*
salt
water to mix to a stiff dough (about ⅛ pint)

Put the flour and salt into a bowl, make a well in the centre, break in the eggs, stir carefully so as to draw the flour gradually into the eggs, add the melted butter and the water as required. Leave the dough in a cold place for 30 minutes before use. Cut out teaspoonfuls of the mixture with a hot spoon. Cook these for 2 or 3 minutes in boiling water. Rinse them under the cold water tap. Heat them without browning them in butter or dripping. Serve with Goulash, etc.

RAVIOLI

8 *oz. flour*
2 *eggs*
1 *oz. melted butter*
salt
water to mix to a stiff dough
(about ⅛ pint)

Put the flour and salt into a bowl, make a well in the centre, break in the eggs, stir carefully so as to draw the flour gradually into the eggs, add the melted butter and the water as required. Knead the dough thoroughly with the hands. Leave the dough in a cold place for about 30 minutes before use.

Roll out the dough very thinly. Cut it in half. Roll one of the ravioli fillings (see below) into small balls and place these balls on one sheet of the rolled out dough about 2 inches apart from one another. Cover this with the other sheet of dough. Press it down carefully between the balls of filling. Stamp out the ravioli with a biscuit cutter of suitable size. Crimp the edges to make them stick firmly together. Cook them in fast-boiling salted water for 15—20 minutes, according to size. Serve in hot sauce or gravy, with browned butter or with melted butter and cheese.

RAVIOLI FILLING (1) (Cheese)

3 *large floury cooked potatoes*
4 *oz. chopped ham*
6 *oz. cream cheese or equal quantities*
   of cream cheese and thick cream
1 *egg yolk*
salt

black pepper
1 *tablespoon chopped chives*
1 *tablespoon chopped parsley*
1 *tablespoon marjoram*

Sieve the potatoes and blend thoroughly with the other ingredients to make a smooth mixture.

RAVIOLI FILLING (2) (Meat)

8 *oz. finely minced lean pork*
8 *oz. finely minced lean veal*
8 *oz. finely minced lean ham*
1 *egg*
2 *minced carrots*
2 *oz. butter*
salt
black pepper

3 *tablespoons stock*
breadcrumbs

Fry the meat, carrot and seasoning gently in the butter for 5 minutes. Add the stock and continue cooking until the meat is done (about 20—30 minutes). Re-mince the mixture, add the beaten egg and parsley and leave to cool before shaping. If it is too moist to shape when cool, add breadcrumbs as necessary.

RAVIOLI FILLING (3) (Meat)

1½ *lb. finely minced cooked meat*
1 *egg*
1 *small onion, finely chopped*
salt
black pepper
2 *tablespoons chopped parsley*
gravy

Blend the egg, parsley and seasoning with the onions and meat. Moisten with gravy if very dry. Shape into balls.

CHICKEN STUFFING

8 *oz. cooked chopped chicken meat*
2 *oz. butter*
1½ *oz. flour*
¾ *pint white stock or milk*
2 *oz. mushrooms*
salt
pepper

Sauté the mushrooms and chicken gently for 5 minutes in the butter. Remove them from the butter and keep them hot. Make a roux with the butter and flour, add the heated stock gradually to make a very thick sauce. Blend the sauce with the chicken and mushrooms.

MEAT OMELETTE

4 *eggs*
4 *oz. flour*
¼ *pint milk*
4 *oz. chopped ham or leftovers,*
    squares of bacon, etc.
salt, black pepper
chopped parsley to garnish
2 *oz. butter for frying*

Mix the flour, seasoning and meat together in a bowl, make a well in the centre and add the egg yolks and milk gradually to make a smooth batter. Leave to stand for 30 minutes. Fold the stiffly beaten egg whites into the mixture. Melt the butter in a heavy frying pan and pour in the egg mixture when it is just turning colour. Fry gently till brown, turn to brown the other side. Tear the mixture into pieces with two forks and continue frying until evenly coloured on all sides.

STUFFED SAVOURY PANCAKES

3 *large eggs*
3 *oz. flour*
¼ *pint milk*
¼ *pint cream*
2 *oz. butter*
salt
black pepper
butter for frying

Warm the milk, cream and butter together just sufficiently to melt the butter. Beat the eggs into this mixture. Put the flour into a bowl, make a well in the centre, gradually sift in the egg mixture to make a perfectly smooth batter. Leave it to stand for 30 minutes. Fry as usual for pancakes. Stuff with any of the fillings given for Ravioli (see p. 34 and above).

FORCEMEAT FILLING

4 oz. breadcrumbs
2 oz. fine suet
2 oz. ham, minced
2 oz. cooked chicken, veal or pork, minced
1 small egg

2 tablespoons parsley
1 tablespoon sage and thyme chopped
1 tablespoon paprika
salt

Mix all the dry ingredients together, using enough beaten egg to moisten the stuffing.

CHEESE PASTRIES

8 oz. flour
4 oz. butter
4 oz. soft cream cheese
¼ teaspoon salt (optional)

Sift the flour and resift it with the salt. With a knife cut the butter and cream cheese into it. When the dough is well blended wrap it in greaseproof paper and put it in refrigerator for 12 hours. Roll it out on greaseproof paper until it is only ⅛ inch thick. Cut the dough into rounds with a biscuit cutter. Place the rounds on an ungreased baking sheet and cook them in a very hot oven (450° F.) for about 12 minutes. Serve them hot.

HAM AND NOODLES

1 lb. pasta of the flat ribbon type, cooked
2 oz. butter
4 oz. chopped ham
3 eggs
⅓ pint sour cream
salt
pepper
breadcrumbs

Cook the noodles and chopped ham gently in the butter for 5 minutes, season with salt and pepper. Blend the egg yolks with the cream, add the ham and noodles. Fold the stiffly beaten egg whites into the mixture. Pour it into a buttered fireproof dish, previously sprinkled with breadcrumbs. Bake in a moderate oven for 45 minutes. Serve with sauerkraut or green salad.

SOUR CREAM DRESSING

1 beaten egg yolk
2 tablespoons wine vinegar
½ pint sour cream
1 tablespoon chopped chives or onion
black pepper

Mix the vinegar into egg yolk, blend in the slightly beaten cream and the onion, season with freshly ground black pepper.

SCHNITZEL SAUCE (1)

4 oz. butter
12 anchovy fillets, pounded
1 tablespoon paprika

Blend and heat the ingredients and pour them over the hot cooked schnitzel.

SCHNITZEL SAUCE (2)

¼ *pint cream*
¼ *pint water*
1 *tablespoon chopped capers*
1 *tablespoon paprika*
salt

pepper
juice of 1 *lemon*

Blend the cream and water. Add the capers and the seasoning. Heat in the pan in which the schnitzel was cooked. Pour over the schnitzel.

KREN (Austrian horseradish sauce)

beetroot
horseradish
cream
very little vinegar
pepper

salt
sugar

Grate the horseradish and beetroot finely. Add enough cream to bring it to the consistency of horse-radish sauce. Mix well and add the seasonings to taste.

CHOCOLATE SAUCE

4 *oz. plain chocolate*
2 *oz. castor sugar*
¼ *pint water*
½ *vanilla pod*

Melt the ingredients in a double saucepan until hot and well blended. Remove the vanilla pod before serving.

BACKHANDEL (Spring chicken)

1 *spring chicken*
4 *oz. flour*
1 *beaten egg*
breadcrumbs

Clean a young chicken and cut it up into joints. Remove the meat from the bones of the carcass. Remove the skin from all the pieces of chicken. Dip them into flour and then into the beaten egg and finally into the breadcrumbs. Fry the pieces in deep fat and drain them on soft paper. Serve very hot with a green salad and new potatoes.

ROAST GOOSE

1 *young goose*
4 *eating apples*
4 *lumps of sugar*
2 *tablespoons chopped marjoram*
salt
black pepper

dripping for roasting
red currant jelly

Rub the goose inside and out with salt and pepper and chopped marjoram. Peel and core the apples. Put a sugar lump into each and stuff the goose with them. Baste frequently while roasting. Serve with red currant jelly.

CHICKEN PAPRIKA

1 *young chicken*
1 *oz. butter*
1 *oz. lard*
3 *onions, chopped*
2 *tablespoons paprika*
1 *pint vegetable or light stock or*
   water
1 *teaspoon flour*
salt
½ *pint sour cream*

Cut the chicken into joints and sprinkle it with salt. Melt the butter and lard in a heavy pan, add the chopped onions and simmer them until they are browned. Add the paprika and the stock. Bring these ingredients to the boil and then add the chicken. Cover the pan and simmer the chicken until it is tender (about 1½ hours). Stir the flour into the sour cream and pour it slowly into the pan. Cook, without boiling, for a further 5 minutes.

ROAST PIGEON

4 *young pigeons*

STUFFING:
4 *oz. calves' liver*
1 *dessertspoon chopped thyme*
2 *oz. butter*
4 *anchovy fillets*
4 *juniper berries (optional)*
salt
black pepper
1 *large onion*

butter for roasting
breadcrumbs fried in butter
¼ *pint sour cream*
apple or red currant jelly

Chop all the stuffing ingredients finely and fry them in the butter until tender. Stuff the pigeons and roast them in butter, baste well. When they are cooked, pour a little sour cream over each of them and serve with the fried breadcrumbs and apple or red currant jelly.

HARE OR RABBIT GOULASH WITH WINE

2 *lb. hare or rabbit, boned and*
   cut in cubes
4 *oz. bacon, chopped*
1 *large onion, chopped*
1 *oz. dripping*
2 *oz. flour*
1 *pint dry red wine or cider*
¼ *pint stock*
1 *tablespoon paprika*
salt
2 *cloves garlic (optional)*
¼ *pint sour cream*

Fry the bacon and onions gently in the dripping for 10 minutes. Brown the meat on all sides. Sauté the meat, onions and bacon over a low heat for 10 minutes. Sprinkle in the flour, paprika, salt and pepper and the garlic. Stir and blend thoroughly. Add the wine and enough stock to cover the meat well. Cook in a slow oven for 2 hours or till tender. Five minutes before serving stir in the sour cream. Reheat without boiling. Serve with rice or nockerl (see p. 33).

HARE

1 *young hare*
3 *carrots*
3 *small turnips*
3 *onions*
2 *cloves garlic, crushed*
parsley
1 *sprig each of rosemary and thyme*
1 *bay leaf*
peel of ½ lemon
12 *peppercorns*
red wine
¼ *pint sour cream*

salt
black pepper
stewed currants or red currant
jelly

Rub the hare with salt and pepper. Simmer the sliced vegetables and herbs for 30 minutes in equal quantities of wine and water. Add the hare and enough extra wine and water to cover. Simmer in a covered pan until tender. Remove the hare. Joint it ready to serve. Strain the sauce, blend with the cream and pour over the hare. Serve it with stewed currants or red currant jelly.

GOULASH

1 *lb. lean stewing beef cut into*
  cubes
1 *lb. onion, sliced*
1 *lb. potatoes*
2 *oz. dripping*
stock
1 *tablespoon paprika*
salt
½ *teaspoon caraway seeds*

pinch of marjoram
2 *cloves garlic*

Fry the onions and the garlic for a few minutes in the dripping. Add the paprika, salt, marjoram and caraway seeds. Just cover the meat with the stock and cook in a covered pan in a slow oven for 3 hours or until perfectly tender. 30 minutes before serving add the potatoes. Long and very slow cooking improves this dish. Serve with nockerl (see p. 33).

CARAWAY SEED ROAST

2 *lb. sirloin or rib of beef, rolled*
  and boned
2 *lb. beef bones*
2 *oz. bacon fat or dripping*
2 *large onions, finely chopped*
salt
black pepper
2 *tablespoons caraway seeds*
2 *tablespoons vinegar*
2 *tablespoons flour (for roux)*
2 *oz. dripping or butter (for roux)*

Mix 2 tablespoons of chopped onion with 1 tablespoon of caraway seeds and a good pinch of salt. Unroll the meat, spread with this mixture, re-roll and tie. Put the rest of the onion and the bacon fat into a roasting tin and sauté in the oven for 5 minutes. Then put in the meat and sprinkle it with the remaining caraway seeds and the vinegar, salt and freshly ground black pepper. Arrange the bones round the meat and pour in enough water to come a quarter of the way up the meat. Roast in a moderate oven for about an hour. Baste frequently. Make a brown roux with 2 oz. flour, 2 oz. dripping or butter and seasoning, and mix this gradually with the strained juice from the roasting pan. Season. Serve with nockerl (see p. 33).

MINCE ROAST

8 oz. beef
8 oz. pork
1 small onion
1 egg
2 Vienna rolls
salt, pepper, parsley
fat
flour

GRAVY:

1 oz. butter or dripping
1 oz. flour
2 oz. fat bacon
salt
pepper
1 dessertspoon chopped capers
2 tablespoons sour cream
¼ pint stock, hot

Remove crust from rolls and soak in milk or water. Mince meat finely. Squeeze out moisture from rolls and add to meat, together with salt, pepper, egg, chopped parsley and finely chopped onion previously fried in a little fat. Knead well and shape into a roll. Dust with flour.

Heat the dripping in a pan with a lid. Put in the meat roll covered with the bacon. Baste the roll with the melted dripping, put the lid on and roast in a moderate oven for 45 to 60 minutes according to the thickness of the roll. Fifteen minutes before the roll is cooked remove the lid and the fat bacon to allow the meat to brown. When it is cooked, remove the roll to a hot dish. Drain the surplus fat from the pan, stir in the flour, cook for a few minutes and then gradually add the stock and the sour cream, seasoning and capers. Do not boil the sauce after adding the cream. Serve the roll and the sauce separately.

TYROLEAN LIVER

1 lb. calves' liver, sliced thin
1 onion, sliced thin
2 oz. dripping
black pepper
1 teaspoon marjoram, chopped
¼ pint stock (optional)
1 oz. flour (optional)

Fry the onions in the dripping until they are just turning colour. Increase the heat, move the onions to one side of the pan, put in the liver, marjoram and pepper and fry fast for about 4 minutes, turning the liver frequently. Add the salt just before serving to avoid toughening the meat. If gravy is required, remove the cooked onions and liver to a hot dish, stir the flour into the fat in the pan, cook for 3 to 4 minutes, add the stock gradually and season to taste. Serve with rice or nockerl (see p. 33).

WIENER SCHNITZEL

1 large veal escalope per head, cut
   ⅓ inch to ½ inch thick, either fillet
   or cut slantwise from the leg
1 egg, beaten
6 oz. fine breadcrumbs
3 oz. flour
4 oz. melted butter
salt
black pepper
2 lemons

Beat the escalopes gently to half their original thickness. Pour the juice of one of the lemons over the meat. Leave it for 1 hour, turning several times. Mix the flour with the seasoning. Dip the marinated veal first into the flour and then into the beaten egg. Last of all, dip it into the breadcrumbs. Fry the schnitzel in the butter for about 1½ minutes on each side. Drain the schnitzel on soft paper, keeping it hot. Serve with quarters of lemon.

VEAL ESCALOPE

1 *lb. veal cut in slices from fillet*
6 *oz. butter*
1 *or 2 quartered lemons*
juice of 1 lemon

Marinate the escalope in the lemon juice for 1 hour, turning frequently. Fry it in the butter, allowing 1 minute for each side. Serve with quartered lemons and the frying butter.

PAPRIKA BEEF

1 *lb. fillet of beef cut in*
  ½ inch thick slices
2 *oz. dripping or butter*
1 *oz. flour*
3 *onions, chopped*
2 *lb. sliced potatoes*
½ pint sour cream
2 *tablespoons tomato purée*
salt
pepper
2 *teaspoons paprika*
½ pint water

Beat the slices of beef to half their original thickness and rub them with salt and pepper. Sear the beef quickly on both sides in the dripping. Remove the beef from the pan, put it into a fireproof casserole with lid. Fry the onions golden, add flour, paprika and tomato purée and stir in the water. Pour this sauce over the meat, cover the casserole and cook in a slow oven for 3 hours. Add the potatoes 45 minutes before serving and the cream 5 minutes before serving. After adding the cream, heat but be careful not to boil. Serve with quarters of lemon or with kren (see p. 37).

SAUTÉED KIDNEYS

1 *lb. ox kidney*
1 *large onion, sliced thinly*
2 *oz. dripping or lard*
salt
black pepper
½ teaspoon marjoram

Skin the kidneys and slice them thinly, removing all the core. Steep the slices in cold water for 30 minutes. Change water, rinse and repeat. Rinse thoroughly, drain and dry carefully with a clean cloth. Sauté the onions until just turning colour, draw them to the side of the pan and raise the heat. Add the kidney slices, the marjoram and the pepper, and sauté quickly for 5 minutes, turning frequently. Add salt just before serving. Serve with green salad.

PORK AND SAUERKRAUT

1 *lb. pork, cut into cubes*
12 *oz. sauerkraut, fresh or tinned*
1 *onion, thinly sliced into rings*
salt
pepper
1 *tablespoon paprika*
1 *clove garlic, crushed*
water

Fry the onion rings in the butter until just turning colour. Add the seasoning, sauerkraut and meat and stir to mix thoroughly. Just cover the meat with water and simmer gently with the lid on for about 1 hour. Serve with dumplings.

BEEF AND SAUSAGE ROAST

2 *lb. lean roasting joint*
4 *long frankfurters*
1 *large onion, finely chopped*
2 *oz. dripping*
1 *oz. flour*
salt
black pepper
paprika
approx. 1 *pint water*

Cut 8 holes through the meat with an apple corer. Thread half a sausage through each hole, trimming the sausages to the thickness of the meat. Rub the meat with salt, black pepper and paprika. Simmer the meat trimmings with the water, and some salt and pepper. Melt the onion in the dripping in a metal casserole. Add the meat and sear quickly on both sides. Sprinkle in the flour and blend it with the onions. Just cover the meat with the stock made from the meat trimmings. Cook it in a slow oven for about an hour and a half until tender. Serve the meat sliced so that rounds of sausages appear in each slice. Strain the gravy over it.

STUFFED SADDLE OF LAMB

saddle of lamb
6 *shallots*
4 *oz. ham*
2 *oz. suet*
4 *slices of bread (soaked and squeezed out)*
2 *tablespoons parsley*
3 *eggs*
salt
pepper
1 *oz. butter*

Remove the bones from the lamb, rub it thoroughly with the cut sides of a shallot and with salt and pepper. Leave it in a cool place for 8 hours. Chop the shallots, ham and parsley and fry them lightly in the butter. Add the 2 beaten eggs and seasoning. Cook gently till set. When the lamb is ready stuff it with this mixture. Tie the joint and roast it in the usual way, basting frequently.

LEG OF PORK

leg of pork
2 *large onions*
2 *carrots*
bouquet garni
2 *sticks celery*
salt
pepper
SAUCE:
2 *lb. tomatoes*
½ *pint white wine or cider*
salt
black pepper
1 *tablespoon brown sugar*

Put the leg of pork, vegetables, herbs and seasoning in a pan with enough water to cover them and cook gently until the meat is tender. Allow roughly 25 minutes per lb. When it is cooked cut a suitable number of slices and serve it with the sauce given below.

Stew the tomatoes in the wine with the seasoning and sugar. Reduce to a thick pulp and strain. Serve with dumplings or nockerl (see p. 33).

ESTERHAZY BEEF STEAK

2 *lb. rump or chuck steak cut into*
  small neat steaks and flattened
4 *oz. good dripping or bacon fat*
3 *carrots, coarsely chopped*
2 *onions, coarsely chopped*
2 *stalks celery, coarsely chopped*
½ *green pepper, coarsely chopped*
salt
black pepper
2 *teaspoons capers*
2 *teaspoons paprika*
1 *oz. flour*
½ *pint good stock*
3 *tablespoons sour cream*
3 *tablespoons Madeira*

Melt half the dripping in a metal casserole, add the seasoning and vegetables, cover and sauté gently without stirring for 10 minutes. Remove the lid and raise the heat. Still without stirring, but shaking the pan, brown the vegetables, adding a little of the stock as necessary. Sprinkle in the flour. Stir gently. When blended, stir in the remaining stock and the sour cream. Heat the other half of the dripping in another pan. Sear the steaks quickly on both sides. Add the steak to the vegetables and gravy. Cover with a tightly fitting lid and cook in a moderate oven for about 30—45 minutes depending on the thickness and quality of the meat. Add the wine 5 minutes before serving.

CALVES' TONGUE

8 *slices calves' tongue*
4 *fillets of anchovy, crushed*
4 *oz. butter*
juice of 2 lemons
salt
black pepper
6 *oz. breadcrumbs*
dripping for frying

Melt the butter and add the lemon juice, seasoning and crushed anchovies. Simmer for 5 minutes. When the sauce is cold, dip the tongue slices first in this and then in breadcrumbs. Fry them till golden. Serve with the sauce heated and poured over the tongue.

APPLE FLAN

short paste (see p. 51)
4 *oz. lump sugar*
1 *oz. ground almonds*
1½ *lb. cooking apples, peeled*
  and sliced
¼ *pint water*
½ *pint whipped cream*

MERINGUE:
4 *oz. castor sugar*
2 *egg whites*

Leave the paste to rest for 30 minutes. Line a buttered, floured flan tin with the paste and bake blind. Boil the sugar and water together for 10 minutes, add the other ingredients and simmer gently until the apples are tender. Meanwhile beat the egg whites stiff and fold the sugar in gradually. When the pastry is cooked fill the shell with the apple mixture, cover this with the meringue and bake for 30 minutes in a slow oven.

COFFEE CREAM

½ *pint strong black coffee*
½ *oz. powdered gelatine*
2 *oz. castor sugar*
2 *oz. vanilla sugar*
½ *pint whipped cream*

Dissolve the gelatine with the plain sugar in a little of the coffee. Bring the rest of the coffee up to the boil and pour over the mixture. Stir to dissolve the gelatine completely. Leave in a cold place to set. When almost set, beat until frothy, add the cream and vanilla sugar, pour into a wetted mould and leave for at least 4 hours.

LOCKSMITH'S APPRENTICES, BAKED

12 *large prunes*
12 *blanched almonds*
8 *oz. flour*
white wine or cider to mix
salt
1 *egg yolk*

GARNISH:

2 *oz. castor sugar*
2 *oz. plain chocolate, grated*

Soak the prunes overnight. Stew until tender. Replace each prune stone with an almond. Make a paste with the flour, salt, and egg yolk and wine. Roll out thin, cut into 12 rounds and wrap one prune in each. Bake on a very well buttered baking sheet in a moderate oven for 30 minutes, turning at half-time to brown both sides. Serve hot rolled in sugar and chocolate.

LOCKSMITH'S APPRENTICES, FRIED

12 *large prunes*
12 *blanched almonds*
4 *oz. flour*
salt
¼ *pint wine or cider*

GARNISH:

2 *oz. castor sugar*
2 *oz. plain chocolate, grated*

Soak the prunes overnight. Stew until soft. Replace the prune stones with blanched almonds. Prepare a batter by beating the wine into the flour and salt. The batter should be runny. Dip the prunes into the batter and fry in deep hot fat until golden. Drain on soft paper. Roll in grated chocolate and sugar. Serve hot.

CANARY MILK

½ *pint milk*
1 *egg yolk*
2 *oz. castor sugar*
1 *vanilla pod*

Cut the vanilla pod into 5 or 6 pieces and bring to the boil with the milk and sugar. Mix the egg yolk with 3 tablespoons of the hot milk while stirring briskly. Pour the remaining milk over this mixture, return to the pan and cook gently until it thickens. Serve hot or cold.

APPLE PUDDING

1½ lb. cooking apples
3 eggs, separated
4 oz. vanilla sugar
3 oz. cake crumbs
1 oz. butter

Peel, slice and core the apples, stew them gently in the butter until tender but not brown. Sieve the cake crumbs. Beat the egg yolks and sugar until pale, stir in the cake crumbs and apple. Whisk the egg whites stiffly and fold them into the mixture. Steam for 1 hour in a well buttered basin covered with greased paper. Serve hot with Canary milk (see p. 44).

APPLE SNOW

1½ lb. cooking apples
4 oz. vanilla sugar
3 egg whites stiffly beaten
juice of 1 lemon

OPTIONAL SAUCE:
½ pint white wine or cider
8 oz. castor sugar
3 egg yolks

Chop the apples with the skins on, stew in very little water until tender. Sieve the apple, add the sugar and lemon juice and whisk over warm water until thick. Remove from the heat, whisk until cool, fold in the egg whites. Serve as cold as possible.

FOR THE SAUCE:
Whisk all the ingredients over hot water until thick. Serve hot.

COLD RICE PUDDING

4 oz. Carolina rice
½ pint milk
½ pint double cream
2 oz. sugar
1 vanilla pod
¼ oz. gelatine

Boil the rice, sugar and vanilla pod in the milk until soft, stir frequently. Soften the gelatine in a tablespoonful of milk, then stir it into the cooked rice. Stir in the cream, remove the vanilla pod and pour into a cold wetted mould. Serve plain or with fruit syrup (see below).

FRUIT SYRUP WITH CREAM

½ pint any fruit juice
sugar to taste
¼ pint double cream whipped
½ tablespoon powdered gelatine

Blend the gelatine with half the fruit juice. Bring the remaining ¼ pint of juice to the boil, add the mixed gelatine and juice and stir over the heat until the gelatine is dissolved. Remove from the heat. When cool beat until thick and light; keep very cold while whipping. Fold in the whipped cream.

CANARY PUDDING WITH CHOCOLATE SAUCE

3 oz. butter
3 oz. sugar
3 oz. flour
3 eggs, separated
grated rind of ½ lemon

Cream the butter and sugar and beat until light. Add the beaten egg yolks gradually. Fold in the sifted flour and stiffly beaten egg whites alternately, add the lemon rind, and steam in a buttered basin for 1 hour.

For the sauce for Canary pudding see p. 37.

FRUIT JELLY

4 oz. fresh red currants
  topped and tailed
4 oz. fresh black currants
  topped and tailed
4 oz. strawberries, hulled
4 oz. black cherries, stoned
¼ pint white wine or cider
¼ pint water

½ oz. gelatine
¼—½ lb. castor sugar to taste

Lightly stew the currants with the sugar and water and then sieve them. Mix the gelatine with a little of the wine, then pour the hot purée over it. Add the rest of the fruit and the wine and pour into a mould to set. Serve with whipped cream or Canary milk (see p. 44).

CANTALOUPE WITH BRANDY

1 cantaloupe melon
1 small glass brandy
4 oz. icing sugar
juice of 1 lemon

Peel the melon finely, remove the seeds and cut the flesh into neat cubes. Mix the other ingredients together and pour over the melon pieces. Cover tightly and stand in a cool place for at least 2 hours. Mix gently and serve with whipped cream.

COMPOTE OF APPLES OR PEARS

1½ lb. cooking apples or pears
¾ pint water
12 oz. sugar
juice and peel of 1 orange
8 oz. cherry jam

Boil the sugar and water together fast without a lid for about 15 minutes until it thickens. Peel, halve and core the apples or pears. Cook these halves in the syrup a few at a time, being careful to keep them whole. When cooked remove from the syrup, arrange on a dish and fill the core hollow with jam. When all the halves are cooked, reboil the syrup with the orange peel and juice and half the apple cores and peel for 15 minutes or until it will set on a cold plate. Strain the syrup over the fruit. Serve cold with whipped cream or Canary milk (see p. 44).

MAGDA (Coffee and chocolate jelly)

½ *pint strong clear coffee*
1 *level teaspoon granulated*
  gelatine
4 *teaspoons chocolate powder*
sugar to taste
little vanilla
pinch of salt
whipped cream to garnish

Heat the coffee and the salt. Dissolve the gelatine in it. Add the chocolate powder, sugar and vanilla. Cook for a few minutes, until it is smooth and the chocolate is completely melted. Cool it, stirring from time to time. Pour into glasses when it is on the point of setting. Chill thoroughly. Top with whipped cream just before serving. Serve with sweet biscuits or sponge fingers.

LITTLE APPLE TURNOVERS

short crust pastry (see p. 51)
4 *cooking apples peeled and*
  quartered
4 *oz. castor sugar*
1 *tablespoon rum*
1 *egg yolk*
1 *tablespoon milk*

Leave the pastry dough to rest for 30 minutes after mixing. Mix the rum with the sugar, pour over the apple. Leave to stand for half an hour. Roll out the dough and cut into 16 squares. Put one apple quarter on each square, draw up the corners and press the edges together but leave the tips open. Arrange on a buttered floured baking sheet. Brush with egg and milk and bake in a hot oven for 20 to 30 minutes. Dust with vanilla sugar and serve hot or cold.

APPLE STRUDEL

strudel dough (see p. 51)
1½ *lb. cooking apples*
2 *oz. currants*
2 *oz. stoned raisins*
2 *oz. dry breadcrumbs fried in butter*
4 *oz. castor sugar*
½ *teaspoon ground cinnamon*
grated peel of ½ lemon
4 *oz. melted butter*

While the strudel dough is resting before being pulled out, prepare the filling. Peel, core and slice the apples thinly, then mix them without breaking them with the rest of the ingredients. When the dough is ready, trim off the thick edges and spread with the apple mixture, leaving an inch uncovered all round the edges. Roll the dough very gently and pinch the edges together and place on a buttered baking sheet. Brush with melted butter and bake in a hot oven for 20 minutes, lower the temperature to moderate and bake for a further 30 minutes. Brush with the melted butter 2 or 3 times during baking. Serve sliced hot or cold.

LEMON SOUFFLÉ

4 *eggs, separated*
2 *oz. icing sugar*
juice and grated rind of 1 lemon

Line a soufflé mould with buttered paper and sprinkle with icing sugar. Beat egg yolks with the sugar, lemon juice and rind until thick. Fold in the stiffly beaten egg whites, turn into the prepared mould and bake in a hot oven for 15 to 20 minutes.

CREAM CHEESE STRUDEL

strudel dough (see p. 51)
4 oz. sieved cream cheese
4 oz. castor sugar
4 oz. butter
⅛ pint sour cream
1 egg, beaten

While the strudel dough is resting before being rolled out, beat all the other ingredients together to blend thoroughly. Then proceed as for Apple Strudel (see p. 47).

VANILLA CREAM

½ pint milk
1 large egg
2 oz. castor sugar
1 oz. cornflour
1 vanilla pod cut into 4 or
    5 pieces

Mix the cornflour, sugar and egg yolk to a paste with a little of the milk. Heat the remainder of the milk with the vanilla pod in a double saucepan. Pour the hot milk over the other ingredients, stirring all the time. When blended, return to the double saucepan, cook and stir until thick.

FRIED YEAST CAKES (Gebackene Mäuse)

8 oz. flour
2 oz. butter
⅛ pint milk (approx.)
1 egg, beaten
½ oz. yeast
½ oz. sugar
2 oz. sultanas
½ teaspoon salt
1 tablespoon rum
frying fat

Scald the milk with the butter and cool to lukewarm. Cream the yeast with the sugar and stand in a warm place for 5 minutes. Warm the flour in a large mixing bowl. Make a well in the flour and, using the hand, gradually beat in the egg, yeast mixture, milk mixture, salt and sultanas. Knead thoroughly. Cover the bowl with a cloth and stand in a warm place to rise. When the dough has doubled its bulk, in about an hour and a half, knock down lightly. Scoop out teaspoonfuls of the dough and fry in deep hot fat. Turn the 'buns' to brown on both sides evenly. Drain on soft paper, serve hot with fruit syrup or vanilla cream (see above).

CHERRY STRUDEL

strudel dough (see p. 51)
1½ lb. black cherries
4 oz. breadcrumbs fried in butter
2 oz. currants
4 oz. castor sugar
½ teaspoon ground cinnamon

grated peel of ½ lemon
4 oz. melted butter

Proceed exactly as in the recipe for Apple Strudel (see p. 47) but use black cherries instead of apples.

EMPEROR'S SCHMARREN

4 oz. flour
¼ pint cream
2 eggs separated
1 oz. castor sugar
salt
1 oz. raisins stoned
1 oz. butter

Beat together the egg yolks and cream, stir these into the flour, raisins, salt and sugar. Fold in the stiffly beaten egg whites. Melt the butter in a shallow baking pan, pour in the batter and bake in a hot oven for 10 minutes or until brown underneath. Turn the batter over and brown the other side, then tear into small pieces with two forks, return to the oven for a further 3 or 4 minutes. Serve hot with vanilla cream (see p. 48).

BREAD OMELETTE

4 thick slices stale bread or 4 rolls
  or brioches
½ pint milk
2 oz. sultanas
1 apple peeled, chopped
1 egg
1 oz. sugar
salt
4 oz. butter for frying

Cut the bread into cubes. Mix all the other ingredients together and pour them over the bread. Leave to stand for 15 minutes. Heat the butter in a frying pan, pour in the batter, fry until brown, turn and brown the other side. Tear the omelette into small pieces with two forks, continue frying for a few minutes, shaking the pan. Serve with hot vanilla sugar.

CREAM CHEESE AND JAM PUFFS

4 oz. flour
4 oz. butter
4 oz. cream cheese
4 oz. approx. jam, jelly or
  strained stewed fruit

Sift flour on to pastry board. Cut butter into small pieces, crumble cream cheese and butter into flour, handling dough very lightly.

Roll out the dough to ¼ inch thickness, and cut into squares. Put a dab of jam or fruit on each square, gather up the corners and press them firmly together. Bake in a hot oven for about 15 minutes. Serve hot sprinkled with icing sugar.

APPLE SLICES

short crust paste (see p. 51)
1½ lb. cooking apples peeled
  and sliced thickly
4 oz. sugar
3 oz. cocoa or 2 oz. stoned raisins
1 egg white
salt

Divide the pastry in half. Roll each half out to a square, spread one square with apple slices, sugar and cocoa or raisins. Bake for 15 minutes in a moderate oven. Cover with the other half of the pastry, brush with beaten egg white and bake in a hot oven for about 30 minutes. Serve cold, sliced and dusted with icing sugar.

BUCHTELN

6 *oz. butter for glaze*
dough as for rich streusel cake
  (see p. 57)
8 *oz. jam*

Melt the butter in a roasting tin. When the dough has doubled its size, knock down and roll out to ¼ inch thick. Cut into 2½-inch squares. Put a good teaspoonful of jam on each. Draw up the corners to enclose the jam, put them gathered side down on the prepared roasting dish, brush all over thoroughly with the melted butter in the tin. Pack the buns closely together, stand in a warm place for 30 minutes. Bake in a moderate oven for 45 to 50 minutes. Remove from the tin, separate, dust with icing sugar. Serve hot or cold.

DALKEN (1)

rich streusel cake dough (see p. 57)
4 *oz. melted butter*
8 *oz. apricot jam (approx.)*
1 *oz. melted lard (approx.)*

When the dough has doubled its bulk, knock it down and roll out to ¼ inch thick. Cut into 2- or 3-inch rounds and leave on a floured board in a warm place for 30 minutes. Brush a griddle or heavy frying pan with lard and lightly fry the Dalken on both sides. Keep hot until all are done, brush quickly with melted butter, spread with apricot jam and serve very hot.

DALKEN (2)

4 *oz. flour*
3 *eggs*
½ *pint milk*
2 *oz. castor sugar*
pinch salt
2 *oz. melted butter*
8 *oz. apricot jam*
¼ *pint whipped cream*

Make a smooth batter with the flour, eggs, milk, sugar and salt. Leave it to stand for 30 minutes. Brush large shallow bun moulds with melted butter. Half fill the moulds with the batter and bake for 10 to 15 minutes in a hot oven, turn them over and return to the oven for a further 5 minutes. Keep the Dalken hot until all are done, then spread with apricot jam and cream, and serve at once.

TO WASH BUTTER

Fill a large bowl with very cold water, preferably with ice cubes added. Stand this bowl with the butter in it under a running cold tap. Squeeze the butter between the fingers for 5 minutes. Squeeze in a floured cloth to remove surplus moisture. Keep in a cold place (not a refrigerator) until needed.

PUFF PASTE WITH YEAST

8 *oz. flour*
6 *oz. butter*
1 *egg*
approx. ⅛ *pint milk*
½ *oz. yeast*
½ *oz. sugar*
salt

Mix the yeast with the sugar. Scald the milk, add the salt, 2 oz. butter, cool to lukewarm, add the yeast mixture. Meanwhile warm the flour in a large mixing bowl. Make a well in the flour and beat in the beaten egg and the milk and yeast mixture. Mix with the hand to form a smooth elastic dough adding milk or flour as necessary. Stand in a warm place, covered with a cloth until the dough has doubled its bulk (1½ hours approx.). Turn the dough on to a floured board and knead a little, roll out into a long strip 3 times as long as its width. Wash the remaining butter (see p. 50). Spread a third of the butter over the middle third of the dough, fold the ends to form a three-tiered square, give a quarter turn and repeat this process twice more so that the dough has had three rollings and all the butter is used. If possible stand the dough in a cold place for 30 minutes, between rollings and again before use.

SHORT PASTE

8 *oz. flour*
6 *oz. butter*
1 *egg yolk*
salt
3 *tablespoons sour thin cream*
(approx.)

2 *oz. castor sugar*
½ *teaspoon lemon juice*

Sift the flour with the salt and sugar. Rub or cut the butter into it. Mix with the egg yolk, cream and lemon juice to form a rather dry dough. Cover and stand in a cool place for 1 hour before use.

STRUDEL DOUGH

8 *oz. flour*
1 *egg yolk, beaten*
salt
¼ *pint warm water (approx.)*
1 *tablespoon melted butter*

Put the flour and salt into a warmed basin. Make a well in the centre and with the hand stir in the beaten egg yolk, butter and enough warm water to make a soft dough, knead thoroughly on a warmed, well floured board. When smooth, cover with a warm bowl and a cloth. Cover a table with a clean cloth. Sprinkle the cloth with flour, place the dough in the middle and roll it out as thin as possible with a warmed floured rolling pin. Slip your hands palm down under the dough and gently pull it out thinner from the middle, using mainly the balls of the thumbs. Ideally it should be pulled out thin enough to read through but this takes much patience and practice.

CROISSANTS

12 oz. flour
8 oz. butter, washed (see p. 50)
½ pint milk
1 oz. butter to mix with milk
1 egg beaten
1 oz. yeast
½ oz. sugar
½ to 1 teaspoon salt
1 egg yolk ⎫ for glaze
2 tablespoons milk ⎭

Cream the yeast with the sugar. Scald the milk, add 1 oz. butter and the salt, cool to lukewarm, add the yeast mixture. Meanwhile warm the flour in a large mixing bowl. Make a well in the flour and beat in the beaten egg and the warm milk mixture. Mix with the hand to form a smooth elastic dough adding milk or flour as necessary. Stand in a warm place covered with a cloth until the dough has doubled its bulk, about 1½ hours. Put the dough, covered with a cloth, in the refrigerator or as cold a place as possible for 3 or 4 hours. Knock the dough down, roll it out into a strip three times as long as it is wide. Spread a third of the butter over the middle third of the dough, fold the ends over to form a three-tired square, give the dough a quarter turn and repeat this process twice more so that the dough has had three rollings and all the butter is used. Stand the dough in a cold place between rollings and again before shaping. Roll the dough out to ¼ inch thickness and cut it into 4-inch squares, then into triangles. Roll each triangle up, starting at the wide base so that the point is in the centre, curve the ends round to form a crescent. Arrange on a buttered floured baking sheet, brush with egg and milk and bake in a hot oven for about 20 minutes. Cool on a wire rack.

GUGELHUPF

12 oz. flour sifted with
  ½ teaspoon salt
6 oz. butter
3 eggs
½ pint warm milk (approx.)
1 oz. yeast
½ oz. sugar
1 10-inch diameter centre tube
  mould
2 oz. raisins, stoned
2 oz. currants
grated rind and juice of 1 orange
2 oz. blanched sliced almonds

Blend the yeast with the sugar, stir in the warm milk. Stand in a warm place for 5 minutes. Rub the butter into the warm flour and salt in a large warm mixing bowl. Make a well in the centre and add the beaten eggs, warm milk, raisins, currants, orange rind and juice and yeast mixture. Stir to mix thoroughly. Prepare the mould by buttering it and dusting it with cornflour and strewing it with the almonds. Fill the mould half full and stand it in a warm place to prove. When the dough reaches the top of the mould it is ready to bake in a moderate oven for 45 minutes to 1 hour. Turn out on a rack to cool.

RICH GUGELHUPF

8 oz. flour
10 egg yolks
8 oz. butter
4 oz. sugar
⅛ pint warm milk (approx.)
10-inch centre tube mould
salt
1 oz. yeast
4 oz. stoned raisins
4 oz. blanched chopped almonds
cornflour or breadcrumbs to line tin

Cream the yeast with a teaspoon of the sugar, add the warm milk and stand in a warm place. Cream the butter, add the eggs gradually, alternately with the flour, add the sugar, salt and raisins and beat thoroughly. Stir in the milk and yeast mixture gently until thoroughly blended. Butter the mould, dust with cornflour or dry breadcrumbs and strew with chopped almonds. Fill the mould not more than three-quarters full, stand in a warm place to rise. When the mixture is just above the top of the tin, bake in a moderate oven for 45 minutes to 1 hour. Turn out and cool on a cake rack.

CAKES (GENERAL)

Austrian sponge cake mixtures should be beaten by hand for 30 minutes. If an electric mixer is used it must be set at a very low speed, otherwise the air bubbles are too large and the mixture too light and frothy. Fatless sponge cakes are best beaten by placing the bowl in which they are mixed in a larger bowl of very hot water.

The tins in which they are baked are greased and dusted first with flour and then castor sugar.

The secret of the celebrated Sacher Torte was very carefully guarded and there are therefore various different recipes for it. I have included two of these.

CLASSIC AUSTRIAN SPONGE CAKE

3 eggs
5 oz. castor sugar
3 oz. flour

Beat the eggs with the sugar until white. Fold in the sifted flour very gently. Bake in tin prepared according to general direction above in a moderately slow oven for 1 hour. Turn out when cold.

VARIATIONS:

1. Use vanilla sugar instead of castor sugar, ice with chocolate frosting and fill with the filling for Sacher Torte.
2. Add melted cooking chocolate to the mixture after the flour. Cover with white icing and fill with thick vanilla cream (see p. 48).

DOUGHNUTS

8 *oz. flour*
2 *eggs*
⅛ *pint warm milk*
½ *oz. yeast*
1 *oz. sugar*
1½ *oz. melted butter*
salt
8 *oz. jam (approx.)*
deep fat for frying

Mix the yeast with a teaspoonful of the sugar and half the warm milk. Warm the flour in a large mixing bowl. Make a well in the centre and pour in the yeast mixture. Sprinkle with flour and stand in a warm place for 30 minutes. Then add the rest of the warm milk, the butter, melted, one whole egg and the egg yolk beaten, the salt and the remaining sugar. Mix well and beat until smooth and the dough leaves the sides of the bowl clean. Add more milk and flour as necessary. Cover the bowl and stand in warm place to double its bulk, about 1½ hours. Turn on to a floured board and knead lightly, roll out to a quarter of an inch thick. Cut into rounds, arrange the rounds in pairs. Put half a teaspoonful of jam in the middle of one round, brush round the edges with beaten egg white and cover with the other round, press the edges together firmly. Leave the doughnuts to rise in a warm place until well risen and light. Fry a few at a time in deep hot fat. Brown the first side with a lid on the pan, turn and brown the other side without the lid. Drain on soft paper and roll in castor sugar.

SACHER TORTE (1)

8 *oz. cooking chocolate*
8 *oz. butter*
8 *oz. ground almonds*
8 *eggs*
6 *oz. castor sugar*
1 *tablespoon cornflour*

Melt the chocolate with a little water. Cream the butter, add the chocolate, beaten egg yolks, ground almonds and sugar. Beat all ingredients together until very light and creamy. Add the cornflour and beat again. Fold in the stiffly beaten egg whites. Transfer gently into a prepared cake tin (see p. 53) and bake in a moderately slow oven (300°F.) for 1 hour. Leave in the tin to cool thoroughly before turning out.

FILLING:
apricot jam or sauce (see p. 56)
4 *egg yolks*
2 *oz. sugar*
2 *oz. cocoa*
¼ *pint double cream*
1 *oz. vanilla sugar (see p. 57)*

FILLING: Cook the beaten egg yolks, sugar and cocoa in the top of a double saucepan, stirring all the time, until the mixture thickens. Whip the cream, add the vanilla sugar and fold into the cocoa mixture when it cools.

Cut the cake in half and spread the lower half with the filling. Replace top half and spread with sieved apricot jam or apricot sauce. Ice with chocolate frosting (see p. 56).

Serve with whipped cream.

SACHER TORTE (2)

8 *oz. cooking chocolate melted in a little coffee*
8 *oz. butter*
8 *oz. sugar*
6 *oz. self-raising flour*
5 *eggs*
filling and icing as in (1)

Cream the butter and sugar until white, beat in the egg yolks one at a time. Beat the egg whites until stiff, add them alternately with the sifted flour, keeping the mixture as light as possible. Fold in the chocolate. Transfer to a tin prepared according to the instructions above. Bake in a moderately slow oven (300°F.) for 1 hour. Leave to cool in the tin, turn out. Fill and ice the cake in the same way as for Sacher Torte (1).

ALMOND CAKE

10½ *oz. ground almonds*
5 *large or 6 small eggs*
9 *oz. castor sugar*
grated rind of 1 *lemon*

Beat the sugar and egg yolks together for 30 minutes. Whip the egg whites stiff and add them to the yolks and sugar. Stir in the ground almonds. Bake in a well buttered and floured tin for 45 minutes in a moderate oven. Cool on a rack. When cold, top with whipped cream and chopped mixed nuts if liked.

CHOCOLATE CAKE

6 *oz. butter*
9 *oz. castor sugar*
6 *eggs, separated*
3 *oz. breadcrumbs*
4 *oz. milk chocolate*
5 *oz. bitter chocolate*
5½ *oz. ground almonds*
2 *tablespoons water*

Beat the butter and sugar until very light, about 30 minutes. Add the egg yolks and stir for a further 30 minutes. Add the breadcrumbs. Melt the chocolate in the water and add the mixture with the ground almonds. Beat the egg whites stiff and beat them into the mixture. Turn into a well buttered and floured cake tin and bake for 1 hour in a moderate oven. Cool on a cake rack, when cold spread with apricot jam and chocolate frosting (see p. 56).

SPITZBUBEN (Nut Biscuits)

8 *oz. butter*
8 *oz. sugar*
8 *oz. flour*
4 *oz. ground almonds*
1 *teaspoon vanilla*
red currant jelly

Cream the butter and add the other ingredients. Mix thoroughly. Pat out with the hands on to a floured board. Cover the dough with greaseproof paper and roll it out until it is only ⅛ inch thick. Cut out biscuits with a small-size biscuit cutter. Put them on a greased baking sheet and bake them for 35 minutes in a slow oven. Allow them to cool. Stick them togehter with a little red currant jelly.

LINZER TORTE

6 *oz. flour*
½ *teaspoon cinnamon*
4 *oz. sugar*
2 *oz. ground almonds*
2 *oz. butter*
2 *egg yolks*
juice and grated rind of 1 *lemon*
raspberry jam

Sift the flour, sugar and cinnamon. Cut in the butter, add the almonds, egg yolks and lemon peel. Work to a smooth paste with a little lemon juice. Roll on a floured board, leave in a cool place for an hour. Roll again and line a greased tart tin with pastry, fill with raspberry jam, cover with criss-cross strips of pastry. Sprinkle with sugar and bake in a moderately hot oven for 30 minutes.

APRICOT SAUCE

8 *oz. apricots or* 4 *oz. dried apricots*
sugar to taste

Cook the apricots with the sugar and a little water until tender. Pass through a sieve.

CHOCOLATE FROSTING

1 *egg yolk*
1 *lb. icing sugar*
⅛ *pint hot strong black coffee*
3 *oz. butter*
1 *tablespoon cocoa*

Cream the butter and egg yolk, add the sugar and cocoa gradually, alternately with the hot coffee, adding just enough of the coffee to make a spreading consistency.

PLAIN STREUSEL CAKE

DOUGH:
8 *oz. flour*
1 *oz. fat*
½ *oz. yeast*
¼ *oz. sugar*
¼ *pint milk*
¼ *teaspoon salt*

STREUSEL:
8 *oz. butter*
8 *oz. sugar*
4 *oz. flour*
1½ *tablespoons cinnamon*

GLAZE:
2 *oz. melted butter*

Proceed exactly as in the recipe for yeast puff paste (see p. 51). When the dough has doubled its bulk, knock down lightly and pat into a round cake about ¼ inch high. Put this cake on a well buttered and floured roasting tin. Put in a warm place until the dough has nearly doubled its bulk. Brush the top with melted butter and cover evenly with the following streusel:
Cut together the ingredients listed until crumbly and well mixed. Bake in a moderate oven for 30 minutes to 45 minutes.

RICH STREUSEL CAKE

8 oz. flour
  large egg beaten
5 oz. butter
¼ pint milk
½ oz. yeast

¼ oz. sugar
salt

FILLING:
as for plain streusel cake
Follow the method for plain streusel cake.

RUM DOUGHNUTS

4 oz. flour
2 oz. butter
½ pint water
3 eggs
salt
2 tablespoons rum
1 teaspoon powdered cinnamon
2 oz. castor sugar
deep fat for frying

Boil water and butter, add flour and salt and beat over low heat until it forms a smooth ball of paste which will leave the sides of the pan clean. Chill slightly, add lightly beaten eggs. Beat these in gradually, making mixture smooth after each addition. When cool stir in the rum. Using an icing bag with a half-inch nozzle, force 3-inch strips of the paste into the hot fat. Fry golden on both sides keeping the lid on the pan during the cooking of the first side. Drain on soft paper, serve hot, dusted with sugar and cinnamon.

MOCHA COFFEE

1 pint strong coffee
1½ pints milk
4 oz. cooking chocolate
4 oz. sugar

Strain the coffee, mix it with 1 pint hot milk. Dissolve the chocolate and the sugar in ½ pint milk. Stir the chocolate mixture into the coffee. This can be beaten until frothy and served hot with whipped cream or used for flavouring.

VANILLA SUGAR

1 vanilla pod
2 lb. castor sugar

Cut the vanilla pod into 4 or 5 pieces. Put it with the sugar into an airtight jar. Screw the lid down firmly. The same pod can be used for about 2 months, the jar being refilled with sugar as required.

CHESTNUT TORTE

8 *oz. butter*
4 *tablespoons single cream*
2—3 *drops lemon juice*
10 *oz. flour*
2 *egg yolks*
pinch salt
chestnut filling

Put the flour into a bowl and cut the butter into it with a knife. Mix the lemon juice with the cream. Add the egg yolks and salt to the flour mixture. Stir and finally add the cream to make a soft rather crumbly dough. Wrap in a cloth and chill in the refrigerator. Roll out the cold pastry and line the bottom of a deep cake tin. Let it come up the sides about 1 inch. See that the walls are greased as well as the bottom. Fill with chestnut filling (see below) and bake in a moderate oven for 1 hour.

CHESTNUT FILLING

1 *lb. cooked chestnuts*
  (weight after peeling)
5 *eggs*
½ *pint milk*
2 *oz. butter*
4 *oz. sugar*

After the chestnuts have been boiled soft and peeled cover with the cup of milk and cook slowly until they are very soft. They will then sieve easily. Cream the butter, add the sugar and egg yolks alternately. Beat well. Beat the egg whites very stiffly. Add the chestnut mixture to the egg yolk mixture and lastly fold in the whites. The filling is now ready to use.

PEACH BOWL

6 *large ripe peaches*
2 *bottles white wine*
½ *bottle champagne*
8 *oz. sugar*

Peel and slice peaches in a bowl, sprinkle with sugar, pour over 1 bottle wine and chill in refrigerator for 2—3 hours. Add second bottle of wine and champagne and serve immediately.

CARDINAL

1 *bottle sweet white wine*
1 *orange*
½ *pint pineapple juice*
8 *oz. lump sugar*
ice

Rub the lump sugar well with orange rind and place in a punch bowl with the orange juice, pineapple juice and the white wine. When the sugar has dissolved serve very cold with ice. Half a bottle of white wine and half a bottle of champagne may be used instead of 1 bottle of white wine.

The Balkans

COOKING IN THE BALKANS

Aubergines, yoghourt, vine leaves, and strong Turkish coffee served in tiny cups immediately conjure up the colourful Balkans. I can see an almost Eastern bazaar scene, with its smells of mutton fat, and charcoal braziers in the street. Shady-looking little restaurants in Bucharest and Athens serving heavenly Pilaf — the rice dish with endless variations. You will find the chicken pilaf amongst these recipes a boon for left-over chicken or any other fowl. I think it must be the chopped walnuts which gives this pilaf its exceptionally delicate flavour. Aubergines have become a familiar sight at the greengrocer and you could do worse than turn to the Balkan countries for variety in the cooking of aubergines.

I remember being told once that the secret of long life is eating yoghourt every day — no doubt the pronouncement of a village elder in Greece. I have stored this statement away in my memory as an advice never to be forgotten — because I would like to live long, and I am also inordinately fond of yoghourt.

Try aubergines with yoghourt for a light luncheon once, and I am sure you will join the ranks of long-living yoghourt eaters too.

There is hardly any need to introduce Dolmas or Stuffed Vine Leaves to most readers — I just want to mention the fact that you can buy vine leaves in tins. So don't discount this very tasty morsel if you do not happen to have vine leaves growing in front of your kitchen window.

Mousaka is my other great favourite — try it next time when your thoughts turn to shepherd's pie. Believe me, it is an extremely clever and tasty way of using up left-over cold meat.

Lemon and Egg Sauce (Avgolemono) is the pride of culinary Greece. Served with young lamb, it adds a most delicate and piquant flavour to the roast.

Turkish skewered lamb invaded the Western picnic scene at some unspecified time — here you will find the original recipe as it is fried in the streets and cafés.

If you have a sweet tooth, you may be tempted to make a Balkan Honey Soufflé. It is a straightforward, easy pudding, but quite often a trifle too sweet for the Western palate. On the other hand, Semolina Mould will be enjoyed by even the most conservative eaters and is an unequalled winner with children.

AUBERGINE SALAD (Greek)

4 *large aubergines*
2 *cloves of garlic*
2 *tablespoons olive oil*
½ *lemon*
3 *teaspoons chopped parsley*
salt, pepper

Boil enough water to cover the aubergines and simmer till tender, about 15 minutes. Peel them and pound in a mortar with the garlic, salt and pepper. Add the oil drop by drop, stirring with a wooden spoon, then the lemon juice and parsley. Spread on bread or toast, or, as in Greece, serve in a bowl and each guest dips his bread in the purée.

ISTANBUL EGGS

olive oil
Turkish coffee
outside skins of onions
eggs

Take as many eggs as are required, cover with an equal quantity of olive oil, Turkish coffee and the brown skins of 2 large onions. Cover the pan and simmer very gently for 12 hours. The egg whites will be coffee-coloured when done and the yolks brilliant saffron yellow and the eggs will taste like chestnuts.

COLD LEEK SALAD (Greek)

8 *leeks*
boiling water
1 *tablespoon cornflour*
1 *tablespoon olive oil*
juice of 1 lemon
salt, pepper

Wash the leeks thoroughly. Cut off the green part. Cover with salted boiling water, boil for 20 to 30 minutes till soft. Drain, keeping ½ pint of liquid. Cool the liquid and mix with the cornflour. Pour over the leeks in the pan and cook gently till the sauce has thickened, stirring all the time. Add the lemon juice and oil, stir for another 3 minutes. Season with salt and pepper. Chill and serve very cold.

TARAMÁ (Dried Grey Mullet Eggs)

4 *oz. Taramá or*
8 *oz. smoked cods' roe*
juice of 1 or 2 lemons
¼ *pint olive oil*
black pepper

If smoked cods' roe is being used, scoop the roe out of skin. Put this or the mullet eggs into a mortar, pound it very slowly with the lemon juice and pepper, add the olive oil slowly and pound till it forms a thick smooth paste. Serve very cold on bread and butter or hot toast.

AVGOLEMONO (Chicken, Egg and Lemon Soup)

2 *pints chicken stock*
2 *oz. rice*
2 *eggs*
juice of 1 lemon
salt, pepper

Bring the stock to the boil, throw in the rice, simmer for 20 minutes. Beat the eggs with the lemon juice. Add 4 tablespoons of the very hot stock to the eggs and lemon, stirring all the time. Remove the chicken and rice soup from the heat, pour in the egg lemon mixture, season with salt and pepper. Serve at once. Never boil again once the eggs have been added.

EGG AND CHEESE SOUP (Greek)

2 *pints chicken stock*
4 *egg yolks*
4 *oz. grated cheese*

Heat the stock. Beat the eggs, add the cheese, stir over a very low heat in the soup pan until the cheese has melted. Slowly pour in the hot chicken stock, stirring all the time, heat again and serve.

GREEK FISH SOUP

2 *lb. any firm white fish*
1 *cod's head*
1 *onion chopped*
1 *leek chopped*
4 *sticks celery chopped*
1 *clove of garlic*
1 *sherry glass white wine*
3 *tablespoons tomato purée*
2 *oz. flour*
½ *pint milk*
2 *tablespoons chopped parsley*
1 *teaspoon chopped fennel*
1 *strip chopped lemon peel*
salt, pepper

Put the fish, cod's head, onion, leek, garlic and celery in a large pan, season with salt and pepper, cover with cold water, bring to the boil and simmer until the fish is soft. Time cannot be accurately given as it depends on the size or sort of fish. When cooked lift the fish out carefully. Cool, remove any bones, and break into large pieces. Simmer the stock for 20 minutes longer, strain and return to the pan. Mix the flour with the milk to a smooth paste, add the tomato juice and white wine, mix well. Add this to the fish stock, simmer and stir till it thickens. Now carefully put the cooked fish back in the soup, add the herbs. Serve with toast, one large piece of fish in each plate.

OKROCHKA (Iced Fish, Meat and Cucumber Soup)

4 *oz. diced fresh cucumber*
1 *oz. diced pickled cucumber*
3 *oz. diced cold cooked chicken*
   or cold meat
4 *oz. cooked shrimps or crab*
   or lobster
1 *oz. chopped leek*
1 *tablespoon chopped fennel*
2 *tablespoons chopped parsley*

1 *bottle yoghourt*
½ *pint milk*
2 *hard-boiled eggs, sliced*
salt, pepper

Mix the yoghourt with the milk, add all the ingredients except the eggs. Chill for 3 hours. Serve very cold with an ice cube in each serving and slices of hard-boiled egg floating on top. Sprinkle with more parsley if wished.

BOILED CHICKEN WITH LEMON

1 chicken
1 lemon
8 oz. carrots, chopped
8 oz. onions, chopped
3 sticks celery, chopped
8 oz. mushrooms, sliced
2 oz. butter
4 oz. blanched almonds
½ glass sherry
1 egg
½ pint chicken stock
4 tablespoons cream

Squeeze the lemon. Rub the bird with lemon juice and plenty of salt and pepper. Put half the lemon in the bird. Boil enough water to cover the bird, put it in with the vegetables. Simmer till tender. An old bird will take about 3 hours. When done put the chicken on the serving dish and keep warm. Now cook the mushrooms in butter till soft. Pour the chicken stock into a saucepan, add the cooked mushrooms, sherry, almonds, heat slowly. Beat the eggs and cream together in a basin, pour the very hot stock on gradually, stirring all the time till it thickens. Pour over the chicken and serve.

CHICKEN PILAF

8 oz. cooked chicken
8 oz. rice
1 medium chopped onion
2 oz. butter
2 pints chicken stock
2 large peeled chopped tomatoes
2 oz. chopped walnuts
salt, pepper
¼ teaspoon chopped thyme

Cut the chicken meat into strips. Fry these with the onion in the butter, in a large pot until brown. Add salt, pepper, thyme. Add the rice, stir well for 5 minutes to prevent sticking. Pour in the stock, tomatoes and walnuts. Cover the pot with a clean cloth and simmer gently till all the liquid has been absorbed and the rice is soft. With a fork stir all together. Leave covered in a warm place for 20 minutes and serve.

ARMENIAN AUBERGINES

10 small aubergines
8 oz. lean minced lamb
2 medium finely chopped onions
2 green or red pimentos, seeded and finely chopped
3 chopped garlic cloves
2 tablespoons chopped parsley
2 oz. pine kernels
2 oz. white fresh breadcrumbs
salt, pepper
¼ pint olive oil

Do not peel the aubergines, cut off the stalks. Heat the oil in a large frying pan, cook the aubergines gently for 10 minutes. Lift them one by one out of the oil. Put the chopped onion and pimentos into the oil and cook very gently for 10 minutes. Meanwhile cut the aubergines in half, longways, and scoop out the flesh without breaking the skins. Add the onions, pimentos, garlic, parsley, pine kernels, breadcrumbs and the minced lamb to the aubergine flesh, season with salt and pepper and mix well. Fill the aubergine skins with the mixture, arrange in a shallow fireproof dish, pour over them the remaining oil in the frying pan and cook in a slow oven for 15 minutes.

SHERKASIYA (Boiled Chicken with Nuts)

1 *chicken*
8 *oz. rice*
½ *pint chicken stock*
2 *medium chopped onions*
2 *oz. butter*
1 *red pepper or pimento, seeded*
  and chopped
3 *oz. walnuts chopped*
3 *oz. almonds chopped*
  and blanched

3 *oz. hazel nuts chopped*
salt

Boil the chicken and rice in the usual way. Carve the chicken in 4 pieces, arrange on the rice and keep warm. Fry the onions in butter till transparent. Pound to a paste, in a mortar, the nuts, red pepper and salt. Add these to the onions in the frying pan, mix well. Pour the chicken stock over; stir over a low heat. Pour this sauce over the chicken and rice.

AUBERGINES WITH PEPPERS AND TOMATOES

4 *aubergines*
4 *peppers (pimentos)*
2 *bottles yoghourt*
2 *large peeled sliced tomatoes*
6 *tablespoons olive oil*
salt, pepper

Cut the aubergines in slices, salt and pepper them. Take out the core and seeds of the pimentos, slice them, add salt and pepper. Salt and pepper the tomatoes.

Heat the oil, first fry the aubergines till soft, remove and drain and put on the warm serving dish. Now do the same to the peppers and put on top of the aubergines. Add the yoghourt. Fry the tomatoes in the oil and put on top. Serve hot.

AUBERGINES WITH YOGHOURT

2 *aubergines*
4 *tablespoons olive oil*
2 *crushed cloves of garlic*
2 *bottles yoghourt*
salt

Cut the unpeeled aubergines in ¼-inch thick slices sprinkle the rounds well with salt, leave for 30 minutes. Wash and dry. Heat the oil and fry till soft. Remove and keep warm on the serving dish. Crush the garlic, stir into the yoghourt and pour over the aubergines. Serve hot.

BALKAN PASTRY TART WITH SPINACH FILLING

1 *lb. chopped spinach*
1 *large chopped onion*
2 *oz. butter or dripping*
1 *tablespoon boiling water*
salt, pepper

Wash and chop the spinach finely. Heat the butter in a stewpan, add the finely chopped onion and cook till transparent, then add the spinach, boiling water, salt and pepper. Stir well, cover and cook quickly, stirring from time to time, for about 20 minutes. Drain well and fill a pastry case.

DOLMAS (Stuffed Vine Leaves)

3 *dozen vine leaves*
2 *cups cooked rice (2 oz.*
  uncooked)
1 *medium finely chopped onion*
1½ *tablespoons olive oil*
juice of 3 lemons
salt, pepper
½ *pint tomato juice*

Throw the leaves into boiling salted water and boil for 3 minutes. Drain. Heat the oil and fry the onions till golden brown. Remove from heat. Mix the onions and the oil with the cooked rice, add salt and pepper. Put 1 teaspoon of this mixture on the smooth side of each leaf, fold up into a little parcel, squeeze in the palm of the hand. Tightly pack the stuffed leaves in a shallow fireproof dish, sprinkle with the lemon juice, pour in the tomato juice. Put a plate on top to prevent them moving about and simmer for 30 minutes. Eat cold.

BALKAN STUFFED PIMENTOS

4 *large pimentos*
2 *cups cooked rice*
2 *small finely chopped onions*
1 *clove of finely chopped garlic*
2 *tablespoons currants*
4 *oz. finely chopped cooked beef,*
  lamb, etc.
salt, pepper
4 *tablespoons olive oil*
2 *tablespoons tomato purée*

Remove the stalks and slit the pimentos down one side, cut out the core and seeds. Wash thoroughly under the tap to remove every fiery seed. Mix all the ingredients except the oil and tomato purée and stuff the pimentos. Arrange them in a fireproof dish, pour over the oil and tomato purée, cover and bake in a moderate oven for 30 minutes.

SAVOURY RICE

8 *oz. rice*
2 *pints boiling meat stock*
  or water
8 *oz. liver*
4 *oz. dripping*
3 *medium finely chopped onions*
1 *large peeled chopped tomato*
1 *oz. sugar*
1 *teaspoon black pepper*
2 *teaspoons salt*
2 *oz. currants*
2 *oz. pine nuts*
1 *teaspoon chopped parsley*
1 *teaspoon chopped sage*
½ *teaspoon mixed spice*

Melt the fat in a large pot, chop the liver in ½-inch pieces, and fry for 3 minutes. Take out the liver, keep warm. Now cook the onion for 4 minutes till soft. Add the nuts and rice and fry for 5 minutes, stirring all the time. Add salt, pepper, currants, tomato, and pour on the boiling stock. Cook as for Plain Pilaf (see p. 66). Add the liver, sage and parsley. Cover and stand, warm, for 20 minutes.

PLAIN TURKISH OR GREEK PILAF

8 oz. rice
2 pints meat stock
3 oz. dripping or butter
1 teaspoon salt
1 teaspoon black pepper
2 oz. melted butter

In a large pot melt the fat, add the rice and fry for 5 minutes. Boil the stock and when boiling pour on to the frying rice, add salt and pepper. Cover the pot with a clean cloth and then clamp on the lid. Cook on a very low heat until there is no liquid left, about 50 minutes. Remove from heat, still covered, and stand for 20 minutes. Pour the melted butter over and mix well before eating.

RISSOLES

1 lb. minced meat, mutton or beef
1 large chopped onion
2 oz. grated cheese
1 tablespoon chopped dill
1 chopped clove of garlic
3 eggs
salt, pepper

3 oz. flour
4 oz. cooked rice

Mix the mince, onion, cheese, garlic, dill, salt and pepper well to make a stiff paste. Add two eggs, mix thoroughly for 2 minutes. Form into small cakes, about 2½ inches across. Dip in 1 beaten egg, roll in flour. Fry in deep fat till brown.
Serve hot with Lemon and Egg Sauce (see p. 72).

PINE NUT AND MEAT RISSOLES

1 lb. minced meat
3 medium boiled potatoes
1 egg
1 oz. pine nuts
1 oz. currants
½ teaspoon chopped thyme
½ teaspoon chopped dill
½ teaspoon chopped parsley

salt, pepper
tomato sauce

Mash the potatoes with a fork, add the mince, stir in the beaten egg. Add the nuts, currants, herbs, salt and pepper. Mix together and form into little round flat cakes about 2 inches across. Fry in deep fat till brown. Serve with tomato sauce.

SPAGHETTI WITH YOGHOURT AND TOMATO PASTE

8 oz. spaghetti
2½ pints boiling water
3 oz. butter
2 bottles yoghourt
1 chopped clove of garlic
2 tablespoons tomato paste
salt, pepper

Throw the spaghetti into the boiling salted water, boil till soft, about 20 minutes. Drain and put under the hot tap. Melt the butter in the pan, add the garlic, tomato paste, and pepper, stir and cook gently for 3 minutes. Add the cooked spaghetti, pour over the yoghourt, stir well and serve.

SPAGHETTI WITH YOGHOURT

8 oz. spaghetti
4 pints boiling water
2 teaspoons salt
4 oz. butter
2 bottles yoghourt
2 teaspoons paprika pepper
1 crushed clove of garlic

Put the salt into the water and bring to the boil. Throw in the spaghetti. Boil for 20 minutes. Strain and run under the hot tap for 2 minutes. Melt 2 oz. butter, add the garlic and the cooked spaghetti, stir gently and cook for 3 minutes. Add the yoghourt. Melt 2 oz. butter, add the paprika and pour over.

BALKAN STUFFED TOMATOES

12 large tomatoes
4 oz. cooked rice
2 finely chopped medium onions
2 oz. currants
2 chopped cloves of garlic
¼ pint olive oil
4 oz. cold mutton or beef, chopped finely
salt, pepper

Cut the tops off the tomatoes, scoop out the flesh. Mix this flesh with the other ingredients, season with salt and pepper, and stuff the tomatoes. Pour the oil into a shallow fireproof dish or roasting pan and heat for 10 minutes in a moderate oven, arrange the tomatoes, cover the dish (greaseproof paper, if no lid available) and bake for a further 20 minutes.

TRAY BOREK (Flaky Pastry with Cheese and Minced Meat)

PASTRY:
8 oz. plain flour
3 oz. melted butter
2 eggs
2 tablespoons cold water

FILLING:

2 oz. cream cheese
3 oz. cooked minced meat
salt

Make a dough with the flour, a third of the butter, 1 egg and the water. Roll into 2 balls and leave for 15 minutes in a cold place.

Roll each piece very thinly, spread with melted butter. Do this again and again until all the butter is used up. Roll into 2 rounds as thinly as possible — paper thin is perfect. Grease a round shallow baking tin and spread one round on the bottom. Pinch it with the finger tips to crumple it. Mix the cheese, minced meat and salt well together, place on the pastry, put the other round on top, damp and seal the edges.

Beat the second egg, brush the top and bake in a moderate oven for 35 minutes.

LAMB PILAF

8 oz. cooked lamb

Proceed as for Savoury Rice (see p. 65), but use cooked lamb cut in strips instead of liver.

BRAISED CALVES' BRAINS

2 *calves' brains*
4 *oz. butter*
1 *cup cooked pearl barley*
4 *oz. cream cheese*
½ *teaspoon chopped sweet basil*
salt, pepper
blanched vine or cabbage leaves

Soak the brains in cold salted water for 1 hour. Clean and dry thoroughly. Melt the butter in a saucepan, add the brains, cook gently for 15 minutes. Chop in ½-inch squares, mix with the barley, cream cheese, basil, salt and pepper. Put a little of the mixture on each blanched leaf, roll up and peg with a matchstick or tie with cotton. Arrange in a shallow fireproof dish, pour over the butter in which the brains have been cooked and bake in a moderate oven for 20 minutes, with the dish covered. Remove pegs or threads and serve hot.

BOILED LAMB

2½ *lb. lamb*
1½ *pints cold water*
8 *oz. carrots, chopped*
3 *sticks celery, chopped*
2 *medium onions, chopped*
2 *oz. dripping*
2 *oz. flour*
4 *egg yolks*
1 *dessertspoon cold water*
uice of 2 lemons
salt, pepper

Cut the meat in 1½-inch squares, add the carrots, celery, onions, salt, pepper and the water. Bring to the boil, remove the scum, and simmer for 1½ hours. Strain the dish. Put the meat and vegetables on the serving dish and keep warm. Melt the dripping, add the flour, stir for 2 minutes, pour over the hot meat liquid gradually, stir and cook for 5 minutes till it thickens. Mix the egg yolks, lemon juice and water, pour into the hot thick sauce, stir well, do *NOT* boil. Pour over the serving dish.

MOUSAKA

1 *lb. minced beef or lamb or mutton*
10 *small onions, finely chopped*
2 *tablespoons olive oil*
4 *sliced unpeeled aubergines*
¼ *pint olive oil*
1 *bay leaf*
salt, pepper
½ *pint meat stock*
1½ *pints tomato sauce*
¼ *pint cream or milk*
1 *egg*

Fry the sliced aubergines till soft in hot olive oil for 3 or 4 minutes. Fry the onions in butter till transparent. Take a medium roasting dish, pour a tablespoon of oil on the bottom. Arrange a layer of aubergines, then a layer of mince, sprinkle with salt and pepper and add the bay leaf, then a layer of onions. Fill the dish with layers like this. Pour over the stock and tomato sauce. Cover the dish and cook in a slow to moderate oven for 45 minutes, or until the liquid has reduced considerably. Beat the egg in the cream or milk, season with salt and pepper and pour over the dish. Cook for 30 minutes or more in a very slow oven, to form a custard on top of the dish.

TURKISH LAMB STEW

2 lb. lamb, cut in 3-inch pieces
1 lb. potatoes, peeled and
   quartered
3 large tomatoes, peeled and sliced
3 large onions, sliced
1 teaspoon chopped sage
1 teaspoon chopped fennel

1 teaspoon dill
2 bay leaves
1 green pimento, seeded and sliced
2 cloves of garlic, chopped
salt, pepper
1½ pints meat stock

Put all the ingredients in a large pot. Simmer for 2½ hours.

PICTI (Pig's head brawn)

1 pig's head
4 bay leaves
20 peppercorns
juice of 4 lemons
salt, pepper

Cover the pig's head with warm water, add the bay leaves, peppercorns, salt and pepper, bring to the boil and simmer for 5 hours. Let it cool in the water, skin and pick off all the good meat. Cut into 1-inch squares. Reduce the stock by half. Strain and add the lemon juice. Arrange the meat in a basin and pour over the stock. Leave it to set.

SKEWERED LAMB (Sis Kebabs)

2 lb. leg of lamb
1 large onion, grated
2 large onions, sliced
4 tablespoons olive oil
1 teaspoon salt
¼ teaspoon black pepper
1 bay leaf

Beat the lamb, rub with the salt, pepper and grated onion. Cut into 1½-inch squares. Put into a bowl and pour on the olive oil and the bay leaf, leave for 2 hours, turning occasionally. Slice the onions thinly and cut the bay leaf into pieces. Impale the meat on skewers with a slice of onion and bay leaf between each piece. Grill under a fierce heat, watch carefully and turn till all sides are cooked.

STIPHADO (Greek Beef Stew)

2 lb. steak
6 tablespoons olive oil
3 lb. small onions
4 cloves of garlic, chopped
½ pint thick tomato paste
¼ pint red wine
salt, pepper

Cut the steak in pieces, 3 × 2 inches. Rub well with salt and pepper. Heat the oil in a stew pan, fry the meat, onions and garlic till brown. Add the tomato purée, and the wine. Cover very tightly and simmer very slowly for 5 hours, till the sauce is thick, like jam.

YOGHOURT AND TOMATO STEW

2 *lb. leg of lamb*
2 *medium sliced carrots*
cold water
salt, pepper
2 *large peeled chopped tomatoes*
1 *pimento, chopped and seeded*

2 *bottles yoghourt*
2 *teaspoons chopped mint*

Cut the meat in 1½-inch squares. Add the carrots, salt and pepper, cover with ¾ pint cold water and stew very gently for 1 hour. Add the tomatoes and pimento and simmer for 1 hour. Stir in the yoghourt, add the mint and serve.

BROAD BEANS AND ARTICHOKES

8 *artichoke 'hearts'*
2 *lb. broad beans*
2 *tablespoons olive oil*
1 *level teaspoon cornflour*
¼ *pint bean stock*
1 *lemon*
2 *teaspoons chopped parsley*

Cook the beans and artichokes separately. Remove the hearts from the artichokes. Strain these, keeping ¼ pint of the bean water. Melt the oil in a thick saucepan large enough to hold the vegetables, stir in the cornflour, add the bean water, the juice of the lemon and the parsley. Add the vegetables and stir gently till they are coated with the oily sauce.

FRIED HARICOT BEANS

4 *oz. haricot beans*
2 *teaspoons chopped parsley*
1 *medium onion*
1 *clove of garlic*
1 *level teaspoon bicarbonate of soda*
2 *oz. white bread*
½ *teaspoon salt*
dripping for frying

Soak the beans overnight. Put the soaked beans, onion, garlic, through the mincer. Soak the bread in water and squeeze dry. Pound the minced mixture, bread, parsley, salt and bicarbonate in a mortar till soft and well mixed. Leave for 2 hours. Flatten on a floured board, cut in 1-inch squares and fry till golden brown in deep fat.

POTATO KEPHTIDES

1 *lb. cold boiled potatoes*
½ *oz. melted butter*
2 *finely chopped spring onions*
2 *large tomatoes, chopped and peeled*
2 *oz. flour*
salt, pepper
olive oil or dripping for frying

Sieve the potatoes and mix with all the ingredients. Knead slightly and roll ¾ inch thick and cut in rounds about 2½ inches across. Heat the oil or dripping till smoking hot, and fry quickly.

These potato rounds can be baked on a greased oven sheet in a hot oven till golden brown. They should be crisp outside but very soft inside.

BALKAN AUBERGINE PURÉE

2 *aubergines*
1 *medium onion, finely chopped*
1 *tablespoon chopped parsley*
2 *teaspoons salt*
¼ *teaspoon black pepper*
3 *tablespoons olive oil*
2 *teaspoons lemon juice*

Take off the stems of the aubergines. Grill the aubergines just as they are under a moderate heat till the skins brown and split. Poke a skewer in to see if they are soft; when they are, remove and peel. Slice and pound in a mortar, with the onion, salt, pepper and parsley, till smooth. Add the oil drop by drop, stirring all the time with a wooden spoon. Add the lemon juice and mix well. Serve on brown bread or toast.

LIME SAUCE

6 *limes*
¼ *pint olive oil*
pinch celery salt
¼ *pint clear honey*
1 *teaspoon paprika*

Cut limes in half and squeeze out ¼ pint juice. Add olive oil, a drop at a time, and whisk. Add salt, paprika and honey and beat hard for 5 minutes.

LEMON AND MUSTARD SAUCE

2 *tablespoons lemon juice*
4 *tablespoons olive oil*
2 *cloves of garlic, crushed*
1 *teaspoon dry mustard*
½ *teaspoon salt*

¼ *teaspoon black pepper*
1 *teaspoon chopped parsley*

Mix the lemon juice and oil together, add the garlic, mustard, salt and pepper. Stir thoroughly, sieve and add the parsley. Good with grilled fish.

THICK TOMATO PASTE

tomatoes
salt
olive oil

Take ½ teaspoon salt for every lb. of tomatoes. Chop the tomatoes, add the salt, cook slowly till all reduced to a pulp. Sieve, then return to the pan and cook slowly to reduce the juice and make the pulp thick and fairly stiff. Spoon into bowls and put in the sun to dry out, or failing this a warm place or cool oven will do. Pour oil over each bowl to seal and store. This paste is used in stews, rice and macaroni dishes in Greece.

AVGOLEMONO (LEMON AND EGG) SAUCE

½ *pint chicken or meat stock*
3 *egg yolks*
juice of 1 *lemon*

Heat the stock. Beat the egg yolks with the lemon juice, pour on the very hot stock, stir till thick. You may make this in a double boiler, if preferred, taking care not to boil, or the eggs will curdle.

Serve with practically any meat dish, especially rissoles and boiled rice.

TOMATO SAUCE OR PURÉE (Greek)

2 *lb. large ripe tomatoes, peeled*
and chopped
4 *lumps sugar*
1 *chopped garlic clove*
1 *medium chopped onion*
2 *oz. minced beef*
salt, pepper

½ *teaspoon chopped basil or*
½ *teaspoon chopped fennel*

Put all the ingredients in a large stew pan. Cover and simmer very slowly, stirring from time to time, for 30 minutes. Sieve this pulp. If the sauce is too liquid, return to the pan and reduce till thick enough.

SKORDALIA (Greek Garlic Mayonnaise Sauce)

2 *egg yolks*
4 *oz. ground almonds*
2 *oz. white breadcrumbs*
6 *cloves of garlic*
1 *pint olive oil*
1 *tablespoon lemon juice*
2 *teaspoons chopped parsley*
¼ *teaspoon salt*
¼ *teaspoon pepper*

Pound the garlic in a mortar, add the egg yolks, almonds, breadcrumbs, stir with a wooden spoon add salt and pepper and the oil drop by drop as for mayonnaise sauce, stirring all the time, lastly stir in the lemon juice and parsley.

Serve with cold fish, cold meats, cooked cold vegetables, potatoes boiled in their skins; in fact, with what you fancy.

SEMOLINA MOULD

4 *oz. semolina*
2 *oz. butter*
4 *oz. castor sugar*
⅜ *pint water*
¾ *pint milk*
4 *oz. blanched chopped almonds*

Heat the butter in a saucepan and add the semolina and almonds. Stir with a wooden spoon till brown. In another pan add the sugar to the milk and water and very slowly bring to the boil. Pour this slowly over the browned semolina and nuts, stirring all the time over a low heat. When thick, cover with a clean cloth, then put the lid on, keeping on the gentlest heat till all liquid has been absorbed. Pour into a wetted mould. Turn out when cold and set.

HONEY SOUFFLÉ

6 tablespoons honey
4 eggs
¼ pint cream

Separate the eggs, whip whites till stiff. Whip cream till thick.

Beat the egg yolks and honey. Put in double saucepan, stir until the mixture thickens: do *NOT* boil. Cool. Fold in the whites and the cream.

Serve very cold.

MAHALLEHI OR MILK PUDDING

1½ pints milk
¼ pint water
4 oz. sugar
2 oz. rice
1 oz. ground rice

Bring the milk and water to the boil, throw in the rice, simmer for 10 minutes. Mix the ground rice to a paste with enough milk from the pan. Add to the cooked rice with sugar and simmer for 10 minutes more. Eat cold, sprinkled with cinnamon or with coarsely ground mixed nuts.

SIPHANIC HONEY TART

8 oz. milk cheese
2 tablespoons honey
1½ oz. sugar
4 oz. plain flour
4 oz. butter
cold water
2 eggs
1 teaspoon cinnamon

Make the pastry of the flour, sugar, butter and water. Roll out and cover a plate or shallow dish. Mix the cheese and honey together, add the beaten eggs and half the cinnamon. Spread on the pastry, sprinkle the rest of the cinnamon on top. Bake in a moderate oven for 35 minutes.

YOGHOURT

Serve as a sweet course with dried apricot, blackcurrant purée, or orange marmalade. Brown sugar is best with it. Any stewed fruit is good hot or cold.

PALACE BREAD (Esh es Seraya)

8 oz. honey
1 lb. crustless stale bread
4 oz. sugar
4 oz. butter
Devonshire cream

Dice the bread. Mix with the honey, sugar and butter in a saucepan over a low heat, stirring into a moist paste. Press into a shallow round dish. When cold cut like a cake. Serve with the cream.

TURKISH COFFEE

coffee
sugar
water

Turkish coffee should be made in a Turkish coffee pot, one to each person. However, it can be made for 4 people in a lipped saucepan. The secret is that it must be strong, sweet and frothy.

For 4 people, take 4 teaspoons coffee, 4 teaspoons sugar and 4 coffee cups cold water. Bring to the boil, remove from the heat and stir. Bring to the boil, remove and stir. Repeat once more, three times in all. Serve immediately while still frothy. If more cups are wanted, boil a fresh brew.

TURKISH DELIGHT

2½ *lb. sugar*
1¼ *pints water*
4 *oz. cornflour*
   mixed to a paste in cold water
½ *teaspoon tartaric acid*
1 *tablespoon rose water*
icing sugar
almond oil
2 *oz. chopped pistachio nuts*

Mix the tartaric acid, rose water and cornflour paste together. Boil the sugar and water together to a thick syrup. Stir the cornflour mixture into the syrup, add the nuts. Pour into a shallow tin, greased with almond oil. Cool, dust well with icing sugar. Ease from the tin, dust with more icing sugar, cut into squares. Roll each piece in icing sugar.

KOURABIEDES

8 *oz. butter*
1 *lb. plain flour*
8 *oz. icing sugar*
1 *teaspoon baking powder*
extra icing sugar to decorate

This is the Greek version of shortbread. Cream the butter and gradually add the mixed flour, sugar and baking powder, working well in. Roll out and cut into 3-inch strips. Bake in slow oven for 45 minutes. When cooked, but not browned, dip each piece in icing sugar, covering completely.

APPLES WITH WINE

6 *cooking apples*
¼ *pint sweet red dessert*
   wine
1 *teaspoon cinnamon*
¼ *pint cream*
4 *oz. soft brown sugar*
4 *oz. butter*

Peel and slice apples. Heat butter and cook apples in this until soft and golden. Add sugar, cinnamon and wine and cook for 5 minutes longer, increasing heat to moderate. Remove apple slices and arrange in a dish. Strain sauce and pour over. Serve with whipped cream.

Belgium

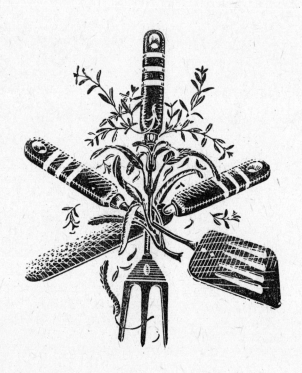

COOKING IN BELGIUM

It is only fitting and fair that the second recipe in a chapter on Belgian cooking should be Brussels Sprouts Soup — though it does not solve one of the minor mysteries which always puzzled me: why are sprouts named after the delightful capital of Belgium?

Belgian cooking is an odd mixture of French, Dutch and Flemish dishes and is justly famed for its excellence. The Belgians have the same live interest in good food as the French. Just ask any taxi driver in Brussels where you ought to take your next meal, and you'll be lucky to get away in half an hour. He will go into long dissertations on the relative value of various establishments, he will make detailed enquiries of your special preference. You will realise that this problem of a meal cannot be treated light-heartedly. It is a big enough problem to give it your whole mind, because good food is IMPORTANT.

To prepare a Belgian Chicken Pâté you must be at leisure, and furthermore of a generous nature to be willing to sacrifice 2 glasses of brandy for a truly royal pâté. It is not an everyday routine dish — but something to be prepared lovingly for special occasions.

Braised Chicory is one of the best internationally known Belgian dishes — ideal for a luncheon party, served with a fresh salad.

Chicken Waterzoie is the oldest national Belgian dish and once you include it in your repertoire it will always stay in it. It is obviously a hearty country dish and has to be served in man-sized soup plates, which are big enough to hold the portions of chicken as well as the vegetables.

Neither rabbits nor prunes will ever send anyone into gastronomic raptures — so I take off my hat to the Belgians for combining the two into an exquisite dish of Rabbit and Prunes — even if you do have to use half a bottle of wine when preparing it. Both the Rabbit dish and the Meat Rolls are perfect for the cook-hostess who wants to finish all the work in the kitchen well before the guests arrive.

CHICKEN PÂTÉ

1 *small roasting chicken*
1 *lb. bacon fat*
8 *oz. lean pork*
2 *glasses brandy*
8 *oz. streaky bacon rashers*
1 *bay leaf*
thyme
salt
pepper

Carve the breast of an uncooked chicken into thin slices. Remove the rest of the meat from the bones and first mince it and then pound it until very smooth, with the bacon fat and the pork. Season with salt and pepper. Add the brandy. Line a shallow earthenware dish with bacon rashers, lay a bay-leaf and a sprig of thyme on them. Put half the minced meats into the dish, cover with the sliced breast, fill the dish with the rest of the minced meats. Arrange bacon rashers on the top. Cook very slowly in a *bain-marie* for 2 hours. Put weights on top of the dish and leave to cool.

BRUSSELS SPROUTS SOUP

2 *lb. Brussels sprouts*
2 *pints chicken stock*
2 *egg yolks*
½ *pint cream*
1 *oz. butter*
½ *oz. flour*
salt
pepper
nutmeg

Cook the sprouts in boiling salted water. Drain. Toss them in the butter, stir the flour into the fat, gradually add the hot stock. Cook until sprouts are very soft. Pass through a sieve. Beat the eggs with the cream. Stir the soup into the egg mixture gradually. Season with salt, pepper and nutmeg. Reheat, but do not boil. Serve in warmed plates.

FRICADELLES (Minced Meat Balls)

2 *lb. minced pork*
2 *small onions, sliced*
2 *slices bread*
1 *gill milk*
1 *glass white wine*
2 *eggs*
2 *oz. lard*
1 *pint stock*
bouquet garni
4 *medium potatoes*

salt
pepper

Fry the onions lightly in 1 oz. lard. Mix with the meat. Add the bread, previously soaked in a little milk, the wine and the egg yolks. Season with salt and pepper. Beat well together and fold in the stiffly beaten egg whites. Shape into balls, roll in flour and fry in the lard until brown. Poach the meat balls in the stock with the *bouquet garni* and quartered potatoes for 30 minutes. Remove the bouquet. Serve the balls in their sauce, sprinkled with parsley.

STEWED EEL WITH FRESH HERBS

2 lb. eel
2 oz. butter
2 glasses white wine
2 egg yolks
mint
salt
chervil
parsley
sorrel

juice of 2 lemons
pepper

Cut the eel into 2-inch lengths. Stew in the butter with the chopped herbs for 15 minutes. Add the wine and enough water to cover the fish. Simmer for 10 minutes. Put the fish in a shallow earthenware dish. Mix the egg yolks and lemon juice together, add gradually to the stock, season with salt and pepper. Pour over the fish. Leave to cool.

BRAISED CHICORY

8 heads chicory
8 slices cooked ham
2 oz. grated Gruyère cheese
½ pint white sauce (see p. 206)
1 oz. butter
nutmeg
lemon juice

Simmer the chicory in salted water with a few drops of lemon juice for 25 minutes. Drain. Add half the grated cheese and a little nutmeg to the sauce. Wrap a slice of ham round each head of chicory. Lay them in a shallow fireproof dish. Pour the sauce over them. Sprinkle with the rest of the grated cheese. Dot with butter. Bake in a moderate oven for 20 minutes.

KIDNEYS WITH JUNIPER BERRIES

4 veal kidneys
4 oz. butter
½ glass white wine
12 juniper berries
salt
pepper

Sprinkle the kidneys with salt and pepper. Brown on both sides in half the butter. Cover the pan and cook slowly for 2 minutes. Add the wine, the crushed juniper berries and the rest of the butter cut into small pieces. Continue to cook slowly until the kidneys are tender.

CHICKEN WATERZOIE

1 boiling fowl
2 onions stuck with cloves
3 sticks celery, chopped
3 leeks, sliced
1 carrot, sliced
bouquet garni
1 lemon
½ bottle white wine
salt

pepper
parsley

Rub the chicken with lemon. Simmer with the vegetables in just enough water to cover. When the water boils add the *bouquet garni* and the white wine. Season with salt and pepper. Continue simmering for 1½ hours. Cut the chicken into pieces, remove the *bouquet garni*, serve the chicken in the stock with the vegetables, garnished with chopped parsley.

CELERIAC WITH CHEESE SAUCE

1 *lb. celeriac, sliced*
4 *oz. grated Parmesan cheese*
2 *oz. butter*
¼ *pint stock*
salt
pepper

Butter a shallow fireproof dish. Fill it with alternate layers of celeriac and grated cheese, and pour the stock over it. Season with salt and pepper. Dot with butter. Bake in a moderate oven for 45 minutes.

RABBIT WITH PRUNES

1 *rabbit, jointed*
½ *bottle red wine*
2 *tablespoons vinegar*
4 *peppercorns*
2 *bay leaves*
thyme
2 *oz. butter*
2 *oz. flour*
salt
pepper

1 *lb. prunes*
1 *tablespoon red currant jelly*

Marinate the rabbit in the wine and vinegar with the peppercorns and herbs for 24 hours. Drain and fry lightly on all sides in the butter. Stir in the flour. Add enough water to cover. Season with salt and pepper. Add the prunes, soaked if necessary, cover the pan and simmer for 1 hour or until tender. Stir in the red currant jelly before serving.

CARBONNADE OF BEEF

1½ *lb. stewing steak*
4 *onions, sliced*
2 *oz. dripping*
½ *pint beer*
2 *tablespoons concentrated tomato purée*
½ *pint stock*
bouquet garni
flour
nutmeg
pepper
salt

Fry the onions lightly in the dripping. Cut the meat into pieces, dredge with seasoned flour. Transfer the onions to a casserole. Seal the meat on all sides in the dripping. Put it with the onions. Pour the beer into the frying pan, simmer uncovered until the beer is reduced by half. Add the stock and the tomato purée, mix well together and simmer for 1 minute. Pour the sauce over the meat, add a *bouquet garni* and a pinch of nutmeg. Cook, covered, in a moderate oven for 2 hours.

CHICORY SALAD

4 *heads chicory*
2 *tablespoons olive oil*
1 *tablespoon lemon juice*
½ *teaspoon sugar*
½ *teaspoon salt*
pepper

Shred the chicory. Mix the olive oil and lemon juice thoroughly. Stir in the sugar, salt and pepper, over the chicory.

MEAT ROLLS

8 *thin slices rump steak*
8 *rashers streaky bacon*
1 *oz. lard*
1 *large onion*
½ *pint stock*
1 *glass red wine*
chopped parsley
salt
pepper

Lay a rasher of bacon on each slice of beef. Season with salt, pepper and chopped parsley. Roll and secure with cocktail sticks. Fry in the lard until all sides are lightly browned. Transfer to a shallow fire-proof dish. Fry the chopped onion until golden. Add it to the meat. Add the stock and the wine, cover the dish and cook in a moderate oven for 1 hour. Season the sauce with salt and pepper and reduce it if necessary.

MEULEMEESTER EGGS

6 *eggs*
2 *oz. butter*
½ *teaspoon French mustard*
1 *dozen shelled prawns*
½ *teaspoon chopped chervil*
1 *teaspoon chopped parsley*
½ *pint cream*
salt and pepper
1 *oz. grated cheese*

Hard-boil the eggs, plunge into cold water then shell them. Chop small and mix with 1 oz. melted butter, chervil and parsley, mustard, prawns, cream, salt and pepper. Arrange the mixture in a buttered dish, sprinkle with cheese and the remaining butter cut in pieces, and cook in a hot oven until the top is nicely brown.

GAUFRES (Waffles)

1 *lb. plain flour*
½ *oz. yeast*
8 *eggs*
½ *pint cream*
2 *oz. butter*
pinch salt
sugar
3 *tablespoons brandy*

Dissolve the yeast in a little warm water, then mix well with 4 oz. flour. Leave for 1 hour and when risen add the rest of the flour, pinch of salt and sugar, the beaten eggs, cream, melted butter and brandy. Work all well together and leave for another 2 hours. Cook in waffle irons until golden brown on both sides. Serve hot sprinkled with sugar.

Canada

COOKING IN CANADA

Have you ever realised how hazy even an ambitious cook's ideas are on the cuisine of some countries? It is very similar to general historical knowledge as represented in *1066 and All That*. In fact one could write a whole book on this subject and call it *Goulash and All That*. In one of my private little surveys to find out what a cross-section of people know about various subjects, I discovered that the only answer to the question of Canadian cookery was 'maple syrup'. Now Canada is a great big country with vast agricultural resources, peopled with home- and good-food-loving individuals of French and English ancestry. This combination naturally produces a rich and varied diet. They have the best home-cured bacon. Eggs and chickens come farm-fresh into the cities' supermarkets. Home grown tomatoes, blueberries, green peppers are all grown in Canada's rich soil. With raw material like this the Canadian cook produces hearty, countrified and absolutely enormous meals. But you can use their recipes without having their produce. Baked Canadian Bacon for instance is just about the best way to prepare a piece of gammon. Their Egg Mousse combines the essentials of a hearty meal with French finesse and their Chicken Pudding will give you good value from one chicken.

Canadians absolutely excel in sweets and pastries. Every self-respecting housewife bakes her pies and cookies regularly — you can never call at a Canadian house without being offered some good home-made pie or wafers. Backwoods Pie, Johnny Cake, Railroad Cake, will all bring you the aroma of wide open spaces and the feeling of a homestead, where a large family gathers round the log fire. Nut Brittles and Brownies I can recommend for any occasion, but especially on Guy Fawkes Night. The Canadian Mum usually makes large quantities of these for Hallowe'en Night 'Handouts' for the children who come roaming along the streets in weird costumes.

Lastly, I find that Canadians show a lot of imagination in preparing tasty and wholesome sandwich fillings — you stop worrying about your waistline after one bite of Canadian chicken sandwich.

TOMATO SOUP WITH MACARONI

1 *oz. butter*
1 *oz. flour*
1 *tablespoon chopped onion*
1 *tablespoon chopped green pepper*
1 *pint brown stock or consommé*
4 *medium tomatoes*
2 *tablespoons macaroni rings*
salt, pepper
cayenne pepper
½ *teaspoon vinegar*

1 *tablespoon grated horseradish or*
2 *tablespoons horseradish sauce*

Cook the chopped onion and pepper in the butter for 5 minutes. Add the flour and blend. Add the stock and tomatoes and simmer for 15 minutes. Pass through a sieve. Season highly with salt, pepper and cayenne pepper. Cook the macaroni separately. Just before serving add the horseradish, vinegar and cooked macaroni. If horseradish sauce is used instead of fresh horseradish less vinegar is necessary.

KIDNEY STEW

2 *medium-sized beef kidneys*
1 *oz. flour*
2 *slices bacon*
1 *oz. butter or dripping*
3 *oz. raw celery*
2 *medium onions*
1 *large tin tomatoes (1¾ pints)*
1 *green pepper*
1 *teaspoon salt*
¼ *teaspoon cayenne pepper*
⅛ *teaspoon curry powder*

Scald kidneys and soak them in salted water for 2 to 3 hours. Change the water 2 or 3 times during that period. Remove the fat, split the kidneys lengthways and take out the white centre and the tubes. Sprinkle the kidneys with flour. Mince the bacon and sauté it slowly until it is light brown. Add the butter. Brown the kidney, chopped into ½-inch slices, in this fat together with the onions and celery chopped fine. Cover the pan and simmer for 10 minutes. Bring to the boil and add the tomatoes, salt, pepper and curry powder. Seed and shred the green pepper and add it. Cover the pan again and simmer the stew for about 15 minutes or until the pieces of green pepper are tender. Stir it often.

Serve with rice or boiled noodles.

LAMB CHOPS WITH TOMATO SAUCE

4 *lamb chops*
1 *oz. butter or dripping*
2 *medium onions*
¼ *pint tomato juice or soup*
¼ *pint water*
flour
salt, pepper

Trim the chops, sprinkle them with salt and pepper and roll in flour. Brown them lightly in the butter. Put them in a fireproof baking dish. Peel the onions, slice them finely and then sprinkle them over the chops. Mix the tomato juice with the water and heat to boiling point. Pour it over the chops. Cover the baking dish and bake in a slow oven for about 1½ hours. Serve with new potatoes or creamed potatoes sprinkled with parsley.

BAKED CANADIAN BACON

2 *lb. gammon*
¼ *pint grapefruit or pineapple juice*
½ *teaspoon dry mustard*
4 *oz. brown sugar*

Combine the brown sugar and the mustard and spread them over the gammon. Bake uncovered for 1 hour in a moderately hot oven and baste with the fruit juice. Add further fruit juice if necessary. Peel off the skin (if the gammon is cooked the skin will peel off easily). Serve with the juice from the pan as sauce.

BREAKFAST SAUSAGE

4 *oz. beef*
4 *oz. pork or bacon*
4 *oz. breadcrumbs*
black pepper
salt
1 *egg, beaten*

Mince the meat finely. Beat in the breadcrumbs, egg and seasoning. Shape into a thick roll, tie in a very well greased and floured cloth and boil for 2½ hours. Remove from the cloth and drain. Serve hot or cold.

CHICKEN PUDDING

PASTE:
1 *lb. flour*
2 *teaspoons baking powder*
8 *oz. lard or butter*
water to mix

FILLING:
1 *medium chicken*
alt
1 *tablespoon flour*
black pepper
2 *oz. butter*

Make a paste with the flour, baking powder, lard or butter, salt and water. Roll out rather thick and line a greased pudding basin with it, saving enough paste for the lid. With a sharp knife cut the chicken meat into small pieces. Sprinkle with flour, salt, and pepper. Fill the prepared pudding basin with the chicken, add a little water and butter. Cover with the paste lid, then with greased paper, then tie down with a cloth. Steam for 2 hours. Meanwhile simmer the chicken bones and the giblets with seasoning. Add the resulting stock as necessary to the pudding when it is served.

EGGS BENEDICT

4 *crumpets*
4 *slices ham or gammon*
hollandaise sauce
butter
4 *eggs*

Toast and butter the crumpets and set aside to keep hot. Fry the ham, and lay a slice on top of each crumpet. Poach the eggs and put one on top of each slice of ham. Cover the eggs with a hollandaise sauce (see p. 161).

EGG MOUSSE

6 *hard-boiled eggs*
¾ *pint mayonnaise (see p. 161)*
½ *pint whipped cream*
black pepper
2 *lb. skinned chopped tomatoes*
1 *tin crab or lobster*
1¼ *tablespoons granulated gelatine*
salt

Dissolve the gelatine in a very little hot water and allow it to cool. Cut the hard-boiled eggs very fine and fold them into the mayonnaise. Fold in the gelatine, which should be cool but still liquid. Fold in the whipped cream and seasoning. Put the mixture into a ring mould and turn out when thoroughly set. The centre may be filled with a mixture of skinned and chopped tomatoes and tinned crab or lobster.

RAGOÛT OF TOMATOES

4 *large tomatoes (or ¾ pint tinned*
  tomatoes)
1 *oz. butter*
1 *green pepper*
1 *large onion*
½ *teaspoon salt*
1 *teaspoon paprika*
2½ *teaspoons brown sugar*
cream
½ *oz. flour*

Chop the onion. Seed and shred the pepper. Peel and slice the tomatoes. Melt the butter in a saucepan. Add all the chopped vegetables and cook until they are tender. This should take about 15 minutes. Add the salt, paprika and brown sugar. Strain the juice from the saucepan. Add to the juice enough cream or evaporated milk to make ½ pint liquid. Combine this carefully with the flour and cook, stirring constantly, until it is thick and well blended. Add the vegetables, bring just to the boil and serve. This makes a good vegetable dish or may be served as a supper dish spread on toast or accompanied by bacon.

TOMATO AND ORANGE SALAD

6 *small tomatos, peeled and*
  quartered
2 *oranges*
tomato ketchup
juice of ½ orange

Peel the oranges and divide into segments. Cut segments into halves if the oranges are large. Mix with the tomatoes and tomato ketchup diluted with the orange juice.

BACKWOODS PIE

8 *oz. short crust pastry*
4 *oz. brown sugar*
12 *oz. syrup (maple if possible)*
¼ *pint milk*
2 *oz. butter*
3 *eggs, separated*
nutmeg to taste

Beat all together except the egg whites. Beat the egg whites stiff and fold them into the mixture. Line a flan tin with good short crust. Pour the mixture in. Bake in a moderate oven for 30 to 40 minutes.

MENNONITE TOAST

8 *slices bread 1 inch thick with crusts*
3 *eggs*
1 *pint milk*
salt

Beat the eggs well and add the milk and salt. Dip the bread slices into the egg and milk, fry in deep hot fat till brown on both sides. Sprinkle with icing sugar and serve hot.

POPOVERS

2 *eggs*
1 *tablespoon sugar*
1 *tablespoon melted butter*
½ *pint milk*
4 *oz. flour*
1 *teaspoon salt*
2 *teaspoons baking powder*

Separate the egg yolks from the whites. Beat the whites until stiff and put aside. Make a batter with the yolks and the other ingredients. Then add the egg whites. Grease castle pudding tins and fill each tin half full of the mixture. Bake for 10 minutes in a hot oven. Serve hot with butter and maple syrup. A piece of fruit added to each tin as the batter is poured in makes a simple variation.

BLUEBERRY PIE

short crust pastry made with 12 oz. flour (see p. 206)
1 *lb. bilberries*
1 *oz. flour*
4 *oz. sugar*
1 *oz. butter*

Line a greased flan tin with half of the pastry. Dredge the washed fruit with the flour. Pour it on to the pastry, sprinkle with the sugar and dot with butter. Cover with the rest of the pastry. Make a hole for the steam to escape. Bake in a hot oven for 25 to 30 minutes.

CREAM FINGERS

1 *lb. flour*
½ *pint cream*
1 *oz. sugar*
⅛ *teaspoon salt*
½ *oz. yeast*
1 *tablespoon sugar* ⎫ *for glaze*
2 *tablespoons milk* ⎭

Cream the yeast with a teaspoonful of sugar. Scald the cream, add sugar and salt, cool to lukewarm, add the yeast mixture. Meanwhile warm the flour and make a well in the centre. When the yeast mixture is ready, add to the flour with the hand, and knead well. Stand the dough in a warm place, covered with a cloth, until it has doubled its bulk. Knock down the dough and roll it out to a quarter of an inch thickness. Cut into strips, 4½ inches long by 1 inch wide, rounded at the corners. Cover and stand in a warm place again. When light, brush over with the milk and sugar. Bake for 20 to 30 minutes in a moderate oven. Cool on a rack, dust with icing sugar when cold.

BROWNIES

8 *oz. sugar*
8 *oz. flour*
4 *oz. plain chocolate*
8 *oz. butter*
4 *eggs*
¼ *teaspoon salt*
4 *oz. ground or chopped nuts*

Melt the butter and chocolate and set aside to cool. Beat the eggs and sugar until thoroughly light and creamy. Fold in the chocolate and butter mixture, add the flour sifted with a pinch of salt and beat until smooth. Fold in the ground nuts. Bake in 9 × 13-inch tin lined with heavy waxed paper or tinfoil in a slow oven for about 45 minutes. Cut into fingers when cold. Brownies should be crisp outside and sticky inside.

PEANUT WAFERS

8 *oz. chopped peanuts*
2 *eggs (well beaten)*
4 *oz. white sugar*
½ *teaspoon salt*
1 *oz. melted butter*
1 *tablespoon milk*
8 *oz. flour*

Mix all the ingredients together, adding more flour if necessary. Roll out the dough ½ inch thick. Cut into strips 4 × 1 inches and cook on a greased baking sheet for 20 minutes in a moderate oven.

CHOCOLATE CAKE

4 *oz. butter*
4 *oz. sugar*
2 *eggs*
½ *pint milk*
8 *oz. flour*
½ *teaspoon salt*
2 **teaspoons** *baking powder*
3 *oz. plain chocolate or cocoa*
1 *teaspoon vanilla*

Cream the butter and sugar, adding sugar gradually. Melt the chocolate over water, add this. Sift together the dry ingredients, and add alternately with liquid and egg yolks to first mixture. Fold in the stiffly beaten egg whites. If a finer-grained cake is wanted, the eggs should be added whole and unbeaten. Bake this cake in a shallow pan or 29-inch layer-cake pans in a moderate oven for about 30 minutes. Ice with chocolate frosting (see p. 91).

CANADIAN GINGERBREAD

6 *oz. plain flour*
¼ *pint sour milk*
4 *oz. sugar*
6 *oz. black treacle (molasses)*
3 *oz. butter*
1 *egg*
1 *teaspoon bicarbonate of soda*

Sift the flour. Add all the other ingredients including the unbeaten egg, mix thoroughly. Pour the mixture into a shallow well-greased cake tin, and bake in a moderate oven for 20 minutes.

MANITOU BLACK CAKE

3 *oz. chocolate*
yolk of 1 *egg*
¾ *pint milk*
1 *oz. butter*
8 *oz. sugar*
1 *teaspoon vanilla*
½ *teaspoon bicarbonate of soda*
2 *teaspoons baking powder*
6 *oz. flour*
salt

Melt the chocolate over hot water, and gradually add it to the well-beaten yolk of egg beaten up with ½ pint of milk. Cook until it thickens slightly. Cream the butter and sugar, add the chocolate mixture and stir well. Add the mixed and sifted dry ingredients alternately with the remaining quarter pint of milk and the vanilla. Mix well. The batter should be quite thin. Pour into a greased tin and bake in a moderately hot oven for 45 to 6o minutes.

CANADIAN BUNS

½ *oz. yeast*
8 *oz. plain flour*
2 *eggs*
1 *tablespoon sugar*
4 *oz. soft butter*
4 *oz. shredded coconut*
water
1 *teaspoon salt*

Dissolve the yeast in the water and stir this into the flour. Set it to rise overnight. In the morning add the eggs, coconut, sugar and salt. Beat all together with a wooden spoon; if necessary, add extra flour to make a stiff dough. Knead well for 15 minutes, then stand in a warm place and leave it to rise until it has doubled its bulk. With the hands, work in the soft butter. Allow it to rise again, and when light shape it into buns. Put the buns close together in a baking pan, and set to rise once more. When light bake in a moderate oven till brown, about 20 minutes. While still hot, brush the tops with sugar dissolved in milk.

JOHNNY CAKE (1)

1½ *pints buttermilk*
8 *oz. sugar*
2 *eggs*
1 *teaspoon salt*
2 *small teaspoons bicarbonate of soda*
1 *lb. ground maize or polenta meal*
6 *oz. flour*
1 *teaspoon cream of tartar*
3 *tablespoons lard*

Mix the buttermilk with the soda, sugar, eggs and salt. Add the ground maize. Sift the cream of tartar with the flour and add to the mixture. Heat 3 tablespoons lard and pour them boiling hot over the mixture. Beat well. Put into a greased tin and bake in a hot oven. Johnny Cake should always be eaten hot and served with butter.

JOHNNY CAKE (2) (with molasses)

½ pint sour milk
6 oz. black treacle (molasses)
pinch of salt
3 oz. lard
6 oz. ground maize or polenta meal
1 teaspoon bicarbonate of soda
2 eggs
8 oz. plain flour

Mix the sour milk with the soda. Then add the black treacle, sugar, eggs and salt. Add the ground maize and flour. Melt the lard and pour it hot into the mixture. Beat well. Put the mixture into a greased cake tin and bake in a hot oven until it is a delicate brown. Johnny Cake should always be eaten hot and served with butter.

RAILROAD CAKE

1 lb. flour
6 oz. butter and lard mixed
6 oz. sugar
2 eggs
½ pint milk
1 teaspoon bicarbonate of soda
1 teaspoon cream of tartar

1 oz. caraway seeds
2 ozs. candied peel

Rub the fat into the flour, add all the other ingredients. Mix well, pour into a well-greased cake tin and bake in a hot oven for 1 hour.

ALMOND MERINGUES

2 egg whites
4 oz. castor sugar
vanilla
nut brittle (see p. 90)
1 oz. shredded almonds

Beat the egg whites until very stiff, gradually fold in 3 oz. sugar, add the pounded nut brittle and vanilla to taste, then fold in the remaining sugar. Arrange spoonfuls on a baking tray covered with waxed paper. Sprinkle the shredded almonds on to it and sift sugar over them. Bake for 25 minutes in a moderately slow oven.

MEAT PASTE FOR SANDWICHES

½ pint milk or cream
1 oz. flour
2 egg yolks
1 oz. butter
½ teaspoon salt
½ teaspoon made mustard
black and paprika pepper to taste
¼ pint lemon juice
1 lb. meat, veal tongue, chicken or
  pork very finely minced

One of the following very finely
  chopped: olives, watercress,
  parsley, lettuce, green pepper

Beat the egg yolks well, then mix with the milk, flour, butter and seasonings. Cook in a double boiler until thick, stirring constantly to prevent lumps. When cool, beat in the lemon juice, minced meat and chopped olives, watercress, etc.

CHICKEN SANDWICH FILLING (1)

8 oz. cold roast chicken
3 stuffed olives
1 tablespoon mustard pickle
1 tablespoon capers
¼ pint mayonnaise (see p. 161)

Mince the above ingredients together and pound to form a paste.

CHICKEN SANDWICH FILLING (2)

1 lb. cold roast chicken
4 oz. blanched almonds
¼ pint thick cream
1 teaspoon lemon juice
black pepper
salt

Mince the chicken and almonds finely, blend them with the cream, lemon juice and seasoning.

NASTURTIUM SANDWICHES

brown bread
nasturtium petals
mayonnaise (see p. 161)
butter

Wash the nasturtium petals and lay them in iced water for 5 minutes. Spread the thinly sliced bread with mayonnaise and a thick layer of the prepared petals. Cover with a thin slice of buttered bread. Serve at once with a few fresh blossoms strewn over the plate.

CHEESE SANDWICH FILLING

8 oz. cream cheese
½ tablespoon paprika
salt
black pepper

4 oz. chopped walnuts
chopped watercress to garnish

Blend the above ingredients thoroughly, add cream if the paste is too dry.

NUT BRITTLE

1 lb. sugar
8 oz. roasted Jordan almonds
pinch of salt

Melt sugar in a heavy pan, stirring constantly until it is a thin syrup. Add the nuts and salt. Stir until well coated, and spread thinly on an oiled pan. When it is cold it may be broken up.

CHOCOLATE FROSTING

8 oz. sugar
5 tablespoons water
⅛ tablespoon cream of tartar
1 egg white beaten stiff
1½ oz. chocolate grated finely
few drops oil of peppermint

Put sugar, chocolate, water, cream of tartar or lemon juice in a saucepan, stir until sugar is dissolved and bring to boiling point. Beat the egg white and add 3 tablespoons of the syrup to it, beating constantly after adding each spoonful. Add the oil of peppermint to the syrup in the saucepan. Boil this syrup without stirring until it spins to a long thread. Pour it slowly over the egg white, beating constantly, until thick enough to stand up in peaks. Spread quickly on the cake before it becomes too stiff.

MOCK MAPLE SYRUP

1½ lb. small potatoes
sugar
½ teaspoon vanilla

Wash the potatoes thoroughly without breaking the skins. Cover with water and boil until done, being careful that the potatoes do not break. Drain off the water and measure it, then take half a pint of sugar to each half pint of the liquid. Boil this mixture for 15 minutes without a lid on the pan. Season with vanilla.

PUMPKIN SYRUP

Take a good-sized pumpkin which is thoroughly ripe, wash well and remove most of the seeds and the soft centre. Cut the flesh with skin on into small cubes, and nearly cover them with water. Boil until soft, then put into a jelly bag. When all the juice has drained, put it in a pan and boil for 30 minutes; then measure the juice and put a cup of sugar to each cup of juice and boil again until thick. Serve with toast or pancakes.

OATMEAL CRISPY SQUARES

4 oz. butter
8 oz. brown sugar
8 oz. rolled oats
1 teaspoon baking powder
½ teaspoon vanilla

Melt butter. Add remaining ingredients and blend thoroughly. Put in a greased tin and pat thin. Bake in a moderately hot oven for 10—15 minutes or until golden brown. Cut into squares while warm.

LEMON SPONGE PUDDING

1 *oz. butter*
6 *oz. castor sugar (scant)*
2 *eggs*
few grains salt
½ *pint milk*
1 *oz. flour*
juice and rind of 1 *lemon*

Cream butter and sugar. Beat egg whites, then egg yolks separately. Add yolks to creamed mixture. Add lemon rind, sifted flour, milk, salt, and juice, in that order. Finally fold in egg whites. Set dish in a pan of hot water and poach in a moderate oven for 30—40 minutes.

CUCUMBER AND PINEAPPLE SALAD

1 *packet lemon jelly*
¾ *pint boiling water*
¼ *pint pineapple juice*
2 *tablespoons vinegar*
½ *teaspoon salt*
¼ *teaspoon onion juice*
1 *cup diced cucumber*

1 *cup canned pineapple, diced*
¼ *pint mayonnaise*

Dissolve jelly in boiling water. Add salt, pineapple juice, vinegar and onion juice. Chill. When slightly thickened, fold in cucumber, pineapple and mayonnaise. This is good served with potato salad and lettuce.

TOMATO JELLY RING

1½ *pints tomato juice*
3 *oz. chopped onion*
2 *oz. chopped celery and leaves*
1 *small bay leaf*
2 *whole cloves*
¾ *teaspoon salt*
2 *oz. brown sugar*
2 *tablespoons gelatine*

4 *tablespoons cold water*
3 *tablespoons vinegar*

Combine juice, onion, celery, bay leaf, cloves, salt and sugar. Simmer for 20 minutes, then strain. Soften gelatine in cold water. Add to hot liquid and dissolve. Add vinegar. Pour into ring mould, and chill until firm.

CHOUX PASTRY FOR ÉCLAIRS ETC.

4 *oz. flour*
4 *oz. butter*
2 *oz. sugar*
3 *small eggs*
pinch salt

Place butter, ½ pint water, sugar and salt in a saucepan and bring to the boil. Add sieved flour, stir and simmer for a further 5 minutes. When it has cooled beat in the eggs gradually. Pipe out on to greased, floured trays and use for making éclairs or cream buns. For savoury choux pastry omit sugar.

To make éclairs, pipe out in oblongs about 4 inches long. Brush over with a little beaten egg yolk. Bake in moderate oven for 25 minutes or until golden. When cold, split open and fill with whipped cream. Top with a thin layer of chocolate icing.

China and Japan

COOKING IN CHINA AND JAPAN

You cannot start thinking about Chinese and Japanese cooking until you consciously try to adopt an Eastern way of thinking, forget your Western hurried notions and accept a completely different rhythm. You must try to realise that people of the East have a completely different idea of time, their philosophy and their aims in life are opposed to ours — and I can't help feeling that they are at times more satisfying. Why should we hurry so much, why can't we spend time, concentration and attention on the subtleties and niceties of a delicately blended meal? One obviously could not spend as many hours in the kitchen as a Chinese or Japanese woman would, but even the busiest Western woman has sometimes the time and the urge to venture into the artistic and intricate ways of her Eastern sisters.

Just to limber you up and whet your appetite, there are a few very simple and easy recipes in this section which you can do without changing your normal routine and transforming your kitchen into an elaborate chemical laboratory. I refer to Chinese Pork with Mushrooms, or Chinese Veal with Cucumber — both using only one unusual ingredient: soy sauce. Once you place a bottle of soy sauce on your cupboard shelf, you can slowly work yourself up to more and more elaborate ingredients and dishes. The final achievement, of course, comes when you can serve a variety of Chinese dishes, fill the table with steaming little bowls of them — but for that you really need the change of philosophy I mentioned before. You must be unhurried and you must also like the actual cooking process, do it with care and detail like a dainty piece of needlework. The Chinese and Japanese are great artists in decorating their tables and making a ceremonial occasion out of every meal time. Psychologically they are doing exactly the same thing that every market research company will advise you to do: put your goods into attractive packages. Those gaily coloured lacquer or porcelain bowls they use will make the food served in them taste much more delicious than they would in more mundane dishes. If you want to make a hobby of Chinese or Japanese cooking, it is advisable to invest in these bowls — they will give the meal an authentic touch.

Rice is the staple food of China, and even if you never want to bother with Eastern cookery I would advise you to learn how to cook rice from the Chinese. It is the only way in this wide world which will keep each rice grain separate.

CHINESE EGG AND PEA SOUP

8 oz. lean raw pork or
  8 oz. raw chicken
8 oz. raw green peas
2 eggs
¼ teaspoon Ve-Tsin (flavouring)
1 teaspoon brandy or dry sherry
1 small knob green ginger
2½ pints cold water
salt

Slice the pork or chicken into thin strips, add the cold water, the peas and ginger. Bring to the boil and simmer for 30 minutes. Beat the eggs, add the brandy or sherry and the Ve-Tsin. Pour this into the soup, bring once more to the boil and serve, having added salt to taste.

CHINESE LOBSTER WITH NOODLES AND VEGETABLES

6 oz. lobster meat
8 oz. noodle pastry cut in strips
  ¼ × 1½ inches
1 8-oz. tin bean sprouts
3 oz. tinned bamboo shoots
1 oz. mushrooms
6 oz. onions
1 teaspoon cornflour
water
salt, pepper
sweet sour sauce
deep fat or oil for frying

Soak the mushrooms in hot water for 15 minutes. Drain and cut in very thin slices. Slice the onions thinly, also the bamboo shoots and lobster meat. Bring the fat or oil to boiling point, plunge the noodles in and cook for 5 or 6 seconds, till crisp. Remove, drain well and place on hot serving dish and keep warm. Heat a little oil in a large frying pan, cook the lobster, onions, bamboo, beans and mushrooms all together for 1 minute, season with salt and pepper. Stir well. Mix the cornflour to a smooth paste in cold water, add two more tablespoons water and pour over the lobster, etc. Cook for 1 minute. Add 1 teaspoon sweet sour sauce. Pour over the noodles, and serve with sweet sour sauce.

CHINESE BEAN AND MEAT ROLLS

8 oz. minced pork or veal
2 oz. butter
1 tin bean sprouts
1 dessertspoon soy sauce
1 clove of garlic, chopped
8 oz. plain flour
¾ pint water
salt, pepper
fat for deep frying

Heat the butter in a frying pan, add the meat, bean sprouts and garlic, fry all together for 5 minutes. Stir in the soy sauce and salt to taste. Leave to cool. Mix the flour and water to a smooth batter, season with salt and pepper.

Heat a 6-inch frying pan, rub with butter, pour in 1 tablespoon of the batter, spread over the pan and cook quickly for a few seconds till set. Turn out on a board. Repeat until all the batter is used up, about 12 times. Put about a dessertspoon of the meat mixture on each round, damp the edges with water and seal tightly, making a neat little 'parcel'. Drop into smoking fat until golden brown and crisp.

SWEET AND SOUR SLICED FISH

8 oz. fillet of cod
1 egg
2 oz. cornflour
1 oz. lard
sweet sour sauce

Slice the fish into small thin slices. Beat the egg, dip in the fish slices and roll in cornflour. Heat the fat till smoking, add the slices and cook for 3 minutes, till brown on all sides. Lower the heat. Pour over sweet sour sauce and cook for 2 minutes more, stirring gently all the time.

CHINESE EGGS

6 eggs
1 oz. butter
3 tablespoons soy sauce

Boil the eggs for 7 minutes, put in cold water and shell them. Melt the butter in a saucepan, add the soy sauce and the eggs. Cook gently for 5 minutes, basting and turning all the time until the eggs are dark brown. Serve cold, cut in slices.

PRAWN OR CRAB CHINESE OMELETTE

3 eggs
½ pint milk
¼ teaspoon salt
4 oz. crab meat or
  4 oz. shelled prawns
2 oz. mushrooms
2 oz. finely chopped spring
  onions or onions
¼ teaspoon Ve-Tsin (flavouring)
2 teaspoons lard
pepper

Peel the mushrooms and plunge into boiling water. Leave for 3 minutes. Remove and slice thinly. Beat the eggs, milk and salt together. Heat the oil in a large thick frying pan, add the prawns or crab meat and the sliced mushrooms. Fry lightly for 3 minutes. Add the onions and a pinch of pepper to the egg mixture. Make the pan containing the prawns, etc., very hot, pour in the egg mixture and cook quickly for 2 or 3 minutes, lifting edges of omelette to let any uncooked mixture run under on to hot pan. Fold over and serve with Chinese brown omelette sauce poured over (see p. 99).

CHINESE BOILED CHICKEN

1 medium boiling fowl
boiling water
½ wine glass of sherry
4 teaspoons salt
1 teaspoon soy sauce
8 oz. spring onions

Have the bird plucked, cleaned and trussed. Place in large saucepan, add the sherry, salt, soy sauce, and spring onions. Pour over enough boiling water to cover the bird. Cover the pan and simmer for 1½ hours, or until the bird is cooked. Leave the chicken in the soup till cold. Remove and carve it, arrange in a shallow dish. Put the carcase, etc., back in the saucepan, pour off half the liquid and simmer for 45 minutes. Strain and pour over the carved meat. Chill thoroughly to set the jelly if served cold.

CHINESE FRIED SAVOURY RICE

6 cups cold cooked rice (12 oz.
  uncooked)
1 egg
8 oz. pork
4 oz. shelled prawns
4 tablespoons chopped spring
  onions or onions
1 dessertspoon soy sauce ⎫
1 dessertspoon water ⎭ mixed
1 dessertspoon oyster sauce
1 dessertspoon minced cooked ham
2 oz. lard
½ teaspoon salt

Shred the pork into fine strips, about 1 × ⅛ inch. Heat the fat in a large thick-bottomed pan, add the shredded pork, rice and salt. Fry gently for 10 minutes, stirring with a fork. Add the prawns, mix well. Make a hole in the mixture and drop in the egg, unbeaten, cook for a few minutes in the heat of the rice, till set. Break up with the fork and stir through the mixture. Add the oyster sauce, the soy and water mixture, and the onions. Sprinkle the ham over the dish and serve hot.

CHICKEN CHOP SUEY ('Chop Suey' means mixture)

the breast of a cooked chicken
1 pint chicken stock
4 oz. spring onions
1 celery stick
2 slices bamboo shoot
2 Jerusalem artichokes
4 oz. heart of white cabbage
6 water chestnuts
2 oz. mushrooms
2 oz. bean sprouts
1 dessertspoon soy sauce
3 tablespoons oil
2 oz. butter
1 oz. cornflour

Slice all the vegetables, except of course the bean sprouts, in thin small strips, also the chicken meat. Mix the cornflour and butter well together. Heat the oil, add all the vegetables, fry quickly stirring all the time for 3 minutes. Add the stock and the soy sauce, bring to the boil and boil for 3 minutes. Add the cornflour mixture, stir well, then the chicken meat. Cook for 3 minutes longer. Serve hot. As the secret of the dish is the taste of each separate vegetable they *must* be very finely sliced, and cooked quickly.

FRIED KOWTZE WITH SWEET SOUR SAUCE

1½ lb. finely minced pork
4 oz. shelled shrimps, crab meat
  or shredded lobster
2 eggs
½ teaspoon Ve-Tsin (flavouring)
2 teaspoons dry sherry, or brandy
1 teaspoon oil
2 teaspoons cornflour
4 tablespoons finely chopped
  spring onions

salt, pepper
Dimsum pastry (see p. 99) cut
  in four 4-inch squares
sweet sour sauce

Mix all the ingredients — except of course the pastry — well together with one egg. Put a quarter of the mixture on each piece of pastry, fold in two, brush the edges with beaten egg, seal tightly. Fry each packet in very hot deep oil or lard till crisp and brown. Serve with sweet sour sauce (see p. 98).

CHINESE PORK AND CELERY

8 oz. pork
1 teaspoon cornflour
1 tablespoon water
1 tablespoon soy sauce
3 oz. mushrooms, sliced
2 hearts of celery, chopped finely

2 oz. butter
¼ teaspoon salt

Prepare and cook exactly as for the 'Chinese Veal with Cucumber' recipe (see below).

CHINESE PORK WITH MUSHROOMS

2 lb. pork
½ pint water
8 oz. mushrooms, sliced
1 tablespoon soy sauce
1 teaspoon sugar
1 teaspoon sherry
½ teaspoon salt

Cut the pork meat into 1-inch cubes. Cover with the cold water, bring to the boil, and simmer for 30 minutes. Strain, keeping the stock. Add the soy sauce to the meat in the saucepan, mix well; now add the sugar, sherry, mushrooms and salt, pour on the stock, mix well. Cover the pan and cook very slowly for 40 minutes. Eat hot, or cold — when it will be a thick jelly.

CHINESE VEAL, LAMB, OR PORK WITH CUCUMBER

8 oz. meat
1 teaspoon cornflour
1 tablespoon water
1 tablespoon soy sauce
3 oz. mushrooms, sliced
1 peeled cucumber cut in cubes
2 oz. butter
¼ teaspoon salt

Mix the cornflour with the water to make a smooth paste. Slice the veal into strips, about ¼ × 2 inches. Mix well in the paste. Heat the butter in a frying pan, add the sliced mushrooms and cucumber cubes, fry for 3 minutes, stirring and turning all the time; now add the veal strips, fry gently for a further 10 minutes. Pour on the soy sauce, stir all together, lower the heat and cook gently for 5 minutes more.

CHINESE SWEET SOUR SAUCE

1 teaspoon oil, lard or butter
2 tablespoons finely chopped mixed pickles
½ teaspoon minced green ginger
1 teaspoon vinegar
3 teaspoons sugar
1 teaspoon tomato sauce
2 teaspoons cornflour
1 teaspoon brandy or sherry
¼ pint cold water

Heat the fat in a saucepan, fry the pickles and ginger for two minutes. Mix the cornflour with the sugar, vinegar, tomato sauce, brandy or sherry to make a smooth paste, pour in the water, mix well. Pour over the pickle mixture and cook fairly briskly for 5 minutes, till the sauce thickens.

CHINESE BROWN OMELETTE SAUCE

¼ *pint cold water*
1 *teaspoon soy sauce*
2 *teaspoons oyster sauce*
1 *teaspoon cornflour*

Mix the cornflour with the sauces to a smooth paste in a small saucepan, add the water gradually, bring to the boil and cook gently for 5 minutes, stirring all the time.

DIMSUM PASTRY

8 *oz. plain flour*
1 *egg*
water
¼ *teaspoon salt*

Mix the flour and salt with the beaten egg and add enough cold water to make an elastic, but not sticky dough. Roll out on a floured board as thinly as possible. Leave to dry out for 1 hour before cutting into whatever sizes required.

CHINESE NOODLE PASTRY

8 *oz. plain flour*
½ *teaspoon salt*
2 *eggs*
2 *egg yolks*
water

Beat the 2 whole eggs, mix with salt and flour, then add the 2 egg yolks, knead lightly to a smooth elastic dough, adding a little water if necessary. Turn out on to a floured board, and roll out very thinly, like paper, twice. Leave for 2 hours, before cutting into squares or strips for whatever dish required.

CHINESE BOILED RICE

1 *lb. rice*
cold water
2 *teaspoons salt*

Wash the rice in 4 changes of cold water till the last water is clear. Put the rice and salt in a large saucepan, pour over cold water, to cover, plus 1 inch above the level of the rice, whatever the quantity. Cover with a tight lid. Bring rapidly to the boil, lower the heat, simmer till the water has evaporated, lower the heat again to almost nothing and leave the rice to cook and swell in its steam for 20 minutes. Keep the lid on all the time. The best way to test the cooking processes is either to put your ear close to the pan and listen for any sounds of bubbling, or to hold the saucepan lid and feel for any vibration. If there is none, all the water will have evaporated and the rice is ready for the 20 minutes swelling process. If this process is successful each rice grain will be separate.

JAPANESE BOILED WATERCRESS

4 or 6 *bundles watercress*
2 *teaspoons 'shoyu' sauce*

Chop the watercress coarsely, put in a saucepan, bring to the boil and simmer in its own juice till tender, about 10 minutes. Drain well, stir in the sauce and serve as a green vegetable.

JAPANESE PICKLED LETTUCE, CUCUMBER AND TURNIPS

2 *lettuce hearts*
1 *cucumber*
1 *turnip*
1 *teaspoon salt*

Cut the lettuces in half, peel the cucumbers and turnip, and slice thinly lengthwise. Sprinkle with the salt and leave for 2 days. This is eaten as a separate vegetable course with rice.

JAPANESE SAVOURY RICE

12 *oz. boiled rice (see 'Chinese Boiled Rice', p. 99)*
8 *oz. cooked chicken*
8 *oz. tinned bamboo shoots*
8 *oz. mushrooms*
2 *oz. butter or oil*
½ *pint chicken stock*
½ *teaspoon sugar*
½ *teaspoon 'shoyu' (soya bean) sauce*

Chop the chicken in ½-inch squares. Slice the mushrooms and bamboo shoots thinly and fry in butter for 2 minutes. Add the chicken, mushrooms and bamboo shoots to the rice, sprinkle in the sugar, add the stock, stir gently. Cover the pan and simmer very gently for 30 minutes till the stock is absorbed. Add the 'shoyu' sauce, mix well and serve.

JAPANESE BLACK NOODLES (Soya Bean)

1 *lb. soya bean flour*
1 *egg yolk*
1 *teaspoon salt*
cold water

Mix the flour, egg, salt with enough cold water to make a thick paste. Leave for 30 minutes. Roll out paper thin and fold in a roll about 14 inches long. Cut in ⅛ inch strips or slices. Throw into boiling water, boil for 5 minutes. Drain and serve.

JAPANESE BOILED RICE AND RED BEANS

1 *lb. dried red beans*
1 *lb. rice*

For special occasions rice is served with red beans. Wash the rice several times and when the water is quite clear place the rice in a saucepan and cover with 1 pint cold water. Bring very slowly to the boil, then simmer for 20 minutes, or until the rice has absorbed all the water. At the same time boil the beans for 1 hour. Drain, then mix rice and beans and steam together for 1 hour.

Creole Cookery

CREOLE COOKERY

The traditional Creole cookery is the most interesting blend of the best traits of Spanish and French cookery, subtly transformed and adapted by the exotic touch of the New Orleans negro cooks.

One cannot help realising how closely connected history and the cuisine of a country are. Louisiana belonged to France in the eighteenth century, a time when the art of cookery was at its height, so the French influence is predominant. The aristocratic exiles from France who settled in Louisiana brought with them traditions of a very high gastronomic standard. When Louisiana was ceded to the Spaniards there came a gradual influence of Spanish cooking, adding a strange and original piquancy to the traditional French dishes. The coloured cooks' ingenious use of herbs gives Creole cookery its exotic but never exaggerated flavour.

Jambalaya is the Creole dish *par excellence* and it has many variations. You will find two on the following pages, both with a real New Orleans flavour.

Political conditions may radically change circumstances in a country, and the era when no proud Creole would associate himself or herself with an American has passed some time ago. The haughty aristocratic Creoles may have given up their prejudices and traditions, but the rest of the world has more than accepted their art in cookery. You will find Creole Chicken served to you in the most unexpected places, because exceptionally fine culinary achievements survive even if their creators relinquish their national traditions. The great merit of these Creole recipes is that most of the ingredients are easy to buy and yet their clever combinations will give you a really original dish — and very palatable to most tastes. Just one word of warning: if you don't like hot food, reduce the amount of chilli peppers used in these recipes, or omit them altogether.

Some of the recipes are extremely simple — for instance the Creole Fried Bananas, which needs no outlandish ingredients and does not take long to prepare. It is one of the most sumptuous desserts you can find in international cookery — a recipe everybody will be glad to adopt.

CREOLE ACHARDS (Hors d'Oeuvre)

3 *teaspoons salt to 1 pint water*
1 *medium finely chopped onion*
1 *pinch saffron*
raw vegetables, cut in dice,
  carrot, French beans, onions,
  cauliflower, cabbage, peas,
  coconuts, pimentos, etc.

¼ *teaspoon salt*
¼ *teaspoon pepper*   } *to ¼ pint olive oil*
¼ *teaspoon chilli pepper*

Soak each vegetable separately in salted water for 24 hours. Drain and place in mounds in a shallow dish. Add the onion, saffron, salt and peppers to the oil and bring to the boil. Pour over the raw vegetables and leave for 48 hours.

CREOLE AUBERGINE (Hors d'Oeuvre)

2 *aubergines*
2 *chilli peppers*
2 *teaspoons lemon juice*
¼ *teaspoon salt*
1 *tablespoon olive oil*
toast, bread or plain biscuits

Peel the aubergines and chop finely. Heat the oil and fry the aubergines gently, till soft. Put in a mortar with the other ingredients and pound to a smooth paste. Pile on small pieces of toast, bread or small biscuits.

CREOLE POTATO SALAD (Hors d'Oeuvre)

1 *lb. potatoes*
½ *pint shrimps*
3 *hard-boiled eggs, sliced*
6 *tablespoons French dressing*
2 *chilli peppers, sliced or*
  1 *pimento*

Boil the potatoes and slice them, mix with the prawns and while still warm pour over the dressing, garnish with the hard-boiled egg and chillies.

PIMENTADE (Creole Boiled Fish)

1½ *lb. thick white fish, cod, hake,*
  turbot, haddock, etc., cut in
  thick slices
juice of 1 lemon
1 *lemon cut in slices*
1 *sprig parsley*
1 *sprig thyme*
¼ *teaspoon cinnamon*
3 *chilli peppers, chopped*

3 *cloves*
¼ *teaspoon salt*
2 *pints water*

Rub the fish slices all over with the lemon juice and leave for 1 hour. Boil all the other ingredients together and simmer for 30 minutes. Add the fish and cook gently for 20 minutes or till soft.

ROUGAIL DE CREVETTES (Creole Prawn Hors d'Oeuvre)

4 *oz. shelled prawns*
2 *chilli peppers*
2 *teaspoons lemon juice*
1 *dessertspoon olive oil*
¼ *teaspoon salt*
bread or toast or biscuits

Chop the chillies finely and pound in a mortar with the prawns, oil, lemon juice and salt to a smooth paste. Pile on small pieces of bread, toast or biscuits.

CREOLE ACRATS

fat or oil for deep frying
1 *lb. salt cod, or smoked*
   haddock, or smoked cod
2 *chilli peppers, chopped*
1 *clove of garlic, chopped*
pinch of salt and pepper
4 *oz. flour*
1 *egg*
¼ *pint milk or water*

Salt cod is sometimes difficult to obtain, so smoked fish can be used instead. Soak the fish in cold water for 12 hours. Take off the fish from the bones and skin, and pound the fish in a mortar with the garlic, chillies and seasoning. Make a batter of the flour, egg and liquid, mix well with the pounded fish. Drop a dessertspoon of this mixture into the boiling fat and fry to a golden brown. Drain and serve.

CREOLE CHICKEN

1 *chicken cut in joints*
2 *medium onions, sliced*
3 *oz. butter*
a pinch of saffron
1 *tablespoon curry powder*
1 *chopped chilli pepper*
¼ *teaspoon salt*
cold water
4 *tablespoons coconut milk*
boiled rice

Melt the butter in a casserole, fry the chicken joints and the onions till brown, add the curry powder, saffron, chilli and salt, add 2 tablespoons coconut milk. Cover the casserole and simmer very gently till tender, turning occasionally. Add the rest of the coconut milk and stir well. Serve with cooked rice.

CREOLE DAUBE DE PORC

2 *lb. pork fillet*
3 *oz. butter or lard*
1 *large finely sliced onion*
1 *tablespoon water*
2 *large peeled aubergines, sliced*
salt, pepper

Melt the fat in a casserole, add the pork and onion and brown well on all sides. Add salt and pepper to taste, and the water. Cover the casserole tightly and simmer gently, turning the meat occasionally, for 50 minutes. Add the aubergines, season with salt and pepper, put the lid back and cook gently for 20 minutes longer.

CREOLE CHICKEN WITH PIMENTOS

1 or 2 chickens, jointed
6 large tomatoes, peeled and sliced
2 large onions, sliced
2 cloves of garlic, chopped
6 red and green pimentos
1 teaspoon chopped parsley
¼ teaspoon chopped thyme
1 bay leaf, chopped
3 oz. butter
2 oz. flour
1 pint chicken stock
salt, pepper
boiled rice

Rub the chicken joints with salt and pepper. Heat the butter in a large saucepan and fry the chicken till brown all over. Add the onion and fry for 2 minutes. Add the flour, stir well and cook till it begins to brown. Add the tomatoes, herbs, pimentos and simmer gently with the lid on for 20 minutes. Pour on the stock, season with salt and pepper and simmer, covered, for 45 minutes. Serve with the hot rice.

CREOLE CHICKEN AND RICE

1 chicken
2 medium carrots, sliced
2 medium onions, sliced
1 medium turnip, sliced
1 bouquet garni
4 oz. rice, washed in 4 fresh
    waters
salt, pepper
cold water

Put the chicken in a saucepan with the vegetables, herbs and seasoning. Pour in cold water to cover two-thirds of it. Bring to the boil and simmer till tender: 45 minutes if a young bird; up to 3 hours if old. When done remove the bird and strain the stock. Put the vegetables round the bird on the dish and keep warm, covered with buttered paper. Replace the stock in the saucepan, add the rice and simmer till tender and dry, about 15 minutes. Heap on to the serving dish.

CREOLE JAMBALAYA WITH SAUSAGES

8 oz. Patna rice, boiled
1 lb. chipolata or Vienna sausages
1 large onion, chopped
1 clove of garlic, chopped
8 oz. tomatoes, peeled and
    quartered
½ chilli pepper or pimento,
    seeded and chopped
salt, pepper, cayenne
butter

Heat 2 oz. butter in a large casserole and fry the onion and garlic till light brown. Add the tomatoes, and crush with a wooden spoon to make the mixture juicy. Fry the sausages separately in butter, if possible; when done cut in 2-inch lengths, pour these and their butter over the tomatoes and onion mixture, add the chilli or pimento, season with salt and pepper and a pinch of cayenne pepper. Fill the casserole with the cooked rice, cover and cook very gently for 35 minutes. Serve hot.

CREOLE STUFFED CABBAGE

1 *white cabbage*
12 *oz. sausage meat*
1 *large onion, finely chopped*
2 *tomatoes, peeled and chopped*
1 *clove of garlic, finely chopped*
1 *teaspoon chopped parsley*
½ *teaspoon chopped thyme*
½ *chilli pepper, or pimento*
½ *bay leaf, chopped*
10 *rashers of bacon*
2 *oz. butter*
salt, pepper
cooked rice

Remove the best of the coarse outer leaves of the cabbage, put the rest of the cabbage in boiling salted water and boil for 10 minutes. Drain well. Fry the onion and garlic in the butter till brown, add salt and pepper, the tomato and the sausage meat, then the herbs and chilli, stir well and cook gently for 20 minutes. Open the cabbage and stuff inside the leaves with the sausage mixture. Wrap the outer leaves round the stuffed cabbage, put 4 rashers on top and tie together with string. Put 6 rashers in the bottom of a covered pan or casserole, put the tied cabbage on top, add ⅛ pint cold water, cover tightly and cook very gently for 1½ hours. To serve, remove the string and the outer leaves, and pour the remaining liquid over the cabbage and bacon rashers. Eat with cooked rice.

JAMBALAYA WITH PRAWNS

Cook this as for Sausage Jambalaya (see p. 105) but add 1 pint of shelled prawns instead of the sausages.

BOEUF CREOLE

3 *lb. rump steak*
6 *rashers fat bacon*
2 *finely chopped chilli peppers*
2 *lb. finely sliced onions*
2 *lb. peeled tomatoes*
salt, pepper

Put the rashers in the bottom of a large casserole, place the steak on top, sprinkle with the chillies, salt and pepper. Cover with the onions and tomatoes. Cover the casserole with a tight-fitting lid and simmer very gently for 5 hours. No water is used for this recipe: the meat cooks in its own juice and the tomato and onion juice.

CREOLE LIVER (Chanfaina)

1 *lb. calves' liver, cut in slices*
3 *oz. butter or 3 tablespoons oil*
1 *tablespoon water*
1 *lb. peeled sliced tomatoes*
2 *chopped chilli peppers*
1 *clove of garlic, chopped*
1 *tablespoon chopped parsley*
salt, pepper

Melt half the fat in a casserole, add the liver slices, salt, pepper, chillies, garlic, parsley and water; cook very gently, turning round and round a wooden spoon for 5 or 6 minutes or till done. Remove from the heat and keep warm. Fry the tomatoes in the rest of the fat and add to the casserole, having seasoned with salt and pepper.

GREEN GUMBO

2 *lb. veal brisket*
12 *oz. lean gammon*
2 *lb. mixed greens (cabbage,*
    spinach, turnip tops, watercress,
    parsley, radish tops)
2 *onions*
½ *red chilli pepper*
1 *clove*
thyme, marjoram, allspice
boiled rice
salt and pepper
2 *oz. butter*

Chop the washed greens, cover with water and boil together for 10 minutes. Drain and keep the water. Cut the veal and ham into 1-inch squares, mix with chopped onion and brown in the hot, melted butter. Chop greens finely, add to the pan and cook all together until well browned. Then add 2—3 quarts boiling water, including the liquid in which the vegetables were cooked, herbs, chilli pepper, salt and pepper. Simmer for 1 hour. Serve with boiled rice.

CREOLE BAKED SWEET POTATOES

Scrub the potatoes well. Bake in their skins in a moderate oven for 1 to 1½ hours till soft throughout. Serve with butter, salt and pepper.

CREOLE RICE PUDDING

1 *pint milk*
2 *tablespoons rice*
1½ *oz. butter*
6 *lumps sugar*
a few drops of vanilla essence
4 *teaspoons grated cinnamon*

Put the milk, rice, butter, sugar and vanilla in a deep casserole, sprinkle the cinnamon on top. Cook in a very slow oven for 5 hours.

CREOLE SWEET POTATO PUDDING

5 *baked sweet potatoes*
3 *eggs*
8 *oz. sugar*
3 *oz. butter*
½ *pint milk*
½ *teaspoon black pepper*
¼ *teaspoon salt*

Peel the potatoes and rub through a sieve. Separate the eggs, beat the whites till stiff. Add the egg yolks and milk to the potato, then the sugar, butter, salt and pepper. Fold in the whites. The mixture should be smooth and 'runny'. Pour into a buttered pie dish and bake in a moderate oven for 1 hour, till brown on top, and eat as a sweet course.

CREOLE CORNFLOUR CAKE PUDDING

4 oz. cornflour
2 pints milk
2 eggs, beaten
3 oz. butter, warmed till soft
1 oz. sugar
a few drops of vanilla essence

Boil the milk, add the cornflour and stir quickly till smooth. Leave to cool. When cold add the soft butter, sugar, eggs and vanilla. Mix all well together. Pour into a buttered fireproof dish and bake in a moderate oven for 10 or 15 minutes till light brown.

CREOLE FRIED BANANAS

deep fat or oil
6 bananas
4 tablespoons rum
1 tablespoon brown sugar
¼ pint batter

Peel the bananas and cut in 4 pieces. Place in a shallow dish, sprinkle with the sugar and pour over the rum. Leave for 30 minutes, turning occasionally. Drain any rum and sugar left into the batter. Mix well, dip each banana piece into this mixture and fry in the boiling fat till light brown. Sprinkle with sugar and serve.

CREOLE COCONUT CAKES

4 oz. finely grated fresh coconut
4 oz. castor sugar
2 egg whites, beaten stiffly

Add the coconut and sugar to the egg whites and beat again till stiff.

Butter a thick baking tin and put spoonfuls of the mixture on it. Bake in a slow oven for 35 minutes, or till they begin to brown.

CREOLE PEANUT PRALINES

1 lb. brown sugar
1 lb. peanuts
4 tablespoons water
1 tablespoon butter, melted

Shell the peanuts and chop them coarsely. Mix with melted butter.

Add the sugar to the water, bring to the boil and cook till it forms a syrup. Add the peanuts, stir till the mixture bubbles, remove from the heat. Take a tablespoon at a time, place on a buttered slab or large dish. Press into rounds ¼ inch thick and 4 inches in diameter. Work fast, leave till dry, lift with a knife. They should be light, crisp and flaky.

Czechoslovakia

COOKING IN CZECHOSLOVAKIA

Poets, philosophers and tourists have long sung the praises of Prague, the capital of Czechoslovakia, the 'Golden City of a Hundred Spires'. In the same way, gourmets all over the world have spread the fame of their 'Wurst' or pork sausages. There is, too, the famous Prague ham, a specially mildly cured specimen, the very king of all hams. If you are addicted to cold meats and pickles, you can spend at least a month in Czechoslovakia without touching any other food and still finding variety. However, the making of these Wurst is the closely guarded secret of individual pork butchers and it is, anyhow, not possible to prepare them in a private kitchen. The rest of the Czech gastronomic scene is rather similar to all the other countries in the erstwhile Austrian Empire. Though they cook basically in the same way as the surrounding countries, the Czechs are exceptionally good at devising solid, filling and economical dishes. The best known and most outstanding speciality of the Czech kitchen are Dumplings. These dumplings are almost as much a staple food of the country as bread, and they are cooked with great skill and art.

Bramborák, the Czech potato pie, is the perfect filling dish for a meatless day. I turned to it very often during the meat rationing days of the War, and I still do when I want to carry out an economy drive of my own. My other favourite has always been Spinach Rolls, also a very economical, but slightly more elaborate dish. The Czechoslovak way with Baked Spaghetti is simple, but very clever. It is in the recipe for Heavenly Favours that the flight of fancy takes them into higher regions — this is an original, light and tasty dessert which most men cherish. Recommended as a sure way to HIS heart.

TOMATO SOUP

1 *lb. tomatoes, chopped*
4 *oz. rice*
1 *oz. butter*
1 *dessertspoon tarragon vinegar*
salt, pepper
sugar
4 *oz. grated cheese*
1½ *pints stock*

Fry the rice in the butter, add 2 pints boiling water and 1 teaspoon salt. Simmer until the rice is just cooked. Pour the rice into a strainer and steam it gently over the pan in which it was cooked. Cook the tomatoes in very little water until tender. Season with salt, pepper and sugar. Pass through a sieve. Put the tomatoes and rice together in a pan with the vinegar, add hot stock gradually. Serve with grated cheese.

BOILED BACON

1½ *lb. boiling bacon (collar is good)*
1 *onion*
1 *lb. French beans*
1 *oz. butter*
salt, pepper
bay leaf

Soak the bacon for 3 hours, or longer if it seems very salty. Drain off the water. Put it in a saucepan with the onion, the bay leaf and 1 pint water. Simmer until tender (about 1½ hours). Cook the beans in boiling salted water. Drain and toss in the butter. Serve the bacon on a dish with the beans around it. Hand the broth separately. Serve with baked spaghetti (see p. 113).

CAULIFLOWER WITH EGGS

1 *small cauliflower*
4 *eggs*
1 *small onion, sliced*
1 *oz. butter*
salt, pepper
caraway seeds

Cook the cauliflower in salted water until just tender. Break into flowerets. Fry the onion in the butter until transparent. Add the cauliflower and caraway seeds. Mix with the onion and fry for 3 minutes. Pour the beaten and seasoned eggs into the pan. Cook slowly, stirring all the time, until the eggs are set.

POTATO PIE (Bramborák)

1 *lb. potatoes*
2 *tablespoons milk*
2 *oz. flour*
1 *clove garlic, crushed*
1 *onion, finely chopped*
salt, pepper

marjoram
1 *oz. butter*

Peel, grate and drain the potatoes. Stir the milk into the flour and add it to the potatoes with the garlic, onion, seasoning. Bake, dotted with butter, in a greased pan for 30 minutes in a hot oven.

POTATO PANCAKES

Use the same mixture as for Bramborák (p. 111), but drop spoonfuls of it into hot fat and fry quickly on both sides.

SPINACH ROLLS

8 oz. spinach
½ pint white sauce
1 slice bread
1 oz. butter
½ pint milk
2 eggs
2 oz. grated cheese

Wash the spinach, reserve 8 large leaves. Cook the rest, drain and chop. Mix with the white sauce, season with salt and pepper. Cut the bread into small dice, fry quickly in the butter. Mix with the spinach mixture. Spread mixture on the blanched spinach leaves, roll and arrange in shallow fireproof dish. Beat the eggs with the milk, cook slowly until the mixture thickens, stir in the grated cheese. Pour over the spinach rolls. Bake in a moderate oven for 20 minutes.

BRAISED BEEF

1½ lb. topside
2 oz. butter
4 oz. streaky bacon
1 onion, sliced
juice of 1 lemon
cayenne pepper
salt

Sprinkle the meat with lemon juice, cover with onion. Leave for 12 hours. Season with salt and cayenne pepper. Brown on all sides in the butter. Lay bacon rashers on the bottom of a casserole, put the meat on top of them. Cover it with more bacon. Put in ½ pint water. Cover with a lid and cook in a moderate oven for 2 hours. Serve with sharp sauce poured over it (see p. 114).

CABBAGE

1 savoy cabbage
2 oz. butter
1 oz. flour
1 small onion
1 clove garlic
1 blade mace
salt, pepper
½ pint stock

Remove hard stalks and shred the cabbage. Blanch it in boiling water and drain. Melt the butter, cook the flour in it, gradually add the stock. Add the mace and the crushed garlic, season with salt and pepper. Put the cabbage into the sauce, with the onion. Simmer for 20 minutes.

BAKED SPAGHETTI

8 oz. long spaghetti
2 oz. butter
2 oz. breadcrumbs
salt

Cook the spaghetti in the usual way (see p. 266). Drain and put into a buttered fireproof dish. Fry the breadcrumbs in the butter until golden. Spread on top of the spaghetti. Bake in a moderate oven until very hot.

BEEF WITH CREAM SAUCE

1 fillet of beef (about 2 lb.)
7 oz. root vegetables (carrot, celeriac, parsley)
½ pint sour cream
1 dessertspoon flour
2 oz. fat bacon
2 oz. lard
1 onion
vinegar, lemon, salt
5 peppercorns
½ bay leaf
1 teaspoon allspice

Wash fillet, clean well and remove fat and gristle. Thread strips of bacon through meat. Lightly fry onion, chopped vegetables and seasoning in baking tin, add meat and cook in moderate oven until brown, adding a little water from time to time. Then take out meat and cut into slices. Add sour cream, mixed with flour, to sauce and simmer for a few minutes. Pass finished sauce through sieve, together with vegetables, so that it is brownish and thick. Add salt, a few drops of vinegar, or a piece of lemon peel and juice, according to taste. Serve with dumplings.

CZECH BREAD DUMPLINGS

8 oz. plain flour
8 oz. fine semolina
4 bread rolls (about 7 oz.)
about 1 pint milk
2 egg yolks
1 teaspoon salt
1 teaspoon butter

Weigh flour and semolina into mixing bowl, add salt and egg yolks mixed in milk. Work dough with wooden spoon until it is smooth and bubbles form. Cut bread into small cubes (rolls from the day before are best), quickly fry in a little butter and mix into dough. Turn part of dough on to floured board, form it into a ball with floured hands and immediately throw into boiling water in large saucepan so it has enough room to float. When the water comes to the boil again, add the next dumpling. Altogether the dumplings should be cooked about 30 minutes. Then using a large wire ladle, take them out and place on board. Cut them into slices with broad knife or wire. These dumplings are served with roast pork, goose, duck and all meat dishes having thick sauces, particularly cream sauce.

PICKLED CELERIAC

1 *celeriac*
1 *large onion*
salt
ginger
vinegar

Clean the celeriac and cut it into thick slices. Slice the onion. Put alternate layers of onion and celeriac into an earthenware dish. Sprinkle each layer with salt and ginger. Cover the vegetables with vinegar and water (4 parts vinegar to 1 part water). This will keep for some time.

APPLE TART

pastry as in 'Heavenly Favours'
  (see below)
2 *oz. butter*
2 *large cooking apples, sliced*
2 *oz. sugar*
2 *oz. seeded raisins*

Line a greased square baking tin with half the pastry. Brush with melted butter. Cover with sliced apples sprinkled with sugar and raisins. Lay the rest of the pastry on top. Brush with melted butter. Bake in a hot oven for 20 minutes.

HEAVENLY FAVOURS

8 *oz. flour*
2 *oz. mixed butter and lard*
2 *eggs*
2 *tablespoons milk*
cinnamon
sugar
fat for frying

Cut the fat into the sifted flour, mix in the beaten eggs and the milk. The mixture should have become an elastic dough. Knead until smooth. Leave in a warm place for 1 hour. Roll on a floured board, fold into 3. Repeat this twice. Roll out to $\frac{1}{4}$ inch thick. Cut into diamonds, fry in very hot fat. Drain and sprinkle with cinnamon and sugar.

SHARP SAUCE

$\frac{1}{2}$ *carrot sliced*
$\frac{1}{2}$ *celeriac sliced*
2 *onions sliced*
3 *tomatoes quartered*
4 *juniper berries*
parsley
1 *glass red wine*
juice of 1 lemon
$\frac{1}{2}$ *bay leaf*
$\frac{1}{2}$ *pint stock*
6 *capers*

cayenne pepper
salt
2 *oz. butter*
$\frac{1}{2}$ *oz. flour*

Cook the vegetables, parsley, juniper berries and bay leaf in 1 oz. butter until tender, adding stock if necessary. Add the wine, lemon juice, capers and stock. Season with salt and cayenne pepper. Rub through a sieve. Thicken with a roux made from 1 oz. butter and the flour.

France

COOKING IN FRANCE

Every country in the world has its gastronomic specialities, its excellent national dishes, but the high art of cookery is essentially French. Any appreciation of French cookery should be written in the best blank verse, because no prose, however flowery, can do it justice. Eating to the French is not merely a physical function, it is an intellectual and aesthetic pleasure. The typically French art of transforming material things into spiritual experiences extends into the department of the cuisine. Not only the creative mind of the great chefs is devoted to the subtle art of cookery — the French peasant and working man are also epicures in their own way.

Accordingly, there are the famous French recipes invented by the masters of the Haute Cuisine and any number of regional, traditional specialities. You will find a rich selection in the following pages — fittingly the longest chapter in this book — but let me point out a few at random.

The Pot-au-Feu of course is the symbol of domesticity in France. It simmers for hours on end in the farmhouses and fills the air with its fragrance. At the other end of the scale you will be introduced to the famous Lobster Soup, indeed the aristocrat of all soups. Winter or summer, this Bisque lends grace and elegance to your dinner table. Or why not try making an onion soup as a pick-me-up after a party and serve it with crisp French bread?

Chicken Marengo is one of the great classical French dishes with an historical tale attached to it. Apparently Napoleon was getting tired of the menus his chef served him during one of his campaigns. The chef was duly worried about the displeasure of Napoleon and invented a brand new dish for him. They had just won a battle in Northern Italy, near Marengo — so the new creation was named Chicken Marengo.

From the French province of Lorraine comes the most superior savoury tart — Quiche Lorraine. It needs no recommendation — make it for a special picnic party once, and you will never think of sandwiches again. All the soufflés and mousses in this section are a 'must' for every housewife who takes pride in her food. Salad dressings and, above all, sauces are unequalled when they are prepared the French way. The list is endless, but the recipes in this section are all reasonably easy to make and are all sure winners.

SALADE NIÇOISE

1 *large lettuce heart*
1 *seeded green pepper cut in rings*
12 *stoned black olives*
4 *medium peeled sliced tomatoes*
4 *oz. cooked French beans*
2 *hard-boiled eggs*
1 *tin tunny fish*
8 *anchovy fillets*
2 *tablespoons chopped fresh*
  herbs, parsley, chives, etc.

1 *tablespoon chopped onions*
1 *clove garlic*
3 *tablespoons olive oil*
1 *tablespoon wine vinegar* } *French*
salt, pepper   } *dressing*

Rub salad bowl with the garlic. Make the dressing and pour into the bowl. Add the lettuce leaves, green pepper, onions, beans, olives, herbs. Mix well in the dressing. Arrange the tunny fish, eggs, tomatoes, anchovies on top. Eat at once.

SALADE DE BOEUF (Cold Beef Salad)

4 *slices lean cold cooked beef*
6 *medium cold cooked potatoes*
3 *peeled seeded tomatoes*
3 *teaspoons chopped mixed herbs*
  (parsley, chives, chervil, etc.)
3 *chopped spring onions or*
  1 *medium onion*
2 *or* 3 *tablespoons French dressing*

Cut the beef in ½-inch squares. Cover with the dressing and leave for 1 hour. Slice the potatoes and onions. Add the herbs. Mix all together with the cold beef. If 'dry'-looking add another tablespoon of dressing.

HARD-BOILED EGGS

6 *eggs*
1 *tablespoon French dressing*
1 *oz. butter*
4 *spring onions, finely chopped*
4 *lettuce leaves*

Boil eggs till hard, peel and cut in half. Remove yolks, mash these with the blade of a knife with the dressing and the butter. Fill whites, sprinkle with onion. Stand three per person on a crisp lettuce leaf.

POTATO AND EGG SALAD

1 *lb. potatoes (not the 'floury'*
  kind)
4 *hard-boiled eggs*
¼ *pint French dressing*
4 *teaspoons chopped herbs*
  (chives, parsley, tarragon, etc.)

Boil the potatoes in their skins. Peel and cool. Remove egg yolks and mash till smooth with the herbs and dressing. Add this mixture to the potatoes and egg whites coarsely chopped, and mix all together. Serve very cold.

FOND D'ARTICHAUTS À L'ORIENTALE

6 *globe artichokes*
3 *tablespoons water*
3 *tablespoons olive oil*
1 *small onion*
2 *tender carrots*
4 *oz. cooked green peas*
4 *oz. cooked new potatoes*
½ *lemon*
½ *teaspoon sugar*
1 *teaspoon chopped herbs (fennel and parsley)*
salt, pepper

Strip the stalk and leaves from each artichoke, keeping the heart. Mix the oil with the water, add the onion and carrots, finely chopped, and boil for 3 minutes. Put in the artichoke hearts, sugar, lemon juice, a pinch of salt and pepper, cover the saucepan and simmer very slowly for 40 minutes. Add the cooked peas and potatoes. When cold sprinkle the herbs on top.

All the vegetables for this hors d'oeuvre must be young and tender.

POTATO, HARD-BOILED EGG, ANCHOVY SALAD

potato and hard-boiled egg salad (see p. 117)
8 *anchovy fillets*

Cut up the fillets and mix with the potato and hard-boiled egg. Serve very cold.

OEUFS MIMOSA

6 *hard-boiled eggs*
6 *teaspoons foie gras*
2 *tablespoons mayonnaise*
6 *tablespoons cold Béchamel sauce (see p. 165)*

Halve the eggs and fill with *foie gras*. Mix the mayonnaise and Béchamel. Pour over. Chop the yolks and sprinkle on top.

MACÉDOINE NIÇOISE

Ravigote sauce (see p. 162)
8 *oz. cold chicken*
8 *oz. cooked lean ham*
1 *kipper fillet*
4 *oz. Mortadelle sausage*
1 *peeled chopped eating apple*
1 *head of celery (use only the inner sticks)*
salt and pepper
3 *hard-boiled eggs*
1 *sweet pepper, very finely sliced, seeds removed*

12 *green olives*
3 *medium cold boiled potatoes*
1 *lettuce heart, chopped*
1 *medium chopped cooked beetroot*

Remove yolks of eggs and chop the whites. Cut all the 'meats' into thin strips. Mix the 'meats' with all the chopped vegetables and the egg whites. Salt and pepper the mixture. Pour over this the Ravigote sauce, put all in a shallow dish, sprinkle with the chopped egg yolks.

CUCUMBER SALAD

½ *teaspoon salt*
1 *cucumber*
1 *tablespoon wine vinegar*
black pepper

Peel the cucumber and slice thinly. Spread out on a flat dish and sprinkle with the salt.

Leave for 1 hour and squeeze in a clean cloth. Add the vinegar and a good sprinkling of black pepper.

TOMATOES AND BLACK OLIVES

8 *medium ripe tomatoes*
16 *black olives*
1 *clove of garlic*
pepper
6 *tablespoons mayonnaise*

Peel the tomatoes. Cut off the tops and scoop out the seeds and pulp. Put this in a bowl, mix with the crushed garlic, add the mayonnaise and pour all over the tomatoes, filling them. Sprinkle very lightly with black pepper. Stone the olives, chop them coarsely and scatter on top of the filled tomatoes.

STUFFED EGGS WITH SARDINES

6 *eggs (hard-boiled)*
1 *tin sardines*
1 *oz. butter*
12 *capers*
1 *teaspoon lemon juice*
salt, pepper

Cut the eggs lengthways. Chop the yolks. Mash the sardines, having boned and skinned them, with the butter and lemon juice; season with salt and pepper. Fill the whites with the mixture and sprinkle with the chopped yolks.

MUSSELS WITH SAFFRON

1½ *pints mussels*
2 *leeks*
1 *small onion*
2 *medium tomatoes*
1 *clove of garlic*
pinch of saffron
pinch of thyme
1 *bay leaf*
2 *small glasses white wine*
3 *tablespoons olive oil*
1 *teaspoon chopped parsley*
salt, pepper

Scrub the mussels under a running tap, very carefully, to remove ALL sand, soak in cold water. Slice all the vegetables. Use only the white parts of the leeks. Melt the oil in a large stew pan, add the leeks and onion, cook for 3 minutes then add the tomatoes and garlic, thyme, bay leaf and saffron; stir together. Put in the wine, season with salt and pepper. Simmer till somewhat reduced, about 20 minutes, stirring now and then.

Add the mussels, put the lid on and toss occasionally. They will soon open; after opening, cook very slowly for 5 minutes more. Remove from their shells and put in a shallow dish. Strain the liquid over them. When cold sprinkle with the parsley.

TUNNY FISH

8 oz. *fresh cooked tunny fish or*
  1 tin
2 *hard-boiled eggs*
2 oz. *butter*
3 *teaspoons chopped herbs*
  (mixed parsley, chives,
  tarragon)
¼ *pint mayonnaise*
sliced lemon or parsley sprigs
buttered brown bread cut in rounds

Mash the fish, butter, eggs, chopped herbs very finely with a fork until creamy. Pile the mixture on the small rounds of buttered bread, cover with the mayonnaise. Decorate with parsley, or small pieces of lemon. Serve three to each person.

TUNNY FISH WITH CELERY

8 oz. *fresh cooked tunny fish*
  or 1 tin
1 *tablespoon wine vinegar*
¼ *teaspoon mustard*
1 *heart of chopped celery head*
3 *teaspoons chopped herbs (chives,*
  tarragon, parsley, fennel)
salt, pepper
lettuce

Cut the fish in tiny pieces, add the inner white parts of the celery head, very finely chopped, also the herbs. Mix all together with the vinegar, mustard, salt and pepper. Fill the inner leaves of a lettuce, three to each person.

POT-AU-FEU

2 lb. *beef (the cheaper cuts)*
1 lb. *shin bones*
the remains of a chicken: bone,
  neck, skin, etc.
2 *large carrots*
1 *turnip*
1 *head of celery*
1 *tomato*
1 *leek*
1 *large onion stuck with cloves*
bouquet garni
½ *teaspoon salt*
pepper
4 *pints cold water*

This is the classic consommé 'bouillon', stock or broth, the basis for many dishes and soups. Some cooks make a week's supply at a time and keep it in the refrigerator. Beef or chicken cubes available today, especially the Swiss makes, are a substitute unless you are the better sort of cook.

Prepare all the ingredients and put in the water, bring to the boil. Boil, skim, skim and skim until no more scum appears. This skimming is the secret of a clear stock. Continue to simmer for 5 hours. Strain and remove the fat — far easier when cold. Of course the vegetables and beef can be eaten as a meal in themselves with boiled potatoes.

BOUILLABAISSE

1 *lb. mixed pieces of fish (cod fillets, whiting, mullet, smelt, turbot, eel, small crabs, lobster)*
3 *finely sliced onions*
4 *finely sliced cloves of garlic*
3 *peeled and seeded tomatoes*
1 *bouquet garni (with a fennel sprig added)*
1 *slice orange peel*
½ *glass olive oil*
¾ *pint hot water*
½ *glass white wine*
¼ *teaspoon nutmeg*
¼ *teaspoon saffron*
2 *teaspoons chopped parsley*
salt, pepper
slices of stale bread or stale rolls

This classic Mediterranean fish dish can be termed either a soup or a fish recipe. It is a meal in itself. There are many ways of making it, but this is as good as any. The fishes should be cut up in fairly equally sized pieces (easy for eating).

Cut up the lobster and or crabs, cover with water and simmer for 20 minutes. In a large pot, put the vegetables, garlic, *bouquet*, saffron, nutmeg, orange peel. On this bed place the pieces of firmer fish all washed and cleaned — such as cod, eel, turbot — add olive oil and wine and the water. Bring to the boil and cook fiercely for 5 minutes. Now put in the softer fish pieces — red mullet, whiting, smelt, etc. Add ½ a cup of the lobster and crab liquid and boil again as before, fiercely for another 5 minutes, or until the pieces of fish are done, but not overcooked or disintegrating. Season with salt and pepper.

Pick out the *bouquet* and the orange peel.

Put the sliced bread or rolls cut lengthways into one dish and pour the liquid over them (you can, if you like, fry the bread or rolls first in olive oil), put the fish pieces in another dish and sprinkle with parsley.

Eat both dishes together.

The lobster and crab are not essential, as they are most extravagant unless you catch them yourselves, but little, otherwise useless, crabs will do.

The secret of bouillabaisse lies in the fierce cooking, to which is due the smooth mixture of oil and the liquid.

MUSSEL SOUP

2 *dozen mussels*
2½ *pints cold water*
1 *glass dry white wine*
1 *medium onion*
1 *teaspoon chopped parsley*
1 *sprig thyme*
1 *clove*
4 *tablespoons cream*
salt, pepper

See that the mussels are cleaned, completely free of sand. Put them in the pot with the onion, sliced, ½ teaspoon of the parsley, the thyme, clove, salt and pepper. Pour on the water and the wine. Boil for 15 minutes. Strain the liquid through a fine sieve or muslin in another pot. Take the mussels from their shells and put them in the warmed tureen. Simmer the liquid until reduced by a quarter. Pour over the mussels in the tureen and stir in the cream, and sprinkle on the parsley. Taste and add more salt and pepper if you think fit.

CONSOMMÉ MADRILÈNE

2½ *pints beef stock*
4 *tomatoes*
3 *oz. lean raw minced beef*
1 *egg white*
salt, pepper

Peel and slice the tomatoes, add to the minced beef, salt, pepper. Stir. Pour on the stock, add the well beaten egg white, stir again, and simmer for 1 hour. Strain and serve.

CONSOMMÉ À LA CHIFFONNADE

3 *lettuce hearts*
3 *handfuls sorrel or spinach leaves*
2 *oz. butter*
1½ *pints boiling water*
1 *pint milk*
3 *oz. vermicelli*
1 *teaspoon chopped chervil*

Wash the sorrel or spinach and the lettuce hearts, chop them very small. Melt the butter, add the vegetables and cook for 4 minutes, stir, add salt and pepper. Pour on the water and milk, bring to the boil, then throw in the vermicelli, stir from time to time and simmer till the vermicelli is soft—about 20 minutes. Sprinkle the chervil on top before serving.

SARDINES

1 *tin sardines*
2 *oz. butter*
juice of 1 lemon
salt, pepper

Mash the sardines and the butter till very smooth with a fork, add the lemon juice and pepper plus a tiny pinch of salt. If the bones and skin seem tough take them out before mashing.

This mixture can be served on rounds of buttered bread, or filling lettuce leaves. Also stuffing the whites of hard-boiled eggs.

POTAGE À LA PURÉE DE GIBIER (Giblet Sou)

remains of cooked game bird (pheasant, partridges, grouse, etc.)
2½ *pints cold water*
3 *carrots*
2 *onions*
½ *head of celery*
1 *bouquet garni*
2 *oz. white breadcrumbs*
2 *tablespoons cream*
salt, pepper

Take whatever you have left of your bird—carcase, bones, skin, giblets, neck, etc.—and put in the pot. Add the chopped vegetables, the *bouquet*, salt and pepper. Pour the water over, bring to the boil and simmer for 1 hour. Strain. Remove any pieces of meat left on the bones and pass them through a sieve, pound them, or 'rub' them as finely as possible on a plate with a wooden spoon. Return this 'paste' to the liquid, add the breadcrumbs, re-heat, but do not boil. Stir in the cream. Serve croûtons with this soup.

SIEVED WATERCRESS SOUP

1 *lb. potatoes*
1 *bunch watercress*
2 *pints cold water*
¼ *pint milk or cream*
½ *oz. butter*
salt, pepper

Peel and boil the potatoes in the water till nearly done, then add the chopped watercress. Cook again till the potatoes are soft. Sieve. Re-heat and add the milk or cream, butter, salt and pepper to taste.

A sprinkling of chopped watercress on top makes this soup look interesting.

LOBSTER SOUP (Potage à la Bisque d'Homard)

1 *lobster*
1 *pint cold water*
1 *onion*
1 *carrot*
2 *oz. butter*
¼ *pint Madeira or white wine*
1½ *pints stock*
4 *slices stale white bread*
salt, pepper
bouquet garni

Dice the vegetables, add the water, salt, pepper and *bouquet*. Bring to a fierce boil, put in the lobster, simmer for 15 minutes. Strain, but keep the liquid. Take the meat out of the lobster tail and put the shell through the mincer, then pound it to a paste. Put this paste into 1 pint of the liquid, simmer for 5 minutes. Strain once more. Now put in the bread (crusts removed) and mash with a wooden spoon till free of any lumps, pour on the stock, the wine and the rest of the liquid, bring to the boil stirring the whole time. Take off the heat, put in the butter and the tail meat. Serve immediately.

WATERCRESS SOUP WITH LEEK

1½ *lb. potatoes*
2 *leeks*
1 *bunch watercress*
2 *oz. butter*
2 *pints water*
1 *egg yolk*
1 *tablespoon milk*
salt, pepper

Chop the prepared vegetables and cook in the melted butter for 4 minutes. Add the salt, pepper and water. Bring to the boil, then simmer for 20 minutes. Beat the egg yolk in the milk and add to the hot soup before serving.

POTAGE VELOURS

6 *cooked carrots*
2 *pints stock*
1 *oz. tapioca*
1 *oz. butter*
½ *teaspoon chopped parsley*
salt, pepper

Mash the carrots. Boil the stock, throw in the tapioca, cook for 6 minutes stirring all the time. Add the mashed carrots, butter, salt, pepper. Stir, boil up once more, stirring quickly the whole time. Sprinkle on the parsley.

SOUPE DE CHASSE

4 *medium onions*
1 *leek*
1 *head celery*
1 *clove of garlic*
2 *oz. butter*
bouquet garni
2½ *pints cold water*
salt, pepper, sugar
1 *clove*
8 *slices thin stale bread fried in butter*

1 *oz. potato flour mixed in ½ cup stock*
3 *egg yolks*

Melt the butter, add the chopped vegetables, stir, add garlic, salt, pepper and a pinch of sugar. Pour on the water, add the *bouquet garni* and simmer for 2 hours. Just before serving stir the egg yolks quickly into the potato flour and stock till smooth and add to the hot soup.

Put the fried bread slices in the tureen and pour the soup over them.

TURNIP SOUP

6 *young turnips*
1 *oz. butter*
2½ *pints boiling water*
½ *teaspoon salt*
¼ *teaspoon sugar*
pepper
1 *egg yolk*
1 *tablespoon cream*

Slice the turnips, melt the butter in the soup pot, and cook slowly for 5 minutes, tossing once or twice. Add the salt, sugar and pepper. Stir. Pour on the boiling water and let the soup simmer till the turnips are soft. Pass through a sieve or mash well with a wooden spoon. Beat the egg yolk in the cream and add to the soup to 'bind' it, just before serving.

TOMATO SOUP

1 *lb. tomatoes*
¼ *bay leaf*
¼ *teaspoon dried thyme or 1 sprig*
1 *medium onion*
2½ *pints cold water*
¾ *teaspoon salt*
½ *teaspoon sugar*
2 *oz. butter*

Quarter the tomatoes and put in a heavy pot, add the bay leaf, thyme, sliced onion. Crush the tomatoes with a wooden spoon and cook very gently for 30 minutes, stirring often to prevent sticking. Sieve. To this purée add the water, salt, sugar, butter. Stir well, bring to the boil and take off heat. Pour over croûtons and serve at once.

MUSHROOM JULIENNE

Prepare vegetables as for Soupe Julienne (see p. 125), but add 8 oz. mushrooms, washed and very thinly sliced (use both caps and stems) 5 minutes before the soup is cooked.

Serve with croûtons.

SOUPE JULIENNE (Vegetable Soup)

2 *carrots*
2 *small turnips*
2 *medium potatoes*
2 *leeks*
4 *cabbage leaves*
2 *oz. butter*
2½ *pints stock*
4 *oz. green peas (or 4 oz. French beans)*
salt, pepper

Cut all the vegetables into very thin strips about 1½ inches long, except of course the peas. Melt the butter in the soup pot and add the vegetables and fry for 4 minutes. Stir them about, gently. Pour on the stock and bring to the boil. Simmer for 15 minutes, add the peas (or beans) and simmer for a further 15 minutes. Add salt and pepper.

The special character of this soup is the look of the vegetables, which should be almost like matchsticks.

TOMATO SOUP WITH TAPIOCA

tomato purée
1½ *pints cold water*
½ *pint hot milk*
¼ *teaspoon salt*
1¼ *oz. tapioca*
2 *oz. butter*

Make the purée as in Tomato Soup (see p. 124).

Boil the water, add the salt and throw in the tapioca, cook for 5 minutes, stir all the time, heating as it thickens; now add the milk slowly, still stirring the mixture. Add the purée and the butter (if too thick add more milk). Stir all together and serve, without croûtons.

POTAGE BOURGUIGNON

3 *oz. cooked haricot beans*
2 *medium onions*
4 *sticks of celery*
½ *pint cold water*
2 *pints stock*
1 *oz. butter*
salt, pepper

Chop up the onions and celery finely, add the cooked beans, salt and pepper, pour on the water and simmer for 20 minutes. Sieve or mash the vegetables thoroughly with a wooden spoon. Add the stock, boil up again, skimming if necessary.

Add the butter before serving, stir and serve with croûtons, fried in bacon fat.

ONION SOUP WITH CHEESE

6 *medium onions*
2½ *pints water*
8 *slices French bread*
4 *oz. grated cheese*
2 *oz. butter*
salt, pepper

Slice the onions finely and fry in the melted butter in a thick pot until brown, but not burnt. Pour in the water and simmer till reduced by a quarter. Add the salt and pepper, be generous with the latter. Ladle into separate fireproof, or earthenware, soup bowls, float 2 slices of bread in bowl, cover generously with the grated cheese (Gruyère is best, but not essential) and brown in a hot oven.

ONION SOUP 'SAVOYARDE'

6 *medium onions*
2 *oz. butter*
1½ *pints beef stock*
1 *pint boiling water*
1 *clove of garlic*
1 *bouquet garni*
1 *beaten egg*
wine vinegar
salt, pepper

Melt the butter, when sizzling add the sliced onions and chopped garlic, cook till soft. Pour on the boiling water, stir, then the stock. Put in the *bouquet*, add salt and pepper. Boil gently for 20 minutes. Remove the herbs. Draw the pot away from the heat and stir in the beaten egg plus 3 or 4 drops of vinegar.

WHITE ONION SOUP

6 *medium onions*
2 *oz. butter*
1 *tablespoon flour*
½ *pint boiling water*
1½ *pints milk*
salt, pepper

Melt the butter; when sizzling, add the sliced onions, cook for 3 minutes. Add the flour, stir, add the hot water, stir. Reduce the heat, season with salt and pepper. Cook for 10 minutes to reduce. Stir again and add the milk. Simmer very gently for 15 minutes or until the onions are soft. This soup may be sieved, but is very good as it is. As in all soups it may be made richer with a beaten egg yolk or a tablespoon of cream added at the last, AFTER it has stopped cooking.

ONION SOUP WITH VERMICELLI

onion soup
vermicelli

Follow the recipe for White Onion Soup. Add the vermicelli broken in half pieces as the soup begins to simmer after the addition of the milk. Stir constantly to prevent sticking, and simmer for 20 minutes.

PEA POD SOUP

1 *lb. young green peas*
1 *lettuce*
1 *small onion*
1 *handful spinach*
1 *sprig mint*
1 *tablespoon flour*
1 *oz. butter*
1½ *pints boiling water*
½ *pint milk*
salt, pepper, sugar

Chop the mint and all the vegetables, pea pods included. Melt the butter in the pot, add the vegetables, cook for 4 minutes, stirring once or twice. Add the flour and stir till absorbed. Pour on 1½ pints of boiling water gradually, stirring all the time, then the milk. Add the salt and pepper and a pinch of sugar. Simmer for 20 minutes.
This soup must be sieved.

ONION SOUP WITH SEMOLINA

onion soup (see p. 126)
2 tablespoons semolina

Follow the recipe for White Onion Soup. Add the semolina with the milk and simmer for 30 minutes, stirring occasionally.

GARBURE

1 *large cabbage*
8 *oz. cooked haricot beans*
   or dried peas
3 *large carrots*
3 *large potatoes*
1 *ham bone or 4 oz. bacon*
2 *pints cold water*
bouquet garni
salt, pepper
1 *tablespoon goose fat*

Shred the cabbage, slice the potatoes and carrots. Put these in a large soup pot with the haricot beans, the bone or bacon, and the *bouquet*. Pour the cold water on and bring to the boil. Simmer for 40 minutes. Take out the *bouquet*. Add the salt and pepper to taste, not too much salt. Remove the meat. Cut the rind off the bacon and chop the meat in pieces, pick any meat off the ham bone and do likewise. Return to the soup. Mash the 'solids' with a wooden spoon to a mush, and just before serving add the goose fat.

SOLE NORMANDIE

2 *large soles, filleted*
1 *pint mussels*
1 *chopped shallot*
12 *oysters*
½ *pint shrimps*
½ *pint dry white wine*
½ *pint cold water*
4 *oz. butter*
2 *oz. flour*
¼ *pint thick cream*
8 *oz. mushrooms, peeled and*
   sliced
salt, pepper

This is a complicated dish, but sole *par excellence*.
   Cook the mushrooms in 2 oz. butter very slowly till tender. Open the perfectly cleaned mussels by heating gently in a covered frying pan. Keep any liquid. Open the oysters, keep any liquid. Peel the shrimps, keep the shells and heads. Pour the wine and water, the mussel and oyster liquid into a small saucepan, add salt and pepper, shrimp heads and tails, the shallot and the butter from the cooked mushrooms. Simmer slowly for 30 minutes. Strain through muslin, re-heat and poach the fillets in this liquid for 10 minutes. Remove the fillets and place lengthwise in a buttered fireproof or baking dish. Keep warm.
   Make a sauce of 2 oz. butter, 2 oz. flour, ½ pint of the fish stock as you would a Béchamel sauce, add the cream, taste for seasoning. Pour this over the fish, decorate with mussels, oysters, shrimps and mushrooms. Put under a hot grill till slightly brown and serve.

SOLE MEUNIÈRE

4 *medium soles*
½ *oz. flour*
4 *oz. butter*
2 *teaspoons lemon juice*
salt, pepper

Dust the fishes with the flour, salt and pepper. Heat the butter, when sizzling hot put in the fish and cook for 30 seconds, turn over and cook for another ½ minute, or till a skewer goes through the thickest part easily.

Arrange in the serving dish, add a pinch of salt and pepper, pour over lemon juice and any butter left in the pan. Serve immediately.

FILLETS OF SOLE FLORENTINE

2 *large or 4 medium filleted soles*
4 *oz. butter*
juice of 1 lemon
salt, pepper
½ *pint Béchamel or Mornay sauce (see pp. 163, 165)*
1½ *lb. cooked spinach, tossed in 1 oz. butter*

Melt the butter, add salt, pepper, lemon juice and when hot put in the fillets. Turn each one. Cook till tender, about 5 minutes in all. Line a shallow fireproof dish with the cooked spinach, put in the cooked fish, pour over the sauce, and brown quickly under a hot grill.

SOLE AU VIN BLANC

2 *medium soles*
2 *tablespoons finely chopped shallots*
5 *oz. butter*
3 *oz. white breadcrumbs*
¼ *pint dry white wine*
salt, pepper

Have your fishmonger prepare the fish and take off the black skin.

Butter a flat fireproof dish, add the fishes, sprinkle with the shallots, salt, pepper, dabs of butter. Pour over the wine. Add the breadcrumbs and dot with the rest of the butter. Cook uncovered in a moderate oven for 25 minutes. Serve in the dish.

You may put the cooked dish under a hot grill to brown if wished.

SOLE MORNAY

4 *medium soles, filleted*
¼ *pint fish stock*
2 *oz. butter*
½ *pint Béchamel sauce (see p. 165)*
3 *oz. grated cheese (Parmesan or Cheshire)*
salt, pepper

Arrange the fillets in a buttered flat fireproof dish, add salt and pepper and the stock. Bake in a moderate oven for 15 minutes. Pour off the liquid and add to the Béchamel mixed with the cheese. Pour over the fillets, lifting them up to let the sauce run underneath. Put back in the oven for 4 minutes.

SOLE BONNE FEMME

4 *medium soles*
1 *teaspoon chopped parsley*
4 *oz. butter*
1 *chopped shallot*
8 *oz. mushrooms*
½ *teaspoon lemon juice*
2 *egg yolks*
SAUCE:
¼ *pint white wine*
4 *tablespoons fish stock*
½ *oz. butter*
½ *oz. flour*
salt, pepper

Chop the mushrooms very finely. Melt the butter in a small saucepan, add the mushrooms, shallot, parsley, lemon juice and cook, covered, very slowly for 10 minutes. Make a sauce with the wine, fish stock, butter and flour as you would White Sauce, put the soles in a flat fireproof dish, pour on this sauce. Cover the dish and cook till the soles are tender, about 15 minutes.

Pour this sauce over the mushrooms, etc. boil for 3 minutes, remove from heat, add salt and pepper and the beaten egg yolks. Pour back again over the fish, put under a hot grill for 3 minutes. Serve.

BAKED CODFISH

1 *small whole cod*
1 *quart fish stock or water*
1 *bouquet garni*
salt, pepper
1 *oz. flour*
3 *oz. brown breadcrumbs*
2 *oz. butter*
1 *pint shrimps, shelled*
1 *tablespoon anchovy essence*
1 *sliced lemon*
parsley sprigs to decorate

Wash and dry the fish. Put it in a baking tin, add the fish stock, or water, the *bouquet*, salt and pepper. Cover with the mixed flour and breadcrumbs and dot with butter. Bake in a moderate oven, basting frequently, about 30 minutes. Take 4 tablespoons of fish liquid out of the dish in the oven, pour over shrimps, with the anchovy essence, stir and pour over the fish and return to the oven for 7 minutes. Decorate the fish with the lemon slices and sprigs of parsley and serve in the dish it is cooked in.

PROVENÇAL CRUSHED SALT COD (Brandade)

2½ *lb. salt cod*
1 *clove of garlic*
½ *pint olive oil*
½ *pint milk*
1 *teaspoon lemon juice*
pepper
a few truffles (optional)
fried bread triangles

This dish is salt cod crushed to a creamy paste.

Soak the fish in cold water for 12 hours, change water twice. Cover with cold water, bring to the boil, remove at once from the heat. Drain, remove bones but not skin. Crush the garlic, and put in a warm large saucepan. Add the fish pieces and place over very low heat. In two other pans warm the milk and the olive oil—only tepid, not hot. (Fish, oil and milk must all be of the same low warmth throughout the making.) With a wooden spoon pound and crush the fish and garlic, add a spoon of milk, stir fiercely, add a spoon of oil, stir fiercely. Continue thus until the mixture is smooth and creamy. Season with pepper and lemon juice. Decorate with truffles, if any. Serve with the fried bread.

SCALLOPS (Coquilles St Jacques)

8 *scallops*
1 *large peeled sliced tomato*
1 *small finely chopped onion*
4 *oz. finely sliced mushrooms*
2 *oz. butter*
⅛ *pint Béchamel sauce*

Ask your fishmonger to open and clean the scallops and give you the shells.

Wash the scallops, cover with cold salted water, bring to the boil and simmer for 7 or 8 minutes till soft. Drain and chop white and red part together and mix with the tomato, onion, mushrooms, salt and pepper. Cook in the butter in a small saucepan, for 3 minutes. Add the Béchamel sauce, mix and fill 4 shells. Brown under a hot grill for a few minutes.

SCALLOPS AU GRATIN

8 *scallops*
4 *oz. mushrooms finely chopped*
2 *oz. breadcrumbs*
2 *oz. butter*
⅛ *pint Béchamel sauce*
1 *sherry glass white wine*
2 *oz. grated cheese*
pepper

Prepare and cook the scallops as in previous recipe.

Melt the butter and cook the mushrooms till soft, about 5 minutes, add the breadcrumbs, pepper, wine and Béchamel sauce, plus the finely chopped cooked scallops. Sprinkle with the cheese, and brown under the grill.

MULLET EN PAPILLOTE

1 *medium mullet*
2 *oz. breadcrumbs*
2 *oz. melted butter*
1 *teaspoon chopped fennel*
salt

Cut off head, tail and fins. Rub in melted butter, mix the breadcrumbs, salt and fennel, put half of this in the fish and the rest sprinkled over. Wrap it up well in buttered paper, and cook under a moderate grill for 25 minutes.

BAKED RED MULLET

2 *mullets*
2 *oz. breadcrumbs*
salt, pepper
2 *teaspoons chopped parsley*
2 *oz. butter*
2 *teaspoons lemon juice*

Ask your fishmonger to clean the fish, keeping the liver. Score the fish on both sides. Butter a shallow fireproof dish, put in the fish, sprinkle with the breadcrumbs, salt, pepper, parsley and lemon juice. Dot on the rest of the butter, bake in a moderate oven for 20 minutes, basting from time to time.

LOBSTER THERMIDOR

2 small boiled lobsters
2 tablespoons butter
½ teaspoon finely chopped onion
dash of cayenne pepper
½ glass dry white wine
8 oz. finely chopped mushrooms
1 tablespoon tomato purée
salt
½ pint Béchamel sauce
2 tablespoons grated Parmesan
   cheese

Pick the meat out of the claws, etc. Chop into dice, coral included, if any.

Heat the butter in a saucepan, add the lobster meat, coral, onion, cayenne and wine. Simmer for 5 minutes, stirring constantly. Add the mushrooms, tomato purée, salt, if necessary, simmer for 5 minutes more. Fill the shells with this mixture and put in serving dish. Cover with the Béchamel sauce, sprinkle on the cheese. Heat thoroughly in a hot oven, then put under a hot grill for 2 minutes.

MUSSELS MARINIÈRE

1 quart mussels
¼ pint cold water
¼ pint dry white wine
1 finely sliced carrot
1 sliced onion
1 crushed garlic clove
bouquet garni
2 oz. butter
salt, pepper
3 teaspoons chopped parsley

Wash and scrub the mussels carefully till no sand is left. A long business, but essential.

Add the carrot, onion, garlic, *bouquet*, butter, salt and pepper to the water and wine. Bring to the boil and simmer for 30 minutes. Strain and put the liquid in a large saucepan. Add the mussels, cover the pan and place over a strong heat, shaking the pan the whole time; after 5 minutes turn the mussels gently so that the top ones go to the bottom, cook for another 4 to 5 minutes till all are open. Take out the mussels, remove top shell, put in a deep serving dish or tureen and pour the liquid over. Sprinkle with the parsley. Serve hot.

LOBSTER À L'AMÉRICAINE

1 hen lobster
4 tablespoons olive oil
1 green pepper, seeded and sliced
2 large ripe tomatoes seeded,
   peeled and quartered
1 small onion, finely chopped
1 pint dry white wine
4 oz. butter
½ teaspoon lemon juice
1 teaspoon meat glaze or ¼ teaspoon Bovril
1 teaspoon chopped parsley
1 teaspoon chopped tarragon
salt, pepper

Cut the lobster in even pieces. Carefully keep the coral and water. Heat the olive oil in a saucepan, add the lobster and cook for 3 or 4 minutes. Add salt, pepper, the pimento, tomatoes and onion and the wine. Simmer for 20 minutes. Remove the lobster and keep warm in the serving dish. Put the saucepan back on a fierce heat and boil to reduce the liquid by half. Meanwhile knead together the butter, coral and lobster water with a wooden spoon. Add this to the reduced liquid, over a low heat stir till creamy and smooth. Add the meat glaze, lemon juice and herbs, stir for another minute and pour over the lobster and serve.

TRUITE AU BLEU

4 trout
2 tablespoons wine vinegar
1½ pints fish stock
2 teaspoons chopped parsley
Hollandaise or Ravigote sauce
  (see pp. 161, 162)

Clean the trout, put in a shallow dish and pour over the vinegar, turn the fish over so that all sides are coated with the vinegar to 'blue' the fish. Boil the stock, put in the fish, bring to the boil again and at once take off the heat, cover the pot, and leave for 5 minutes. Remove the trout, put in the serving dish, sprinkle with parsley and serve with either Hollandaise or Ravigote sauce.

TRUITE MEUNIÈRE

4 trout
1 tablespoon flour
4 oz. butter
2 teaspoons chopped parsley
½ teaspoon lemon juice
salt, pepper

Clean and wash the trout. Dry and roll them in the flour, salt and pepper. Heat 3 oz. butter in a frying pan, put in the trout and fry gently for 10 to 12 minutes, or until the fish is soft all through. Remove from pan and put on warm dish, sprinkle with parsley and lemon juice, add 1 oz. butter to the hot butter in frying pan, mix well and pour over the fishes.

HERRINGS À LA LORRAINE

4 large herrings
1 tablespoon flour
salt, pepper
3 oz. butter
1 small onion finely chopped
juice of 1 lemon
2 tablespoons cream
4 tablespoons breadcrumb

Ask the fishmonger to clean the herrings and cut off the heads. Wash and dry the fish. Mix flour, salt and pepper and roll the fish in this. Melt the butter in a large frying pan, add the chopped onion and cook gently till transparent. Add the herrings and fry gently on both sides for 4 or 5 minutes. Dust with the breadcrumbs, add the cream and lemon juice, stir the fish gently about in the pan, turn each fish over, spoon some of the liquid over each and cook gently with a lid on until the fish are soft through the thickest part.

WHITE FISH IN CUSTARD

4 fillets turbot, halibut, cod,
  plaice
1 pint milk or ½ milk, ½ cream
3 eggs
1 oz. butter
salt, pepper

Butter a shallow fireproof dish and place the fish in it. Beat the eggs, add the milk or milk and cream, salt and pepper, pour over fish. Stand the dish in a baking dish with 1 inch water in it, cook in a very slow oven for 1 hour.

    Any white filleted fish, cod, plaice, halibut, etc. can be cooked in this simple delicious way.

MACKEREL À LA NANTAISE

2 *large mackerel*
1 *tablespoon olive oil*
1 *finely chopped onion* } *marinade*
salt, pepper
1 *pint fish stock*
2 *teaspoons vinegar*
½ *pint Béchamel sauce*
1 *teaspoon chopped chives*
1 *teaspoon chopped capers*

1 *teaspoon lemon juice*
1 *oz. butter*

Take off heads and tails of already cleaned fish and cut open lengthwise. Soak in the marinade for 2 hours. Heat the stock till simmering gently, add vinegar, put in the mackerel and simmer for 30 minutes. Make the Béchamel sauce, add the chives, capers, lemon juice and butter. Pour over the cooked fish and serve.

BAKED TURBOT

4 *slices of turbot*
3 *tablespoons butter*
½ *tablespoon finely chopped onion*
½ *tablespoon chopped parsley*
2 *oz. white breadcrumbs*
1 *sherry glass white wine*
salt, pepper
1 *sliced lemon*
few parsley sprigs } *garnish*

Grease a flat fireproof dish with 1 oz. butter, sprinkle over half the chopped onion and parsley, salt and pepper, place the fish slices on this, dot with the rest of the butter, onion, parsley, another pinch of salt and pepper and the breadcrumbs. Pour the wine over, cover with greaseproof paper, and bake in a moderate oven for 25 minutes. Garnish with lemon slices and parsley.

EEL WITH WINE AND MUSHROOM SAUCE

1 *eel*
¾ *pint dry white wine*
1 *bouquet garni*
1 *chopped onion*
salt, pepper
2 *oz. butter*
2 *oz. flour*
4 *oz. chopped mushrooms*
12 *very small onions or shallots*
1 *egg yolk*
12 *shrimps*
croûtons } *fried in butter*

Cut the cleaned skinned eel in 3-inch pieces and put in a saucepan with the wine, chopped onion, *bouquet*, salt and pepper. Bring to the boil and boil for 30 minutes. In a small saucepan melt the butter, add the flour, pour on ½ pint of the eel liquid, gradually stirring all the time till smooth. Add the small onions and mushrooms and cook till soft. Add more stock, if too thick. Remove from the heat and stir in the egg yolk. Put the cooked eel on the serving dish, pour over the sauce, decorate with the fried shrimps and croûtons.

WHITING À LA BERCY

4 *medium whiting*
4 *teaspoons finely chopped*
  shallots
1 *liqueur glass white wine*
1 *liqueur glass cold water*
juice of 1 lemon
2 *oz. butter*
1 *teaspoon chopped parsley*

Split the whiting and cut along the backbone for easier cooking. Butter a shallow fireproof dish and lay the whiting side by side. Put 1 teaspoon of the shallots in each whiting, salt and pepper them, add the lemon juice and the water and wine. Dot the rest of the butter over and put in a moderate oven for 25 minutes. Baste frequently until there is no liquid left.

CHICKEN MARENGO

1 2-*lb. chicken*
1 *dessertspoon flour*
6 *tablespoons olive oil*
1 *clove of garlic*
bouquet garni
8 *oz. sliced mushrooms*
salt, pepper
2 *tomatoes*
3 *tablespoons stock*
1 *teaspoon chopped parsley*
2 *slices white bread* ⎱
2 *oz. butter* ⎰ *croûtons*
4 *fried eggs*

Carve the bird in seven pieces — wings, thighs, drumsticks and breast. Chop the garlic finely, heat the oil in a casserole. Put the legs in, plus garlic, salt and pepper, cook for 5 minutes, add the rest of the chicken and the *bouquet*. Cook till browned, add the mushrooms, the peeled and sliced tomatoes and the stock. Cover and simmer for 30 minutes. Make the croûtons, fry the eggs meanwhile. Remove the *bouquet* and serve arranged on a flat dish.

CHICKEN À LA BOURGOGNE

1 *young chicken cut in 5 pieces*
6 *mushrooms*
3 *oz. butter*
1 *dessertspoon flour*
12 *button onions*
3 *oz. bacon*
2 *shallots*
6 *tarragon leaves*
¼ *teaspoon nutmeg*
1 *liqueur glass brandy*
1 *pint red Burgundy*
salt and pepper

Slice the mushrooms and fry gently in 1 oz. butter till done. Keep warm. Roll the chicken pieces in the flour, salt and pepper. Melt 2½ oz. butter in a casserole, add the mushrooms and butter, plus the bacon cut into small cubes. Put in the onions, fry for 3 minutes, now add the chicken and fry till brown all over. Add the shallots, tarragon and nutmeg. Stir well. Pour in the wine and brandy. Simmer for 30 minutes. Add the fried mushrooms.

POULET À LA VALENCIENNE

1 3-*lb.* chicken
3 *tablespoons olive oil*
2 *medium onions*
2 *medium tomatoes*
2 *cloves of garlic*
2 *small red chillies*
1 *pinch of saffron*
1 *teaspoon chopped parsley*
4 *oz. Patna rice*
½ *pint stock*
salt, pepper

Cut up the chicken as for Chicken Marengo (p. 134). Peel the tomatoes and chop finely, also the onions, garlic, chillies. Heat the oil in a casserole or thick stewpot, add the garlic, cook for 3 minutes. Add the chicken pieces and the chopped parsley, onions, tomatoes, chillies, salt and pepper. Fry all till browned, stirring all the time. Put in the rice and saffron, pour over the stock. Boil up once, skim, and simmer with no lid for 30 minutes, or until rice grains are tender. Stir in with a fork. Serve with chutney sandwiches.

COQ AU VIN

1 *young chicken*
2 *oz. butter*
2 *oz. lean bacon*
4 *oz. sliced mushrooms*
1 *clove of garlic*
bouquet garni
1 *liquer glass brandy*
1 *pint red wine*
pepper

The blood of the chicken plus ¼ teaspoon vinegar should be kept.

Divide the chicken into 6 pieces. Melt the butter in a saucepan, add the diced bacon, the mushrooms, pepper. Fry all for 5 minutes till browned. Add the chopped garlic and the *bouquet*. Pour the brandy over and set it alight, add the wine, cover the pot and simmer for 20 minutes. Now pour in the chicken blood to thicken the gravy. Serve very hot with pieces of toast.

POULET AU BLANC

1 2-*lb.* chicken
2 *medium onions*
bouquet garni
1 *teaspoon salt*
1 *oz. butter*
1 *tablespoon flour*
¼ *pint milk*
¼ *pint chicken stock*
3 *egg yolks*
2 *lemons*
pepper
½ *pint cold water*

Carve the bird as for Chicken Marengo. Slice the onions, add the salt, *bouquet* and chicken pieces. Pour on the water and simmer covered for 30 minutes. Remove the chicken and put on serving dish. Keep warm. Make a sauce by melting the butter, add flour, ¼ pint hot chicken stock, ¼ pint milk. Boil and stir for 10 minutes. Remove from heat, stir in the beaten egg yolks, the juice of the lemons, pepper. Stir well and pour over the chicken.

CUISSE DE POULET À LA MOUTARDE

4 *chicken legs*
½ *oz. butter*
½ *teaspoon prepared mustard*
1 *oz. white breadcrumbs*
pinch of salt

Skin the legs, rub in the butter and mustard and salt, roll in breadcrumbs. Grill on both sides till tender. Serve with Mousseline sauce (see p. 162).

DUCK WITH ORANGE

1 *4-lb. duck, trussed*
1 *tablespoon wine vinegar*
2 *oz. sugar*
2 *oranges, juice of*
  the grated rind of 1 orange
1 *wine-glass Grand Marnier*
salt, pepper

Dust the duck with salt and pepper and roast for 1 hour. 10 minutes before the duck is cooked make the sauce — take a thick saucepan, boil the sugar and vinegar till it caramels. Add the orange juice, Grand Marnier, grated rind. Stir gently. Pour in the duck gravy, boil once and pour over the duck.

ALICOT

2 *lb. poultry meat*
(any part of uncooked chicken,
  duck, goose, turkey, you may
  have or remains of cold birds)
2 *oz. goose fat*
2 *large onions*
2 *oz. raw ham*
5 *medium tomatoes*
bouquet garni

1½ *pints stock*
salt, pepper

Slice all the vegetables, add the ham, *bouquet,* salt, pepper, cover with the hot stock. Boil for 20 minutes. Meanwhile fry the meat in the goose fat till brown. Put the meat in a casserole. Strain the vegetable stock, pick out the ham, add the ham to the casserole plus the strained liquid. Cover and simmer for 2 hours.

CONFIT D'OIE PÉRIGOURDINE (Preserved Goose)

1 *goose*
enough salt to rub all the pieces
¼ *pint cold water*

The goose must be cut in quarters. Cut away all fat from the inside. If not enough fat, use pork or beef dripping later on.

Rub the goose pieces all over with salt. Leave for 24 hours. Melt the fat, add the pieces plus the water. Cover the pot and simmer very slowly for 3 hours.

Sprinkle salt inside a deep glazed jar or basin, pour in some of the fat; when congealed, add the goose, cover completely with the rest of the fat. Store in a cool place. This will keep for months and may be used in Cassoulet or heated in its fat and eaten with cooked haricot beans or lentils.

PARTRIDGE WITH CABBAGE

2 *partridges, trussed*
1 *oz. butter*
1 *medium cabbage*
1 *medium carrot, sliced*
1 *medium onion, sliced*
2 *oz. fat bacon, diced*
1 *dessertspoon flour*
bouquet garni
½ *pint stock*
6 *chipolata sausages*
salt, pepper

Boil the cabbage, having cut it in 4. Keep warm. Melt the butter in a large casserole, add the bacon, onion, carrot, stir for 3 minutes on a quick heat. Dredge the birds with flour, add them to the casserole, cook, turning occasionally till brown all over. Season, put in the sausages and the *bouquet*. Pour the stock over, cover, and simmer for 20 minutes. Place the boiled cabbage on top, press down till covered by the stock. Cover and simmer for 1 hour or more, until the partridges are tender.

PARTRIDGE WITH WHITE GRAPES

2 *trussed partridges*
1 *oz. bacon fat*
6 *rashers of bacon*
bouquet garni
1½ *lb. white grapes*
salt, pepper

Peel and seed the grapes. Cut each rasher in 3. Melt the fat in a casserole, just large enough to hold the birds, add the rashers, the birds and the *bouquet*, salt and pepper. Press in the grapes to cover the birds and simmer for 1 hour. The casserole lid must fit well: seal with flour paste if necessary.

SADDLE OF HARE BOURGUIGNON

1 *saddle of hare*
3 *oz. butter or dripping*
¼ *pint cream*
¼ *pint chestnut purée*
salt, pepper
red currant jelly

Cover the hare with the fat, salt and pepper it. Cover with greaseproof paper and roast for 45 minutes in a fairly hot oven. Keep warm on the dish. Pour off excess fat from the gravy, add the cream and purée, stir well, re-heat but do not boil. Pour over the saddle and serve with Red Currant Jelly.

CIVET DE LIÈVRE LANDAIS

1 *cut-up hare*
3 *oz. goose fat or lard*
12 *chopped shallots*
3 *chopped cloves of garlic*
4 *oz. diced raw ham or bacon*
2 *oz. butter*
1 *glass red wine*
¼ *pint stock*

1 *tablespoon tomato purée or 6 peeled cooked tomatoes*
4 *oz. sliced mushrooms or cèpes*
salt, pepper

Fry the hare pieces in the fat till slightly brown. Fry the shallots, garlic, bacon or ham in the butter in a casserole till brown. Add the wine, stock, tomato, mushrooms, salt and pepper. Add the fried hare pieces. Simmer for 3 hours. Serve.

RABBIT WITH LENTILS

1 *lb. cooked lentils*
1 *cut-up rabbit*
4 *rashers of bacon*
2 *oz. bacon fat or butter*
¼ *pint cider*
bouquet garni
salt, pepper

Halve the rashers, add to the melted fat, plus the rabbit pieces, and fry till brown. Pour on the cider, cook for 3 minutes, add the *bouquet,* salt and pepper. Cover and simmer for 45 minutes or until the rabbit is tender. Pour the liquid over the lentils, re-heat, cook to reduce. Add the hot rabbit and bacon.

BOEUF À LA PROVENÇALE

3 *lb. lean beef*
¼ *pint olive oil*
2 *medium onions*
2 *bacon rashers*
1 *tablespoon flour*
bouquet garni
¼ *pint white wine*
¼ *pint cold water*
3 *large tomatoes*
12 *green olives*
salt, pepper

Chop the onions, cut up the rashers (always remove the rinds). Peel and quarter the tomatoes, stone the olives. Cut the beef in pieces 2 × 3 inches. Heat the olive oil in the stew pot and when fairly hot add the meat, onions, salt and pepper. Stir and add the flour, stir all the time and cook for 3 minutes. Add the *bouquet,* wine and water. Bring to the boil and simmer very gently for 3 hours. Now lift out the beef and put in another pot, add the bacon, the tomatoes and the olives. Strain the liquid over and cook again slowly for 30 minutes, shaking the pot occasionally.

BOEUF À LA MODE

3 *lb. lean beef*
2 *oz. fresh pork skin — with*
 ¼ *inch of fat left on*
3 *oz. butter*
3 *shallots*
1 *clove of garlic*
6 *medium carrots*
1 *calf's foot — split in 4*
2 *oz. fat bacon — cut in cubes*
½ *pint claret or white wine*
1 *liqueur glass brandy*
12 *small or button onions*
bouquet garni
½ *teaspoon salt and pepper*

Melt the butter in a thick pot large enough to take the meat; when hissing hot put in the piece of meat and brown it on all sides quickly to 'close' it. Turn it with wooden spoons or tongs so as not to prick it and let the juices escape. Take the beef out and in the same pot put the pork skin cut in 2 strips. Now add all the ingredients except the carrots. Cover the pot tightly and simmer very slowly for 3 hours. Lift the lid and put in the carrots, sliced, and cook for a further 3 hours, covered. Take out the *bouquet,* the calf's foot and the pork skin. Put the beef on a dish and pour the vegetable liquid over.

FILET DE BOEUF FLAMBÉ À L'AVIGNONAISE

4 *small thick fillet steaks*
1 *clove of garlic*
5 *oz. butter*
1 *liqueur glass brandy*
4 *slices white bread*
4 *sprigs watercress*
salt, pepper

Cut the crusts off the slices of bread. Cut the garlic clove in half and rub both halves over the steaks to get full flavour, season with salt and pepper.

Fry the bread slices in 2 oz. butter, till golden, arrange on the serving dish and keep warm. In the cleaned frying pan melt another 2 oz. butter; when sizzling put in the steaks and quickly brown all over, use a spoon to turn. When brown add the last 1 oz. of butter, when melted pour on the brandy. Set it alight. Cook another ½ minute. The whole steak frying should only take 3 minutes. Arrange the steaks on the fried bread and pour over the gravy. Serve at once.

TOURNEDOS SAUTÉ

1 *lb. fillet steak*
3 *oz. butter*
¼ *pint stock*
1 *small glass sherry*
1 *teaspoon flour*
salt, pepper

Mix ½ oz. butter with the flour in a small basin. Cut the steak across in ½-inch strips, dust with salt and pepper. Melt 2½ oz. butter in a frying pan and when sizzling add the pieces of meat. Toss these and cook very quickly till brown, only for 2 or 3 minutes. Remove them and keep warm. Pour the sherry and the stock into the frying pan, heat, add the mixed butter and flour, stir and scrape the sides and bottom of the pan to get all the meat essence. Keep stirring quickly until the mixture is smooth, taste and add more salt if necessary, let it simmer for 3 minutes. Pour over the fillets.

PORC AU MARÉCHAL

4 *pork chops*
2 *oz. butter*
1 *teaspoon chopped parsley*
salt, pepper
1 *small orange*
1 *liqueur glass Madeira or sherry*
¼ *pint cold water*

Cut the orange peel into tiny strips, boil in a small pan with the water for 5 minutes. Add the wine, and leave.

Mix the parsley on a plate with 1 oz. butter to make a paste. Leave.

Salt and pepper the chops spread with 1 oz. butter. Grill, when well done (pork must always be well cooked), put on the serving dish and keep warm.

Pour the orange and wine liquid on to the juices and fat that have come from the chops. Slit each chop, rub in the parsley, butter, and serve, with the sauce served separately.

RUMPSTEAK À LA HUSSARDE

2 *lb. lean rumpsteak*
2 *medium onions*
4 *oz. mushrooms*
1 *pint stock*
2 *tablespoons milk*
3 *oz. white breadcrumbs*
3 *oz. calves' liver*
2 *egg yolks*
6 *oz. butter*
salt, pepper

Pick a thick square steak. Chop the liver and onions finely. Soak the breadcrumbs in the milk, squeeze dry, and mix all together, add salt and pepper. Melt 2 oz. butter in a small saucepan, add the mixture and cook till it begins to brown. Cool and then add the egg yolks, stir well and set aside: this is the stuffing.

With a very sharp knife cut five deep slits in the steak in rows, open out like the pages of a book. Fill these with the stuffing up to ½ inch of each slit. Tie with string securely. Fry in a stew pot using the rest of the butter, quickly, till brown all over. Add a little more salt, pour the stock on gradually, add the mushroom caps and any stuffing left over. Bring to the boil, cover and then simmer very gently for 4 hours. Serve with mashed potatoes or spaghetti.

PORC À LA MARSEILLAISE

4 *loin pork chops*
1 *egg*
2 *oz. breadcrumbs*
3 *oz. butter*
2 *lb. onions*
½ *pint stock*
salt, pepper

Chop the onions finely and boil in the stock till quite soft. Mash them well. Dust the chops with salt and pepper, then egg and breadcrumb them and fry in the butter till cooked.

Pile the onion purée in the middle of the dish and arrange the chops around.

AGNEAU JARDINIÈRE

1 *small leg or shoulder of lamb*
4 *small onions, or 2 large ones*
2 *medium turnips*
2 *oz. lard or pork fat*
2 *glasses dry white wine*
1 *tablespoon chopped parsley*
1 *teaspoon chopped tarragon*
3 *tablespoons cream*
salt, pepper

Quarter the vegetables. Melt the lard or pork fat in the casserole or pot, fry the vegetables till they brown. Add salt and pepper. Put in the meat and turn to 'close' it. Pour on the wine, cover tightly and simmer for 2½ hours. Lift out meat and vegetables, keep warm. Remove excess fat from the gravy, add the parsley, tarragon and stir in the cream.

This dish should be served in slices on a plate surrounded by the vegetables with the gravy poured over.

PORK IN CASSEROLE

2 *lb. pork*
2 *oz. butter*
1 *clove of garlic*
¼ *teaspoon chopped sage*
¼ *pint hot water*
salt, pepper

Old, lean pork will do for this dish.

Cut up the meat in 2-inch cubes. Melt the butter in the casserole, add the pork pieces, salt and pepper, stir till browned. Add the sage and chopped garlic, stir again. Cook very slowly in the covered casserole, turning the meat with a wooden spoon occasionally for 2 hours. Add the hot water and stir thoroughly.

Cooked chestnuts are good with this dish.

GIGOT À LA PROVENÇALE

1 *leg of mutton*
1 *clove of garlic*
1 *oz. butter*
salt, pepper
3 *anchovy fillets*
3 *chopped gherkins*

Slit the meat next the bone and push in the garlic about 1 inch down. Dust with salt and pepper and rub with the butter. Roast the meat, 20 minutes to the lb. Keep the meat gravy, to which you add the anchovy fillets and the gherkins, all very finely chopped. Pour over the roast joint.

GIGOT À LA BRETONNE

1 *small leg of mutton*
1 *clove of garlic*
2 *oz. butter*
5 *oz. haricot beans*
1 *large onion*
1 *large tomato*
1 *shallot*
bouquet garni
salt, pepper
water

Soak the haricot beans overnight. Take the beans and whole onion, add the *bouquet,* salt and pepper, cover with water and boil till soft, skimming frequently. Strain. Keep the beans and the onion warm.

Slit the meat and press the garlic in next the bone. Dust with salt and pepper and rub with 1 oz. butter. Roast the ordinary way, 20 minutes to the lb. Keep warm in the serving dish. Keep the gravy in the pan. Make a sauce by melting 1 oz. butter, salt and pepper, add the chopped shallot, the tomato peeled and quartered and the boiled onion. Cook till soft. Stir this mixture into the gravy left in the roasting pan, add the cooked beans and pour over the roast joint.

LAMB CUTLETS À LA MINUTE

8 *lamb cutlets*
4 *oz. butter*
½ *teaspoon lemon juice*
salt, pepper

Beat the cutlets very flat, or ask the butcher to do it.

Sprinkle with salt and pepper. Fry in the sizzling butter for 1 minute each side. Put in the serving dish. Add lemon juice to the butter in the pan, stir and pour over the cutlets.

ROAST LAMB À LA NIÇOISE

1 *leg of lamb*
6 *small vegetable marrows*
  (courgettes)
1 *large tomato*
12 *small potatoes*
½ *teaspoon salt*
pepper
¼ *pint olive oil*

Halve the courgettes, do not peel them; peel and slice the tomato, peel the potatoes. Put these in the flat roasting pan, add salt and pepper. Put the joint on top, pour over the olive oil, cover with grease-proof paper and roast in a hot oven for 20 minutes to the lb.

AGNEAU RÔTI PERSILLÉ

1 *leg of lamb*
2 *oz. white bread-*
  crumbs
2 *teaspoons chopped*
  parsley   } *persillade*
1 *clove of garlic,*
  chopped
pinch of salt, pepper

Roast the lamb, 15 minutes to the lb. When three-quarters cooked, spread the breadcrumbs, parsley, garlic, salt, pepper mixed together on top. Baste once or twice until the meat is cooked and the *persillade* golden brown.

ROAST LAMB À LA BORDELAISE

1 *leg lamb*
3 *oz. butter*
3 *tablespoons olive oil*
8 *oz. mushrooms*
1 *teaspoon chopped parsley*

1 *chopped clove of garlic*
pinch salt, pepper

Roast the lamb in a large casserole or covered stew pot adding all the ingredients, 20 minutes to the lb. and 20 minutes over, in a hot oven.

LAMB STEW

2 *lb. best end neck of lamb*
1 *tablespoon flour*
2 *medium onions*
1 *oz. butter*
1 *pint stock*
2 *large tomatoes*
3 *medium turnips*
1 *dessertspoon mushroom catsup*
1 *glass dry sherry*
salt, pepper

Have the meat cut up by the butcher. Trim excess fat. Peel and slice the tomatoes, chop the onions and turnips. Melt the butter in the stewpan, add the meat and fry till brown on all sides. Remove the meat. Add the flour to the butter, stir till brown, pour on the stock and stir till the mixture boils. Add the meat, the vegetables, salt and pepper. Cover closely and simmer gently for 2 hours. Before serving stir in the sherry and catsup.

More carrots and turnips should be served as a vegetable.

ROAST LAMB À LA BONNE FEMME

1 *leg of lamb*
3 *rashers fat bacon*
12 *small onions*
4 *oz. butter*
pinch salt, pepper

Cut 10 or 12 larding strips of bacon and lard the joint. Cook in a covered casserole, 15 minutes to the lb. with the butter, salt, pepper and onions whole.

PAUPIETTES DE VEAU CLEMENTINE

1 *lb. veal cut in very thin slices*
½ *bacon rasher to each slice*
1 *medium onion*
1 *tablespoon flour*
½ *teaspoon lemon juice*
2 *oz. butter*
salt, pepper
1 *glass white wine*
¼ *pint cold water*
½ *teaspoon chopped parsley*
pinch of thyme
1 *small strip lemon peel*
6 *capers*

Dust the veal slices in flour, salt and pepper and add a few drops of lemon juice to each slice. Put ½ bacon rasher on top of each slice and roll up, peg or tie securely — these make the paupiettes. Slice the onion finely and fry in the butter till soft, add the paupiettes and brown, turning gently. When brown add the parsley, thyme, lemon peel and capers, pour on the wine and water, simmer very gently for 10 minutes. Strain the liquid over the paupiettes and serve — of course remove pegs or cotton.

ESCALOPES DE VEAU AUX OLIVES

4 *veal escalopes*
1 *dessertspoon flour*
2 *oz. butter*
12 *black olives*
1 *glass white wine*
salt, pepper
½ *teaspoon lemon juice*

Dust the escalopes in the flour, salt and pepper, brown quickly in the butter, lower the heat and cook very slowly for 8 minutes. Stone the olives and add them to the meat, cook together for 2 minutes, then lift the meat and olives out of the pan. Keep warm on the serving dish. Add the wine and lemon juice, stir and scrape round the pan, cook till the gravy begins to thicken, pour over the escalopes.

ESCALOPES DE VEAU CHASSEUR

4 *veal escalopes*
1 *dessertspoon flour*
salt, pepper
3 *oz. butter*
2 *tomatoes*
4 *oz. mushrooms*
½ *teaspoon chopped tarragon*

Dust the escalopes in flour, season with salt and pepper and brown quickly in butter. Keep warm. Peel and slice the tomatoes and mushrooms and cook till soft, in 1 oz. butter, add the tarragon. Put in the cooked veal, stir gently and cook slowly for 6 minutes more.

ESCALOPES DE VEAU AU BEURRE D'ANCHOIS

8 *veal escalopes*
6 *oz. butter*
1 *oz. flour*
salt, pepper
¼ *cup white wine*
¼ *cup hot water*
8 *slices stale white bread*
2 *anchovy fillets*
a few drops of lemon juice
parsley

Mash the anchovies and lemon juice in 1 oz. butter to make a paste. Fry the bread (crusts removed) in 2 oz. butter till golden. Take out and spread with the anchovy paste and keep warm, arranged on the serving dish.

Ask your butcher to flatten the escalopes, or beat them with a wooden spoon. Dust with the flour, salt and pepper.

Heat the 3 oz. butter in the frying pan, and fry the escalopes till brown on both sides, quickly, taking about 8 minutes all told. Remove the escalopes and put one on each piece of fried bread, keeping warm in the oven. Pour the wine and water into the pan, and scrape the sides and bottom and stir till the gravy thickens. Cook for 2 minutes more. Pour over the escalopes. Before serving decorate with parsley sprigs.

ESCALOPES DE VEAU À LA ROYALE (A recipe from Dijon)

4 *slices white bread fried in butter*
4 *large veal escalopes*
1 *tablespoon olive oil*
2 *medium onions*
4 *tablespoons cold water*
2 *tablespoons cream*
2 *egg yolks*
2 *tablespoons brandy*
2 *tablespoons port*
salt, pepper

Put the escalopes in the heated oil. Add the sliced onions; cook, turning frequently till brown. Now add the cold water, salt and pepper. Stir and leave to cook very slowly for 8 or 10 minutes. Lift out the escalopes and place one on each slice of fried bread on the serving dish. Keep warm. Beat the egg yolks and stir into the cream, add this to the gravy, also the brandy and the port. Cook very gently, stirring all the time until the sauce begins to thicken, pour at once over the escalopes and serve.

VEAL CUTLETS À LA MARÉCHAL

4 *veal cutlets*
1 *oz. breadcrumbs*
1 *oz. grated Parmesan cheese*
1 *egg*
2 *oz. butter*
1 *orange*
salt, pepper

Pepper and salt each cutlet, brush with the egg and roll them in the mixed cheese and breadcrumbs. Fry in the butter till golden brown. Squeeze the juice of the orange over them. As a vegetable serve spinach.

BLANQUETTE DE VEAU AU RIZ

2 *lb. shoulder of veal*
8 *oz. mushrooms, chopped*
4 *medium onions*
3 *oz. butter*
1 *egg yolk*
¼ *pint cream*
¼ *pint dry white wine*
1 *teaspoon lemon juice*
2 *tablespoons flour*
1 *liqueur glass dry vermouth*
bouquet garni
salt, pepper
2 *pints hot water*
cooked rice

Melt the butter in the stewpan; when hot, put in the veal cut in 1½-inch cubes, stir and cook till slightly brown. Add the chopped onions, stir, then the flour, stir and lower the heat. Cook gently for 3 minutes, stir again, add the wine and the vermouth, salt and pepper and the *bouquet*. Pour on the water, cover the pan, simmer for 1¼ hours, add the sliced mushrooms and simmer for a further 15 minutes. Meanwhile heat the egg yolk and the lemon juice, and add two minutes before serving, also the cream. Remove *bouquet*. Keep warm but do NOT boil, as this will curdle the gravy. Serve with cooked rice.

VEAL AU BOULANGER

4 *veal cutlets*
2 *oz. butter*
1 *teaspoon chopped parsley*
salt, pepper
1 *lb. apples*
1 *small strip lemon rind*
1 *dessertspoon sugar*
¼ *pint water*

Peel and chop the apples, add the water and lemon rind. Stew till soft, add the sugar. Mash them or put through a sieve.

Mix 1½ oz. butter with the parsley to make a paste. Salt and pepper the cutlets, spread with ½ oz. butter and grill till done. Slit each cutlet and press in the parsley butter. Serve the cutlets sitting on a bed of the apple purée.

FRICANDEAU DE VEAU

3 *lb. fillet veal*
salt, pepper
8 *medium carrots or* 12 *small ones*
4 *rashers of fat bacon for larding*
1 *slice fresh pork fat, enough to wrap round the veal*
6 *medium onions*
2 *cups stock*
bouquet garni

Roll the larding pieces of bacon in salt and pepper and lard the meat, and wrap in the piece of pork fat. Put it in a heavy stew pan, add the sliced carrots and onions, the *bouquet* and pour over the stock. Simmer gently for 3½ hours with the lid on.

Now take out the meat, remove the pork fat, and strain the liquid. Put the meat and the liquid back in the pot and cook quickly to reduce by a quarter. Skim off excess fat. Press the vegetables through a sieve into the pot, stir, re-heat and serve. The veal should be soft enough to cut with a spoon. Spinach is the best vegetable to have with this dish.

FOIE DE VEAU SAUTÉ (Fried Calves' Liver)

8 oz. calves' liver
2½ oz. butter
4 rashers of bacon
2 medium onions
1 teaspoon chopped parsley
2 tablespoons water
salt, pepper

Melt 2 oz. butter in a frying pan, add a pinch of salt and pepper, when hot put in the pieces of liver and fry quickly for 3 minutes, turning the pieces till brown all over. Cover the pan and remove from the heat.

Butter a shallow fireproof dish with ½ oz. butter, add the finely sliced onions and bacon cut in ½-inch squares (always remove the rinds), the parsley, salt and pepper. Slip the liver out of the frying pan plus all the juices and butter on to this mixture, add the water. Cover the dish tightly and in a moderate oven cook for 20 minutes.

CALVES' LIVER

8 oz. calves' liver
1 tablespoon flour
salt, pepper
3 oz. butter
1 teaspoon lemon juice
1 small glass white wine
1 teaspoon chopped parsley

Have the liver cut in slices ¼ inch thick. Roll the pieces in a mixture of the flour, parsley, salt and pepper. Melt 2½ oz. butter in a frying pan and fry quickly for 2 minutes on each side, lower the heat, cover the pan and cook very gently for 10 minutes more without disturbing. Remove the liver and put on the serving dish; keep warm.

Pour the wine in the frying pan, stirring and scraping to collect all the juices, add ½ oz. butter and lemon juice. Stir and pour over the liver.

OX TONGUE WITH MUSHROOMS

1 ox tongue
1 large onion
1 stick celery
1 bay leaf
½ teaspoon salt
½ teaspoon pepper
enough cold water to cover
1 oz. butter ⎫
1 oz. flour ⎪
½ pint tongue stock ⎬ sauce
1 dessertspoon French ⎪
  mustard ⎭
4 oz. mushrooms
1 oz. butter
3 pickled gherkins, chopped

1 glass dry white wine
3 tablespoons cream

Put the tongue (previously soaked for 12 hours in cold water) in enough water to cover it, add the onion, celery, bay leaf, salt and pepper. Bring to the boil, skim if necessary, and simmer for 4 hours.

Take the tongue out of the pot, skin it and remove hard root and nerve. Keep warm on the serving dish.

Now for the sauce. Slice the mushrooms and fry in butter. Make the sauce as for Brown Sauce, adding the mustard. Be careful with the salt. Add the fried mushrooms, the gherkins and the wine and cream. Pour over the tongue and serve.

BEEF KIDNEY À LA PARISIENNE

1 *very fresh beef kidney*
1 *clove of garlic*
2 *oz. butter*
1 *teaspoon wine vinegar*
1 *teaspoon chopped parsley*
1 *teaspoon chopped chives or onion*
1 *teaspoon flour*
½ *pint stock*
salt, pepper

Skin and core the kidney, cut in ¼ slices. Melt the butter in a small pan, add the kidney, chives or onions, salt, pepper, fry for 3 or 4 minutes till brown, lower heat, stir in the flour, add the vinegar, stir again. Cook for 1 minute then add the stock. Stir till the gravy begins to thicken, and serve. Do not boil or the kidney slices will become hard.

ROGNON DE VEAU À LA LIÈGEOISE
(Calves' Kidney à la Liègeoise)

4 *veal kidneys*
2 *oz. butter*
1 *small glass dry white wine*
6 *juniper berries*
½ *teaspoon lemon juice*
salt, pepper

Skin the kidneys, leaving on a little of the fat. Melt 1½ oz. butter in a small saucepan; when sizzling, add the whole kidneys, salt and pepper, turn each kidney till brown — a matter of seconds. Lower the heat and add the wine. Cover with a tight lid and cook extremely slowly for 5 minutes. Add the juniper berries, lemon juice, ½ oz. butter, stir, and continue stirring over a very low heat for 5 minutes more. Serve on toast if you wish.

TÊTE DE VEAU VINAIGRETTE
(Calf's Head with Sauce Vinaigrette)

1 *calf's head*
1 *tablespoon flour*
2 *large carrots*
1 *large onion*
2 *lemons or 2 tablespoons wine
   vinegar*
2 *cloves*
1 *bouquet garni*
½ *teaspoon salt*
½ *teaspoon pepper*
5 *quarts boiling water*

Ask the butcher to split the head and remove the tongue and brains. Soak all together in cold water for 12 hours.

Put the flour, pepper, chopped onion, chopped carrot, the juice of the 2 lemons or the vinegar, the cloves and the *bouquet* in a pan large enough to hold the head. Pour on the boiling water and simmer for 15 minutes. Add the head, brains and tongue. Boil for 30 minutes and take out the tongue and brains (easier if previously tied in muslin). Peel the tongue and keep warm with the brains, on a plate over hot water. Simmer the head for another 1½ hours. Cut the hot meat from the head and arrange on the serving dish with the tongue cut in slices and the brains. Serve with Sauce Vinaigrette (see p. 164).

ROGNONS AU MADÈRE (Sheep's Kidneys in Dry Sherry)

4 *sheep's kidneys*
2 *oz. butter*
½ *glass dry sherry*
4 *oz. mushrooms*
½ *teaspoon flour*
few drops of lemon juice
1 *teaspoon chopped parsley*
salt, pepper
4 *pieces toast*

This is a good entrée. Make the toast and put in the serving dish. Skin and halve the kidneys. Cut each half in three pieces. Slice or chop the mushrooms.

Melt the butter in a small saucepan, add the pieces of kidney, the mushrooms, flour, salt and pepper. Cook fairly quickly, for 3 or 4 minutes, stirring all the time. Pour on the sherry, stir again, then the drops of lemon juice and the parsley. Stir to mix, pour over the toast and serve at once. This whole job must be done very quickly to keep the kidneys tender.

CALVES' BRAINS WITH BLACK BUTTER

4 *calves' brains*
boiling water
¼ *pint wine vinegar*
1 *medium onion*
¼ *teaspoon salt*
bouquet garni
1 *oz. butter*
¼ *teaspoon vinegar*
2 *teaspoons chopped parsley*

Soak the brains in cold water for 1 hour. Throw into boiling water for 5 minutes, drain, skin and clean.

Put them in a saucepan, add ½ cup of vinegar, the salt, chopped onion, and the *bouquet*. Simmer for 30 minutes. Remove, drain and keep warm in the serving dish. Melt the butter till dark brown, cook for 2 minutes, add ¼ teaspoon vinegar, stir and pour over the brains. Sprinkle parsley over and serve.

CALVES' FEET À LA MÉNAGÈRE

3 *calves' feet*
cold water
1½ *oz. butter*
1 *large onion*
1 *large tomato*
bouquet garni
salt, pepper
1 *dessertspoon flour*

¼ *pint stock*
1 *liqueur glass white wine*

Have the feet split in three. Cover with cold water, boil for 2 hours. Bone carefully. Melt the butter, add the flesh off the feet, the onion chopped, tomato peeled and seeded, the *bouquet*, salt, pepper; stir, add the flour, stir again; then add the stock and wine, and simmer for 20 minutes.

SWEETBREADS (Ris de Veau, Ris d'Agneau)

Preparation of Sweetbreads: The 'heart' round ones are best. Remove all blood, hard tubes, etc., soak in cold water for 4 hours.

Remove and put in a stewpan, cover with cold water or stock, bring to the boil, simmer for 2½ minutes. Throw into cold water, drain, trim to a tidy shape, and set between two plates or boards with a Weight on top till cold.

ASPARAGUS

1½ *lb. asparagus*
3 *oz. butter*
boiling water
salt, pepper

Asparagus should be cooked standing up, as the stalks take longer than the tips.

Trim the stalks, wash gently and tie in a tidy bundle. Stand in a jug or deep jar, add a little salt, pour in boiling water two-thirds of the way up. Stand this in a pan of boiling water. Cover the pan and boil for 30 minutes. Serve with melted butter, pepper and salt.

TRIPE À LA MODE DE CAEN (1)

2½ *lb. tripe, cut in 2-inch squares*
1 *leek washed and trimmed*
1 *small onion stuck*
  with 3 cloves   ⎫
1 *bay leaf*   ⎬ *bouquet garni*
1 *sprig thyme*   ⎭
4 *large onions*
1 *calf's foot split in 4*
8 *oz. chopped beef suet*
1 *teaspoon salt*
½ *teaspoon pepper*
½ *pint cider*
2 *tablespoons Calvados*
cold water
4 *oz. flour*
2—3 *tablespoons cold water*

Tie the *bouquet* together firmly, or tie up in a piece of muslin. Make a stiff paste with the flour and water.

Slice the onions. Put a layer of onions in the bottom of a large casserole, then a layer of tripe, the calf's foot, a layer of suet, another layer of onions, tripe, the *bouquet* and finish with a layer of suet. Add the Calvados, the cider, salt and pepper and enough water to cover the layers. Put on the lid and seal the edges tightly with the flour paste. Cook in a very slow oven for 12 hours.

When cooked, remove the *bouquet,* and the calf's foot. Pick the flesh off this and put in the casserole. Skim off any excess fat. Serve boiling hot, with boiled potatoes.

TRIPE À LA MODE DE CAEN (2)

2 *lb. tripe cut in 1-inch squares*
1 *cow heel or 2 calves' feet cut in*
  1-inch pieces
4 *leeks*
2 *large carrots*
3 *large onions*
2 *bay leaves*
6 *cloves*   ⎫
2 *sprigs of thyme* ⎬ *bouquet garni*

1 *pint cider or dry white wine*
½ *port glass of brandy*
2 *teaspoons chopped parsley*
enough water to cover everything
salt, pepper

Put all these ingredients, except the chopped parsley, in a large casserole, or stewpan, covered with a very tight lid. Simmer for 11 hours. Take out the *bouquet,* sprinkle with chopped parsley and serve boiling hot.

SWEETBREADS À LA MINUTE

4 *sweetbreads*
1½ *oz. butter*
2 *teaspoons lemon juice*
1 *teaspoon chopped parsley*
salt, pepper

Melt the butter; when sizzling, put in the prepared sweetbreads, fry for 2 or 3 minutes, turning to brown. Remove to serving dish. Add pinch of salt, pepper, lemon juice and parsley to the gravy and pour over the sweetbreads.

JERUSALEM ARTICHOKES

2 *lb. artichokes*
1 *pint cold water*
1½ *oz. butter*
or
1 *pint Béchamel sauce*
salt, pepper

Scrub the unpeeled artichokes thoroughly. Cover with cold salted water, boil till tender, about 20 minutes. Drain, keep the liquid. Cool slightly then rub the skin off. Serve with melted butter, salt and pepper, or Béchamel sauce made with half milk and half the artichoke liquid.

ARTICHOKES (Globe)

Cut off the stems and the top. Remove the very hard outer leaves. Plunge them, stem end down, into boiling water, boil for 30 minutes, uncovered. Drain well upside down. Serve with melted butter, French dressing or Hollandaise sauce (see p. 161).

AUBERGINES WITH HERBS

4 *aubergines or breadfruit*
2 *rashers bacon, diced*
2 *cloves of garlic*
½ *teaspoon mixed chopped marjoram and basil*
salt, pepper
4 *tablespoons olive oil*

In each unpeeled aubergine cut two slits lengthways. Chop each clove of garlic into 4, roll in salt and herbs. Fill the slits with the bacon dice and garlic. Pour over the oil. Put the aubergines in a shallow covered fireproof dish and bake in a slow oven for 1 hour.

BRAISED CELERY

3 *heads of celery*
2 *oz. butter*
2 *tablespoons meat glaze or*
  ½ *teaspoon Bovril*

Cut each thoroughly clean head in half, throw into boiling water and boil for 10 minutes. Drain till dry. Melt the butter in a covered shallow fireproof dish, add the celery and cook slowly for 30 minutes or more, till tender. 5 minutes before serving add the glaze or Bovril.

CREAMED SPINACH

2 *lb. young spinach*
4 *oz. butter*
¼ *pint cream*
¼ *teaspoon nutmeg*
½ *teaspoon sugar*
salt, pepper

Wash and chop the spinach finely. Melt the butter, add the spinach, stir over a good heat until there is no juice left. Add the cream, nutmeg, sugar, salt and pepper. Stir well and simmer gently for 10 minutes.

CREAMED BEETROOT

8 *small young boiled beetroots*
8 *grapes, peeled and pipped*
2 *tablespoons cream*
a few drops of lemon juice
1 *pint Béchamel sauce*
  (see p. 165)

Peel and slice the boiled beetroots, add them to the hot sauce with the grapes. Simmer for 5 minutes. Just before serving stir in the cream and the lemon juice.

CREAMED CUCUMBERS

2 *cucumbers*
½ *teaspoon chopped mint*
salt, pepper
½ *pint thick Béchamel sauce*
  (see p. 165)

Peel and cut the cucumbers in fingers. Season and steam for 20 minutes till soft. Add the chopped mint to the sauce and the cucumbers.

GREEN BEANS MAÎTRE D'HÔTEL

2 *lb. French beans*
2 *pints boiling water*
3 *oz. butter*
1 *tablespoon chopped parsley*
salt, pepper

Pick dark green small young beans. Wash and trim the ends. Boil whole uncovered in salted water for 20 minutes. Drain. Melt the butter, re-heat the beans in it. Sprinkle parsley, salt and pepper over.

SALSIFY

1 *lb. salsify*
½ *teaspoon vinegar*
1 *oz. butter*
salt, pepper

Wash, trim and scrape each root, put in cold water plus the vinegar to prevent turning black. Throw into boiling salted water, boil for 20 minutes. Drain. Heat the butter and toss the cooked vegetables in it, season and serve hot.

GLAZED TURNIPS

12 *small very young turnips*
1 *pint boiling salted water*
1 *teaspoon castor sugar*
2 *oz. butter*

Prepare the turnips, pour over the water and boil for 15 minutes, till soft.

Butter a flat fireproof dish, add the drained turnips, sprinkle with sugar and put dabs of butter on top. Cook very slowly till the sauce turns brown and sticky. Do not burn. Stir the turnips round in the glaze and serve.

GREEN PEAS WITH LETTUCE

2 *lb. peas in pod*
  or 1 *large packet frozen peas*
1 *tablespoon warm water*
1 *small lettuce*
3 *small chopped onions*
1 *oz. butter*
salt, pepper

Shell the peas — thaw if the frozen sort. Wash and pull apart the lettuce.

Melt the butter, cook the onions till soft, add the lettuce leaves, salt, pepper, peas, warm water; stir, cover the pan and cook gently for 20 minutes, shaking the pan occasionally.

PURÉE OF CHESTNUTS

½ *lb. chestnuts*
2 *pint water*
pepper
1 *oz. butter*
3 *tablespoons cream*
3 *tablespoons stock*

Prick each nut and bake in a moderate oven for 20 minutes. Peel off both skins.

Put the chestnuts in a casserole, pour on the water, add pepper, cover and cook slowly for 1½ hours.

When done, sieve or mash very finely, add the butter, cream and stock, stir and re-heat slowly.

CHICORY IN BUTTER

4 *heads of chicory*
2 *oz. butter*
½ *teaspoon lemon juice*
salt

Prepare the heads of chicory, but do not cut them. Melt the butter in a casserole with a tight lid, add chicory. Turn well in the butter. Cook slowly till tender for about 20 minutes and golden brown. Add salt and lemon juice.

ROAST ONIONS

8 *or* 12 *medium onions*

Do not skin the onions. Bake them in a hot oven for 1½ hours. Peel off the skins.

Serve with butter, salt and pepper.

POTATOES À L'ÉCHIRLETTE

1½ *lb. small potatoes*
½ *pint stock or cold water*
2 *cloves of garlic*
1 *tablespoon goose or pork fat*
salt, pepper

Put the peeled potatoes in a large pan. Add the liquid, salt, pepper, plus the garlic. Cover the pan and cook till the liquid is absorbed. Melt the fat in a frying pan, add the potatoes and cook slowly, turning from time to time till brown all over.

GALETTE OF POTATOES

1½ *lb. potatoes*
1 *tablespoon olive oil*
1 *tablespoon butter*
¼ *teaspoon ground nutmeg*
salt, pepper

Peel and slice potatoes very thinly, wash well in cold water. Dry them well.

Melt the oil and butter in a large frying pan. When hot arrange the slices flatly. Add nutmeg, salt and pepper. Fry for 5 minutes. Lower the heat, cover the pan and cook gently for 15 minutes. Turn them over, continue for 4 minutes.

Serve whole as a pancake or cut in 4.

PUFF PASTRY FOR VOL-AU-VENT

1 *lb. plain flour*
1 *teaspoon salt*
⅜ *pint water*
11 *oz. washed butter*

Squeeze the butter in your hands under a running tap for 3 minutes. Put the flour on a board, make a hole in the middle, put in the salt and some of the water, work with your finger tips, adding the rest of the water, very quickly, until it forms a ball. Flatten it with your hand. Leave for 10 minutes. Roll the butter into a ball half as big as the dough and put it on top of the dough. Flour the rolling pin and roll quickly and lightly into a strip 8 × 24 inches by ¼ inch thick. Fold each end towards the middle to make a square. Leave for 15 minutes. Now roll again, having turned the strip round; fold as before and leave for 15 minutes. Repeat these two processes 4 times. Work in a cool place.

PROVENÇAL TOMATOES

4 *large tomatoes*
2 *cloves of garlic*
4 *teaspoons chopped parsley*
salt, pepper
2 *tablespoons olive oil*

Do not peel the tomatoes. Halve them. Pound the garlic, salt and pepper together. Score the pulp of each tomato half and press in the garlic mixture. Sprinkle with parsley, pour on the oil. Arrange in a flat fireproof dish and put under the grill for 6 or 7 minutes. Increase the heat and slightly blacken the surfaces.

POMMES ANNA

2 *lb. potatoes*
3 *oz. butter*
salt, pepper

FLOUR PASTE:
2 *oz. flour*
1 *tablespoon cold water*
salt, pepper

Butter a straight-sided fireproof dish. Cut the peeled potatoes in very thin rings, soak in cold water for 10 minutes. Drain and dry them thoroughly. Fill the dish with the rings in layers, dotting each layer with dabs of butter, salt and pepper. Spread the top layer with butter. Seal the lid with the paste. Bake in a moderate-to-slow oven for 45 minutes, take out the 'cake' and put back upside down. Re-cover and bake another 45 minutes. Pour off excess butter and turn out the golden cake.

VOL-AU-VENT

Roll out the puff pastry ½ inch thick. Cut out 4 rounds, say 7 inches in diameter. Keep 2, and cut out a circle 4 inches across in the other two. Moisten each round ring with water and build up in layers. Keep one 4-inch circle to make the lid. Put in a refrigerator or cold place for 20 minutes. Beat 2 egg yolks with 2 tablespoons water and brush the whole case, sides top and lid. Moisten the baking sheet with water, put on the case with the lid on top, bake in a very hot oven for 5 minutes, then in a moderate oven for 30 minutes longer. Scoop out the soft middle to make room for the stuffing.

MUSHROOM, CHICKEN, LOBSTER, SHRIMP OR HAM VOLT-AU-VENT

Take enough cooked chopped mushrooms, ham, chicken or lobster meat or shrimps and mix with a thick Béchamel sauce; make a fairly thick mixture (see p. 165). Fill the vol-au-vent, place the lid on top and re-heat gently in the oven.

PLAIN OMELETTE

8 *eggs*
2 *oz. butter*
½ *teaspoon salt*
black pepper
1½ *teaspoons cold water*

Break each egg into a cup first before putting in the mixing bowl; if any egg looks even slightly 'off', discard it. Add the salt, pepper and water. Beat with a fork for ½ a minute, not longer. Meanwhile, the frying pan, a heavy iron one not less than 8-inch diameter at base, should be heating slowly. Put in the butter, or butter and lard, turn up the heat. In a moment when the butter stops frothing, stir the egg mixture and pour it into the pan. Reduce the heat a little, and with a fork loosen the edges and let the excess mixture flow under; do this for 2 minutes. Fold the omelette over, press round the unfolded edges with the fork and slip on to serving dish. Rub some butter on the top and eat at once. If cooked quickly like this the omelette will be brown outside and wet inside.

MUSHROOM OMELETTE

6 *eggs*
4 *oz. mushrooms*
2 *oz. butter*

Slice the mushrooms finely, fry till soft in the butter, add salt and pepper. Cool, then add to the beaten eggs and cook as for plain omelette.

OMELETTE AUX FINES HERBES

6 *eggs*
salt
pepper
1 *teaspoon water*
1 *tablespoon chopped parsley*

1 *tablespoon chopped chives* or
   tarragon

Mix the herbs into the egg mixture, add salt, pepper and water and cook as for plain omelette.

QUICHE LORRAINE (1) (Cream Custard and Bacon Tart)

6 *oz. flour*
2 *oz. butter*
1 *oz. dripping*
6 *rashers bacon*
½ *pint cream*
2 *eggs*
salt, pepper
⅛ *pint water*

Make a pastry with the flour, butter, dripping, salt and water. Roll it 2 or 3 times, leave in a ball for 1 hour.

Line a flan tin (6—8 inches in diameter) with the pastry. Dice the bacon, of course having taken off the rind, and fry for 1 minute. Spread over the bottom of the pastry. Now beat the eggs into the cream, add salt and pepper, pour over the bacon and bake in a moderate oven for 25 minutes. Serve with tomato salad, dressed with French dressing.

QUICHE LORRAINE (2) (Cheese Custard and Bacon Tart)

pastry
6 bacon rashers
1 cup grated cheese, Parmesan
1 cup grated cheese, Gruyère
2 eggs
¼ pint milk

black pepper
watercress salad

Make the pastry and line the tin with the bacon as in the previous recipe. Mix the cheese with eggs, milk and pepper, pour over the bacon. Bake in a slow-to-moderate oven till brown, about 20 minutes. Serve with watercress salad, with French dressing.

PISSALADIÈRE

1 lb. dough
2 lb. onions
20 stoned black olives
12 anchovy fillets
¼ pint olive oil

Ask the baker to give you the dough. Pull it out and spread on a baking dish. Slice the onions and cook in the oil very slowly for 40 minutes, till they make a thick purée. Pour the purée over the dough, decorate with the olives and anchovies. Bake in a moderate oven for 30 minutes.

If dough is hard to get, unsweetened pastry can be used or slices of a sandwich loaf cut lengthways 1 inch thick with the crusts removed. If bread is used, fry each slice on one side only, spread the purée, etc., and cook for only 10 minutes.

Serve with lettuce salad and French dressing.

SAVOURY RICE WITH CABBAGE

1 small white cabbage
4 oz. peeled, sliced tomatoes
4 oz. sliced onions
2 oz. sliced mushrooms
2 oz. bacon fat
1 oz. sultanas or currants
2 rashers bacon, diced
1 tin tomato juice
½ teaspoon nutmeg
½ teaspoon thyme, chopped
2 sugar lumps
⅛ of rind of 1 lemon, chopped finely
1 clove of garlic

salt, pepper
8 oz. rice

Undercook the rice in boiling salted water for only 15 minutes. Fry the bacon, onions and mushrooms in the bacon fat. Slice the cabbage thinly. Mix together the tomatoes, mushrooms, onions, sultanas or currants, nutmeg, thyme, pinch of salt and pepper with the rice. Put a layer of cabbage in a deep casserole, then a layer of the rice mixture. Repeat this till the casserole is three-quarters full. Add the garlic, lemon rind, salt and pepper to the tomato juice, and pour this into the casserole. Cover. Cook in a very slow oven for 2 hours.

ONION TART LORRAINE

8 *oz. plain flour*
4 *oz. butter*
¼ *teaspoon salt*
4 *tablespoons cold water*
2 *lb. sliced onions*
3 *oz. bacon fat*
2 *eggs*
2 *oz. grated Gruyère cheese*
salt, pepper

Make the pastry of the flour, butter, salt and water. Roll out and line tart tin. Melt the bacon fat, add the onions, salt and pepper. Cook gently, stirring now and then, for 30 minutes till soft, in a covered pan. Cool, add the beaten eggs, cheese, stir well. Pour into the tart tin and bake in a moderate oven for 20 minutes.

STUFFED LOAF

1 *sandwich loaf*
8 *oz. chicken livers* ⎫
1 *pair sweetbreads* ⎬ *fried*
8 *oz. mushrooms* ⎭
½ *pint Béchamel sauce*
  (*see p. 165*)
½ *teaspoon chopped parsley*
½ *teaspoon chopped chives*
½ *teaspoon chopped tarragon*
16 *rashers bacon*

Scoop the crumb out of the sandwich loaf by opening one end. Mix the finely chopped fried chicken livers, sweetbreads and mushrooms previously fried, with the Béchamel and herbs. Line a deep casserole with 8 bacon rashers, of course no rinds, put in the stuffed loaf and put 8 more rashers on top. Cover the casserole and bake in a slow oven for 40 minutes. Serve cut in slices with a vegetable. Spinach, cabbage or cauliflower are good with this dish.

STUFFED MARROWS

STUFFING:
4 *oz. cooked pork*
2 *oz. cooked beef or mutton*
4 *oz. white breadcrumbs*
salt, pepper
1 *medium onion, chopped*
1 *shallot*
1 *clove of garlic*
2 *eggs*
2 *teaspoons chopped parsley*
4 *small young marrows*

2 *medium peeled sliced tomatoes*
3 *oz. grated Gruyère cheese*
1 *oz. butter*

Wash and cut the marrows lengthways. Scoop out the seeds and flesh, leaving ¼ inch on edge. Butter a shallow fireproof dish and put in the 8 pieces. Make stuffing and fill each half marrow. Sprinkle with the cheese and bake in a moderate oven for 20 minutes, place the tomato slices on top and bake 10 minutes longer.

STUFFED RED CABBAGE LANDAIS

1 *medium red cabbage, sliced*
1 *lb. cooking apples, peeled, cored and sliced*
1 *lb. onions, sliced*
2 *red peppers, seeded and sliced*
¼ *of peel of 1 orange, cut in strips*
1 *clove of garlic, chopped*
1 *tablespoon mixed herbs, chopped*
1 *teaspoon pepper*
1 *teaspoon salt*
1 *teaspoon ground cloves*

1 *teaspoon ground nutmeg*
8 *smoked frankfurter sausages*
¼ *pint red wine*
¼ *pint wine vinegar*

In a large casserole put a layer of cabbage, then a layer of onions, then one of apples. Sprinkle with some of the sugar, red peppers, orange peel, garlic, herbs, salt, pepper, cloves and nutmeg. Repeat this until everything is used up. Pour in the wine and vinegar. Cover and cook in a slow oven for 3½ hours. Now, bury the sausages deep in the dish and cook for a further 20 minutes.

CHEESE SOUFFLÉ

4 *oz. butter*
2 *oz. flour*
1 *pint milk, hot*
¼ *teaspoon salt*
4 *eggs*
5 *oz. grated Parmesan cheese*

Butter a soufflé dish. Separate the eggs, beat the whites till stiff. Melt the butter in a saucepan, add the flour and salt, add the hot milk gradually, stirring all the time, cook for 3 minutes, stirring, till smooth. Remove from the heat, beat in the yolks one at a time, add the cheese, stir well. Fold in the whites. Mix carefully. Bake in the buttered dish in moderate oven for 20 minutes. Eat immediately.

FISH SOUFFLÉ

Proceed as for Cheese Soufflé, but add 6 oz. cooked flaked white fish instead of cheese.

RATATOUILLE (Provençal Vegetable Stew)

2 *aubergines*
2 *large onions, sliced*
4 *medium tomatoes, peeled and quartered*
2 *red or green pimentos, sliced*
¼ *pint olive oil*
2 *cloves of garlic, finely chopped*
salt, pepper

Slit the pimentos in the side and pull out seeds and core, wash thoroughly to remove every seed. Cut the aubergines into 1-inch squares.

Warm the oil in a large frying pan, add chopped onions and stew gently for 8 minutes. Now add the sliced pimentos, aubergines, stew gently for 10 minutes. Add garlic, salt and pepper, then the quartered tomatoes. Cover the pan and simmer gently for another 10 minutes, or until all the oil has been absorbed.

RATATOUILLE WITH FRIED EGGS

1 *lb. potatoes*
12 *oz. onions*
2 *cloves of garlic*
3 *small young marrows*
3 *tomatoes*
3 *green or red peppers*
¼ *pint olive oil*
2 *tablespoons lard*
salt, pepper
4 *fried eggs*

Peel all the vegetables, remove the seeds from peppers, slice thinly. Melt the lard in a large heavy frying pan, add the oil, salt and pepper and all the cut-up vegetables. Mix well together, cover the pan and simmer gently for 45 minutes, take the lid off and simmer for another 30 minutes.

Fry the eggs and place on top of the vegetables on the serving dish. If a substantial dish is wanted, serve with boiled rice.

FROGS' LEGS À LA PROVENÇALE

2 *lb. medium-size frogs' legs*
8 *oz. butter*
1 *tablespoon olive oil*
1 *tablespoon chopped parsley*
2 *cloves of garlic, finely chopped*
¼ *pint milk*
2 *tablespoons flour*
juice of ½ lemon
1 *teaspoon chopped chives*
½ *teaspoon salt, pepper*

Add salt and pepper to the milk, dip in the legs and roll in flour. Heat 2 oz. butter and the olive oil, add the floured legs, gently fry for 12 minutes, till browned. Add the lemon juice, parsley, chives and a pinch of pepper, stir and keep warm in the serving dish. Melt the remaining butter, add the garlic and brown quickly, pour over the dish. Cut slices of lemon may be used as a garnish.

PÂTÉ OF PIG'S LIVER PÉRIGORD

6 *rashers of bacon*
8 *oz. pig's liver*
8 *oz. bacon*
½ *teaspoon black pepper*
2 *cloves of garlic*
3 *shallots*
1 *liqueur glass brandy*
¼ *teaspoon nutmeg*
¼ *teaspoon ground cloves*
1 *pig's foot, cut in two*
2 *medium sliced carrots*
2 *medium sliced onions*
1 *sprig thyme* }
1 *sprig rosemary* } *bouquet*
1 *bay leaf*

1 *wine glass white wine*
1 *wine glass cold water*
lard for sealing

Mince liver and bacon with the garlic and shallots. Pound to a smooth paste, add pepper, nutmeg and cloves. Line a deep small casserole or terrine with the bacon rashers, put in the mixture, pour in the brandy. Put on top the pig's foot, carrots, onions, *bouquet*, and add wine and water. Cover the casserole tightly, stand in a dish of water and cook very slowly for 4 hours. Take out the pig's foot, carrots, onions, *bouquet*. Seal the pâté with melted pure lard.

SNAILS

50 *snails*
1½ *pints Chablis or* 1½ *pints
salt water*
a small handful of thyme
a large handful of fennel
4 *oz. butter*
2 *cloves of garlic*
*a handful of parsley, finely
.chopped*
¼ *teaspoon ground nutmeg*
salt, pepper

Add the thyme and fennel to the wine or water, simmer the snails in this for 1 hour. Strain. Keep snails warm.

Pound the garlic to a pulp in a mortar, remove any hard pieces that refuse to be pulped, add the butter and parsley, salt, pepper and nutmeg. With a wooden spoon work thoroughly till everything is mixed well together. Put over the warm snails in the serving dish and let the garlic butter melt and run into the snails.

MIROTON

6 *or* 8 *slices of cold boiled beef*
3 *oz. butter*
1 *tablespoon wine vinegar*
1 *teaspoon chopped parsley*
2 *oz. breadcrumbs*
4 *medium onions, sliced*
1 *oz. flour*
¾ *pint meat stock*
1 *tablespoon tomato purée*
salt, pepper
1 *tablespoon tomato sauce*

Melt 2 oz. butter in a stewpan, add the onions, cook gently till turning brown, add the flour, stir and cook for 2 minutes. Add the vinegar, stir well, then gradually pour in the meat stock and stir till smooth. Add the tomato sauce, parsley, season generously with salt and pepper. Pour half this mixture into a shallow fireproof dish, arrange the meat slices on top, add the other half. Sprinkle with breadcrumbs, dot with the rest of the butter and brown in a moderate oven.

CASSOULET

1½ *lb. haricot beans*
3 *medium onions, sliced*
2 *large tomatoes, peeled and sliced*
4 *cloves of garlic, chopped*
8 *oz. bacon, cut in* 1-*inch squares*
2 *oz. white breadcrumbs*
1 *lb. garlic sausage*
2 *pints stock*
1 *leg and* 1 *wing preserved goose*
bouquet garni
salt, pepper

Any good pieces of duck, chicken or turkey can be used as well.

Soak the beans overnight, and simmer for 2½ hours. Melt the bacon in a stewpan, add the onions, garlic, tomatoes, *bouquet*, salt and pepper. Pour over the stock and simmer for 30 minutes.

Take a large casserole, rub with garlic. Put the goose, sausage and any other pieces of poultry in the bottom, with plenty of goose grease. Pile the beans on top and pour in the strained stock. Bring slowly to the boil, lower the heat, and spread the breadcrumbs over all. Cook in a slow oven for 1 hour.

Serve exactly as it is, with a green salad and red wine. This is a meal in itself and should be the only course, except perhaps cheese or fruit as dessert.

FRENCH DRESSING

3 *tablespoons olive oil*
1 *tablespoon wine vinegar*
½ *teaspoon salt*
¼ *teaspoon pepper*

Mix all together. You can if you like add a pinch of sugar and ¼ teaspoon of made mustard.

MAYONNAISE

1 *egg yolk*
½ *pint olive oil*
1 *dessertspoon wine vinegar*
salt, pepper

Make this sauce in a cool place, use cool ingredients and utensils. Stir with a silver spoon and 'keep cool' as you work.

Put a carefully broken yolk (no white at all) into a basin. Add the oil, drop by drop, stirring gently all the time. When the sauce begins to thicken stir in the vinegar, salt and pepper. Add more oil drop by drop till it once again thickens, when the oil can be poured in slowly, stirring always, until finished. Taste and add more salt and pepper if you wish.

Should the mayonnaise refuse to thicken and look curdled when finished, do not panic. Break a new yolk into another basin and stir the mixture on to it slowly. Taste and if it has not enough 'bite' stir in a few drops of vinegar to sharpen the extra yolk.

HOLLANDAISE SAUCE

3 *egg yolks*
2 *oz. butter*
1 *tablespoon wine vinegar*
salt, pepper

The secret of this sauce is that it must not ever boil; also good fresh butter must be used.

Melt the butter in a double saucepan or in a basin over hot water. Mix the egg yolks, vinegar, salt and pepper, add to the melted butter, stir briskly without stopping until the sauce is smooth and thick. Taste and add more salt and pepper if you think it needs it.

TARTARE SAUCE

mayonnaise sauce
3 *shallots or very small onions*
*green herbs — parsley, chives,
   chervil, tarragon, watercress, etc.*
½ *teaspoon mustard*

Chop the shallots, all or any of the herbs very finely. Stir these, plus the mustard, into the mayonnaise sauce.

BÉARNAISE SAUCE

2 *shallots*
1 *sprig tarragon*
3 *stalks chervil*
2 *tablespoons dry white wine*
1 *tablespoon wine vinegar*
2 *egg yolks*
2 *oz. butter*
1 *teaspoon cold water*
salt, pepper

Chop the shallots and herbs extremely finely. Put the wine and vinegar in a saucepan, add the chopped shallots and herbs. Simmer till reduced by two thirds. Strain and cool.

Put the egg yolks in a basin over very hot but NOT boiling water, add the cold water and the herbs and wine mixture. Whip with an egg whisk, gently but steadily, adding the butter bit by bit, as you whip, until the sauce is thick and creamy. Season with salt and pepper.

Should the sauce curdle try adding another teaspoon of cold water to it, remove from the heat and whip furiously.

RAVIGOTE SAUCE

½ *a bunch of watercress*
4 *teaspoons chopped parsley, chives, tarragon, chervil*
1 *clove of garlic*
½ *teaspoon mustard*
2 *tablespoons wine vinegar*

¼ *pint olive oil*
salt, pepper

Pound or squash the herbs with a wooden spoon in a basin, add the oil, vinegar, salt and pepper. Good with cold meats.

MOUSSELINE SAUCE

¼ *pint Hollandaise sauce (see p. 161)*
¼ *pint fresh cream*
salt, pepper

Whip cream till stiff and add to Hollandaise sauce, already made, and heat extremely carefully in a bowl over hot water. If it gets too hot it will be a failure. Season to taste.

SAUCE PIQUANTE

½ *pint brown sauce (see p. 165)*
3 *tablespoons wine vinegar*
1 *chopped shallot or grated onion*
1 *teaspoon chopped parsley*

1 *oz. butter*
2 *tablespoons chopped gherkin*

Heat everything slowly in the butter, except the gherkins. When melted, add the lot to the brown sauce. Last add the chopped gherkins.

SAUCE MADÈRE (1) (Madeira Sauce)

½ *pint brown sauce (see p. 165)*
bouquet garni
1 *wine glass of Madeira*

Add the *bouquet garni* to the sauce when thickened and cook very gently for 10 minutes, then take it out. Add the Madeira.

If the sauce should need thinning, add another tablespoon stock.

SAUCE MADÈRE (2) (Madeira Sauce)

½ *pint brown sauce (see p. 165)*
4 *medium mushrooms, finely sliced*
2 *tablespoons gravy*
1 *wine glass Madeira wine*

Add the mushrooms and gravy to the brown sauce. Five minutes before serving add the Madeira and simmer very gently with the lid on the pan till the mushrooms are tender, for 5 or 6 minutes.

MAÎTRE D'HÔTEL SAUCE

4 *oz. butter*
2 *teaspoons finely chopped parsley*
2 *teaspoons lemon juice*
salt, pepper

With a wooden spoon knead the butter, parsley, strained lemon juice, salt and pepper together, till smooth.

MORNAY SAUCE

½ *pint Béchamel sauce*
(see p. 165)
2 *oz. grated Parmesan cheese*
or 4 oz. 'cooking' cheese
(Cheddar or Cheshire)
cayenne pepper

Make the Béchamel and stir in the cheese. A tiny pinch of cayenne pepper is an improvement.

MAYONNAISE AU RAIFORT

2 *tablespoons grated horseradish*
mayonnaise (see p. 161)

Add the horseradish to the mayonnaise. Bottled horseradish will do, but fresh is better by far.

BLACK BUTTER SAUCE (Beurre Noir)

4 oz. butter
2 tablespoons wine vinegar
1 teaspoon chopped parsley

Melt the butter until dark brown, but do not burn, put in the parsley and cook for 1 minute. Pour this over the cooked dish (fish, brains, etc.). Put the vinegar in the used saucepan, heat for half a minute or less, till hot, and pour this too over the dish.

SAUCE AU FENOUIL (Fennel Sauce)

½ pint Béchamel sauce
  (see p. 165)
½ teaspoon finely chopped fennel

Fennel is delicious with fish.
  Add ½ teaspoon finely chopped fennel to ½ pint Béchamel sauce, mix well. Fennel is strong; do not use too much.

AILLOLI (Garlic Mayonnaise)

3 cloves of garlic
½ pint mayonnaise sauce
  (see p. 161)

Crush or pound the garlic as finely as possible, in the bowl in which you make the mayonnaise.

GARLIC SAUCE

2 cloves of garlic
1 slice white bread
2 tablespoons milk
½ pint mayonnaise sauce
  (see p. 161)

Remove the crust from the bread, soak in the milk, mash with a fork. Chop or pound the garlic and crush into the mashed bread, drain excess milk. Add this mixture to the mayonnasie.
  Good, if you like the taste of garlic, with all cold meats and poultry.

SAUCE VINAIGRETTE

4 tablespoons olive oil
2 tablespoons wine vinegar
1 teaspoon salt
1 teaspoon black pepper
1 teaspoon chopped onion

1 teaspoon chopped chives
1 teaspoon chopped parsley

Mix the herbs, salt and pepper with the vinegar. Stir thoroughly, add the oil.

BÉCHAMEL SAUCE

2 oz. butter
2 oz. flour
½ pint hot milk
salt, pepper

Melt the butter. Add the flour gradually, stir over a slow-to-medium heat until the mixture leaves the sides of the pan. Add the hot milk slowly, stirring all the time, till thick and creamy. Add salt and pepper. Flour and butter must be of equal quantities always; this, with the continual stirring and fairly slow cooking, is the secret of a smooth creamy 'white' sauce, and not a paste full of lumps.

BROWN SAUCE

2 oz. butter
1 oz. flour
½ pint hot meat stock or water
salt, pepper

Melt the butter, stir in flour and cook gently until it browns. Add the hot liquid gradually, stirring all the time until the sauce thickens. Add salt and pepper to taste.

MEAT GLAZE

any pieces of meat, bones,
  carcases, etc.
1 sliced carrot
1 sliced onion
1 sliced leek
1 bouquet garni
1 clove of garlic
salt, pepper

Chop any bones, break up carcases. Put vegetables, *bouquet*, salt, pepper and garlic in a baking dish, add the meat, etc., and put in the oven till brown and shrivelled, but *not* burnt. Take out, cover with boiling water and simmer for 15 minutes, remove all bones, simmer again, stirring and scraping the pan to collect essence which may stick to the pan, until reduced to one third. Strain through muslin. This glaze will keep in a cool place almost indefinitely.

TOMATO SAUCE

8 large ripe tomatoes
1 medium finely sliced onion
1 bouquet garni
1 clove of garlic, chopped
1 oz. butter
1 teaspoon cornflour
salt, pepper

Cut up the tomatoes and crush them with a wooden spoon in a thick saucepan. Add the sliced onion, garlic and the *bouquet*. Simmer gently till soft for 10 minutes. Sieve this purée. Mix the cornflour with the butter, add to the purée, return to the pan and simmer for 15 minutes. Season with salt and pepper.

LARDING

bacon
a larding needle

Cut the bacon in strips, ¼ inch square, 3 to 4 inches long. Thread the needle and stitch into the meat in 1 inch 'tacking' stitches going down about ½ an inch; pull through till the needle is empty each time, leaving the lardons embedded in the meat.

BOUQUET GARNI (Herbs of various kinds)

2 *or* 3 *heads of parsley*
1 *sprig of thyme*
1 *bay leaf*

This recipe is the basic *bouquet garni:* the herb or spice flavouring often used in cookery.

Tie the ingredients together firmly with string or cotton. If cloves, fennel, lemon peel or other herbs are included in any recipe, they are specially mentioned.

Some cooks find it better to tie all together in a small piece of clean muslin.

COURT-BOUILLON (for boiled fish)

1 *large onion, sliced in rings*
1 *bouquet garni*
1 *clove garlic*
1 *shallot*
1 *carrot, sliced*
1 *clove*
2 *peppercorns*
pinch of curry powder

1 *tablespoon coarse salt*
2½ *quarts water*
1 *tumbler dry white wine*

Simmer spices and vegetables for 1 hour in the water and wine. Then poach your fish in the court-bouillon until it is cooked. This stock may be used as a basis for soup.

CROÛTONS

Bread, toast, or croûtons are served with French soups: bread or toast with meat or fish soup, croûtons with vegetable soups

Cut the crusts off slices of stale white bread, then cut the bread in 1-inch squares. Fry in butter or oil, or bacon fat till golden. 1 slice of bread per person is ample. Serve separately on a warm plate or scatter on top of the soup if to be served immediately, or put in the bottom of the tureen and pour the soup over them.

FRENCH APPLE SAUCE

8 *cooking apples*
2 *oz. butter*
4 *oz. sugar*
½ *teaspoon grated lemon rind*
3 *tablespoons water*
1 *tablespoon mixed candied peel*

Peel, core and quarter the apples. Put the apples, butter, sugar, rind and water and candied peel in a thick saucepan. Cook slowly over a low heat, stirring frequently until the apples are quite soft, about 20 minutes.

APPLE SAUCE MERINGUE

½ oz. butter
2 egg whites
2 tablespoons castor sugar
apple sauce

Butter a soufflé dish, pour in the apple sauce. Whisk the egg whites till stiff, sieve in the sugar gradually, beating continually. Spread the meringue over the apple mixture and bake in a moderate oven for 20 minutes.

BANANA TRIFLE

7 bananas
2 tablespoons apricot jam
3 tablespoons sherry
½ pint cream

Peel and cut 6 bananas lengthways. Spread with the jam and pour on the sherry. Leave for 1 hour. Whip the cream for 4 minutes, spread over and decorate with 1 banana cut in thin slices.

CREAMED BANANAS

3 large bananas
2 oz. castor sugar
½ pint cream
¼ pint sherry

Peel the bananas, sieve them. Add the sugar, stir, add the cream and whisk for 10 minutes or until thick, beat in the sherry gradually. Chill for 2 hours.

BANANAS AU RHUM

6 large bananas
3 tablespoons Demerara sugar
juice of 1 lemon
3 tablespoons water
1 sherry glass rum
1 nut butter
cream to serve

Butter a shallow fireproof dish. Cut the bananas in half lengthways and arrange overlapping in the dish. Sprinkle the sugar over, add the lemon juice and water. Bake in a moderate oven for 20 minutes or till brown. Add the rum 5 minutes before the end. Serve with whipped cream, which may be flavoured with rum, if wished.

CHOCOLATE MOUSSE (1)

4 oz. bitter chocolate
4 tablespoons water
6 oz. castor sugar
5 eggs
1 tablespoon brandy

Separate the eggs — whip whites till stiff.
   Melt the chocolate over a very low heat, add water and sugar, stir till sugar is dissolved. Remove from heat. Add the yolks one by one, beating vigorously, then the brandy. Stir. Fold in the egg whites, stir till thoroughly mixed. Serve in separate, small moulds or glasses. Serve very cold.

CHOCOLATE MOUSSE (2)

3 *heaped tablespoons cocoa powder*
3 *oz. castor sugar*
3 *eggs*
3 *tablespoons cream or milk top*
1 *tablespoon very strong coffee*

Separate the eggs — whip whites till stiff.

Melt the cocoa, sugar, cream or milk top on a very low heat. Take off the heat. Add the eggs, one by one, stir quickly, also the coffee. Fold in the whites, whip all together till well mixed. Serve in separate moulds, glasses, or failing these a soufflé dish or glass bowl. Chill and serve. All chocolate mousse improves with keeping, so make the day before if wished.

APPLE TART

2 *lb. apples*
5 *oz. sugar*
apple peels
rind of 1 lemon
2 *oz. sugar*
¼ *pint cider*
pastry case

Pastry tart case as in Cold Cheese Tart (see p. 172). Prick the bottom of the pastry. Peel, core and slice the apples very finely. Fill the tart tin in layers of apple and sugar. Bake in a moderate oven for 30 minutes. Boil the peels, lemon rind, cider till syrupy and pour over the cooled tart.

RASPBERRY AND RED CURRANT TART

1 *cooked flan or tart case*
1½ *lb. raspberries*
8 *oz. red currants*
6 *oz. castor sugar*
1 *tablespoon red currant jelly*

Prepare the fruit, add the sugar, and cook stirring gently for 4 minutes, or until the sugar has melted and made a syrup. Keep the fruit whole. Strain the fruit and put in the cooked case. Bake in a moderate oven for 10 minutes. Add the red currant jelly to the juice, pour over the cooled fruit.

Eat cold, with cream if possible.

PEARS WITH CHOCOLATE

8 *pears*
¼ *pint water*
2 *oz. sugar*
⅓ *vanilla pod*
4 *oz. chocolate*
½ *oz. butter*

Peel and quarter the pears. Put the pears, water, and vanilla pod in a saucepan and stew till nearly cooked. Place in a shallow fireproof dish.

Melt the chocolate in 1 dessertspoon pear liquid, add the butter, stir. Pour over the pears, cover and bake in a moderate oven for 15 minutes till the pears are quite soft.

PEACH MELBA

8 *oz. vanilla ice cream*
4 *ripe peaches*
8 *oz. raspberries*
2 *oz. sugar*

Melt the raspberries and the sugar, stir and bring to the boil, simmer till the fruit is soft, about 4 minutes, stirring all the time. Sieve to make the purée. Cool.

Peel and stone the peaches. Put 2 halves on 2 oz. ice cream, pour a quarter of the cold purée on each.

BOMBE GLACÉE

8 *oz. sugar*
¼ *pint water*
3 *egg yolks*
1 *pint thick cream*
½ *tablespoon powdered coffee
essence*

Beat the cream till it begins to thicken, add the coffee essence. Dissolve sugar and water, add beaten egg yolks. Stir all the time in a double boiler over simmering water until mixture thickens. Do not overcook. Whip for 15 minutes. Fold in the flavoured cream. Pour into a chilled mould and freeze.

CHESTNUT MOULD

2½ *lb. chestnuts*
cold water
¼ *pint milk*
6 *oz. castor sugar*
2 *tablespoons brandy*
6 *egg whites*
3 *tablespoons water*
½ *pint cream*

Roast the chestnuts in a slow oven for 20 minutes. Skin and peel them. Cover with cold water and boil till soft. Drain and sieve or mash very finely. Beat in milk. Add 2 oz. sugar and the brandy to the purée, stir well, then fold in the egg whites.

Make a caramel of 4 oz. sugar with the water. Coat the bottom and sides of a cake tin. Pour in the chestnut mixture and cook in a moderate oven for 1 hour. Turn out on serving dish. Serve very cold with the cream, whipped.

PLUMS ON BUTTERED BREAD

4 *large slices white bread*
2 *oz. butter*
24 *ripe plums*
2 *oz. brown sugar*

Butter the bread on one side only, stone the plums, put six on each buttered side, press down well, dab with the rest of the butter and sprinkle with sugar. Arrange the slices flatly in a buttered fireproof dish, plum side up, cover with buttered paper and bake in a moderate oven for 30 minutes, when the plums should be cooked in a syrup on golden crisp bread.

ST. ÉMILION AU CHOCOLAT

4 *oz. butter*
4 *oz. sugar*
1 *egg*
8 *oz. chocolate*
1 *tablespoon water*
½ *pint milk*
2 *lb. macaroons*
1 *liqueur glass rum*

Soak the macaroons in the rum. Cream the butter and sugar. Scald the milk and when cool beat in the egg yolk. Melt the chocolate in the water over a low heat, stir in the milk and egg mixture, then the creamed butter and sugar. Stir till quite smooth.

In a soufflé dish put a layer of rum-flavoured macaroons, then a layer of the chocolate cream; repeat until the dish is full, finishing with macaroons. Chill for 12 hours or more and serve.

JACQUES (These pancakes are special to the Périgord)

4 *oz. flour*
¼ *pint milk*
¼ *pint water*
1 *dessertspoon olive oil*
2 *oz. sugar*
2 *eggs*
3 *eating apples*
1 *teaspoon lemon juice*

Peel and core the apples, slice them very thinly, spread on a dish, sprinkle each one with 2 teaspoons sugar and lemon juice.

Make the batter, including the olive oil but using only 1 teaspoon sugar. Grease a small very hot frying pan with lard or butter and pour in a little batter, about 1 tablespoon. Place 2 apple slices on the pancake, cook ½ minute, pour in another tablespoon of batter, cook ½ minute, turn, and cook for another minute or till the apple is soft. Serve the pancake flat, sprinkle over the rest of the sugar. Keep warm and work quickly. Serve at once when all cooked.

CRÊPES OR FRENCH PANCAKES

6 *oz. flour*
2 *oz. sugar*
3 *eggs*
2 *oz. melted butter*
¾ *pint milk*
2 *tablespoons brandy or rum*
1 *teaspoon grated lemon rind*
⅛ *teaspoon salt*

Sift the dry ingredients, add the eggs one at a time, beating well till quite smooth. Add the sugar, brandy or rum, lemon rind and salt plus the melted butter, and mix well. Now gradually pour in the milk, beating all the time. Always make the batter 2 hours before using.

The frying pan should be rubbed with butter and lard and the pancakes cooked very quickly on both sides with only enough batter to cover the pan very thinly. Keep pancakes warm in a covered dish over hot water, never in the oven as this dries and hardens them.

CARAMEL RICE

4 oz. rice
1 pint milk
1 slice lemon rind or vanilla pod
4 tablespoons cream
6 oz. castor sugar
juice of 1 lemon
2 oz. candied peel

Put the milk, rice, 4 oz. sugar, lemon rind or vanilla pod in a double saucepan. Simmer for 2 hours, when the mixture will be creamy. Stir in the lemon juice and cream and the candied peel. Pour into a soufflé dish and chill thoroughly. Spread 2 oz. sugar on top evenly, and put under a very hot grill for about 1 minute or till the sugar looks like toffee; watch it all the time, as it burns easily. Serve very cold.

CRÊPES SUZETTE

3 oz. butter
3 oz. sugar
grated rind of 1 orange or lemon
2 teaspoons brandy, or cointreau, or curaçao or kümmel
1 liqueur glass brandy, or cointreau, or curaçao or kümmel

Make the pancakes. Keep warm. Cream the butter and sugar, add the grated rind and the brandy or liqueur. Spread each warm pancake with this mixture, fold, and arrange on warmed serving dish. Pour the liqueur glass of brandy or liqueur over the top of the pancakes as they are put on the table and set alight.

HOME-MADE MILK CHEESE WITH FRESH FRUIT

5 pints sour milk
sugar and fresh raspberries or red currants to serve

This is a favourite French sweet dish for the pudding course and an excellent way of using surplus milk.

Pour 5 pints of milk into a large bowl and leave overnight. Skim off the cream and keep cold. Leave the milk for 12 hours more, pour into muslin and hang up to drip in the usual way for several hours until all the liquid has run out. Fill separate little moulds, pour cream over each and serve with sugar and the prepared fruit. 5 pints of milk should make 1 lb. cheese and 6 oz. cream.

PASTRY FOR FRUIT, CUSTARD OR CHEESE TARTS

6 oz. flour
4 oz. butter
3 oz. sugar
1 egg
a pinch of salt

Sieve the flour, add the sugar and the butter in small pieces, work till crumbly, add the beaten egg, work as quickly as possible. Roll out on greaseproof paper, large enough to fit bottom and sides of the tin, place the flan or tart tin on top and turn upside down otherwise you will find the pastry will break in handling. Fill with beans or crusts and bake in a moderate oven for 20 minutes, covered with greaseproof paper to prevent burning.

CREAM CHEESE TART

1 *cooked pastry flan or tart case*
6 *oz. Pommel cheese or demi-sel,*
  or home-made cream cheese
2 *egg yolks*
4 *tablespoons sugar*

grated rind of 1 orange
¼ *pint milk, cream or milk top*

Mix the cheese, egg yolks, sugar, rind, milk together thoroughly. Add the stiffly beaten egg whites, pile into the already cooked pastry case and bake for 15 minutes in a very moderate oven.

COLD CHEESE TART

8 *oz. flour*
4 *oz. butter*
1 *egg*
¼ *teaspoon salt*
2 *tablespoons cold water*
6 *oz. cream cheese*
3 *eggs*
4 *oz. castor sugar*

2 *tablespoons cream*
2 *tablespoons chopped angelica*

Make a pastry of flour, butter, salt, egg and water. Leave for 2 hours, roll and line the tart or flan tin.

Mix the cream cheese, eggs, sugar, cream and angelica well together, fill the flan tin and bake in a slow oven for 40 minutes. Eat it cold.

ALMOND TART

3 *eggs*
2 *oz. sugar*
4 *oz. ground almonds*
⅛ *pint milk*
1 *cooked pastry flan case*

Mix all the ingredients thoroughly. Fill the case and bake in a moderate oven for 15 minutes.
Serve with whipped cream and sugar.

CUSTARD (1)

3 *egg yolks*
1 *egg white*
¾ *pint milk*
1 *oz. sugar*

Heat the milk. Beat the eggs. Pour the hot, not boiling milk over in a double saucepan or basin above simmering water. Stir until the mixture thickens, add the sugar. Never boil custard or the mixture will curdle. This is proper custard, quite unlike the custard powder variety usually served.

CUSTARD (2)

1 *pint milk*
4 *oz. sugar*
3 *egg yolks*
1 *vanilla pod*

Scald the milk, in which is the vanilla pod. Take out pod and cool milk till warm. Beat the yolks with the sugar, add the milk gradually, stirring all the time. Put in a double boiler over simmering, not boiling, water and cook till it thickens, stirring gently all the time.

Germany

COOKING IN GERMANY

German cooking is esssentially homely — delicious, but a bit on the heavy side. The German Hausfrau caters for the hearty appetite of outdoor people and has no feeling for French finesse. She cooks wholesome and substantial meals — tasty but not frivolous. One of the national features of German cookery is their fondness for mixing sweet flavours with sour ones. This can be very effective as in their recipe for Pork Chops with Plums.

The greatest German achievement in the gastronomic field is changing that most ordinary and dull, respectable cabbage into their own Sauerkraut. You can buy sauerkraut all over the world now, either loose in delicatessen shops or tinned, and it is certainly a great addition to any larder.

Their other world-famous recipe is Sauerbraten — a meat course with a real kick to it, beautifully flavoured and satisfying.

German cakes and pastries are wonderful — just the thing for a farmhouse-tea type of meal. A good German Coffee Cake will be sufficient for a large party and it will be enjoyed by all.

Another recipe I would like to point out is Cinnamon Stars. In most households there is an occasional accumulation of egg whites waiting to be used up. You use the yolks for mayonnaise, or thickening soups, and most housewives can only think of meringues to use up the left-over whites. Now Cinnamon Stars will give you a new use for those redundant egg whites — they are light and dainty biscuits and will keep for a long time in an airtight tin.

One cannot write about German food and not mention dumplings. The German are the master dumpling cooks and like to add dumplings to a number of their main dishes. They are jolly good dumplings too. Your waistline is your own responsibility.

ANCHOVY SALAD

8 *anchovy fillets*
4 *oz. ham sausage*
4 *oz. smoked salmon*
½ *pint prawns*
pickled cucumber
capers
½ *lemon*

2 *tablespoons olive oil*
1 *tablespoon wine vinegar*

Mix the oil and vinegar well. Arrange the anchovy fillets in the middle of a dish, surround them with slices of ham sausage and smoked salmon and prepared prawns. Pour the oil and vinegar over them. Garnish with pickled cucumber, capers and slices of lemon.

LEEK AND LETTUCE HORS D'OEUVRE

1 *round lettuce*
2 *leeks*
½ *rasher gammon*
½ *oz. lard*
2 *tablespoons wine vinegar*
salt

Shred the lettuce, finely chop the leeks. Cut the gammon into small pieces and fry lightly in the fat. Stir the vinegar into the fat in the pan, season with salt. Pour over the lettuce and leek.

POTATO SALAD WITH ROLLMOPS

2 *medium potatoes*
4 *rollmops*
gherkins
2 *tablespoons olive oil*
1 *tablespoon wine vinegar*
parsley

salt, pepper

Boil the potatoes in their skins, peel and slice them when still warm and dress with olive oil and vinegar. Slice the gherkins and add them to the salad. Season with salt and pepper and sprinkle with chopped parsley. Serve with rollmops.

ROLLMOPS

herrings
capers
shallots
gherkins
wine vinegar
pickling spice
peppercorns
onion
lemon

Fillet the herrings. Mix sliced gherkins and sliced shallots and capers and spread a layer of this mixture on each fillet. Roll and secure with cocktail sticks. Put them in a glass preserving jar with wine vinegar, a teaspoonful of pickling spice, a little sliced onion and a squeeze of lemon juice. Screw down the lid and leave for 4 days or longer.

BEER SOUP

1 *pint dark lager*
1 *pint milk*
juice of ½ lemon
2 *egg yolks*
cinnamon
sugar
salt

Heat the lager in a saucepan with the lemon juice and a pinch of cinnamon. Heat the milk and beat in the egg yolks, add them to the beer. Season with sugar and salt.

CABBAGE SOUP

1 *cabbage*
1 *onion*
1 *lemon*
8 *oz. tomatoes*
2 *pints stock*
2 *apples*
sugar

salt, pepper

Shred the cabbage, mince the apple and onions. Cook the tomatoes with a little water and pass through a sieve. Cook the cabbage, onion, apple and tomato purée in the stock for 30 minutes. Season with salt, pepper, lemon juice and sugar.

KIDNEY SOUP

1 *calf's kidney*
2 *pints stock*
2 *onions*
1 *oz. flour*
1 *oz. butter*
parsley
thyme
½ *bay leaf*

1 *egg yolk*
1 *gill milk*

Blanch the kidney, skin it and remove the core, slice thinly. Brown the kidney in the butter with the sliced onion and the herbs, stir in the flour and cook till brown. Add the stock, season with salt and pepper. Simmer for 30 minutes. Mix the beaten egg yolks with warm milk, add to the soup just before serving.

LENTIL SOUP

8 *oz. lentils*
1 *onion*
2 *sticks celery*
bacon bones
1 *dessertspoon wine vinegar*

salt, pepper

Soak the lentils for 12 hours. Chop the celery and onion and cook with the strained lentils and bacon bones in 3 pints water until tender. Season with salt and pepper. Stir in the vinegar.

FISH BALLS

2 *lb. white fish (bream, fresh*
    haddock or cod)
2 *eggs*
2 *onions*
1 *carrot*
1 *stick celery*
1 *oz. ground almonds*
1 *oz. breadcrumbs*
parsley
salt, pepper

Remove the skin, head and bones from the fish. Cook them with the onion, sliced, half the carrot, sliced, and the celery in 1½ pints of water for 30 minutes. Strain.

Mince the fish and the remaining onion, add the ground almonds, some chopped parsley and season with salt and pepper. Beat the eggs into this mixture and blend well. Add the breadcrumbs, shape into balls. Slice the rest of the carrot, add it to the strained stock. Bring the stock to the boil, simmer the fish balls in it for 1 hour. Arrange the fish balls on a dish with a little stock strained over each. Serve cold.

FISH CAKES WITH SPINACH

2 *lb. cod on the bone*
1 *slice bread*
1 *onion*
1 *egg yolk*
1 *gill milk*
2 *oz. breadcrumbs*
8 *anchovy fillets*
salt, pepper
butter
1 *lb. spinach*

Dot the fish with butter and cook slowly in a covered fireproof dish. Chop the onion and fry it in a little butter until transparent. Soak the bread in milk. Remove the skin and bones from the fish, pound it with the onion and bread, from which the milk has been squeezed. Season with salt and pepper. Shape into balls, roll in egg and breadcrumbs and fry quickly in hot fat. Chop the anchovy fillets, mix with the cooked spinach and serve with the fish balls.

BRUNSWICK STEW

1 *rabbit, cut in pieces*
1 *lb. tomatoes, peeled and*
    quartered
1 *lb. runner beans, sliced*
3 *spring onions, chopped*
1 *lb. small new potatoes*
1 *glass red wine*
½ *bay leaf*
thyme

salt, pepper
2 *oz. dripping*

Dredge the rabbit in seasoned flour. Fry lightly in the dripping until browned. Transfer to an oven-proof dish, add the vegetables, wine, herbs and seasoning. Cover the pan. Cook in a moderate oven for 1½ hours.

HAMBURG STEAK

1 *lb. raw beef, finely chopped*
4 *oz. raw pork, finely chopped*
chopped parsley
1 *small onion, chopped*
1 *slice bread soaked in milk*
5 *eggs*
salt, pepper

breadcrumbs
fat for frying

Mix the meat with the parsley, onion and soaked bread (from which the milk has been squeezed) and 1 egg, season with salt and pepper. Shape into 4 flat cakes. Roll in breadcrumbs. Fry fairly slowly on both sides. Fry the eggs lightly and place one on top of each meat cake.

HAM WITH POTATOES

1½ *lb. cooked ham*
6 *raw potatoes, sliced*
4 *green peppers*
2 *large onions*
½ *pint milk*
1 *egg*
4 *oz. grated cheese*
salt, pepper
butter

Peel and slice the potatoes. Remove the seeds and slice the green peppers. Slice the onion. Cut the ham into 1-inch dice. Put a layer of potatoes in the bottom of a fireproof dish, cover with layers of onion, green pepper and ham. Repeat the layers until the dish is full, ending with a layer of potatoes. Beat up the egg with the milk. Season with salt and pepper and pour into the dish. Dot with butter. Cook in a moderate oven for 1½ hours. Sprinkle with grated cheese and brown in the oven or under a grill.

PANCAKE PUDDING

8 *oz. minced cooked meat*
1 *oz. butter*
2 *shallots or small onions, finely*
   chopped
2 *tablespoons stock*
½ *oz. flour*
salt, pepper
oil for frying
½ *pint pancake batter (see p. 183)*

Fry the shallots in the butter, stir in the flour, add the stock and cook slowly until the onions are soft. Add the meat, season with salt and pepper and mix well together, and keep hot. Make the pancakes in the usual way. Put the first one on a fireproof dish, spread a little of the meat mixture over it. Continue with alternate layers of meat and pancakes. Put in a moderately hot oven to reheat if necessary.

POTATOES WITH COTTAGE CHEESE

2 *lb. potatoes*
8 *oz. cottage cheese*
½ *pint thick sour cream*
1 *bunch spring onions, chopped*
1 *oz. caraway seeds*
salt

Boil the potatoes in their skins in salted water. Peel. The potatoes should be served hot. The cheese, cream, onions and caraway seeds should be handed separately in individual dishes. Each person takes as much of the side dishes to eat with potatoes as he fancies.

FRANKFURTERS WITH SAUERKRAUT

8 *oz. sauerkraut*
8 *oz. haricot beans*
bacon bones
4 *rashers bacon*
4 *frankfurters*
salt, pepper

Soak the beans overnight. Drain and cook with the bacon bones and 2 pints water until tender, pass through a sieve, season with salt if necessary and pepper. Fry the bacon and remove to keep warm. Heat the sauerkraut in the bacon fat. Arrange the bean purée in the middle of a dish, surrounded by the sauerkraut, and put the bacon and frankfurters on top. Put in a moderate oven until the frankfurters are hot.

PRAWNS WITH MIXED VEGETABLES

1 *pint prawns*
8 *oz. cooked peas*
8 *oz. cooked new carrots*
1 *small cauliflower, cooked*
4 *oz. mushrooms*
8 *oz. asparagus*
2 *oz. butter*
1 *oz. flour*
sugar
salt

Remove the heads and tails of the prawns, cook them in the butter until tender. Remove and keep hot. Separate the cauliflower flowerets, fry them lightly in the butter with the peas, carrots and prawns. Season with salt and a little sugar and add to the mushrooms. Cook the asparagus in boiling salted water until tender. Break off the tips and put them with the other ingredients. Stir the flour into the butter and gradually add enough of the water in which the asparagus was cooked to make a fairly thick sauce. Arrange the vegetables and prawns on a dish and pour the sauce over them.

RABBIT

1 *rabbit cut into pieces*
1 *pint mild beer*
2 *onions*
1 *tablespoon flour*
8 *oz. prunes*
2 *oz. dripping*

salt, pepper

Dust the pieces of rabbit with seasoned flour. Brown them in the dripping. Add the sliced onions and the prunes (previously soaked if necessary). Cover with water, cook with a lid on the pan in a slow oven for 1½ hours.

MEAT BALLS

8 oz. beef
4 oz. pork
4 oz. liver
1 slice bread
chopped parsley
½ lemon
1 teaspoon Worcester sauce
2 pints stock
2 oz. dripping
1 oz. flour
1 onion
2 eggs
½ oz. butter
capers

salt, pepper

Mince the onion, fry it lightly in a little butter. Mince the meat and the bread (previously soaked in water and the water squeezed out). Mix the onion, minced meat, bread and eggs and beat well. Add the parsley, grated lemon rind, lemon juice and sauce and beat again. Shape the mixture into balls and poach them in the stock for about 15 minutes. Remove them and drain. Put aside to keep hot. Melt the dripping, cook the flour in it for 1 minute, gradually add enough stock to make a fairly thick sauce. Season with salt and pepper and capers. Pour the sauce over the meat balls.

BRAISED TOPSIDE (SAUERBRATEN)

3 lb. topside
2 oz. lard
salt
6 peppercorns
1 teaspoon dry mustard
1 bay leaf
1 sprig thyme
4 cloves
1 onion, sliced
1 carrot, sliced
2 glasses red wine
2 tablespoons wine vinegar

1 oz. flour
½ pint sour cream
¼ pint stock

Put the wine, vinegar, carrots, onion, cloves, bay leaf, thyme, salt and mustard into a pan. Marinate the meat in this mixture for 48 hours, turning it every 12 hours. Drain the meat and fry it lightly on all sides in the lard. Pour the marinade over it and cook, covered with a lid, in a slow oven for 3 hours. Strain the sauce and thicken with the flour, add stock if necessary and the cream. Slice the meat and pour the sauce over it. Serve with noodles.

GOULASH WITH SAUERKRAUT

2 lb. veal
2 oz. dripping
2 onions
8 oz. tomatoes
½ pint sour cream
¼ teaspoon paprika
1 lb. sauerkraut
salt

Cut the veal into 1-inch squares. Slice the onion and brown in the dripping, add the meat and fry it, turning the pieces so that all sides are browned. Add the peeled and quartered tomatoes, season with salt and paprika. Cover with water, put a lid on the dish and simmer for 1½ hours. Strain the sauce, simmer it gently to reduce it, add the cream and simmer for 3-4 minutes. Pour the sauce over the meat, re-heat and serve with sauerkraut.

MEAT CAKES WITH SAUERKRAUT SAUCE

8 oz. beef
8 oz. pork
2 slices bread
1 gill milk
1 onion, chopped
6 anchovy fillets
1 egg
2 oz. butter
1 oz. flour
½ pint stock
1 glass white wine
1 teaspoon capers
1 teaspoon French mustard
1 dessertspoon sugar
juice of ½ lemon
2 egg yolks

salt, pepper

Soak the bread in the milk, squeeze it gently and mix it with the minced meat, chopped onion, and minced anchovies. Season with salt and pepper. Bind with the egg. Shape into flat cakes and fry in the butter; keep warm.

FOR THE SAUCE:

Melt the butter, cook the flour in it for 1 minute, gradually add the stock and the wine. Add the capers, mustard, sugar, lemon juice, salt and pepper. Pour the sauce over rissoles, cook slowly for 15 minutes. Mix the beaten egg yolks with a little melted butter and stir carefully into the sauce just before serving.

PORK CHOPS WITH MADEIRA SAUCE

4 large pork chops
¼ pint white wine
½ tablespoon wine vinegar
½ bay leaf
1 clove garlic
1 glass Madeira
salt, pepper

Rub the chops with the garlic and put them in a shallow fireproof dish, pour the wine and vinegar over them and enough water to cover the meat. Season with salt and pepper. Cover the dish and cook in a moderate oven for 1 hour. Strain the sauce and add the Madeira and simmer for 2−3 minutes. Pour it over the meat. Serve with cooked slices of apple.

PORK CHOPS WITH PLUMS

4 pork chops
8 oz. plums
1 oz. sugar
cinnamon
4 cloves
1 glass red wine
salt, pepper

Trim the chops and fry lightly in the surplus fat. Stew the plums with the sugar in a little water. Pass through a sieve. Put the chops in a shallow fireproof dish. Mix a pinch of cinnamon and the cloves with the strained plums. Pour on top of the chops. Add the wine. Season with salt and pepper. Cover with lid and bake in a moderate oven for 1 hour, adding a little water from time to time if necessary.

PORK WITH SAUERKRAUT

1 *lb. pork fillets*
caraway seeds
1 *lb. sauerkraut*
¼ *pint sour cream*

Cook the pork with the sauerkraut for 40 minutes. Remove the meat and keep it hot. Stir the cream into the sauerkraut, flavour with a few caraway seeds. Put the sauerkraut on to a hot dish, arrange the pieces of pork on it, serve immediately.

PORK CHOPS WITH SOUR CREAM

4 *pork chops*
¼ *pint sour cream*
juice of ½ *lemon*
1 *teaspoon sugar*
thyme
flour
salt, pepper

Trim the chops and melt the surplus fat. Season the chops, and dust with flour. Fry lightly on both sides in the fat. Transfer to a casserole, add the sour cream, lemon juice, sugar and a pinch of thyme. Pour in enough water to cover the chops. Put a lid on the casserole. Cook in a moderate oven until tender (about 1 hour).

MIXED VEGETABLE STEAMED

peas
new carrots, sliced
small new potatoes
cauliflower, broken into flowerets
broad beans
celeriac, sliced

salt
1 *oz. butter*

Mix all the vegetables together, put them in a pudding basin with the butter and a pinch of salt. Steam until tender.

RED CABBAGE

1 *red cabbage*
1 *onion*
2 *rashers streaky bacon*
1 *oz. dripping*
2 *glasses red wine*
1 *dessertspoon vinegar*
salt, pepper
allspice

Shred the cabbage and blanch it in boiling water, drain. Fry the sliced onion in the fat, add the bacon, the wine, the shredded cabbage, the vinegar; season with salt and pepper. Add a little allspice in a muslin bag. Cook slowly in a covered pan for 1 hour. Remove the allspice before serving.

PORK WITH PRUNES

loin of pork weighing about 3 lb.
8 oz. prunes
1 clove garlic

Rub the boned pork with a cut clove of garlic. Soak and stone the prunes and stuff the pork with them. Roll the meat. Roast it in a hot oven for 30 minutes per lb.

SAUERKRAUT

2 lb. sauerkraut
1 grated potato, raw
1 onion, chopped
4 oz. butter
10 juniper berries
¾ pint stock
1 small glass kirsch or white wine

Lightly brown the onion in the butter. Add the sauerkraut and the juniper berries. Pour in a little stock, simmer for 1½ hours, adding a little stock every 15 minutes. Add the potato 15 minutes before serving. Add the kirsch. If white wine is used, it should be substituted for some of the stock during the cooking.

SAVOY CABBAGE

1 savoy cabbage
1 onion
1 apple
1 dessertspoon wine vinegar
½ teaspoon sugar

¼ pint stock
2 oz. dripping
salt, pepper

Fry the sliced onion lightly in the dripping. Add the shredded cabbage, sliced apple and all the other ingredients. Simmer in a covered pan for 30 minutes.

APPLE PANCAKES

6 oz. flour
½ pint milk
1 egg
1 oz. melted butter
salt
3 apples
cinnamon
2 oz. sugar
juice of 1 lemon

Break the egg into the sifted flour, pour on the milk and beat the batter well. Add the melted butter and a pinch of salt just before using. Slice and chop the apples, flavour them with the lemon juice, sugar and a pinch of cinnamon. Heat a very little fat in a heavy pan, put in a tablespoon of the batter, cover with the apple mixture, fry quickly, turn and fry the other side.

APPLE TART

8 oz. pastry (see p. 284)
1 lb. apples
2 oz. sugar
nutmeg
cinnamon
½ lemon
1 egg
¼ pint milk

1 oz. melted butter
2 oz. almonds

Cut the apples into thin slices. Beat the egg in the milk, add the sugar, melted butter and flavourings. Put the apple slices in the mixture and leave to stand for 2 hours. Roll out the pastry and line a Swiss Roll tin with it. Fill it with the apple mixture, sprinkle the top with chopped almonds and bake in a hot oven for 30 minutes.

CHESTNUT MOUSSE

1 pint milk
4 egg yolks
2 oz. sugar
1 lb. chestnuts
1 oz. gelatine
½ pint whipped cream

Make a thick custard by cooking the eggs and milk very slowly in a double saucepan. Peel and sieve the chestnuts (see p. 398, Spanish section). Stir them and the sugar into the custard. Add the gelatine, dissolved in a little warm water. Whip the cream and fold it into the mixture. Pour it gently into a glass dish. Serve cold.

FRUIT KUCHEN

½ pint milk
4 oz. flour
1 egg
1 oz. sugar
2 oz. melted butter
fruit

2 oz. almonds
cinnamon

Beat the egg into the flour, beat in the milk, sugar and lastly the melted butter. Pour into a shallow greased pie dish. Put small pieces of tinned or fresh fruit in the batter, sprinkle with cinnamon and chopped almonds. Bake in a moderate oven for 45 minutes.

FRUIT PANCAKE

½ pint milk
3 oz. flour
3 eggs
1 oz. sugar
1 oz. stoned chopped raisins
1 oz. ground almonds
2 oz. butter

Beat the egg yolks into the flour, beat in the milk, add the sugar, raisins, ground almonds and the stiffly beaten egg whites. Heat the butter in a large frying pan, pour in the mixture. Cook quickly until the underside is brown, brown the top under a hot grill and serve sprinkled with sugar.

TRIFLE

½ *pint thick rice pudding*
½ *pint boiled egg custard*
damson cheese
vanilla
½ *pint cream*

Cover the bottom of a glass dish with damson cheese, or with a thick purée of any sharp tasting fruit. Cover this with the rice pudding and pour the egg custard over the top. Add a drop of vanilla to the cream, beat it and arrange it on the custard and serve chilled.

ANISEED CAKES

4 *oz. sugar*
3 *eggs*
6 *oz. flour*
1 *teaspoon baking powder*
1 *tablespoon aniseed, crushed*
vanilla

Beat the eggs and sugar until white and creamy. Sift the flour with the baking powder and fold it into the egg mixture. Flavour with a few drops of vanilla and the aniseed. Drop teaspoonfuls of the mixture on to greased baking tins, leave to stand for 12 hours. Bake in a moderate oven for 10 minutes.

CINNAMON STARS

8 *oz. icing sugar*
6 *egg whites*
1 *teaspoon grated lemon peel*
1 *teaspoon cinnamon*
1 *lb. ground almonds*
salt

Whisk the egg whites stiffly with a pinch of salt. Fold in the sugar, cinnamon and lemon peel. Put aside one third of the mixture. Fold the ground almonds into the rest. Roll out the mixture to ¼ inch thick. Cut into star shapes, cover with spoonfuls of the meringue. Bake on a greased tin for 15 minutes in a slow oven.

GERMAN SULTANA CAKE

8 *oz. sugar*
2 *oz. butter*
2 *oz. lard*
5 *eggs*
4 *teaspoons baking powder*
salt
1 *lb. flour*
½ *pint milk (scant)*
4 *oz. sultanas*
1 *teaspoon lemon peel*

1 *teaspoon vanilla*
4 *oz. flaked almonds*
icing sugar

Cream the butter and sugar. Beat the eggs in one at a time. Fold in half the flour sifted with the baking powder. Beat in half the milk. Repeat with the rest of the flour and milk. Add the sultanas, lemon peel and vanilla. Bake in a moderate oven for 40 minutes. Ice with very thin white icing, sprinkle with almonds.

ORANGE CAKE

3 *oz. sugar*
3 *eggs*
3 *oz. flour*
2 *oz. melted butter*
1 *tablespoon rum*
1 *orange*

Beat the egg yolks and the sugar until white. Beat in the orange juice and the rum. Add the sifted flour and the butter. Fold in the stiffly beaten egg whites. Bake in a greased and floured tin for 40 minutes in a slow oven. Ice with rum icing (see p. 187).

PRETZELS

8 *oz. flour*
2 *oz. butter*
2 *egg whites*
2 *egg yolks*
milk
salt

pepper
coarse salt

Work the creamed butter, beaten egg whites and egg yolks into the flour with a little salt and pepper. Roll out on a floured board, shape into figures of eight. Brush with milk, sprinkle with coarse salt. Bake in a moderately hot oven for 10 minutes.

SPICED BISCUITS

4 *oz. butter*
7 *oz. sugar*
3 *eggs*
6 *oz. flour*
vanilla
cinnamon
4 *oz. almonds*

Cream the butter with 3 oz. sugar. Beat in the egg yolks and then the sifted flour. Roll out between sheets of greaseproof paper until $\frac{1}{4}$ inch thick. Cut into rounds with a small pastry cutter. Put into greased baking tins. Cover with meringue made as follows:

Whisk the egg whites stiffly, fold in the sugar, flavouring and finely chopped almonds. Bake in a moderate oven for 15 minutes.

TARTELETTES

4 *oz. sugar*
6 *oz. butter*
6 *oz. flour*
2 *egg yolks*
1 *egg white*
4 *oz. almonds*
2 *oz. sugar*
cinnamon

nutmeg
lemon peel

Cream the butter with the sugar and a little grated lemon peel. Beat in the egg yolks, fold in the sifted flour. Drop small spoonfuls of the mixture on to greased baking tins. Beat the egg white with 1 tablespoon water. Brush the biscuits with it. Mix the almonds with the sugar, cinnamon and nutmeg. Sprinkle over the biscuits. Bake in a moderate oven for 10 minutes.

RUM ICING

8 oz. icing sugar
2 oz. lump sugar
1 strip lemon peel
1 tablespoon rum

Rub the lump sugar with the lemon peel. Heat the icing sugar, the lump sugar and the rum slowly with a little water until it thickens.

SPICED CAKES

8 oz. brown sugar
4 oz. butter
2 eggs
¼ pint sour milk
8 oz. flour
2 teaspoons baking powder
cinnamon
nutmeg

salt
4 oz. currants

Cream the butter and sugar. Beat in the eggs one at a time. Add the sour milk, fold in the flour, sifted with the baking powder, a pinch of salt, a little cinnamon and nutmeg. Beat well, add the currants and beat again. Bake in 24 small greased tins for 20 minutes in a moderate oven.

EGG DUMPLINGS

2 eggs
6 oz. flour
salt
½ teaspoon baking powder
2 oz. breadcrumbs
4 oz. butter

Beat the eggs, beat in the flour sifted with salt and baking powder. Cut very small pieces off the dough and poach in boiling water. Roll in breadcrumbs as for potato dumplings (see p. 188).

SAUSAGE BALLS FOR SOUP

8 oz. sausage meat
1 egg white
parsley
basil
1 tablespoon fine breadcrumbs

Mix the ingredients well together, shape into balls about 1 inch in diameter. Poach them in boiling stock for 15 minutes. Drain and serve with pea, bean or lentil soup.

POTATO DUMPLINGS

6 *medium potatoes*
2 *eggs*
4 *oz. flour*
2 *oz. butter*
salt
2 *oz. breadcrumbs*

Steam the potatoes in their skins until tender. Leave to cool, peel, pass through a sieve. Beat in the eggs, then the flour and a good pinch of salt. Shape into balls and poach for 10 minutes in gently boiling salted water. Melt the butter, brown the breadcrumbs in it. Roll the dumplings in the browned breadcrumbs. Traditionally served with Sauerbraten (see p. 180).

SWEET STEAMED DUMPLINGS

1 *lb. flour*
5 *oz. butter*
5 *oz. sugar*
pinch salt
2 *egg yolks*
¼ *teaspoon powdered cinnamon*
½ *oz. yeast*
¼ *pint milk*
½ *pint water*
2 *oz. lard*
½ *teaspoon salt*

Put the butter, sugar and pinch of salt into a warmed bowl and beat together thoroughly. Add the egg yolks and beat together until you have a thick smooth cream. Dissolve the yeast in the lukewarm milk, and add to the creamed mixture alternately with the sifted flour and cinnamon. Keep just a little of the flour aside. Knead until the dough will leave the sides of the bowl cleanly. Cover with a cloth and leave in a warm place until it has doubled in bulk. Roll out the dough to about 1 inch thickness on a floured board. Cut into small rounds and then roll them into little balls. Arrange these in a large skillet or frying pan which can be covered with a lid. There should be plenty of space between the dumplings as they will spread in cooking.

Melt the lard with the water and 1 teaspoon salt, pour over the dumplings, cover with a lid and cook over a moderate heat for about 30 minutes. The liquid will have evaporated and the dumplings should be well-risen and have a golden crust. Serve with a sweet fruit or vanilla sauce.

STRAWBERRY BOWL

3 *lb. strawberries*
juice of 1 lemon
½ *pint light sweet red wine*
8 *oz. castor sugar*

Divide the strawberries into half, reserving the best fruit and sprinkling them with half the sugar. Mash the rest of the berries smoothly with the lemon juice, 4 oz. sugar and wine. Pour this purée over the whole berries, stir well together and serve with sponge fingers or biscuits. Raspberries can be used in the same way.

Great Britain

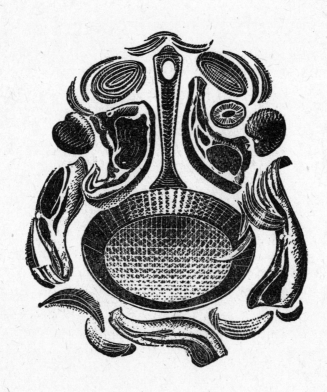

COOKING IN GREAT BRITAIN

Recently, when I opened the chapter on England, Wales and Northern Ireland in an American round-the-world cook book, I read with quite a shock the following sentence: 'For their own protection, visitors to England should understand British food habits.' Come, come, it is not as bad as all that. The main trouble is the British attitude to food — not its inferior quality. I mean the attitude of 'I eat because I have to live, not because I enjoy my food'. But even this attitude is only characteristic of a small section of the British people and is changing from day to day. In fact I am not at all alone in thinking that British cooking can be exceptionally good, especially the dishes which hail from the North. A really light Yorkshire pudding can be served to gourmets from all over the world and win praise for you. The West of England has given us a recipe which should make a regular appearance in every household: Cornish Pasty, Jugged Hare, Irish stew, Welsh Rabbit and Lancashire Hot Pot are all solid foundations to any kitchen. To say nothing of a nice joint of sirloin for the traditional English Roast Beef — a dinner which you can put before the choosiest Frenchman and feel sure that he will tuck in happily. I have been very happy to notice that, during the last few years, an old favourite of mine, Steak and Kidney Pudding, has at last taken its rightful place on the menus of large hotels and restaurants.

I shall defend British cooking for all I am worth against any onslaught if only in gratitude for one of the best sauces of the world: Cumberland Sauce. I could mention a dozen other recipes which have originated in Britain and have infiltrated into the cookery of the world — from Plum Pudding to Christmas Cake, all institutions which the world has accepted, while they crack their little jokes about British cooks.

You will also find a number of traditional Scottish recipes in this section which are well worth trying. They include the famous Cock-a-Leekie Soup, Scotch Eggs, Scotch shortbread, Cream-Crowdie, an excellent Dundee cake, Musselburgh Pie made with steak and oysters, and of course a recipe for haggis. The traditional haggis involves a tremendous amount of preparation and you must obtain the large stomach bag of a sheep — but we have given a pot version which anyone can make without difficulty and which will look and taste every bit as authentic as the real haggis which is piped in at a Burns Supper.

CABBAGE SOUP

8 oz. streaky bacon, diced
2¼ pints boiling water
1 large cabbage, chopped
1 large onion
1 large carrot
4 sticks of celery
½ pint dried peas, soaked
  overnight

salt, pepper
rolls or slices of bread (optional)

Put everything in a large saucepan, pour over the boiling water, simmer for 4 hours. Serve, if liked, with a roll or a slice of bread in each soup plate with the hot soup poured over.

CREAM OF CAULIFLOWER

1 medium cauliflower
1 pint milk
1¼ pints vegetable stock
2 oz. butter
4 celery sticks, finely chopped
1 small onion, finely chopped
1 oz. flour
1 bay leaf
salt, pepper
croûtons

Cook the cauliflower in boiling salted water for 20 minutes. Cut in half. Save half of the white flower and coarsely sieve the rest. Fry the celery and onion in the butter for 5 minutes in a large saucepan, add the flour, mix well, add the stock and the bay leaf, bring to the boil and simmer for 10 minutes. Strain. Add the sieved cauliflower and the milk to the stock. Add salt and pepper to taste. Separate the cauliflower into small heads, add to the soup, re-heat and serve with croûtons.

COCK-A-LEEKIE SOUP

1 small fowl
salt, pepper
6 leeks
3 oz. butter
2 tablespoons rice (optional)
2½ quarts stock or water
a few sprigs of thyme and
  parsley tied together

Joint the fowl. Wash the leeks thoroughly and chop finely.

Heat the butter in a large saucepan and add the pieces of fowl lightly seasoned with salt and pepper. Fry gently on all sides till brown, add the leeks and fry for a further 3 minutes. Pour on the stock, add the thyme and parsley, bring to the boil, skim if necessary, and simmer for 2 hours, or until the bird is tender.

Remove the pieces of fowl, take out any bones and chop the meat, return to the soup, remove the thyme and parsley. If rice is used add after 1 hour's cooking. Add more salt and pepper to taste.

This soup is better if made 24 hours before eating and re-heated when wanted.

OXTAIL SOUP

½ *oxtail, cut into joints*
2 *carrots*
1 *onion*
bouquet garni
2 *quarts water*
2 *oz. butter*
3 *oz. flour*
1 *teaspoon tomato purée*
1 *teaspoon red currant jelly*
½ *glass sherry*
salt, pepper

Slice carrots and onion and place in a saucepan with the oxtail, *bouquet garni* and water. Bring to the boil, remove scum from top and simmer for 2 hours. Take out the oxtail and strain stock. Cut off the meat from the oxtail. Melt butter and stir in flour, then stir in the stock. Bring to the boil, simmer for 5 minutes, then add tomato purée, red currant jelly, sherry, chopped meat, salt and pepper. Simmer together very gently for a further 5 minutes.

HADDOCK SAVOURY

2 1½ *lb. smoked haddocks*
8 *rashers of bacon*
4 *oz. butter*
3 *oz. flour*
2½ *pints milk*
6 *peeled tomatoes, sliced*
1 *onion, finely chopped*
pepper
3 *oz. grated cheese (Parmesan is best)*

Soak the fish in cold water for 30 minutes.

Drain, this will have got rid of excess salt. Put the fish in the milk, bring to the boil and simmer for 15 minutes. Strain the milk into a basin. Pick all the skin and bones off the fish and flake the flesh. Cut the bacon rashers in half, fry them with the chopped onion.

Make a white sauce with milk the fish has cooked in, flour, butter; season with pepper. Add the grated cheese. Arrange the fish, bacon and onion and tomatoes in layers in fireproof dish, pour over the sauce, brown in the oven and serve hot. This is a substantial dish, and with a green salad an brown bread and butter makes a very adequate supper for four or six hungry people.

SOUSED MACKEREL

4 *cleaned mackerels, heads and tails removed*
1 *large onion, cut in thin rings*
½ *teaspoon salt*
¼ *teaspoon black pepper*
a pinch of dried thyme
1 *cut up bay leaf*
1 *carrot, finely sliced*
1 *teaspoon olive oil*

enough cold water mixed with
1 *teaspoon vinegar to cover*

Put the fish in a shallow fireproof dish, add all the other ingredients. Bake in a cool oven until the vegetables are tender, basting frequently. Leave to cool in the liquor if eaten cold; but they are good eaten hot.

White wine and a good squeeze of lemon juice may be used instead of the vinegar and water.

STUFFED HERRINGS

4 *large herrings, with soft roes*
3 *oz. fresh breadcrumbs*
2 *teaspoons chopped parsley*
salt, pepper
2 *oz. butter*
1 *egg*
2 *tablespoons milk*
1 *teaspoon lemon juice*

Split the fish, remove the roes.

Mix the roes, parsley, breadcrumbs, salt and pepper together. Melt 1 oz. butter in a saucepan, add the egg and the breadcrumbs mixture, stir well together and cook gently till the egg is just cooked in the mixture. Cool and stuff the fish with this. Place the stuffed fish in a shallow fireproof dish, dot with 1 oz. butter, sprinkle with lemon juice, salt and pepper. Pour the milk in the dish, cover with grease-proof paper and bake in a moderate oven for 20 minutes, or till soft throughout. Serve with lemon slices

HERRING PIE (Yorkshire)

4 *herrings, boned and filleted*
salted water
1 *oz. butter*
4 *medium potatoes, cut in thin slices*
2 *medium cooking apples, peeled and finely chopped*
salt, pepper

Having prepared the fish leave them to soak in salted water for 1 hour. Drain. Rub the butter over the sides and bottom of a straight-sided pie dish. Line sides and bottom with some of the potato slices. Arrange the fillets and chopped apple in layers in the dish, season each layer with salt and pepper, finish with a layer of potatoes.

Cover with a wall-buttered paper. Bake in a moderate oven for 45 minutes. 15 minutes before the end remove the paper to brown the top.

MACKEREL AU GRATIN

4 *cleaned mackerel, heads and tails removed*
4 *shallots*
2 *medium onions*
2 *teaspoons chopped parsley*
2 *oz. white breadcrumbs*
1½ *oz. butter*
salt, pepper

Butter a shallow fireproof dish. Chop the onions, shallots very finely. Arrange the fish in the dish, sprinkle with the onions, shallots, breadcrumbs, a sprinkling of salt and pepper and the parsley. Pour over enough white wine to come up to one third of the fish, dot with butter. Cover with a buttered paper and bake in a moderate oven for 25 minutes.

BOILED MACKEREL WITH GOOSEBERRY SAUCE

4 *fresh cleaned mackerel, heads and tails removed*
boiling water
¼ *teaspoon salt*
gooseberry sauce (see p. 203)

Have enough boiling water to cover the fish, add the salt. Make several incisions in the back of each fish, put into the boiling water, simmer very gently for 15 minutes. Drain and serve with the hot gooseberry sauce.

CRIMPED COD

1½ *lb. cod cutlets*
3½ *pints water*
2 *teaspoons salt*
1 *teaspoon vinegar*
1 *medium chopped onion*
1 *bay leaf*
2 *peppercorns*
1 *oz. butter*
juice of 1 lemon
parsley

Put 1½ teaspoons salt in 2 pints of water and the vinegar, add the fish and leave for 3 hours.

Add the onion, peppercorns, bay leaf and ½ teaspoon salt to 1½ pints of water. Bring to the boil and simmer for 20 minutes. Boil up, put in the fish, lower heat and simmer 10 minutes or till tender. Drain well, place on a hot dish, squeeze a little lemon juice on each cutlet, dab with butter. Serve with ½ pint white sauce to which you can add 2 teaspoons chopped parsley, or 1 chopped hard-boiled egg.

HAGGIS

8 *oz. sheep's liver*
4 *oz. beef suet*
2 *onions*
4 *oz. oatmeal*
salt and pepper

Cover the liver with water and boil for 40 minutes. Drain and keep the liquid. Mince the liver finely. Parboil the onions then chop small with the suet. Brown the oatmeal by tossing quickly in a thick pan over the fire. Now combine the minced liver, suet, onions and oatmeal and season with salt and pepper. Moisten with the liquor in which the liver was boiled. Turn into a greased bowl, cover with greaseproof paper and steam for 2 hours.

JUGGED HARE

1 *hare, well hung*
salt, pepper
¼ *pint red wine, preferably port*
1 *pint meat stock or water*
2 *oz. butter*
2 *oz. bacon, chopped small*
1 *tablespoon lemon juice*
1½ *tablespoons flour*
1½ *tablespoons butter*

TIED IN MUSLIN:
4 *cloves*
4 *bay leaves*
4 *sprigs of parsley*
1 *sprig thyme, or marjoram*
¼ *teaspoon nutmeg powder*

¼ *teaspoon cinnamon powder*
12 *peppercorns*

Ask you butcher to skin, clean and cut up the hare in pieces the size of an egg. Dust these with salt and pepper. Fry these in the 2 oz. butter and bacon till browned. Put the pieces in a jar or deep casserole and pour over the wine. Cover tightly and cook in a moderate oven for 30 minutes. Now add the lemon juice, stock and herbs. Stand the jar or casserole in a pan of water, cover and cook in a moderate-to-cool oven for 3 hours or simmer very gently on top of the stove. Strain the gravy. Mix the 1½ tablespoons butter with the flour, pour on the hot gravy, bring to the boil, stirring all the time, pour over the hare and serve hot.

CASSEROLE OF HARE WITH PRUNES AND RAISINS

1 *hare, with the blood*
2 *oz. butter*
6 *medium onions, chopped*
8 *oz. prunes*
4 *oz. seedless raisins*
¾ *pint meat stock*
½ *teaspoon salt*
¼ *teaspoon pepper*
¼ *teaspoon sugar*
1 *sherry glass red wine*
1 *tablespoon red currant jelly*
fried croûtons of bread

Separate the front from the back part of the hare. Cut up the front part in egg-sized pieces. Roast the back part in the usual way, so that it will be done by the time (1½ hours) it takes the casserole to cook. Fry the cut-up pieces in the butter till brown, add salt, pepper, the onions, prunes, raisins and the stock. Bring to the boil and simmer for 1½ hours with the lid on the casserole. Add the sugar, wine and jelly and cook uncovered for 30 minutes. Now add the blood and the roasted back.

Heat and serve with the croûtons in the gravy.

ROAST TURKEY

turkey
rasher of fat bacon

CHESTNUT STUFFING:

1 *lb. chestnuts*
2 *oz. bacon*
3 *oz. breadcrumbs*
1 *teaspoon chopped parsley*
1 *oz. butter*
salt and pepper
1 *egg*
¼ *pint stock*
grated rind of ½ lemon

BREAD SAUCE:

1 *onion*
2 *cloves*
5 *tablespoons white breadcrumbs*
salt and pepper
½ *pint milk*
1 *oz. butter*
bacon rolls
sausages
gravy

Prepare chestnut stuffing as follows:

Slit skins of nuts and boil in water for 10—15 minutes. Skin, then place in a pan with the stock and simmer gently until they are tender. Mash well. Pound with chopped bacon, breadcrumbs, parsley, lemon rind and butter, season with salt and pepper and bind with beaten egg. Stuff the turkey — but not too full as this stuffing will swell during cooking. Extra stuffing can be made into balls and roasted with the bird.

Cover the breast with the rasher of fat bacon and roast in a moderately hot oven for about 3 hours for a 12-1b. bird. When the breast is brown, cover with greaseproof paper. Serve the turkey with sausages, bacon rolls, gravy and bread sauce, made as follows. Stick the cloves into the onion and simmer with the milk for 10—15 minutes. Remove onion and bring milk to the boil. Stir in the crumbs and simmer for 5 minutes, stirring all the time. Add salt, pepper and butter, reheat and serve.

FRICASSÉE OF RABBIT

1 *young rabbit, cut in joints*
3 *oz. butter*
4 *oz. bacon rashers, chopped small*
4 *medium onions, chopped*
4 *cloves*
a *small bunch of mixed herbs,*
 parsley, thyme, marjoram, etc.
¼ *teaspoon nutmeg*
½ *teaspoon salt*
¼ *teaspoon pepper*
½ *pint water*
1 *oz. flour*
1 *sherry glass white wine*

2 *egg yolks*
grated rind of ½ *lemon*

Heat 1 oz. butter and bacon in a stew pan, add the rabbit pieces and chopped onions, fry for 3 minutes, add the cloves, herbs (tied in a muslin bag), nutmeg, pepper, salt and water, bring to the boil and simmer for 50 minutes with the lid on.

Mix the flour with 2 oz. butter, pour on some of the stock from the saucepan to make a thick gravy, return this to the pan, stir well and simmer for 5 minutes. Beat the yolks, add the wine, the lemon rind and pour over the hot, but not boiling, dish. Stir well and serve.

PIGEONS IN CASSEROLE

4 *pigeons or 2 wood-pigeons*
2 *oz. butter*
4 *oz. bacon, diced*
4 *medium onions, chopped*
4 *medium carrots, chopped*
1 *oz. flour*
1 *bay leaf*
2 *teaspoons chopped parsley*
¼ *teaspoon dried thyme*
½ *teaspoon salt*
¼ *teaspoon pepper*

½ *pint meat or chicken stock*
2 *sherry glasses red or white wine*

Fry the diced bacon in a thick saucepan for 2 minutes, add the butter and the pigeons and brown quickly on all sides. Remove them and add the chopped vegetables, the herbs, salt, pepper and flour. Mix well. Replace the birds, pour on the stock and the wine, bring to the boil and simmer very gently for 1½ hours or until the birds are tender. Serve with red currant jelly.

CORNISH PASTIES

1 *lb. short pastry (see p. 206)*
8 *oz. raw steak*
4 *oz. kidney*
8 *oz. potatoes or a mixture*
 of onions, turnips and potatoes
salt, *pepper*
1 *beaten egg*

Cut the steak, kidneys and peeled potatoes, etc. into ½-inch dice, season with salt and pepper. Roll out the pastry and cut in six rounds the size of a saucer. Place a sixth of the mixture on each round, moisten the edges with cold water, fold over and seal tightly. Brush with the beaten egg.

Cook on a baking sheet in a hot oven for 15 minutes, lower the heat to moderate and cook for a further 40 minutes.

TOAD IN THE HOLE

1 *lb. steak, cut in 1-inch pieces*
4 *oz. flour*
½ *pint milk*
1 *egg*
salt, pepper
1 *oz. dripping*

Mix the flour, milk, beaten egg and ½ teaspoon salt to make a smooth batter and leave for 1 hour or longer. Heat the dripping in a flat tin or fireproof dish in a hot oven, when smoking hot pour in a quarter of the batter and bake till set, for about 10 minutes. Now put in the meat, seasoned with salt and pepper. Pour over the rest of the batter and bake quickly till risen, for 25 minutes. Lower the heat to moderate and cook for a further 20 minutes. Cut up kidney, small rolls of bacon may be added to the meat. Any of these are far better than the usual sausage.

ROAST BEEF

1 *sirloin or middle rib*
salt, pepper
dripping

Sprinkle the joint all over with salt and pepper and rub well in. If the joint has not much fat put 2 oz. dripping on the fat side.

Make oven very hot, stand the joint in a roasting dish or on oven bars with pan underneath and cook for 20 minutes. Reduce to a moderate heat and cook; for underdone beef 16 minutes to the pound, 22 minutes for medium and even 30 minutes for those who like it overdone. Serve with Horseradish Sauce and Yorkshire Pudding and potatoes, peeled (halved if too big), cooked round the joint for 30 to 40 minutes in the roasting dish, or until quite soft inside when pricked with a skewer or fork and crisp and brown outside.

IRISH STEW

2 *lb. neck or loin of mutton*
3 *large onions*
2 *lb. potatoes*
¾ *pint cold water*
1 *teaspoon salt*
¼ *teaspoon pepper*

Remove any excess fat from the meat and cut the rest into 2 × 1-inch pieces, or smaller. Peel and slice the onions and potatoes into ⅛-inch thick rounds. Fill a casserole or thick pan with alternate layers of meat, onions, then potatoes, with a sprinkling of salt and pepper on each. Pour in the water and bring to the boil, skim if necessary, reduce the heat, cover the casserole or pan tightly, cook very slowly in the oven or on the stove for 3 to 4 hours until the meat is tender and almost all the liquid has disappeared. Serve hot, straight from the pot.

WELSH RABBIT

4 *slices of thick toast (crusts removed)*
8 *oz. grated cheese*
2 *oz. butter*
¼ *pint beer or stout*
½ *teaspoon paprika*
1 *teaspoon mustard*
2 *beaten egg yolks*

Make the toast, keep warm. Melt the butter in a double-boiler or over a very low heat, add the cheese, stir, then add the beer or stout slowly, stirring all the time till smooth, now the paprika and the eggs. Keep stirring till warm throughout, pour over the toast and serve. Never let this mixture boil or bubble; if you do it will become 'stringy' and lumpy.

SCOTCH EGGS

4 *oz. minced ham*
3 *anchovy fillets*
2 *oz. fresh breadcrumbs*
¼ *teaspoon pepper*
1 *beaten egg*
4 *hard-boiled eggs*
fat for frying

Chop the anchovies very finely, add to the minced ham, breadcrumbs and pepper, stir in beaten egg. Cover each egg with a coating of this forcemeat and fry in hot fat until brown all over. Cut in half and serve on fried bread, if wished.

DEVILLED KIDNEYS

4 *pieces toast*
8 *sheep's kidneys*
2 *oz. butter*
1 *tablespoon dry mustard*
1 *dessertspoon Worcester sauce*
salt, pepper

Skin the kidneys, cut them in half and core them. Mix the sauce and the mustard together. Heat the butter in a saucepan, add the kidneys, season with salt and pepper, brown quickly for 2 minutes, lower the heat and cook very gently for 6 minutes with the pan covered, add the mustard mixture, stir well and cook slowly for 2 minutes more. Stir and serve on the hot toast.

LANCASHIRE HOT POT

2 *lb. neck of mutton*
2 *lb. potatoes*
3 *large onions*
8 *oz. mushrooms*
3 *sheep's kidneys*
1 *pint meat stock*
2 *oz. butter*
12 *oysters (optional)*
salt, pepper

Cut the meat into cutlets and remove excess fat. Peel and slice the potatoes fairly thickly, slice the onions thinly. Wash, but do not peel, the mushrooms and cut in two. Skin and core the kidneys, cut in halves. Take a deep casserole and place in each ingredient in layers, finishing with potatoes on top. Season each layer with salt and pepper, pour in the butter, melted, and the stock. Cover the casserole tightly and cook very slowly for 3 hours.

BOILED MUTTON WITH DUMPLINGS AND CAPER SAUCE

1 3- to 4-*lb. leg of mutton*
1 *teaspoon salt*
1 *large turnip*
3 *medium carrots*
3 *medium onions*
2 *tablespoons pearl barley*
2 *teaspoons chopped parsley*

Boil enough water to cover the meat, put in the meat best side down. Bring again to the boil, skim add the vegetables cut in medium-sized pieces and the salt. Lower the heat and simmer for nearly 2 hours for a 4-lb. joint, 20 minutes less for a 3-lb. joint. Garnish with chopped parsley over the joint and the vegetables round the dish. Serve with dumplings (see p. 206) and caper sauce (see p. 203).

MUSSELBURGH PIE

1 *lb. beef steak*
12 *oysters*
2 *shallots*
1 *oz. flour*
1½ *gills stock*
salt and pepper
small piece bacon fat
puff pastry (see p. 205)
beaten egg for glazing

Beat the steak very flat and cut into strips. Beard the oysters then cut them in half. Wrap each half, with a tiny piece of bacon fat, in a strip of steak. Season the flour with salt and pepper, dip each roll in this and pack in a pie dish. Add the stock, cover with pastry, brush with beaten egg and bake in a hot oven for 5 minutes. Turn oven to moderate and continue baking for 1½ hours, lowering the heat again if necessary.

ROAST STUFFED SHOULDER OF MUTTON

4 *lb. shoulder of mutton*
1½ *lb. potatoes*
STUFFING OR FORCEMEAT:
3 *oz. breadcrumbs*
1 *finely chopped small onion*
4 *oz. finely chopped mushrooms*

1 *egg*
pepper, salt

Ask your butcher to bone the shoulder.
    Mix all the stuffing ingredients together and stuff the meat. Skewer or tie into a neat shape. Peel and cut the potatoes in halves, if too big. Arrange the potatoes round the joint in the roasting tin, add the dripping and roast in a moderate-to-hot oven for 1½ hours. Serve with onion sauce.

POT ROAST

2½ *lb. rump or rolled rib of beef*
1 *large chopped onion*
2 *tablespoons beef dripping*
½ *pint hot water or beef stock*
2 *peeled chopped tomatoes*
1 *chopped head of celery*
3 *medium sliced carrots*
1 *bay leaf*

1 *teaspoon salt*
¼ *teaspoon pepper*

Take a thick-bottomed pot and melt the dripping in it, add the onion and fry till brown. Put in the meat and brown it all over, pour in the hot liquid, add the vegetables, bay leaf, salt and pepper. Bring to the boil, cover the pot tightly and simmer very slowly for 3 hours.

STEWED OXTAIL WITH TOMATOES

1 *oxtail, jointed*
1 *oz. dripping*
1 *large onion, sliced*
1 *lb. tomatoes*
1 *oz. flour*
parsley, thyme, bay leaf or other
   herbs tied together
cold water or stock
2 *cloves*
2 *teaspoons lemon juice*
salt, pepper
2 *teaspoons flour*
½ *oz. butter*

Wash the tail well. Heat the dripping in a stew pan or casserole, add the oxtail pieces, fry till browned, add the onions, sprinkle in the flour, stir well. Pour in enough water or stock to cover the meat, add the cloves and herbs, salt and pepper. Bring to the boil, cover and simmer very gently for 2 hours. Skin the tomatoes, add them, re-cover and simmer for another 30 minutes. Leave until cold, then lift off the fat formed on top.

Melt the butter in a small saucepan, add the flour, stir, pour on enough of the meat stock to thicken, add this to the stew plus the lemon juice. Bring again to the boil and simmer for 15 minutes longer. If the oxtail is old this dish may take longer to cook — it is essential that the meat should be iust falling off the bone.

PORK PIE

1 *lb. lean pork*
1 *lb. flour*
½ *teaspoon salt*
6 *oz. lard*
1 *egg, beaten*
¼ *pint cold water*
salt, pepper

Cut the pork in ½-inch squares, put in a pan with the water, bring to the boil. Pour off the water on to the lard. Sieve the flour and salt in a basin, pour on the lard and hot water slowly, stirring all the time to make the dough. Leave till cool, turn on to floured board and knead for 4 to 5 minutes. Cut off a quarter of the dough. Roll out to about ⅛ inch thick and line a buttered pie-dish, which should be round with straight sides. Season the meat with salt and pepper and fill the pie. Roll the quarter of dough into a round and cover the top, moisten and seal the edges. Cut leaves out of any left-over rolled pastry, make a small hole in the middle of the top, decorate with the leaves. Brush well with beaten egg and bake in a moderate oven for 2 hours.

BOILED SILVERSIDE AND DUMPLINGS

3 *to 4 lb. silverside*
2 *lb. carrots, cut in two*
   lengthways
2 *lb. medium onions*
1 *bay leaf*
cold water

Put the meat in a large saucepan, add the prepared vegetables and bay leaf, cover with cold water. Bring to the boil gradually, skim if necessary, cover the pan and simmer gently for 2½ to 3 hours.

Serve with hot dumplings.

TERRINE OF PORK, VEAL AND LIVER

1 *lb. fat pork (belly)*
1 *lb. lean veal*
8 *oz. liver*
2 *tablespoons brandy*
6 *tablespoons dry white wine*
1 *clove of garlic*
6 *black peppercorns*
6 *juniper berries*
¼ *teaspoon ground mace or nutmeg*
3 *oz. fat bacon*
2 *teaspoons salt*

Mince the pork, veal and liver. Mix well. Add 2 oz. of the bacon cut into ¼-inch dice, chop the garlic very fine and the berries, add these, the salt, the brandy and the wine. Mix thoroughly and leave for 2 hours. Put into a 2-pint-size terrine dish or a straight-sided casserole. Cut the rest of the fat bacon into ¼-inch wide strips and arrange on the top of the pâté or terrine decoratively. Place the dish in a roasting tin filled with water. Cook uncovered in a slow oven for 1½ hours. When the mixture begins to come away from the sides of the dish it is done. Remove and cool. They are better if pressed down with weights when half cold.

Cover with melted lard or butter when cold, if to be kept more than a week.

STEAK AND KIDNEY PUDDING

suet crust
1½ *lb. rump steak*
8 *oz. kidney*
1 *clove of garlic (optional)*
2 *oz. flour*
1 *teaspoon salt*
1 *teaspoon pepper*
8 *oz. mushrooms*
½ *pint meat stock*

Cut the steak into thin slices, 4 × 3 inches. Cut the kidney in ½-inch squares. Slice the mushrooms. Mix the flour, salt and pepper together, and roll the steak, kidney and mushrooms in it. Wrap a piece of kidney and mushrooms in a slice of meat. If using garlic, cut it in two and rub the inside of the basin well with it. Roll out the suet crust, line the basin with it, sides and bottom and cut a round for the top. Pack the steak rolls in the lined basin, add any extra pieces of kidney or mushroom, pour over the stock, cover with the round of pastry, damp the edges and seal tightly. Tie two pieces of greased paper tightly over the top. Steam for 4 hours.

JUGGED PEAS

2 *lb. shelled peas*
1 *oz. butter*
½ *teaspoon salt*
1 *teaspoon castor sugar*
12 *mint leaves*
a pinch of pepper

Put everything in a screw-top jar. Screw the lid on tightly and stand in a saucepan of boiling water coming half way up the jar. Boil for 30 minutes. Take out the mint leaves before serving. If the peas are old they may take a little longer, but cooked in this way peas are delicious and tender.

VEAL AND HAM PIE

2 *lb. veal*
4 *oz. ham*
2 *hard-boiled eggs*
salt, pepper
pinch of dried herbs
enough meat stock to cover the
   meat, etc.
6 *oz. flour*
2 *oz. lard*
⅜ *pint hot milk*
½ *teaspoon salt*

Cut the veal into slices 1 × 2 inches, also the ham. Slice the eggs. Arrange these ingredients in layers in a pie-dish, season with salt, pepper and a sprinkling of herbs. Pour over the stock.

Make the pastry by melting the lard in the warmed milk, stir slowly into the sieved flour and salt, mix to a soft dough. Turn on to a floured board, roll out fairly thinly, cover the pie-dish, moisten and seal the edges. Decorate with any left-over pastry, make a hole in the middle and bake in a moderate-to-hot oven for 1 hour.

APPLE AND QUINCE SAUCE

1 *quince*
4 *small or 2 large cooking apples*
¼ *pint cider*
3 *oz. sugar*
1 *oz. butter*

Peel, core and grate the fruit coarsely or chop very fine. Put the grated quince in a small saucepan, pour in the cider, bring to the boil and simmer for 10 minutes, till tender. Add the apple and simmer for 10 minutes longer, till tender. Stir well with a wooden spoon to make a thickish pulp (if too thin drain off some of the liquid), add the sugar and cook gently till melted, stir well and add the butter. Stir again. Serve hot with roast pork or roast goose.

BRANDY BUTTER

4 *oz. butter*
1 *oz. sugar*
brandy

Work the sugar into the butter till smooth. Add enough brandy (or rum) into the mixture gradually stirring all the time until the mixture will absorb no more brandy while remaining stiff.

BREAD SAUCE

½ *pint milk*
1 *small onion*
2 *cloves*
1 *blade mace or a good pinch*
   of ground nutmeg
2 *oz. white fresh breadcrumbs*
½ *oz. butter*
1 *teaspoon cream*
½ *teaspoon salt*
pinch of pepper

In a double boiler heat the milk, the onion stuck with the cloves and nutmeg or mace until just not boiling, for 30 minutes. Remove the mace, if used, add the breadcrumbs, stirring and beating with a fork, now the salt, pepper and half the butter. Cook gently, beating frequently, for 20 minutes. Remove the onion, add the other half of the butter and the cream. Serve hot.

CAPER SAUCE

2 oz. butter
2 oz. flour
¼ pint milk
¼ pint mutton stock
salt, pepper
1 tablespoon capers
1 dessertspoon vinegar

Heat the milk and mutton stock till nearly boiling. Melt the butter in the saucepan, add the flour, stir well, pour in the nearly boiling liquid and, stirring all the time, simmer for 3 minutes. Add salt and pepper to taste. Just before serving stir in the capers and the vinegar. Serve hot.

CUMBERLAND SAUCE

1 lemon rind and juice
1 orange rind and juice
½ gill port wine (⅛ pint)
½ gill water
2 tablespoons red currant jelly
2 tablespoons vinegar
½ tablespoon made mustard
pinch of salt
pinch of cayenne pepper
2 oz. glacé cherries, chopped

Shred the lemon and orange rinds very finely, no white pith must be attached. Squeeze the juice of both fruit and strain. Boil the shredded rinds in the water for 5 minutes, strain and put the liquid back in the saucepan. Add the wine, red currant jelly, mustard, cayenne, salt, the fruit juice and the vinegar. Boil all together for 3 minutes. When cold, add the chopped cherries.

CUMBERLAND RUM BUTTER

1 lb. dark brown soft sugar
¼ teaspoon grated nutmeg
1 sherry glass rum
8 oz. best fresh butter
icing sugar for dusting

Melt the butter very slowly, do not let it froth. Put the sugar in a bowl, add the nutmeg. Pour in the rum and mix well. Pour the melted butter over the sugar mixture and beat for 10 minutes until it begins to set. Turn into a pretty china bowl and sprinkle with icing sugar. Delicious with unsweetened biscuits and bread and butter at tea time.

GOOSEBERRY SAUCE

½ pint young green gooseberries
¼ pint water
1 oz. butter
1 oz. sugar
salt, pepper
¼ teaspoon ground nutmegs
cooked sorrel or spinach leaves

Boil the gooseberries in the water for 4 or 5 minutes, till tender and mushy. Drain and sieve them. Add a tablespoon of sorrel leaves chopped finely, the butter, sugar, salt and pepper to taste and the nutmeg. Re-heat and serve with mackerel or other fish.

If wished, this concentrated sauce may be mixed with ¼ pint white sauce.

HARD SAUCE

4 oz. castor sugar
2 oz. butter
1 egg white, stiffly beaten
2 tablespoons brandy

Cream the sugar and butter. Add the egg white, mix well, then the brandy. Stir all together. Serve very cold.

HORSERADISH SAUCE (1)

4 tablespoons finely grated horse-
    radish
1 teaspoon sugar
1 teaspoon salt
½ teaspoon mustard
1 teaspoon pepper
2 tablespoons vinegar

3 tablespoons cream

Heat the vinegar in an enamel saucepan, add the sugar, salt, mustard and pepper, stir over a very low heat for 2 minutes, add the horseradish and cook for a further 2 minutes, cool, then add the cream. Stir well and serve cold.

HORSERADISH SAUCE (2)

2 tablespoons finely grated
    horseradish
¼ teaspoon made mustard
¼ pint cream
1 tablespoon white wine vinegar
2 tablespoons castor sugar

½ teaspoon salt
¼ teaspoon pepper

Mix the horseradish with the sugar, salt and pepper, mustard and vinegar. Whip the cream and stir gradually into the mixture. Serve very cold.

ONION SAUCE

2 oz. butter
2 oz. flour } white sauce
1 pint hot milk
¼ teaspoon ground nutmeg
3 large finely chopped onions
salt, pepper

Cover the onions with water, salt and pepper to taste, bring to the boil and simmer till tender. Add to the white sauce, season with salt and pepper, if necessary, add the nutmeg. Stir well. Serve hot.

MINT SAUCE

2 level tablespoons finely chopped
    mint
¼ pint white wine vinegar
3 oz. sugar
½ teaspoon salt

2 tablespoons water

Boil the sugar, vinegar, water and salt for 4 minutes, pour over the chopped mint, cover tightly while cooling. Stir well before serving, when quite cold.

RED CURRANT JELLY

1 lb. sugar to 1 pint juice

Pick the fruit off the stems and wash it. Put it in a large basin or casserole, stand this in a saucepan of simmering water and steam for several hours until all the juice has run out of the currants or leave in a cool oven; the length of time depends, naturally, on how many pounds of fruit you have.

Pour the currants into a jelly bag — one made of thick flannel is best — and leave them to drain until they stop dripping. Measure the juice. For each pint take 1 lb. sugar. Put both in the preserving pan, bring to the boil and boil for 5 minutes, or until the jelly sets. Bottle at once in warm jars and seal.

SAGE AND ONION STUFFING

1 lb. chopped onions
boiling water
1 teaspoon salt
pinch of pepper
4 oz. breadcrumbs
1 teaspoon finely chopped sage
1 oz. butter

Put the onions and salt in a small pan and just cover with boiling water, simmer for 8 to 10 minutes till tender, add the breadcrumbs, sage and pepper, and butter, stir to make a smooth 'dryish' mixture.

PUFF PASTRY

1 lb. flour
2 8-oz. blocks of butter
  or margarine
1 egg yolk
the juice of 1 lemon
¼ pint cold water

Ingredients, utensils and hands must be cold. Sieve the flour into a basin. Beat the egg. Cut the butter into small dice and with the finger tips mix with the flour, but do not rub it in. Add the beaten egg, water and lemon juice spoon by spoon, mix quickly and lightly until the dough leaves the sides of the basin. Turn on a floured board and roll quickly all over into an oblong, rolling with quick short pushing strokes away from you. Fold the pastry in three, top edge a third down, and bottom edge over the two thicknesses, making three thicknesses. Turn the pastry round on the board, folded edges at the sides, and repeat the process of rolling. Repeat twice more, four times in all. Put into a very cold place and leave for at least an hour before using.

WHITE SAUCE

(This is the basis for many sweet and savoury sauces)

2 *oz. butter*
2 *oz. flour*
1 *pint hot milk*
½ *oz. butter*

Melt the butter in a saucepan, stir in the flour with a wooden spoon on a low heat, pour over the hot milk gradually, stirring all the time, till smooth and creamy, cook gently for a further 2 or 3 minutes. Stir in the ½ oz. butter before serving.

DUMPLINGS

4 *oz. flour*
2 *oz. chopped suet*
¼ *teaspoon baking powder*
1 *medium finely chopped onion*
1 *teaspoon finely chopped parsley*
1 *teaspoon salt*
¼ *teaspoon pepper*
cold water to mix
plenty of boiling water or stock to boil

Mix all the ingredients together in a basin, add a little cold water, teaspoon by teaspoon to make a soft but firm dough: when it comes cleanly away from the sides of the basin it is right. Roll into 12 small balls. Have the water or meat stock, as in Boiled Silverside, boiling; put in the dumplings and cook, uncovered, for 20 to 30 minutes till dry inside and nicely swollen in size.

SHORT CRUST PASTRY

8 *oz. flour*
¼ *teaspoon baking powder*
¼ *teaspoon salt*
4 *oz. butter, lard or dripping*
cold water

Sieve the flour, baking powder and salt together, rub the fat in lightly with the fingers till the mixture looks like breadcrumbs. Add enough — only a little — cold water to make stiff paste that comes cleanly away from the sides of the basin. Roll out at once. Work quickly throughout the proceeding.

SUET CRUST

8 *oz. flour*
4 *oz. chopped suet*
1 *ievel teaspoon baking powder*
½ *level teaspoon salt*
cold water

Sift the flour, salt and baking powder, add the suet and mix well. Add a little cold water gradually and mix well until the paste forms a soft dough. When it leaves the sides of the basin cleanly, it is done.

YORKSHIRE PUDDING

1 *pint milk*
4 *oz. flour*
2 *eggs, beaten*
½ *teaspoon salt*
1 *oz. dripping*

Sift the flour and salt, add the milk gradually, stirring all the time till quite smooth, then stir in the beaten eggs. Always make this batter at least an hour before it is to be cooked.

Melt the dripping in a shallow baking tin in the oven; when smoking hot, stir the mixture and pour in the batter. Cook in a moderate-to-hot oven for 30 minutes. A most delicious way of cooking this batter is to place the tin in which it is to be cooked under the meat which is roasting on the oven shelf. The essence of the meat drips into the pan and the batter is put in the tin 30 minutes before the meat is fully cooked. This, however, means a roast with no separately served meat gravy.

APPLE CHARLOTTE

1 *lb. cooking apples, peeled and cored*
8 *oz. sugar*
rind and juice of ½ a lemon
2 *oz. butter*
3 *tablespoons apricot jam*
¼ *teaspoon cinnamon*
2 *oz. almonds, skinned*
puff pastry (see p. 205)

Cut the apples in ½-inch dice, put in a saucepan, add the sugar, lemon rind and juice, butter, jam and cinnamon. Cook very slowly, stirring all the time until the apples are soft. Add the almonds.

Line a pie-dish, preferably one with straight sides, with puff pastry. Pour in the mixture. Bake in a moderate oven for 45 minutes. Serve with cream or hard sauce (see p. 204).

APPLE DUMPLINGS

4 *cooking apples, peeled, cored and halved*
2 *teaspoons sugar*
1 *teaspoon cinnamon*
½ *oz. butter*
8 *oz. self-raising flour*
¼ *teaspoon salt*
2 *oz. butter*
milk

Sift the flour and salt, add the 2 oz. butter and mix till the mixture is like fine breadcrumbs. Add enough milk to make a soft dough. Roll till ⅜ inch thick. Cut 8 squares large enough to hold half an apple. Mix the sugar, cinnamon and ½ oz. butter. Put an equal amount on each apple half. Wrap the apples in the dough, moisten and seal well. Steam for 45 minutes or till the apple is soft. Serve with cream or hard sauce (see p. 204).

BAKEWELL TART

short crust pastry (see p. 206)
  with 1 oz. sugar added
4 oz. flour
2 teaspoons baking powder
pinch salt
2½ oz. cooking fat or butter
3 oz. castor sugar
2 eggs

3 dessertspoons milk
½ teaspoon almond essence
raspberry jam

Roll out the pastry and line a 7-inch flan tin. Put a little jam in the bottom. Sift the flour, baking powder, salt and sugar in a bowl, then rub in the butter or the cooking fat, eggs, milk and almond essence. Stir until smooth and pour into pastry case. Bake for 30 minutes in a moderate oven.

NORFOLK PUDDING

Yorkshire pudding batter
  (see p. 207)
1 lb. cooking apples
2 oz. sugar
1 oz. lard

Peel and slice apples. Heat fat in a shallow baking tin and place the apples in it. Add sugar, then cover with the batter mixture and bake in a hot oven for 30 minutes.

SPOTTED DICK

8 oz. self-raising flour
4 oz. chopped suet
3 oz. sugar
pinch salt
4 oz. currants
milk

Add suet, sugar and currants to sieved flour and salt and mix with sufficient milk to make a soft dough. Grease and flour a pudding cloth and place the dough, moulded into a roll, on this. Roll up and tie at both ends, leaving room for the pudding to swell. Steam for 3 hours. Serve with custard.

SCOTS CREAM-CROWDIE

1 pint double cream
2 oz. coarse oatmeal
2 oz. castor sugar
1 tablespoon rum
4 oz. fresh raspberries or blackberries

Toss the oatmeal in a thick-bottomed saucepan over the fire for a few moments. Beat cream to a thick froth and stir in the oatmeal, sugar, rum and fresh fruit. Serve at once.

AUNT NELLY PUDDING

8 oz. *chopped suet*
8 oz. *golden syrup*
8 oz. *plain flour, sifted*
juice and grated rind of 1 *lemon*
3 *tablespoons milk*
2 *eggs, beaten*

Add the syrup to the suet and stand in very hot water, or in a cool oven till the suet begins to melt. Beat well till the mixture forms a smooth cream. Add the rind and the juice of the lemon, stir in the flour, the eggs and the milk. Pour into a buttered basin and cover tightly with greased paper. Steam for 4 hours.

A sauce made with 3 tablespoons warmed syrup diluted with 1 tablespoon warm water may be served with this.

BREAD AND BUTTER PUDDING

4 *slices of bread*
2 oz. *butter*
2 oz. *currants*
1 oz. *sultanas*
3 *tablespoons sugar*
4 *eggs, well beaten*
1⅛ *pints milk*
grated lemon rind to taste
½ *teaspoon nutmeg*

Remove the crusts and butter each slice of bread. Cover the bottom of a greased dish with slices, sprinkle over some of the fruit and 2 tablespoons sugar. Repeat until bread and fruit and sugar are finished. Mix the eggs well into the milk, add the lemon rind and pour into the dish. And, this is important, leave for 2 hours. Sprinkle 1 tablespoon sugar and nutmeg on top and bake in a very slow oven for 1 hour or till the custard is set.

COLD LEMON WHIP (uncooked)

3 *eggs*
2 *teaspoons powdered gelatine*
1 *tablespoon cold water*
2 *tablespoons hot water*
6 oz. *castor sugar*
grated rind of 1 *lemon*
5 *tablespoons lemon juice*

Soak the gelatine in the cold water for 10 minutes. Separate the eggs. Beat the yolks with the lemon rind and sugar till creamy, add the lemon juice. Pour the hot water over the gelatine, stir till dissolved and add to the yolk mixture. Mix well. Whip the egg whites till stiff, fold lightly into the yolk mixture until completely mixed. Turn into a mould or glass dish. Chill and serve with sweetened cream, if possible.

LEMON SOUFFLÉ

5 *eggs*
2 *lemons*
8 oz. *icing sugar*

Sieve the sugar. Separate the eggs, beat the whites until stiff. Grate the peel of 1 lemon, and squeeze the juice from both. Add the peel and the juice to the egg yolks, stir in the sugar and whip till creamy. Fold in the stiff whites. Put in a buttered soufflé dish and bake in a moderate-to-hot oven for 20 minutes. Serve at once.

DUKE OF CAMBRIDGE PUDDING

short crust or puff pastry
  (see pp. 205, 206)
3 oz. butter
3 oz. castor sugar
2 egg yolks
2 oz. finely chopped candied peel

Line a shallow dish or flan ring with the pastry. Cover the bottom with the candied peel. Melt the butter in a saucepan, add the sugar, stir till melted, add the egg yolks and bring to the boil. Pour, at once, over the candied peel and cook in a slow oven till the top is nicely browned and crinkled.

GOOSEBERRY FOOL

1 lb. green gooseberries
4 oz. sugar
¼ pint water
½ pint cream or 2 bottles of
  yoghourt (in which case use
  6 oz. sugar)

Stew the gooseberries, water and sugar till tender. Sieve them and add the cream, whipped, or the yoghourt. Sponge fingers or digestive biscuits are good served with this.

QUEEN OF PUDDINGS

4 oz. fine white breadcrumbs
3 eggs, the yolks and whites
  separated
1 whole egg, beaten
1 pint milk
3 or 4 tablespoons raspberry jam
3 tablespoons castor sugar

Beat the 3 yolks and the 1 egg, add to the milk and mix well. Add the breadcrumbs. Put the jam on the bottom of a pie dish, making a layer of about ½ inch. Pour over the milk, egg and crumb custard and leave for 30 minutes. Bake in a very cool oven for 1 hour, till set. Whip the whites very stiffly, add the sugar. Pile on top of the custard, sprinkle a little sugar on top and put back in the very cool oven till the meringue is set and delicately browned.

GUARDS PUDDING

4 oz. flour
4 oz. butter
4 oz. castor sugar
2 eggs
2 oz. white breadcrumbs
2 tablespoons sieved raspberry jam
  or raspberry jelly
pinch of bicarbonate of soda

SAUCE:
3 tablespoons raspberry jam
3 tablespoons water
1 teaspoon lemon juice

Butter a soufflé dish and put a round of buttered paper on the bottom. Cut another round of paper to be tied over the top of the dish.

Cream the butter and sugar till quite white and fluffy. Beat in 1 egg, half the flour and half the breadcrumbs, then the other egg and the rest of the flour and breadcrumbs and the bicarbonate. Add the sieved jam or jelly. Pour into the dish. Tie over the buttered paper. Steam for 1½ hours. When done leave cooling for 8 minutes before turning out.

Make the sauce by heating all the ingredients mixed together. Sieve and serve separately.

RHUBARB PUDDING

short crust pastry
12 oz. rhubarb, finely chopped
2 oz. flour
4 oz. soft brown sugar
grated rind of ½ lemon
3 tablespoons thick cream

Line a plate with pastry. Cover with the rhubarb mixed with the cream, sugar and rind. Bake in a moderately hot oven for 10 minutes, lower the heat and cook till the mixture is firm and the top crisp, about 25 minutes. Serve with whipped cream if possible.

RUM BUMBLE PUDDING

¾ tablespoon gelatine
water
4 oz. sugar
2 tablespoons rum
2 egg whites, beaten stiff
¼ pint cream
almonds, skinned and chopped

Soak the gelatine in a basin in 1 tablespoon cold water, then dissolve in 3 tablespoons boiling water. Add the sugar and rum. Stir till the sugar is dissolved. Strain and leave to cool.

When the mixture begins to set, whisk until frothy, add the egg whites and the cream gradually, whisk all together. Chill and serve sprinkled with almonds.

Skin the almonds by placing in boiling water for 1 or 2 minutes, when the brown skins will come off easily.

PLUM PUDDING (1)

10 oz. chopped suet
10 oz. breadcrumbs
5 oz. flour
8 oz. raisins, seedless and washed
10 oz. sultanas, washed
5 oz. chopped apples
4 eggs
5 oz. candied peel, chopped small
1 oz. chopped almonds
grated rind and juice of ¼ lemon
½ teaspoon nutmeg
3 oz. brown sugar
¼ teaspoon salt
1 sherry glass rum

½ sherry glass sherry
1 sherry glass stout

Soak the raisins and sultanas in the rum and sherry. Sieve the flour, add the breadcrumbs, suet, salt, sugar, lemon rind, almonds, nutmeg, peel, apples and the fruit and rum mixture. Beat the eggs, add to the stout and lemon juice, stir well. Add gradually to the flour mixture, stirring for a long time till completely and well mixed. Put the mixture into greased basins. Tie two layers of greaseproof paper firmly over the top of each basin and tie the whole in a cloth. Boil for 6 hours.

This pudding will keep for months. Before using boil again for 3 hours.

Serve with brandy butter (see p. 202).

PLUM PUDDING (2)

8 oz. flour
8 oz. grated suet
8 oz. brown sugar
4 oz. breadcrumbs
2 teaspoons mixed spice
2 teaspoons cinnamon
2 teaspoons nutmeg
juice and grated rind of 1 lemon
juice and grated rind of 1 orange
2 tablespoons golden syrup
4 eggs
½ pint ale or beer
1 grated carrot
8 oz. grated apple
8 oz. mixed candied peel
1 lb. raisins

2 oz. dried chopped apricots
2 oz. stoned chopped prunes
8 oz. chopped blanched almonds
8 oz. currants
8 oz. sultanas

This recipe makes 3—4 puddings. Clean fruit, grate the carrot, chop peel and nuts and beat eggs. Mix all the ingredients well together, stir thoroughly and leave for 12 hours. Stir again, then put the mixture into well-greased pudding basins, cover with cloth or greaseproof paper, boil for 4—6 hours. Remove covers and put on dry covers. Store the puddings for several weeks before eating. Steam or boil for a further 2—3 hours on the day they are to be eaten. Serve with hard sauce or rum sauce (see p. 204 and below).

RUM SAUCE

½ oz. cornflour
½ pint water
1 tablespoon sugar
¼ teaspoon cinnamon
1 tablespoon rum
1 oz. butter

Mix cornflour with a little cold water, pour on the rest of the boiling water to make a sauce. Add sugar, cinnamon, rum and butter cut in pieces. Stir gently until boiling.

ANGUS TOFFEE

1½ lb. sugar
2 oz. ground almonds
1 oz. butter
¼ pint milk

Melt the butter in a saucepan, stir in the ground almonds, sugar and milk and bring to the boil. Stirring well all the time, boil for 7 minutes, then remove from heat and stir for 2 more minutes. When thick pour into a shallow buttered tin and cut up when cold.

GOOSEBERRY PUDDING

FRUIT MIXTURE:
12 *oz. gooseberries*
3 *oz. butter*
3 *oz. soft brown sugar*
1 *oz. chopped nuts*

CAKE MIXTURE:
4 *oz. self-raising flour*
¼ *teaspoon salt*
4 *oz. castor sugar*

4 *oz. butter*
2 *eggs, beaten*

Wash and prepare the fruit. Melt the 3 oz. butter, add the brown sugar, stir well, add the nuts. Butter a deep fireproof dish and pour in this mixture. Place the gooseberries in a layer on top. Sieve the flour and the salt. Cream the 4 oz. butter with the castor sugar, add the eggs and flour gradually, stirring well. Pour over the fruit and bake in a moderate oven for 35 minutes. When done turn the pudding on to a dish so that the gooseberries are on top.

SUMMER PUDDING

currants, black, red or white,
strawberries, raspberries
1½ *lb. ought to be enough*
for 4 people
slices of stale white bread,
crusts removed
sugar to taste

Choose a soufflé dish or basin that will half fill with the fruit. Butter the bottom and sides and line with the slices of bread, so that they just overlap. Add enough sugar to taste to the fruit in a saucepan and heat until the sugar melts and the juice begins to run, but do not boil. Pour the fruit into the lined dish, cover the top with bread. Put a plate or saucer on top and a heavy weight on this. Leave overnight in a cold place.

Serve very cold with whipped cream.

TRIFLE

3 *small sponge cakes*
6 *macaroons*
¼ *pint medium sweet sherry*
3 *tablespoons brandy*
2 *oz. blanched almonds, cut*
in strips
strawberry jam
½ *pint custard*
¼ *pint cream*

¾ *oz. sugar*
1 *white of egg*

Put the sponge cakes and macaroons in a dish, pour over the brandy and sherry, keeping back 1 teaspoon, leave to soak for 10 minutes. Cover with a thick layer of strawberry jam. Pour over the cooled custard. Whisk the cream, sugar, egg white and 1 teaspoon sherry till fluffy, cover the cake and jam mixture. Stick the almond strips all over the cream mixture. Serve cold.

WHIPPED RASPBERRIES

1 *lb. raspberries*
1 *lb. sugar*
2 *egg whites*

Bruise the fruit with a wooden spoon, add the sugar. Stir well. Beat the egg whites till stiff, stir into the raspberry mixture and beat with the egg whisk till everything is well mixed. Serve cold with cream.

CHRISTMAS CAKE

1 *lb. seedless raisins*
1 *lb. currants*
2 *oz. almonds, shredded*
3 *oz. glacé cherries, chopped*
4 *oz. mixed peel, chopped*
8 *oz. flour*
8 *oz. butter*
8 *oz. soft brown sugar*
1 *tablespoon black treacle*
grated rind of 1 orange and
   1 lemon
¼ *teaspoon mixed spice, cinnamon,*
   nutmeg and ginger
a few drops of vanilla essence
4 *eggs*
¼ *pint brandy or sherry*
almond paste
royal icing

Line an 8-inch cake tin with 1 layer of brown and 2 layers of greaseproof paper to come 2 inches higher than the tin.

Wash and dry the fruit. Take a large basin, put in the fruit, almonds, cherries, peel and 1 tablespoon flour. Mix well.

In another basin cream the butter and sugar, add treacle, orange and lemon rinds, essence and the spices. Beat well, then add the eggs, one by one, beating between each. Sieve the flour and add with the fruit mixture. Pour in 2 tablespoons of brandy or sherry and mix well. Pour into the tin, make a hollow in the middle, for a flat top result. Tie a band of newspaper round the tin and bake in a slow oven for 1½ hours, reduce the heat to very slow and cook for a further 4 hours. Test with a skewer or knife, which will come out clean if the cake is done.

Leave the cake in the tin for 40 minutes, turn upside down, prick deeply with a skewer and pour over the remaining sherry or brandy and let it run into the cake.

Cover with almond paste and royal icing (see p. 215).

ALMOND PASTE

2 *eggs*
4 *oz. castor sugar*
4 *oz. icing sugar*
8 *oz. ground almonds*
4 *drops lemon juice*
3 *drops almond essence*
1 *dessertspoon brandy or sherry*
2 *tablespoons warm apricot jam*

Spread the warm jam on top of the cake. Beat the eggs with the sugars in a basin over hot water till light and fluffy. Cool, add the almonds, lemon juice, almond essence and brandy.

Roll out to fit the top of the cake. These quantities are sufficient for 8-inch diameter cake.

ROYAL ICING

8 *oz. icing sugar*
1 *egg white*
1 *teaspoon lemon juice*
a drop of laundry blue (optional)

Sieve the icing sugar, beat the egg white not stiffly, but till no longer slimy. Add gradually to the sugar, beating all the time, also the lemon juice and blue, if any. Beat for 20 minutes. Spread over the cake, smoothing on at the end with a stainless steel knife dipped in boiling water.

CORNISH SPLITS

1½ *lb. flour*
4 *oz. butter*
1 *oz. lard*
1 *oz. yeast*
½ *teaspoon sugar*
¼ *pint warm water*
¼ *pint milk*
cream
jam

Put the yeast, sugar and 1 teaspoon flour in a basin, pour on the warm water, mix well and leave in a warm place for 15 minutes. Sieve the flour in a large basin and leave in a warm place. Heat the milk gently, add the lard and butter, leave to melt.

Make a well in the middle of the flour and gradually pour in the yeast water and the warmed milk, and butter and lard, mixing all to a soft dough. Leave in a warm place for 1½ hours to rise. Knead for 4 minutes, roll out ½ inch thick. Cut in pieces and form small balls about the size and shape of a tangerine, or small rissole. Bake in a moderate oven for 20 to 30 minutes till golden brown. Serve cold, split in half, and filled with Cornish cream and jam, especially raspberry.

SPONGE CAKE

8 *eggs*
the weight of the eggs in castor
  sugar
the weight of 5 eggs in flour
the grated rind and juice of
  1 *lemon*

Butter a large cake tin and sift sugar all over the inside. Put the sieved flour on a piece of paper in a cool oven to warm.

Put the sugar in a basin, add the yolks of 4 eggs and 4 whole eggs. Beat the 4 whites very stiffly in another basin. Stand the basin with the sugar and egg yolks over nearly boiling water, grate the lemon rind on to them and whisk for 15 minutes, add the lemon juice, then the stiff whites and lastly the flour, stirring it in as lightly and quickly as possible. Bake in a moderate oven for 1¼ hours.

DIGESTIVE BISCUITS

4 *oz. butter*
1 *lb. wholemeal flour*
1 *beaten egg*
1 *oz. sugar*
pinch of bicarbonate of soda
½ *pint cold water*
1 *teaspoon milk*

Rub the butter well into the flour. Mix the soda in the milk. Add this to the eggs and the sugar, mix well. Gradually pour in the water, mixing quickly. Roll out on a floured board as thick as a penny. Cut into rounds, prick all over with a fork and bake in a moderate-to-cool oven for 25 minutes.

VICTORIA SANDWICH CAKE

6 *oz. flour, self-raising*
6 *oz. castor sugar*
6 *oz. butter*
3 *eggs*
grated rind and juice of ½ *lemon*
2 *tablespoons raspberry, strawberry*
  or apricot jam

Grease two cake tins and dredge them with flour. Sieve the flour. Cream the butter and sugar till fluffy, add the flour and eggs spoonful by spoonful, beating all the time, and lemon rind and juice. Pour into the tins, bake in a moderate oven for 20 minutes. When done turn out on a wire rack. Spread one cake with jam and place the other on top.

JUMBLES

5 *oz. sugar*
5 *oz. butter*
1 *egg*
10 *oz. flour*
1 *teaspoon grated lemon rind*
2 *oz. ground almonds*

Cream the butter and sugar, add half the egg, stir in the sieved flour, lemon rind, almonds and the rest of the egg. Form the mixture into rolls the thickness of a finger, shape as the letter 'S', place on a greased baking sheet and bake in a moderate oven for 10 minutes.

PARKIN

1 *lb. flour*
12 *oz. medium oatmeal*
4 *oz. butter*
1 *teaspoon salt*
2 *oz. sugar*
8 *oz. syrup*
8 *oz. treacle*
½ *pint milk*
½ *teaspoon bicarbonate of soda*
1 *teaspoon ground ginger*
1 *egg*

Dissolve the soda in the milk. Melt the treacle, syrup and butter together. Beat the egg. Mix all the dry ingredients together, pour in the melted butter and treacle and syrup, stir well, add the egg, then the milk, stirring all well together.

Bake in a flat square greased tin for 45 minutes in a moderate oven. Turn out of the tin when cold. Half these quantities may be used, as this makes a big cake, but it keeps well and matures by keeping.

DUNDEE CAKE

10 *oz. flour*
8 *oz. butter*
4 *eggs*
8 *oz. sugar*
1½ *lb. mixed dried fruit*
2 *oz. cherries*
2 *oz. candied peel*
2 *oz. chopped almonds*
2 *tablespoons milk*
1 *teaspoon mixed spice*
split almonds to decorate
egg white to glaze

Cream butter and sugar and add beaten egg. Sieve flour and spice and add to the mixture, with the milk. Flour the cherries, fruit and chopped peel and stir in with the chopped almonds. Pour the mixture into a greased and floured 8-inch cake tin and decorate the top with split almonds. Brush with beaten egg white. Bake in a very moderate oven for 3—3½ hours.

WALNUT LAYER CAKE

12 *oz. self-raising flour*
8 *oz. butter*
8 *oz. sugar*
4 *eggs*
4 *oz. chopped walnuts*
milk to mix

BUTTER FILLING:

4 *oz. butter*
6 *oz. icing sugar*
1 *tablespoon strong black coffee*
  or coffee essence

ICING:

10 *oz. icing sugar*
3 *tablespoons coffee*
walnuts to decorate

Cream butter and sugar, then beat in the eggs. Fold in the sieved flour and chopped nuts, adding sufficient milk to give a soft dropping consistency. Grease and line two sandwich tins and divide the mixture between them. Bake in a moderate oven for 30—35 minutes. When cold split each cake and spread each layer with butter filling. Make this by creaming together butter and icing sugar, then beating in coffee essence. To make icing for the top of the cake, heat the icing sugar and flavouring very gently, stirring until the icing is smooth and glossy. Ice the cake and decorate with halved walnuts.

SHREWSBURY BISCUITS

8 oz. flour
½ teaspoon baking powder
grated rind of 1 lemon
4 oz. sugar
4 oz. butter
1 egg
2 oz. currants

Cream together butter and sugar. Add grated lemon rind and beaten egg, then sifted flour, baking powder and currants. Knead and roll out thinly. Prick and cut into rounds. Bake in a moderate oven for 15 minutes.

BRANDY SNAPS

2 oz. plain flour
3 oz. butter or cooking fat
2 oz. sugar
3 oz. golden syrup
1 teaspoon ground ginger
whipped cream

Melt syrup, sugar and fat in a pan, cool slightly then stir in flour and ginger. Mix well and place teaspoons of the mixture well apart on greased baking sheets. Bake in a moderate oven for 10—15 minutes. Remove with a palette knife when they are just beginning to get crisp, and roll up — an easy way to do this is round the greased handle of a wooden spoon. When cold fill with whipped cream.

MINCE PIES

puff or short crust pastry
  (see pp. 205, 206)
mincemeat
castor sugar
brandy

Roll out pastry to ⅛ inch thick and cut out lids for individual pies. Then fold up trimmings, roll out ⅛ inch thick, and cut out rounds to line patty tins. Fill generously with mincemeat and sprinkle each pie filling with a little brandy. Damp the edges with cold water then press together. Sprinkle with castor sugar and bake in a hot oven for 10—15 minutes.

SCOTCH SHORTBREAD

6 oz. flour
4 oz. butter
2 oz. castor sugar
pinch salt

Mix flour and salt and rub in butter and sugar. Knead to a dough, then roll out and form into a round cake. Crimp the edges, prick all over with a fork and mark into portions with a knife before baking. Place on a baking sheet lined with greased paper and bake in a slow oven for 1 hour. Dredge with castor sugar.

HOT CROSS BUNS

1 *lb. flour*
1 *oz. yeast*
½ *teaspoon salt*
3 *teaspoons sugar*
2 *oz. lard*
½—¾ *pint lukewarm milk*
1 *teaspoon mixed spice*
1 *oz. candied peel*
2 *oz. currants*

Warm flour, spice and salt. Cream yeast and sugar. Rub fat into flour, then add candied peel and currants. Make a well in the centre. Add yeast and liquid and mix to a soft dough, just firm enough to be shaped after it has risen. Beat the dough well until it is smooth and elastic. Put to rise in a warm place until it is twice its size — this will take about 45 minutes. Knead and shape into buns. Flatten slightly and make a deep cross on top with a knife. Allow to rise again in a warm place for 15 minutes. Bake in a hot oven for 20 minutes, lowering the heat slightly after 5 minutes. Rub over with butter to glaze.

SALLY LUNN

1 *lb. flour*
2 *oz. butter*
1 *oz. sugar*
1 *oz. yeast*
½ *pint milk*
1 *egg*
pinch salt

Sieve flour and salt. Cream the yeast and sugar, then stir in the warm milk and pour into a well in the centre of the flour. Add the beaten egg and butter and mix to a soft dough. Grease large round patty tins and half fill with the dough. Leave in a warm place until the dough has doubled its size (about 30 minutes), then bake in a hot oven for 15—20 minutes.

CHELSEA BUNS

4 *oz. butter*
2 *eggs*
4 *oz. castor sugar*
¼ *pint milk*
½ *oz. yeast*
2 *eggs*
1 *lb. flour*
3 *oz. currants*
lard

Warm together butter, 3 oz. sugar and all but 1 tablespoon of the milk. Cream the yeast with this. Add the warmed ingredients and creamed yeast to the sieved flour, together with beaten eggs. Mix all together. Put to rise in a warm place until the dough has doubled in size. Roll out to an oblong, brush with lard, sprinkle on fruit and the rest of the sugar, and roll up. Cut slices 1 inch thick and place close together on a greased baking sheet. Leave for 20 minutes, then bake in a hot oven for 15—20 minutes. A few minutes before removing from the oven, brush over with a sugar and water glaze.

FRUIT SCONES

8 *oz. self-raising flour*
2 *oz. butter or cooking fat*
pinch salt
2 *oz. sugar*
1 *egg*
2 *oz. sultanas*
milk to mix

Sieve flour and salt and rub in fat. Add sugar and cleaned dried sultanas, beaten egg and sufficient milk to make a soft dough. Roll out on a floured board and stamp in rounds ½-inch thick. Bake in a hot oven for 10—15 minutes.

WHOLEMEAL SCONES

8 *oz. wholemeal flour*
pinch salt
2 *oz. butter or cooking fat*
1 *level teaspoon bicarbonate of soda*
2 *level teaspoons cream of tartar*
1 *oz. sugar*
milk to mix
egg to glaze

Sieve dry ingredients, rub in fat and sugar, then add sufficient milk to make a soft dough. Roll out and cut into rounds, brush with a little beaten egg and bake for 10 minutes in a hot oven.

DROP SCONES

3 *oz. self-raising flour*
1 *oz. cooking fat*
1 *egg*
½ *oz. sugar*
pinch salt
4 *tablespoons milk*
fat for frying

Beat the egg and add flour, milk, salt and sugar gradually to make a batter. Beat for 1 minute. Drop spoonfuls of the mixture either on to a greased hotplate or into a lightly greased frying pan. Cook till bubbles appear on surface, then turn and cook on the other side until golden brown. Keep the scones in a linen cloth as you cook them; this keeps in the steam and prevents their becoming dry.

ECCLES CAKES

1 *lb. puff pastry*
  (see p. 205)
4 *oz. jam*
8 *oz. currants*
2 *oz. butter*
2 *oz. chopped candied peel*
½ *teaspoon mixed spice*
sugar to coat

Melt butter and add jam, washed dried currants, chopped peel and mixed spice. Heat gently in a saucepan. Roll out the pastry thinly, cut into squares and when cool place a spoonful of filling in the centre of each square. Pinch together edges of pastry over the filling to make a round flat cake. Brush with water, sprinkle with sugar and make two cuts in the top of each cake. Bake in a hot oven for 10—15 minutes.

STRAWBERRY JAM

5 *lb. strawberries*
5 *lb. sugar*
juice of 4 lemons

Cook fruit and juice until tender. Add sugar, dissolve and boil up for 15—20 minutes until it will set. Cool slightly, stir, and pour into jars.

GOOSEBERRY JAM

3 *lb. gooseberries*
3 *lb. sugar*
1 *pint water*

Stew fruit and water until tender and broken. Add sugar, dissolve and boil until it will set when tested.

BLACKCURRANT JAM

4 *lb. blackcurrants*
4 *lb. sugar*
2 *pints water*

Simmer fruit and water until fruit is tender, then add sugar, dissolve and boil until it will set.

RHUBARB AND GINGER JAM

4 *lb. rhubarb*
3 *lb. sugar*
2 *teaspoons ground ginger*
1 *teaspoon citric acid*

Cut up rhubarb and arrange fruit and sugar in layers in a bowl. Leave to stand for 12 hours. Then place in a pan, add acid and ginger and boil for 10—15 minutes until the jam will set.

QUINCE JELLY

quinces
water
sugar

Peel washed quinces. Weigh the parings and put into a pan with ½ pint water to each lb. parings. Boil until soft. Place the sliced fruit in another pan and strain the liquid over, adding enough water to cover the fruit. Simmer gently until the fruit is soft. Strain through a jelly bag, leaving overnight. Next day add 1 lb. sugar to each pint of juice. Stir these together, then boil rapidly until jelly sets when tested (about 15 minutes).

CRANBERRY CHEESE

1 *pint cranberries*
½ *pint water*
12 *oz. sugar*
2 *oz. seedless raisins, chopped*
2 *oz. walnuts, chopped*
1 *orange, peeled and thinly sliced*

Cook the cranberries in the water till soft. Sieve them. Add the sugar, raisins and walnuts. Bring slowly to the boil, stirring all the time, add the orange. Simmer for 20 minutes. Pour into jars and seal.

DAMSON OR BULLACE CHEESE

12 *oz. sugar to* 1 *pint pulp*

Cook the fruit slowly till soft, either in a saucepan, no water added, or in a slow oven. Sieve the fruit. Add ¾ to 1 lb. sugar to every 1 pint of pulp. Bring to the boil stirring all the time, until it stiffens and grows thick. Pour into warm jars and seal.

Crack the stones and boil the kernels with the sugar and pulp to make it most delicious.

LEMON CURD OR CHEESE

6 *oz. castor sugar*
4 *egg yolks*
1 *egg white*
grated rind and juice of 1 *large*
lemon
2 *oz. butter*

Whip the egg yolks and white very well. Melt the butter, sugar, lemon rind and juice in a saucepan, add the eggs, mix well and cook very slowly, stirring all the time till thick, for about 15 minutes preferably over boiling water in a double saucepan. If over-heated or not stirred, the eggs will scramble and the curd be ruined.

Pour into pots and seal with paper if not to be eaten at once.

DARK COARSE MARMALADE

1 *lb. Seville oranges*
2 *pints water*
2 *lb. Demerara sugar*
1 *teaspoon lemon juice*

Wash the oranges. Put in the preserving pan, cover with the water and cook very slowly till the oranges are soft throughout. Remove, cool and cut into ½-inch squares. Save the pips, add these to the orange liquid and simmer for 10 minutes. Strain, throw away the pips. Add the sugar and orange pieces and lemon juice to the liquid. Stir gently till the sugar has dissolved, bring to the boil, boil rapidly for 15 minutes. Test for setting. When 'jelled' leave to cool for 15 minutes. Stir well, pour into warm jars and seal.

JAPONICA JELLY

These fruits of the garden shrub make a tart amber-coloured jelly. They are of the quince family, and are excellent eaten with cold meats.

Cut the fruits in quarters, unpeeled and uncored, cover with water and cook till soft. Strain overnight or for 12 hours in a flannel jelly-bag. Take 1 lb. sugar for 1 lb. juice. Warm the sugar, bring the juice to the boil, add the sugar, stir till the sugar is dissolved, bring to the boil and boil for 15 minutes. Test, pour into jars and seal.

RHUBARB WINE

5 *lb. rhubarb*
1 *gallon water*
3 *lb. loaf or preserving sugar*
⅜ *oz. isinglass*
grated rind and juice of 1 *lemon*

Wash the rhubarb and cut into ½-inch slices. Put into a large basin and press and pound them well, pour in the water. Cover the basin, leave for 10 days, stirring once a day. Strain it, add the sugar and stir till dissolved, with the lemon juice and rind. Add the isinglass, stir well and pour into the cask. Leave uncorked for 10 days, but cover the bung hole with a folded cloth. After 10 days cork tightly. Drink it after 12 months.

HOT CIDER AND RUM

3 *quarts cider*
¾ *pint rum*
4 *tablespoons brown sugar*
1 *lemon*
1 *orange*
1 *teaspoon ground cinnamon*
1 *teaspoon ground ginger*
8 *cloves*

Peel the fruit very thinly and chop the rind. Slice the fruit. Put ½ pint cider in a small saucepan with the sugar and spices, cover and simmer for 30 minutes. Pour the rest of the cider into a large saucepan, add the strained fruit and spice liquid. Heat slowly to a comfortable drinking temperature, add the rum and warm once more. Never over-heat any alcohol mixture or all the 'power' will disappear. Taste, and if more sugar is wished add more, as the sweetness of cider varies. Sufficient for 10 or 12 people.

RUM PUNCH

3 *parts rum*
2 *parts brandy*
1 *part lemon juice*
6 *parts hot, not boiling, water*
sugar to taste

Mix the rum, brandy, lemon juice, together. Heat the water, add the sugar, stir till dissolved and pour over the rum, etc.

WASSAIL BOWL

3 *quarts beer*
1 *lb. sugar*
1 *grated nutmeg*
1 *teaspoon grated ginger*
4 *glasses sherry*
3 *slices of lemon*
3 *slices of toast, crusts removed*

Warm to comfortable drinking temperature 1 quart of beer, add the sugar, nutmeg and ginger, stir till sugar is dissolved. Add the sherry, the rest of the beer and the lemon slices. Warm once more. Serve with the toast floating on top.

SLOE GIN

sloes
white sugar
gin

Wash and prick the sloes. Mix with an equal weight of white sugar. Half fill the bottles with this and fill up with the gin. Cork tightly. Drink in 3 months time.

SYLLABUB

An old English rich frothy drink, originally made from the milk straight from the cow. This is a modern version:

¼ *pint lemon or orange juice*
1 *tablespoon sherry (optional)*
sugar to sweeten
¼ *pint cream*
¼ *pint milk*
2 *egg whites, stiffly beaten*

Put the sweetened juice and sherry in a large bowl, add the cream and milk and whisk till fluffy, be careful not to over-whisk and make buttery. Add the egg whites, whisk again, chill and serve in glasses. This will keep in a cold place for several days.

MULLED CLARET

2 *nutmegs, grated*
2 *pints claret*
2 *oranges*
12 *sugar lumps*
12 *cloves*
½ *teaspoon ground cinnamon*
1 *pint boiling water*
1 *sherry glass curaçao*
1 *sherry glass brandy*

Slice one unpeeled orange finely, pare the rind thinly off the other. Add these to the claret in a saucepan, plus the sugar, cloves and cinnamon. Heat slowly to comfortable drinking temperature, add the boiling water just off the boil, stir well, add the curaçao and the brandy. Pour into glasses and sprinkle the nutmeg over each. Serve at once.

Holland

COOKING IN HOLLAND

The interesting aspect of Dutch cookery is its very solid national Netherlands background, thickly overladen by a definite Indonesian spice-veneer. Historically it is very easy to explain, because the Dutch have always possessed a traditional characteristic cuisine, but they also used to own the Dutch East Indies, the Spice Islands — an archipelago now called Indonesia. From there they acquired and brought back the taste for unusual condiments. This fraternisation in the kitchen seems to have worked both ways, as I discovered as soon as I landed in Djakarta, the capital of Indonesia. Breakfast at the Hotel des Indes invariably brings with it some chocolate vermicelli — the typical Dutch ingredient for the breakfast table. In all my travels I only met chocolate vermicelli for breakfast in Holland and in Indonesia.

The Dutch housewife, like the German one, has to cater for huge appetites. So first of all, she specialises in good filling soups — soups which could mean a whole meal for daintier appetites.

Fish is plentiful and cheap in Holland and consequently they have quite a few good fish specialities. By grating a little nutmeg into their Fish Cakes, they add a special little touch to the ordinary fish cake recipe — a tip well worth accepting.

Veal Olives is another national dish which the Dutch housewife prepares with care and love. Most housewives could learn the art of dealing with veal from the Dutch — remember that beating the slices of veal is absolutely essential. If you don't possess the proper tool for this beating process, I can recommend doing it with the base of an empty milk bottle.

A dish of Minced Meat Balls is one of the richest and tastiest one-course meals — the very thing for a career woman's dinner party, as it can all be prepared well beforehand and heated up when wanted.

BROWN BEAN SOUP

8 oz. brown beans
1 onion
2 oz. dripping
2 oz. flour
bouquet garni
nutmeg
salt, pepper

Soak the beans for 12 hours. Simmer in 2 pints of water with the *bouquet garni* until tender. Cook the chopped onion in the dripping until tender, stir in the flour. Cook for 1 minute. Add to the soup. Season with salt and pepper and grated nutmeg. Pass through a sieve. Serve with croûtons of fried bread.

PEA SOUP

8 oz. dried peas
2 leeks
1 stick celery
1 pig's trotter
8 oz. boiling sausages
salt, pepper

Soak the peas for 12 hours. Put into a pan with the sliced leeks, chopped celery, pig's trotter and 4 pints water. Simmer for 4 hours, add the sausages 30 minutes before serving. Season with salt and pepper.

SPINACH SOUP

1 lb. spinach
2 oz. butter
1 oz. flour
¼ pint cream
salt, pepper
nutmeg

Cook the spinach in a little salted water until tender. Pass through a sieve. Melt the butter, cook the flour in it for 1 minute, gradually add the spinach purée or some hot milk if necessary. Season with salt, pepper and nutmeg. Stir in the cream just before serving. Serve with croûtons of fried bread.

DRIED COD

1½ lb. dried cod
potatoes
4 onions
2 oz. butter
1 oz. flour
1 teaspoon mustard
8 oz. cooked rice

Soak the cod for 24 hours. Remove the skin and bones. Cut into slices, roll and secure with a cocktail stick. Cook in boiling salted water for 45 minutes. Remove the fish from the water. Melt the butter, stir in the flour and the mustard, cook for 1 minute, gradually add the fish water to make a medium thick sauce. Put the fish and the rice in a shallow fireproof dish, pour the sauce over them. Bake in a moderate oven until the top browns. The same recipe can be used for fresh cod or any other white fish.

FISH CAKES

1 *lb. fish fillet*
2 *oz. butter*
2 *slices bread*
1 *egg*
chopped parsley
nutmeg
salt, pepper
flour

milk
fat for frying

Cook the fish in a court-bouillon (see p. 166) until tender. Flake the fish. Soak the bread in a little milk. Mash the fish and soaked bread well together, beat in the egg and the butter. Season with salt, pepper and nutmeg. Shape into flat cakes, dust with flour. Fry quickly in hot fat.

HERRINGS WITH RED CABBAGE

4 *herrings*
salt
pepper
flour
fat for frying

Split the herrings. Dust with seasoned flour. Make the fat very hot. Fry the insides first and then the outsides. Serve with red cabbage (see p. 231).

STEWED MACKEREL

4 *small mackerel*
2 *tomatoes, peeled and quartered*
1 *onion, finely chopped*
salt, pepper
juice of ½ lemon
1 *tablespoon chopped parsley*

2 *oz. breadcrumbs*
1 *oz. butter*

Put the mackerel in frying pan with a little water and the tomato, onion and parsley. Season with salt and pepper. Sprinkle with lemon juice. Spread the breadcrumbs over the top. Dot with butter. Simmer for 30—40 minutes.

HUNTSMAN PIE

1 *lb. minced meat, fresh or cooked*
2 *lb. cooked potatoes, diced*
2 *onions, sliced very thin*
2 *large cooking apples, sliced*
½ *pint stock*
salt, pepper
nutmeg

4 *oz. breadcrumbs*
2 *oz. butter*

Arrange alternate layers of potatoes, cooked meat, onion and apple in a deep casserole, beginning and ending with a layer of potato. Season the stock with salt, pepper and grated nutmeg. Pour this into the dish. Sprinkle with breadcrumbs. Dot with butter. Bake in a moderate oven for 1 hour.

MEAT AND BEETROOT SALAD

1 *cooked beetroot*
8 *oz. chopped cooked meat*
2 *cooked potatoes*
1 *hard-boiled egg*
1 *cooking apple*
parsley
2 *tablespoons olive oil*
1 *tablespoon wine vinegar*
salt, pepper

pickled onions

Mix cold sliced potatoes, sliced beetroot, chopped meat and peeled and chopped cooking apple. Mix the oil and vinegar well together, season with salt and pepper and pour over the salad. Garnish with chopped parsley, slices of hard-boiled egg and pickled onions.

MINCED MEAT BALLS

8 *oz. minced beef*
8 *oz. minced veal*
8 *oz. minced pork*
1 *large onion, minced*
2 *oz. breadcrumbs*
1 *egg*
salt, pepper
lard for frying
2 *tablespoons concentrated tomato purée*

¼ *pint sour cream*
½ *pint stock*

Mix the minced meats with the onion and breadcrumbs. Bind with the egg. Season with salt and pepper. Form into small balls and fry quickly in the lard. Gradually add the tomato purée and the stock, simmer for 15 minutes. Leave to stand for several hours. Reheat and stir in the cream just before serving.

MINCED MEAT SCALLOPS

8 *oz. minced beef, fresh or cooked*
½ *pint brown sauce (see p. 165)*
2 *oz. breadcrumbs*
1 *oz. butter*
parsley

Mix the meat with the sauce. Fill 4 scallop shells with the mixture. Sprinkle with breadcrumbs. Dot with butter. Bake in a moderate oven for 30 minutes. Garnish each one with a sprig of parsley.

SAUSAGE WITH CURLY KALE

2 *lb. curly kale, cooked*
2 *lb. potatoes, cooked*
½ *pint stock*
8 *oz. smoked sausage, sliced or frankfurters*
2 *oz. rolled oats*
2 *oz. butter*
salt, pepper

Put the curly kale, potatoes and sausage in a saucepan with ½ pint stock. Add the rolled oats and simmer for 15 minutes without a lid; the stock should almost all have evaporated. Remove the sausage, mash the vegetables with the butter. Season with salt and pepper. Arrange on a flat dish, garnished with the sausages.

MIXED SALAD

8 *oz. peas*
8 *oz. new carrots*
2 *new potatoes*
½ *onion*
8 *oz. cooked meat, minced*
gherkins
salt, pepper
parsley
1 *tablespoon wine vinegar*
2 *tablespoons olive oil*

Cook the peas and diced carrots in boiling salted water until just tender. Steam the potatoes in their skins, peel and chop them. Mix lightly together with the raw chopped onion. Arrange the meat in the middle of a flat dish, surround it with the mixed vegetables. Garnish with gherkins and chopped parsley. Mix vinegar and olive oil well together, season with salt and pepper. Pour over the vegetables.

SAUSAGES WITH RICE, ONION AND POTATOES

8 *small pork sausages*
2 *lb. onions*
1 *lb. potatoes*
4 *oz. cooked rice*
salt, pepper

Cook the potatoes and roughly chopped onion together in boiling salted water until tender. Drain and mix with the rice. Season with pepper and salt if necessary. Arrange the fried sausages on a dish with the rice and vegetable mixture round them. Serve with vinegar or Worcester sauce.

SCRAMBLED EGG SALAD

3 *eggs*
1 *oz. butter*
2 *grated raw carrots*
½ *onion, chopped*
2 *tomatoes, sliced*
cucumber, sliced
mint
parsley
marjoram

salt, pepper
2 *tablespoons olive oil*
1 *tablespoon vinegar*

Beat the eggs lightly, season with salt and pepper and the chopped herbs. Scramble with the butter in the usual way. When cold, cut into small pieces, mix with the carrot and onion, surround with the sliced tomatoes and cucumber. Mix the oil and vinegar well together and pour over the tomato and cucumber.

VEAL OLIVES

8 *slices lean veal (4 oz. each)*
2 *oz. butter*
½ *pint stock*
1 *lemon*
salt, pepper

Beat the veal, season with salt and pepper. Roll and secure with string. Brown all over in the butter. Arrange in a shallow fireproof dish, put a slice of lemon on each roll. Pour the stock over. Cover and cook in a moderate oven for 1 hour. Remove the string before serving.

STUFFED BREAD ROLLS

8 *long bread rolls*
8 *oz. meat or ham, minced*
½ *pint stock*
1 *oz. butter*
parsley
1 *oz. flour*
salt, pepper

Make a sauce with the butter, flour and stock. Mix the meat with it. Season with salt, pepper and chopped parsley. Scoop out the insides of the rolls and fill with the mixture, brush with melted butter. Replace the lid and bake for 10 minutes in the oven or under the grill.

PORK CHOPS WITH CHESTNUTS AND RED CABBAGE

4 *pork chops*
2 *oz. butter*
½ *pint chicken stock*
½ *small red cabbage*
16 *chestnuts*
salt, pepper

Shred the cabbage and remove the hard stalks. Soak in cold water for 1 hour. Peel and cook the chestnuts (see p. 398, Spain). Lightly fry the chops on both sides in the butter. Drain the cabbage and place at the bottom of a deep casserole, put the chestnuts on top of it and then the chops. Season with salt and pepper. Pour in the stock. Cover with a lid, bake in a moderate oven for 1½ hours.

STEWED STEAK

1½ *lb. beef steak*
1 *onion*
½ *bay leaf*
2 *cloves*
nutmeg
salt, pepper
lard
1 *tablespoon vinegar*

Cut the meat into 8 slices. Season with salt and pepper. Brown the meat on both sides in the fat. Add the sliced onion and the flavourings, ½ pint water and vinegar. Cover the pan and stew slowly for 2 hours, or longer if necessary.

RED CABBAGE

½ *red cabbage*
1 *onion*
1 *cooking apple*
1 *oz. butter*
salt, pepper
3 *cloves*
1 *dessertspoon wine vinegar*

Shred the cabbage and remove the hard stalks. Soak in cold water for 1 hour or longer. Drain. Fry the sliced onion in the butter for a few minutes. Add the cabbage, sliced apple and flavourings. Stew very slowly for 2 hours, adding a little stock or water if necessary.

YOGHOURT PUDDING

1 *pint yoghourt*
2 *oz. mixed sultanas and glacé cherries*
2 *oz. sugar*
½ *oz. powdered gelatine*
juice of ½ *lemon*
2 *tablespoons water*

Dissolve over hot water the gelatine, sugar and 2 tablespoons water. Mix together the lemon juice, sultanas and cherries, then add the yoghourt and dissolved gelatine, and stir well. When on the point of setting, pour into a wet mould and allow to set; cool for 30 minutes. When firm, turn out and garnish with glacé fruits, then decorate with whipped cream.

BOTERCAKE

8 *oz. Dutch unsalted butter*
8 *oz. self-raising flour*
8 *oz. castor sugar*
4 *eggs*
5 *oz. dried fruit*

Cream the butter and sugar well. Blend in beaten eggs, a little at a time, keeping the mixture stiff. Fold in sieved flour and the fruit. Spread mixture in a large buttered loaf tin and bake for 1—1½ hours in a cool oven, until golden brown.

APPLE OR PLUM CAKE

8 *oz. flour*
2 *teaspoons baking powder*
3 *oz. sugar*
2 *oz. butter*
2 *tablespoons milk*
1 *lb. plums or cooking apples*
cinnamon

Sift the flour with the baking powder, rub in the butter lightly, mix in 2 oz. sugar. Add enough milk to make a stiff paste. Roll it out to ¼ inch thick, lay it on a greased Swiss Roll tin. Peel and slice the apples or halve and stone the plums. Arrange them on top of the pastry. Sprinkle with sugar and cinnamon. Bake in a hot oven for 25 minutes.

SEMOLINA WITH SULTANAS

1 *pint milk*
1 *oz. semolina*
1 *oz. butter*
1 *egg*
cinnamon
1 *oz. sugar*
2 *oz. sultanas*

Bring the milk to the boil, stir in the semolina and the sugar. Cook very slowly, stirring from time to time. Add a pinch of cinnamon, the butter, beaten egg and sultanas when the mixture thickens.

Hungary

COOKING IN HUNGARY

I suppose that it is a great achievement for a very small country like Hungary to have become internationally famous for two things: Paprika (red pepper) and Goulash, but if you know Hungarian cookery fairly well you cannot help being slightly peeved that the goulash and paprika cloak gets thrown over such excellent cuisine as the Hungarian.

Hungarian cooking does, of course, use the national condiment of paprika rather lavishly, but always remember that they use the sweet paprika, which has a very pleasing flavour, makes the dishes bright and red, but is *not hot*. After this staunch defence of Hungarian cooking, let me turn to some of the recipes in this chapter and point out their virtues.

Let us start with Sauerkraut Soup — commonly known in Hungary as Tippler's Soup, and consumed ritually by almost everybody at about 6 a. m. on New Year's day. Christmas is a purely family holiday in Hungary — but everybody goes wild on New Year's Eve — and by the next morning they all need their Tippler's Soup, which works miracles after a gay night.

Goulash is, of course, on the menu of restaurants and households all over the world — sometimes a goulash which would make Hungarians flinch — so why not try the original version given in this chapter? Pörkölt is the Hungarian stew, for which any kind of meat can be used — I find it perhaps best when made of pork. Chicken Paprikash with its succulent red sauce is a perfect main course for a dinner party — remember to have some fresh bread on the table and let your guests dunk with it. You will hardly need to wash the plates afterwards.

Ham and Pancake Pudding and Mushroom Paprikash are such delightful dishes, that you can serve them as a main course, or as an entrée to a special dinner. That dream of a gâteau, which you can find in good pastry shops and espressos all over the world, Dobosh, was created by a Hungarian chef of the same name. With its layers of chocolate fillings and thin sponge and its caramel top, it looks most elaborate — yet it is neither difficult nor expensive to make.

Once you have tried some of these recipes, you will realise that Hungarian cooking blends the flavours of East and West and has an imagination which is uniquely its own.

FISH SOUP

8 oz. skate
8 oz. pike
1 onion
1 tomato
1 oz. butter
4 potatoes
salt, pepper
1 teaspoon paprika

Fillet the fish and cut into small pieces. Boil the heads, tails, bones and skin to make fish stock. Chop the onion and cook it in the butter until it is golden, add the peeled and chopped tomato, the paprika and the fish. Fry the fish until all pieces are well browned. Pour in 2 pints of strained fish stock, add the potatoes, cut into long pieces. Simmer for 20 minutes. Season with salt and freshly ground pepper.

HARICOT BEAN SOUP

8 oz. haricot beans
1 pint bacon stock
2 carrots
1 parsnip
1 oz. bacon fat
1 tablespoon flour
½ pint sour cream

Soak the beans overnight. Pour off the water and substitute bacon stock made by boiling bacon bones, rinds or a small knuckle. Add the sliced carrot and parsnip. Season with salt and pepper. Simmer until tender. Sieve the soup and mix it with the flour, cooked and slightly browned in the fat. Reheat and sprinkle with chopped parsley. Serve with croûtons of fried bread.

POTATO SOUP

2 lb. potatoes
1 onion
2 oz. lard
¼ pint sour cream
1 green pepper
2 pints stock
nutmeg
salt, pepper

Fry the diced potatoes and the chopped onion in the lard, until well covered with fat. Add the chopped flesh of the green pepper. Pour in the stock and simmer until all vegetables are tender. Season with salt, pepper and nutmeg. Stir in the sour cream and bring to the boil. Serve with croûtons of fried bread.

BACON AND POTATO CASSEROLE

2 lb. potatoes
8 rashers bacon
1 onion
¼ pint milk
1 teaspoon paprika
salt
butter

Arrange alternate layers of thinly sliced potato, chopped bacon and sliced onion in a well-buttered fireproof dish, ending with a layer of potato. Mix the paprika with the milk, add a pinch of salt and pour over the potatoes. Dot with butter. Cook in a moderate oven for 1½ hours.

SAUERKRAUT SOUP

1 *lb. sauerkraut*
1 *lb. bacon bones*
1 *onion, chopped*
1 *oz. lard*
2 *oz. flour*
1 *teaspoon paprika*
salt
caraway seeds (optional)
¼ *pint sour cream*
8 *oz. boiling sausage*

Simmer the sauerkraut with 2 pints water and the bacon bones for 30 minutes. Fry the onions in the lard until transparent, stir in the flour and cook for 1 minute. Add the paprika and caraway seeds, mix them well with the flour. Pour in the stock from the sauerkraut stirring all the time, add the sauerkraut and the sausage cut into small pieces. Simmer for 10 minutes.

CABBAGE PANCAKES

pancake mixture (see p. 275)
4 *oz. cabbage*
butter
2 *oz. ham*

Shred the cabbage and boil until cooked. Chop finely, fry lightly in a little butter then add to the pancake batter. Make pancakes in the usual way, and before rolling them up sprinkle with chopped ham.

HAM AND PANCAKE PUDDING

12 *small pancakes*
8 *oz. minced cooked ham*
½ *pint thick white sauce*
2 *oz. grated cheese*
salt, pepper

Make 12 small pancakes (see p. 275). Line a greased pudding basin with one of them and reserve one for the top, cut the rest into strips. Mix with the ham and sauce, season with salt and pepper, pour into the basin. Cover with the remaining pancake. Sprinkle with grated cheese. Bake in a moderate oven for 15 minutes.

HUNGARIAN MARROW

1 *12-inch marrow or*
2 *6-inch marrows*
3 *onions*
4 *oz. butter*
1 *teaspoon paprika*
½ *pint sour cream*
1 *dessertspoon parsley*

Cut up the marrow, without peeling it, into finger-sized strips. Melt the butter in a frying pan. Chop the onions finely and fry light brown in the butter. Now add the marrow pieces. Cover the pan, lower the heat and simmer for 30 minutes. Stir the paprika into the sour cream and pour over the marrow. Heat thoroughly without boiling and serve with chopped parsley sprinkled over the top.

HUNGARIAN BEANS

1 *lb. French beans*
1 *oz. butter*
½ *oz. flour*
3 *tablespoons sour cream*
salt

String and slice beans. Simmer in butter with a very little water until tender. Sprinkle over the flour and add a little more water, stir gently and simmer for a further 10 minutes, then finally stir in the sour cream.

MUSHROOM PAPRIKASH

8 *oz. mushrooms*
½ *onion*
½ *teaspoon paprika*
½ *oz. butter*
¼ *pint sour cream*
1 *dessertspoon flour*

Fry the chopped onion in the butter until golden. Stir in the paprika, add the thinly sliced mushrooms, cover the pan and cook slowly for 10 minutes. Stir in the flour and gradually add the sour cream. Reheat but do not boil.

SMOKED SAUSAGE WITH SCRAMBLED EGG

4 *oz. smoked sausage*
2 *rashers bacon*
1 *green pepper*
1 *small tomato*
4 *eggs*
1 *oz. butter*
salt and pepper

Peel the tomato and cut into small pieces. Remove the seeds from the pimento and cut it and the sausage and bacon into small dice. Fry all these lightly together in the butter. Beat the eggs and stir them into the mixture. Season with salt and pepper. Cook fairly slowly, stirring from time to time until the mixture thickens. It should have the consistency of lightly scrambled eggs.

CHICKEN STEW

8 *portions young chicken*
chicken giblets
2 *onions*
1 *oz. butter*
2 *tablespoons chopped parsley*
½ *teaspoon salt*
2 *teaspoons paprika*
1 *pint chicken stock*
2 *tablespoons tomato purée*

Melt the butter in a deep saucepan and fry the chopped onions and parsley in it. Add the chicken portions and giblets. Sprinkle with salt and paprika. Cover with chicken stock and simmer very slowly until tender. Add tomato purée and cook for another 5 minutes. Remove chicken portions from pan and place on a hot dish. Serve the strained liquid separately.

STUFFED AUBERGINES

4 *aubergines*
2 *oz. breadcrumbs*
1 *small onion*
1 *clove garlic*
1 *tablespoon olive oil*
8 *oz. cooked minced pork*
1 *rasher bacon, minced*
parsley
salt, pepper

Scoop out the insides of the aubergines and chop the flesh. Fry the finely chopped onion and the garlic in the olive oil, add the pork and bacon and cook for 10 minutes. Mix with the chopped aubergine and a little chopped parsley. Fill the aubergines with this mixture, cover with breadcrumbs and bake in a moderate oven for 20 minutes.

CHICKEN PAPRIKASH

1 *large chicken*
1 *onion*
1 *green pepper*
2 *tomatoes*
2 *oz. lard*
1 *tablespoon paprika*
¼ *pint sour cream*
1 *tablespoon flour*
salt
½ *pint water*

Cut the chicken into pieces and dust with flour. Fry the finely chopped onion in the lard until golden, fry the chicken pieces until browned on all sides. Add the peeled and chopped tomatoes, the chopped flesh of the green pepper, paprika and water. Cover the pan and simmer until the chicken is tender. Strain off the liquid, season with salt and stir in the sour cream. Heat but do not boil the sauce, arrange pieces of chicken on a hot serving dish and pour the sauce over them. Serve with sauté potatoes and watercress.

PORK CHOPS (1)

4 *pork chops*
½ *bottle white wine*
2 *carrots, sliced*
1 *onion, sliced*
1 *bay leaf*
1 *sprig parsley*
1 *clove garlic*
1 *sprig rosemary*
2 *oz. butter*
2 *oz. breadcrumbs*
1 *teaspoon paprika*

1 *oz. flour*
salt
pepper

Put the carrots, onion, bay leaf, parsley, rosemary, garlic and wine into a shallow dish and marinate the chops in it for 12 hours. Drain the chops and brown them in the butter. Stir in the flour, cook for 1 minute and add the strained marinade. Simmer for 20 minutes. Add the paprika and simmer for another 5 minutes. Arrange the chops in a shallow dish, pour the sauce over them, cover with breadcrumbs and brown them in the oven.

PORK CHOPS (2)

4 *pork chops*
1 *oz. lard*
1 *onion, chopped*
1 *teaspoon paprika*
juice of ½ lemon
salt, pepper
small savoy cabbage
¼ pint sour cream

Fry the onion lightly in the lard. Add the chops and brown them on both sides. Stir in the paprika and lemon juice, season with salt and pepper. Add a little water. Cook, covered with a lid, in a moderate oven for 45 minutes. Cook the shredded cabbage in boiling salted water for 8 minutes. Drain and stir in the sour cream. Arrange the chops on a hot dish, pour the sauce over them and surround them with the cabbage.

GOULASH

1½ *lb. stewing beef*
1 *oz. dripping*
1 *onion, sliced*
4 *medium potatoes*
8 *oz. tomatoes*
1 *teaspoon paprika*
salt

Cut the beef into 1-inch pieces. Cook the sliced onion in the dripping until golden, add the meat, the peeled and quartered tomatoes and ½ pint water. Season with salt and paprika. Cover the dish and cook in a moderate oven for 1 hour. Peel the potatoes and cut them into long pieces, add them to the stew and simmer for another 30 minutes. Serve with plain boiled rice.

GOULASH WITH RUNNER BEANS

2 *lb. pork*
1 *onion*
2 *oz. dripping*
1 *lb. tomatoes*
1 *teaspoon paprika*
salt
2 *lb. runner beans*

Cut the pork into cubes, brown them in the dripping, add the chopped onion and brown it with the meat. Peel and quarter the tomatoes and cook them slowly with a little water until tender, rub through a sieve. Add them and the sliced beans to the meat. Season with salt and paprika and cook slowly in a covered pan for 1½ hours. Serve with mashed potatoes.

PÖRKÖLT: PORK STEW

2 *lb. pork, goose or duck*
1 *onion*
2 *potatoes*
2 *teaspoons paprika*
salt
1 *oz. dripping*

Fry the chopped onion in the dripping. Cut the meat into 2-inch cubes and brown it in the dripping with the onion. Stir in the paprika, season with salt, cover with water and cook in a moderate oven with a lid on the pan for 1½ hours. Add the potatoes, cut into ½-inch cubes, and cook for another 30 minutes.

TOKAY GOULASH

2 *lb. shoulder of pork*
2 *tomatoes*
1 *green pepper*
1 *lb. sauerkraut*
1 *teaspoon paprika*
salt
½ *pint sour cream*
1 *oz. butter*

Peel and quarter the tomatoes, remove the core and seeds of the pepper and cut it into slices. Melt the butter and cook tomatoes and pepper in it slowly until tender. Cut the pork into 1-inch pieces and add them to the vegetables. Brown slightly and add the sauerkraut, the salt and the paprika. Put a lid on the pan and cook slowly for 1½ hours. Stir in the sour cream and serve immediately.

TOKANY (Beef Stew)

2 *lb. stewing steak*
1 *onion*
4 *oz. mushrooms*
parsley
1 *teaspoon paprika*
2 *oz. butter*
salt
½ *pint sour cream (optional)*

Cut the meat into strips about 1 inch wide and 3 inches long. Brown them in the butter, add the finely chopped onion and fry until it is golden. Slice the mushrooms and add them to the meat. Season with paprika and salt, cover the pan and cook in a moderate oven for 1½ hours. Stir in the sour cream before serving.

VEAL CUTLETS

4 *veal cutlets*
2 *oz. butter*
1 *teaspoon paprika*
1 *oz. flour*
8 *rashers streaky bacon*
salt, pepper
¼ *pint sour cream*

Season the flour with salt and pepper. Dust the cutlets with it. Fry them on both sides in the butter until golden. Remove the cutlets and keep warm. Stir the paprika into the fat in the pan, cook for 1 minute, add the cream and heat gently. Pour this sauce over the cutlets and heat in a slow oven for 5 minutes. Roll the bacon rashers and cook them separately in the oven while making the sauce. Arrange them round the cutlets.

APPLE FOOL

2 *lb. cooking apples*
2 *egg whites*
4 *oz. sugar*
4 *fresh plums*

Peel and core the apples. Cook with very little water until tender. Rub through a sieve. Beat the egg whites until very stiff. Fold in the sugar, gradually add the apple purée. Decorate with fresh plums, stoned and cut in half, or with any fresh fruit in season. Serve cold.

RICE SOUFFLÉ

2 oz. rice
1 pint milk
4 oz. sugar
2 eggs
strawberry jam
apple purée
1 small glass brandy

Put the rice and milk in a double saucepan and cook slowly until thick and creamy. Beat the egg yolks with 1 oz. sugar and add them to the rice. Put one third of the rice mixture into a buttered fireproof dish, cover it with a thin layer of jam, repeat these layers twice. Cover the top layer with apple purée. Whip the egg whites stiffly, fold in 3 oz. sugar, arrange this on the top and bake in a moderate oven for 20 minutes. Warm the brandy, pour it over the pudding, set light to it and serve immediately.

PANCAKES WITH CHOCOLATE SAUCE

8 pancakes
2 oz. ground almonds
2 oz. seeded raisins
3 oz. castor sugar
vanilla
1 oz. butter
4 oz. cooking chocolate
1 tablespoon strong black coffee
¼ pint milk

Pound the raisins with the ground almonds, 2 oz. sugar and a drop of vanilla. Put one pancake into a greased round fireproof dish, cover with a layer of the almond mixture, repeat the layers until all the pancakes have been used. Sprinkle with sugar, dot with butter and bake in a moderate oven for 10 minutes. Serve with chocolate sauce made by melting the chocolate in the coffee and milk.

CHOCOLATE ICE CREAM

5 oz. cooking chocolate
½ pint double cream
2 tablespoons black coffee

Melt the chocolate in the coffee. Whip the cream and beat in the coffee and chocolate mixture. Pour into the freezing tray of a refrigerator and leave to freeze.

CHOCOLATE CAKE

4 oz. sugar
5 eggs
2 oz. flour

FOR THE FILLING:
4 oz. sugar
4 eggs
4 oz. cooking chocolate
vanilla
2 oz. butter

FOR THE GLAZE:
3 oz. sugar

Beat the egg yolks, beat in the sugar until white and creamy. Beat in the finely sifted flour. Fold in the stiffly beaten egg whites. Grease and flour 2 8-inch baking tins. Fill with the mixture. Bake in a moderate oven for 15—20 minutes.

TO MAKE THE FILLING:
Pour the sugar and eggs into the top of a double saucepan, cook slowly, stir until thick. Melt the chocolate and a drop of vanilla in a little water. Cream the butter and beat the chocolate into it. Add this gradually to the egg mixture. Spread this between the layers of cake. Dissolve the sugar in a little water, cook gently until it begins to colour. Spread over the top of the cake. The cake should not be cut for at least 12 hours.

DOBOSCH GÂTEAU

4 *eggs*
4 *teaspoons castor sugar*
4 *tablespoons flour*

FILLING:

1 *egg*
2 *oz. cocoa*
4—5 *tablespoons milk*
4 *oz. castor sugar*
4 *oz. unsalted butter*

ICING:

3 *oz. castor sugar*

Beat the egg whites very stiff, add the sugar and go on beating. Next add the yolks, still beating the mixture with the whisk. Fold in the flour lightly and carefully. Grease and flour the outside bottom of two sandwich tins, pour a little of the cake mixture on each inverted tin and spread evenly with the help of a palette knife. Put them into a very hot oven for 3—4 minutes. Do not let it brown — it should be a pale yellow colour when ready. The cake on the higher shelf will be ready first; take it off the tin immediately, grease and flour the tin and put another portion of mixture on it and into the oven. By this time the layer on the cooler shelf will be ready, so take it out and repeat the procedure, till all is used up. With the above quantity you should be able to make 5—6 layers. Put the layers aside while you prepare the filling.

Heat milk in a saucepan, add the cocoa to it when hot, and mix it well to make a smooth paste. Add a little extra milk if you find the paste too dry. Take off the heat and let cool while you beat up the egg and sugar. Add this to the paste. Add the butter to this mixture by beating in small pieces, and go on beating till the filling is light in colour and consistency. Use this filling generously between the layers of sponge, but remember to keep a little for the sides of the cake. Do not put the top layer on till you have covered it with the caramel icing. For this you melt the sugar in a pan and heat it till it turns into a nice brown runny caramel. Pour this caramel quickly over the sponge layer, smoothing and spreading it with a buttered knife. Before it has time to cool, cut sections into it with another buttered knife. These sections in the hard caramel top make it easy to cut the cake.

SOUR MILK CHEESE

3 *pints sour milk*
butter
1 *oz. chopped capers*
4 *anchovies*
½ *teaspoon chopped onion*
1 *teaspoon German mustard*
1 *teaspoon paprika*
salt and pepper

Use the milk when it has become solidified. Drain through a muslin bag for 12 hours, then combine together equal quantities of the cream cheese and butter. When you have a smooth paste add the other ingredients, finely chopped, and season with salt, pepper and paprika.

India

COOKING IN INDIA

The mentality of the British and that of the Indians could not be more different — they are worlds apart in every aspect. Yet, due to the political association between the two nations, Indian culinary art has become part of the conservative British kitchen. One finds curry, kedgeree, mulligatawny soup, and chutney belonging to the daily routine cooking of housewives who would refuse to allow a single pair of Frankfurters to pollute their traditional ideas. If this proves anything, it proves that it is easy to break down nationality barriers in the kitchen and learn new ideas even from people totally different from you and who live under completely different circumstances.

The Indians believe that cookery is one of the Divine Arts, one of God's revelations to man, and therefore cooking should be approached as a sacred ceremony. In Indian civilisation — a civilisation much older than the Western — there is a reverence and love towards the preparation of food, which makes the art of cookery part of the ritual life of the people. Naturally, this attitude created a national gastronomy which is subtle and pleasing, which balances the ingredients with devoted care and judgement.

You will find the recipes on the following pages very clear and workable, yet much more genuine than the over-anglicised version of some Indian recipes. The first step towards making a good curry is to master the art of cooking rice. The rice should be well cooked, soft and yet each grain separate and dry. So before you venture into the preparation of these fascinating curries take serious heed of how the Indians boil their rice. The washing and soaking of the rice is very important — it gets rid of the surplus starch in rice and makes it lighter and whiter.

There are two excellent recipes for making chutney in this section — another Indian speciality which has become part of the Western world. These chutney recipes are more authentic than most I have met and will lift a dull cold-**meat** supper into quite an occasion.

Indian spices and condiments can be obtained from many good grocers and from shops specialising in Indian food.

INDIAN BOILED RICE

8 oz. *Patna rice*
2 teaspoons *salt*
3 pints *cold water*

Wash the rice in two changes of water. Soak in cold water for 30 minutes. Drain the rice and put in a large saucepan, add the salt and pour over 3 pints of cold water. Bring to the boil quickly and simmer for 20 minutes or more until each grain is soft, but not mushy. Drain in a colander and rinse under the cold tap for one minute. Cover the colander with a clean cloth only, no lid, and stand over simmering water till the rice is warmed throughout.

MULLIGATAWNY SOUP

2 pints *chicken or meat stock*
1 oz. *butter*
1 *medium minced onion*
1 *minced clove of garlic*
1 *heaped dessertspoon
  mulligatawny paste*
1 *heaped dessertspoon tomato
  purée or paste*
salt, *lemon juice*

Heat the fat in a saucepan, fry the onion, garlic, paste and purée very gently for 3 minutes. Pour on the stock, add salt and lemon juice to taste, bring to the boil and serve.

If a thicker soup is liked, add 1 tablespoon flour to the mixture and mix well, before the stock is poured over.

MADRAS FRIED FISH

4 cod cutlets, 2 *filleted plaice
  or other white fish*
1 egg, *beaten*
1 teaspoon *ground turmeric*
¼ teaspoon *ground chillies*
1 *medium finely chopped onion*
1 *finely chopped clove of garlic*
juice of ½ *a lemon*

salt to taste
fat for deep frying

Make a pickling mixture of all the ingredients and leave the fish in it for 1 hour, turning from time to time. Fry in the very hot fat till golden brown, drain and serve. Garnish with parsley and a cut lemon if wished.

KEDGEREE

1½ lb. *cooked fish (the flaky sort)
  haddock, cod, turbot, etc.*
8 oz. *cooked rice*
2 oz. *butter*
2 *medium chopped onions*
1 *clove of garlic chopped*
1 teaspoon *ground turmeric*
2 *hard-boiled eggs*
salt, pepper

a few red and green chillies,
  cut lengthwise

Heat the butter in a large pan, fry the onions and garlic till transparent. Add the turmeric and fry gently for 3 minutes. Add the flaked fish and the rice. Turn over and over gently with a fork or knife till warmed through, add pepper and salt to taste.

Pile on a warm dish and decorate with slices of egg and the chillies.

PLAIN PEPPER WATER

the juice of 1 *large lemon*
1 *teaspoon vinegar*
2 *pints hot water*
1 *oz. butter*
2 *cloves of garlic, finely chopped*
2 *teaspoons ground coriander*
1 *teaspoon ground turmeric*
½ *teaspoon ground cummin seed*
½ *teaspoon ground mustard seed*
6 *peppercorns*

2 *dry chillies*
salt to taste

In a large saucepan melt the butter, and fry gently all the other ingredients for 2 or 3 minutes. Add the lemon juice and vinegar and hot water, add salt to taste, and simmer for 15 minutes.

This is to be used to moisten the rice served with dry curry.

PORK VINDALOO (Hot Curry)

1 *lb. fat pork, cut into* ½-*inch squares*
4 *medium finely chopped onions*
1 *clove of garlic finely chopped*
2 *tablespoons vindaloo mixture, mixed to a paste with vinegar*
2 *oz. butter*
salt to taste
cold water

Fry the onions and garlic in the fat until transparent, add the vindaloo paste, fry very gently for 3 minutes. Add the pork, mix well, cover the pan lightly and cook on the lowest possible flame, as it easily burns, for 30 minutes or until the pork is tender. Add enough cold water to make a thick gravy, stir well, add salt to taste.

TOAST CURRY

1 *medium onion, sliced*
2 *cloves of garlic, chopped*
2 *bay leaves*
8 *cardamom seeds* } *tied in muslin*
12 *cloves*
2 *oz. butter*
1 *tablespoon curry powder*
½ *pint tomato ketchup*

1 *teaspoon tarragon vinegar*

Heat the butter, add the onions, garlic and fry till brown. Stir in the curry powder, pour over the tomato ketchup and vinegar, add the bag of spices. Simmer gently for 20 minutes, until thick.

This paste can be spread warm on hot buttered toast, or cold on biscuits for a picnic.

COOKED VEGETABLE CURRY

1½ *lb. cooked mixed vegetables, cut into small pieces*
2 *oz. butter*
1 *medium finely sliced onion*
1 *tablespoon curry powder*
½ *pint meat stock*

Heat the butter in a saucepan, fry the onion till brown, stir in the curry powder, add the vegetables, pour over the stock, simmer for 30 minutes.

VEGETABLE CURRY

8 oz. green beans, sliced
8 oz. potatoes, cut in 1-inch cubes
8 oz. tomatoes, peeled and
　chopped
2 oz. fat
1 large finely chopped onion
1 clove of garlic, finely chopped
1 heaped tablespoon curry powder
salt

a squeeze of lemon juice
cold water

Heat the fat, fry the onions and garlic till transparent, add the curry powder, fry gently for 3 minutes. Add the tomatoes, stir well. If too dry add a little cold water to make a thick gravy. Now add the beans, simmer for 12 minutes, add the potatoes and simmer for another 6 or 7 minutes. Season with the lemon juice and salt, to taste.

VINDALOO CURRY

6 medium sliced onions
5 oz. butter
2 tablespoons medium hot curry
　powder
1 lb. chopped rump steak
¼ pint wine vinegar
½ teaspoon salt

Heat 4 oz. butter in a saucepan and fry the onions till brown, add the curry powder. Have the steak cut in ½-inch cubes and brown these in 1 oz. butter. Add to onion mixture. Put on a low heat and add the vinegar drop by drop, stirring all the time, add the salt, cover and simmer very gently for 2 hours.

BENGAL CURRY

1 young chicken or rabbit or 2 lb.
　mutton cutlets
4 oz. butter
4 medium thinly sliced onions
1 clove of garlic, chopped
2 tablespoons medium hot curry
　powder or
　1 tablespoon hot curry powder
2 tablespoons tomato juice
1 tablespoon milk
1 teaspoon salt

¾ pint meat stock

Parboil the chicken, rabbit or mutton for about 20 minutes. Cut in small pieces, about ½ inch square. Heat the butter in a saucepan, add the onions and garlic, fry till brown, add the chopped meat, curry powder, tomato juice, milk and salt. Cook for 35 minutes, stirring all the time with a wooden spoon, until the butter separates from the curry and the liquid has been absorbed. Serve on a hot dish, eat off hot plates with boiled rice served separately.

PISH-PASH

8 oz. rice
1 chicken, cut in pieces
2 pints water
1 tablespoon milk
2 tablespoons salt
2 oz. raisins
2 medium finely chopped onions

Boil the chicken pieces in the water, milk and salt till quite tender. Remove the chicken meat and keep warm. Add the washed rice and onion to the chicken stock and boil for 25 minutes until the stock is absorbed. Put in the chicken meat and the raisins, cover with a clean cloth. Keep warm.

DHALL RISSOLES

4 *oz. lentils*
1 *large minced onion*
1 *clove of garlic, minced*
¼ *pint boiling water*
2 *oz. breadcrumbs*
¼ *teaspoon ground turmeric*
a pinch of ground chillies
1 *oz. flour*
1 *beaten egg*

salt
fat for deep frying

Put the lentils, minced onions and garlic in boiling water and simmer gently; stir till the mixture cooks to a stiff paste. Cool and add the rest of the ingredients, mix well. Flour your hands and form into rissoles. Have the fat smoking hot and fry the rissoles till golden brown. Drain on paper and serve.

COLD MEAT 'KOOFTAH' CURRIED RISSOLES

2 *teaspoons 'Kooftah' mixture*
1 *lb. minced cooked meat*
4 *medium finely chopped onions*
1 *beaten egg*
2 *cloves of garlic, finely chopped*
1 *oz. flour*
2 *oz. butter, oil or fat*
1 *tablespoon curry powder*
1 *dessertspoon tomato paste*
½ *pint cold water*
salt to taste
juice of 1 lemon

Mix meat, 1 tablespoon chopped onion, 'Kooftah' mixture, flour, salt with the beaten egg and make with floured hands into small balls, the size of a walnut. Put aside. Heat the fat and fry the onion and garlic till transparent, add the curry powder and tomato paste, mix well and cook slowly for 4 minutes, add the cold water gradually to make a thick gravy, stirring all the time, add salt and lemon juice to taste. Add the meat balls and simmer for 10 minutes more.

PILLAU RICE

1 *lb. Patna rice*
boiling water
8 *oz. butter*
1 *large onion chopped finely*
2 *cloves of garlic, chopped finely*
½ *teaspoon saffron (soaked in ¼ pint warm water)*
12 *cloves*
12 *whole cardamoms*
2 *2-inch cinnamon sticks*
½ *teaspoon whole allspice*
4 *oz. sultanas*

2 *oz. skinned almonds, fried in butter*
salt

Boil the rice in a large pan. Heat the butter, add the onions, garlic and dry spices, fry but do not brown. Add the rice, cook for 5 minutes, stirring with a fork. Pour in the saffron and water, add salt to taste and pour in boiling water to cover and come 2 inches above. Cover the pan and cook very slowly till the liquid is absorbed and each grain is separate — for about 35 minutes. Add the sultanas and fried almonds and stir all together.

'KOOFTAH' PILLAU RICE

cooked Pillau rice
1 lb. minced mutton or beef
1 tablespoon finely chopped onions
1 clove of garlic, finely chopped
1 heaped dessertspoon 'Kooftah'
  mixture
1 oz. flour
1 beaten egg

salt to taste
fat for frying

Mix all these ingredients well together, make into walnut-sized balls and fry in fat till brown all over. Add to the prepared Pillau. Keep the pan covered till ready to eat to preserve the flavour.

CHICKEN CURRY

1 chicken, cut in pieces
½ pint sour milk
1 tablespoon ground coriander
1 tablespoon desiccated coconut
1 level teaspoon ground turmeric
½ teaspoon ground chillies
2 teaspoons ground almonds
2 oz. butter, oil or other fat

1 large finely chopped onion
2 cloves of garlic, finely chopped
salt to taste
juice of 1 lemon

Fry the onions and garlic in the butter, but do not brown. Add everything else and simmer gently in a covered pan for 30 minutes, or until the chicken is tender. Serve with Pillau rice.

COCONUT CURRY

1 chicken
2 oz. butter
1 coconut, or an equal amount
  of desiccated coconut
2 medium onions, sliced
1 tablespoon hot curry powder
½ pint meat or chicken stock,
  or gravy

Joint and skin the chicken. Heat the butter and fry lightly till brown. Crack open the coconut and pour off the milk, keep it. Chop very finely or pound the flesh of the nut and put it, or the desiccated coconut, in a heated frying pan, add the onions and the curry powder and fry till brown. Put the fried chicken in a stew pan, add the coconut mixture, pour in the stock and simmer gently for 45 minutes.

EGG CURRY

8 eggs, hard-boiled
3 medium onions, sliced
½ tablespoon curry powder
3 oz. butter
½ pint meat or chicken stock

Fry the onions in butter till brown, add the curry powder and stock, bring to the boil and simmer for 5 minutes, add the shelled hard-boiled eggs, and simmer for 30 minutes. Cut the eggs in halves, and pour the curry gravy over them on a bed of boiled rice.

HOOSEINEE COOKED MEAT CURRY

cooked lamb or mutton or beef
green ginger, sliced
onions, sliced
2 oz. butter
1 tablespoon hot curry
2 small sliced onions
1 tablespoon cold water
1 tablespoon cold milk
½ pint meat stock

Cut the cold meat in 1-inch squares and put on skewers, one slice of meat, one of ginger, one of meat, one of onion, until the skewers are packed tight. Pound the 2 small onions with the curry powder and moisten with water to form a paste. Heat the butter and cook this paste gently for 3 minutes. Add the milk and the water and cook for 10 minutes more, stirring all the time. Add the skewered meat and cook gently for 2 minutes, pour in the stock. Cover the saucepan and cook gently until the butter separates from the curry — for about 30 minutes.

KHEER

1 pint milk
1 oz. ground rice
1 oz. sugar
2 oz. chopped almonds
2 oz. chopped pistachio nuts
coconut milk
a few drops of rose, orange or
    lemon flavouring

Boil the milk, sprinkle in the ground rice, lower the heat and stir till it begins to thicken, add the nuts, flavouring and gradually pour in enough coconut milk to make as thin as an ordinary custard. Cook gently for 3 or 4 minutes longer. This dish is sometimes decorated with gold and silver leaf.

RHUBARB CHUTNEY

2 lb. rhubarb
1 lb. sultanas
2 lb. sugar
2 lemons
8 cloves of garlic
1 tablespoon salt
1 oz. root ginger
1 pint vinegar

Cut up the rhubarb into 1-inch pieces. Peel the lemons, remove seeds, chop pulp and skin finely. Chop or crush the garlic finely. Bruise the ginger. Put everything in a large saucepan, bring to the boil slowly, stirring all the time, stir and cook until the mixture turns to a thick pulp. Take out the ginger, put chutney into jars and seal. Keep for a month before using.

GREEN TOMATO CHUTNEY

2 lb. green tomatoes
2 oz. mustard powder
1 oz. cinnamon
1 oz. ground cloves
1½ lb. brown sugar
3 pints vinegar

1 pinch of cayenne pepper

Slice the tomatoes, put in a saucepan, add all the other ingredients, bring slowly to the boil and cook till thick. Pour into jars and seal. Eat after one month.

JELLABIES

BATTER:
4 oz. flour
1 *pint cold water*
deep fat for frying

SYRUP:
8 oz. sugar
½ *pint water*
2 *sprigs of saffron*
3 *inner seeds of cardamoms*

Make a smooth batter of the flour and water and leave in a warm place for 24 hours to ferment.

Put the sugar, saffron, cardamom seeds and water in a saucepan, bring to the boil slowly, and boil gently till a heavy syrup is formed. Keep warm. Heat the fat in a large deep pan till smoking. Stir the fermented batter. Take an ordinary funnel, put your finger over the hole and fill the funnel; let the batter run into the boiling fat in figures of eight or double circles. When set turn them over in the fat. They should be joined together. When crisp and golden brown, remove and drain them of fat. Separate and put them in the syrup for 3 minutes. Remove and drain. The syrup will run through the tubes and the jellabies should keep crisp.

CHUPPATIES

4 oz. *plain flour*
4 oz. *wholemeal flour*
1 oz. *butter or ghee*
⅛ *pint water (approximately)*
salt

Make a dough with the flour, butter, pinch of salt and water. It must be elastic, but not sticky. Knead well, cover and leave for 1 hour, then separate into small balls. Roll out on a floured board as thinly as possible. Have a slightly greased frying pan very hot, put in the chuppatie, remove from the heat and cook on the hot metal until a light brown skin has formed, turn and do the other side. Keep in a warm oven. Immediately re-heat the pan till very hot, put in the chuppatie last cooked side down and wait till it puffs up the top skin, but do not let it burst. Put at once in a warm oven. Each of the balls of dough must be cooked like this.

TO MAKE SOUR MILK DHYE OR TYRE

Warm 2 pints of milk to blood heat, add the juice of 3 lemons. Cover the pan and set aside for 24 hours to set. Put the curd in a clean cloth and hang up to drip for several hours till ry.

This can be kneaded into little balls, which are often served in rose-flavoured sugar syrup as a sweetmeat called Rasgollah.

BHUGIAS

4 oz. flour
1 teaspoon ground turmeric
¼ teaspoon ground chillies
1 medium minced onion
1 clove of garlic, minced
2 small finely chopped chillies
4 oz. finely chopped cooked
   vegetables—peas, carrots,
   turnips, etc.
2 eggs, beaten
milk

salt
fat for deep frying

Mix the flour, turmeric, chillies, minced onion and garlic well together, add the beaten egg and mix into a thick batter. If too thick add a little milk. Add the vegetables and salt to taste and stir gently so as not to break the vegetables.

Heat fat till smoking and drop in dessertspoons of the mixture. The Bhugias will swell up like doughnuts; when golden brown, drain well and serve hot.

DHALL

8 oz. lentils
1 medium onion
2 oz. butter
½ tablespoon curry powder
1 pint meat or chicken stock
½ teaspoon salt

Soak the lentils in cold water for 1 hour. Chop the onion very finely. Drain the lentils and put them, with the onion, butter, curry powder and stock in a saucepan, bring to the boil, cover the pan and simmer for 30 minutes. Add the salt and cook a little longer until the mixture looks like thick soup.

TO COOK BOMBAY DUCK

Fresh or tinned Bombay Ducks

These salt dry fishes are either roasted in the oven with 2 oz. fat, or fried till crisp. The fish should be held down while cooking as otherwise it will curl up; weighted in the oven or held down with a spoon or slice while frying. It has a strong smell but is a great appetiser to be eaten with curries.

RICE BALLS

8 oz. rice
2 pints milk
4 oz. sugar
small stick of cinnamon
desiccated coconut

Wash the rice, then simmer in the milk with sugar and cinnamon until cooked. Remove cinnamon and let the rice cool. When cold form into small balls and roll in desiccated coconut. Serve with cream and sugar.

BOMBAY PUDDING

2½ *tablespoons semolina*
½ *tablespoon salt*
1 *pint milk*
2 *oz. butter*
¼ *oz. flour*
fat for frying
SAUCE:
juice of 3 lemons
2 *tablespoons sugar*

Boil the milk, sprinkle in the semolina and cook until the semolina becomes clear and thick. Stir in the butter. Spread thinly on two or three plates. Leave to cool and harden. Dust each piece with flour and fry in butter or lard. Cut in segments and serve with the sugar melted in the warmed lemon juice.

COCONUT MILK

Grate the kernel of a fresh coconut or take the same amount of desiccated coconut and pour over enough boiling water to cover the coconut. Leave for 20 minutes. Squeeze the milk out with a vegetable presser or by the hands. Save this milk and do exactly the same again with the coconut pulp. This milk is excellent for cooking rice for curries, or for making the sweetmeat Kheer. Cows' milk and water mixed will make an even better 'milk'.

PINEAPPLE BALLS (Anglo-Indian)

2 *eggs*
4 *oz. sifted flour*
a *pinch of salt*
¼ *pint milk*
2 *tablespoons finely chopped*
   pineapple
fat for deep frying
castor sugar

Make a thick batter of the flour, eggs, salt and milk, add the pineapple, mix well. Have the fat smoking hot, drop in the mixture a dessertspoonful at a time. Fry till golden brown, drain well and serve with castor sugar sifted over them. They should puff up into golden balls.

HALWA

8 *oz. semolina*
8 *oz. butter*
8 *oz. sugar*
4 *oz. raisins*
4 *oz. blanched almonds*
1 *teaspoon cinnamon*
½ *teaspoon ground cardamoms*

Cook the sugar with 1 pint of water to form a thick syrup. Melt the butter and brown the semolina in it, then add the stoned raisins, almonds, cinnamon and cardamoms, stirring well. Finally add the syrup and simmer for a little longer. Pour into moulds to set.

NARRI GORENG (Javanese Fried Rice)

1½ lb. rice
2 pints boiling water
½ teaspoon salt
3 large onions, finely chopped
2 cloves of garlic, finely chopped
1 teaspoon finely chopped red
　chillies
4 oz. lard
8 oz. cooked meat, ham or chicken
　chopped in ½-inch cubes
½ tablespoon ground coriander
　seed
4 oz. shelled shrimps
an omelette made from 2 eggs

Boil the rice, drain and keep warm over hot water with a clean cloth over the colander.

Heat 3 oz. of the fat in a frying pan and fry gently for 10 minutes onions, garlic and chillies. Remove and keep warm. Fry the meat in 1 oz. lard for 5 minutes in a large pan, add the coriander and the cooked rice, onion mixture and the salt. Mix with a fork till everything is well blended, lower the heat, add the shrimps, cover the pan and heat slowly for 10 minutes. Meanwhile make the omelette, cut in strips, serve the rice mixture in a shallow dish and decorate with the omelette strips.

BAHMI

8 oz. vermicelli (Chinese if
　possible)
1 teaspoon salt, pinch of pepper
2 large finely chopped onions
2 cloves of garlic, finely chopped
4 tablespoons oil
8 oz. pork
2 lb. mixed vegetables, chopped
　small (cauliflower, cabbage
　heart, beans, peas, sprouts,
　spinach)
2 lb. leeks, chopped
2 heads of celery, chopped
4 oz. shelled shrimps
an omelette made from 2 eggs

soy sauce, tomato salad, cucumber
　salad
cut lemon served separately

Throw the vermicelli in plenty of salted boiling water and boil for 10 minutes. Fry the onion and garlic in the oil until brown. Remove and keep warm. Fry the meat in the same oil, quickly at first on both sides, then more slowly for 10 minutes, cool, and cut in ½-inch cubes. Put all the finely chopped vegetables, the pork cubes, shrimps and vermicelli in a large saucepan, mix well, cover the pan and heat slowly for 10 minutes. Meanwhile make an omelette with the eggs, pepper and salt; when done, cut in strips. Serve the Bahmi in a shallow dish; decorate with criss-cross strips of omelette.

Italy

COOKING IN ITALY

There is something glowingly happy and sunny in the Italian character, an enthusiasm and dash which shines through in their paintings, their music and in their cooking. They have their chefs and their Haute Cuisine — but the succulent and rich basis of Italian cookery springs from the people, the laughter, food and wine-loving people in all strata of society. The Italians have a rich heritage of traditional dishes, which have not changed for centuries and are part of the Italian way of life.

From ancient villages and farm kitchens come the great soups of the Italians, such as Minestrone. This must have been dreamed up by an Italian Mum who had more children than money and who wanted to put all she had into a bowl of soup.

Italy is blessed with sea, sunshine and good black soil — so they have a variety of fish and the finest array of vegetables and fruit. And do they cook them to perfection! It is all very simple: good material, good olive oil, the right flavouring — and a sprinkling of Parmesan cheese. You will notice this directness of approach amongst the fish recipes in the following pages — there is nothing over-elaborate or complicated, but each recipe is just right.

One of my favourite entrée dishes, which makes an excellent supper party dish too, is risotto — meat or chicken. I find risotto a blessing when I have more guests than dining room chairs because you can eat it with a fork sitting round the fire.

Pizza is a wonderful dish for a meatless lunch or dinner. Let me whisper to you that if you have no time to make the bread dough you can beg a little from your local baker and, following the instructions for the top, your pizza will be just as good as if you made the dough at home. There is hardly any need to point out that when it comes to making spaghetti or any other Pasta-siutta dishes you must inevitably follow the Italian recipes. The same thing applies to the cooking of veal, for which you will find a number of valuable recipes here — veal cutlets made with cheese are a real gourmet's joy and are really no trouble to prepare.

Last, but not least, let us not forget those gems which the Italians have given the world: their ice creams and sorbets.

ANCHOVIES AND CAPERS

4 *unsweetened biscuits*
8 *anchovy fillets*
8 *stoned olives*
12 *capers*
1 *tablespoon olive oil*

Soften the biscuits with a little water. Chop the anchovies and olives. Mix them with the softened biscuits, the capers and the olive oil. Spread on bread or biscuits.

ANTIPASTO

tomato salad (see p. 259)
potato salad (see p. 258)
1 *green pepper*
2 *hard-boiled eggs*

Slice the pepper. Arrange it and the tomato and potato salads on a dish. Cover with sliced hard-boiled eggs.

FENNEL ANTIPASTO

2 *heads Florence fennel*
4 *tablespoons olive oil*
1½ *tablespoons lemon juice*
freshly ground black pepper
salt

Wash fennel and soak for 2—3 hours in cold water. Slice thinly and arrange in a dish. Serve with dressing made from oil, lemon juice, black pepper and salt.

MUSHROOMS AND SCAMPI

1 *packet frozen scampi*
  or prawns
8 *oz. mushrooms*
3 *tablespoons olive oil*
1 *tablespoon lemon juice*
chopped parsley
salt, pepper
1 *clove garlic*

Slice the raw mushrooms thinly. Mix olive oil, lemon juice, salt, pepper and crushed garlic. Pour half of the dressing over the mushrooms and half over the scampi. Mix the two together just before serving.

PESTO

8 *anchovies, chopped*
4 *oz. grated Parmesan cheese*
2 *oz. pine kernels or walnuts,*
  chopped
1 *clove garlic, chopped*

basil
1 *tablespoon oil*

Put all the ingredients in a bowl. Beat with a wooden spoon until they form a smooth paste. Serve spread on bread or dry biscuit.

POTATO SALAD

4 *potatoes*
2 *tablespoons olive oil*
1 *dessertspoon wine vinegar*
salt, pepper
garlic
parsley

Steam the potatoes until cooked but very firm. Peel and slice them. Dress them while still warm with the oil and vinegar, add crushed garlic, chopped parsley, salt and pepper.

RADISH, TOMATO AND YELLOW PEPPER SALAD

2 *yellow peppers*
2 *tomatoes*
3 *radishes*
1 *stick celery*
2 *tablespoons olive oil*
salt, pepper

Peel and slice the tomatoes. Cut the peppers into rings. Slice the radishes and the celery. Mix together. Pour the olive oil over them. Season with salt and pepper.

RICE AND SCAMPI

4 *oz. Patna rice*
1 *packet frozen scampi*
3 *tablespoons olive oil*
1 *tablespoon wine vinegar*
chopped chives
salt, pepper

Cook the rice in boiling salted water. Drain and mix with the olive oil, vinegar, salt and pepper while still warm. When cold add the scampi and sprinkle with chopped chives.

RICE AND TUNNY FISH

4 *oz. Patna rice*
4 *oz. tunny fish*
3 *tablespoons olive oil*
1 *tablespoon wine vinegar*
½ *onion, finely chopped*
garlic
parsley

salt
pepper

Cook the rice in boiling salted water. Drain and dress with oil and vinegar while still warm. Mix with onion, salt, and crushed garlic. Sprinkle with freshly ground pepper. When cold add the tunny fish.

TOMATO SALAD

8 oz. tomatoes
2 tablespoons olive oil
salt, pepper
sugar

basil (optional)
chopped onion (optional)

Slice the tomatoes. Pour the olive oil over them, season with salt and pepper. Add sugar, onion or basil to taste.

TUNNY FISH WITH FRENCH BEANS

1 lb. cooked French beans
4 oz. tunny fish
3 tablespoons olive oil
1 tablespoon lemon juice
salt, pepper

Mix the olive oil and lemon juice, season with salt and pepper. Pour over the beans while they are warm. Cut the tunny fish into ½-inch squares, arrange them on top of the beans before serving.

TUNNY FISH SALAD

potato salad (see p. 258)
4 oz. tunny fish

Add tunny fish broken into fairly large pieces to potato salad, half an hour before serving.

BACON SOUP

1 bacon knuckle
1 onion, sliced
1 oz. butter
4 peppercorns
2 oz. flour
4 oz. grated Parmesan cheese

4 oz. Patna rice
salt

Cook the bacon, rice and peppercorns in 2 pints of water for 1 hour. Cook the onion in the butter until golden, add the flour, finely chopped bacon from the bone, the bacon stock and the rice. Reheat and serve with grated cheese.

CHICKEN SOUP WITH EGGS (for two people)

¾ pint chicken stock
2 eggs
2 oz. grated Parmesan cheese
2 slices bread
2 oz. butter

Fry the bread in the butter. Spread with grated cheese. Cut each piece into 3 strips. Bring the stock to the boil, poach the eggs in it. Pour into warmed soup bowls. Arrange 3 strips of bread round each plate.

CREAM OF CHICKEN SOUP

1½ *pints rich chicken stock*
  (a bouillon cube will not do
  for this)
1 *oz. ground rice*
2 *eggs*
1 *dessertspoon lemon juice*
nutmeg
½ *gill milk*
pepper

Mix the ground rice with the milk and a little of the stock. Heat the stock and add it to the ground rice paste. Simmer for 20 minutes. Season with the lemon juice, nutmeg and pepper. Beat up the eggs in a basin, pour a little of the hot soup over them, being careful not to allow the egg to curdle. Pour back into the pan and reheat carefully.

HARICOT BEAN SOUP

1 *lb. haricot beans*
½ *a small red cabbage*
2 *or 3 onions*
2 *leeks*
a small head of celery
a crushed clove of garlic
a sprig of thyme
salt, pepper

4 *tablespoons olive oil*
2 *tablespoons concentrated tomato purée*
3 *pints beef stock*

Soak the haricot beans for 12 hours. Put them in a casserole with the olive oil, tomato purée, and the chopped vegetables, season with salt, pepper and herbs. Add the stock and simmer slowly for at least 2 hours.

MINESTRONE (1)

1 *small head celery, chopped*
1 *small marrow, sliced*
2 *carrots, sliced*
½ *a small cabbage, shredded*
8 *oz. tomatoes, skinned*
2 *leeks, sliced*
4 *oz. spaghetti*
1 *small onion, sliced*
4 *pints stock*
4 *oz. streaky bacon*

4 *oz. grated cheese*
parsley
salt, pepper

Put the bacon, celery and carrots into the boiling stock. Simmer for 30 minutes. Add the other vegetables and the spaghetti, cook for a further 30 minutes. Stir the grated cheese into the soup before serving.

MINESTRONE (2)

8 *oz. bacon*
3 *pints stock*
8 *oz. broad beans*
8 *oz. peas*
1 *small head celery, chopped*
1 *onion, sliced*
8 *oz. spinach*
2 *carrots, sliced*
8 *oz. tomatoes, peeled and
quartered*

4 *oz. Patna rice*
4 *oz. grated Parmesan cheese*
salt, pepper
parsley

Cut the bacon into 1-inch squares, put it into the boiling stock with all the vegetables and the rice, season with salt and pepper, add the parsley. Simmer for 1 hour. Stir in the grated cheese before serving.

MUSHROOM SOUP

8 *oz. mushrooms, sliced*
2 *oz. butter*
2 *oz. flour*
1 *pint milk*
¼ *pint stock*
1 *clove garlic*
½ *glass Marsala*
salt, pepper

nutmeg
chopped parsley

Melt the butter and cook the mushrooms in it. Add the Marsala and cook gently for 2 minutes. Add the flour, cook for 1 minute, pour in the warmed liquids gradually. Season with salt, pepper and nutmeg. Sprinkle with parsley.

TOMATO SOUP (1)

2 *lb. ripe tomatoes, chopped and
skinned (or a large tin of
Italian tomatoes)*
2 *pints stock*
parsley
salt, pepper
1 *teaspoon sugar*
2 *tablespoons ground rice*

Cook the tomatoes slowly without water for 5 minutes. Add the stock and the parsley. Simmer for 10 minutes. Season with salt, pepper and sugar. Sieve the soup into the ground rice which has first been mixed with a little water. Return to the pan and simmer for 10 minutes.

TOMATO SOUP (2)

8 *oz. tomatoes, skinned and
    chopped*
1 *tablespoon olive oil*
2 *pints stock*
1 *clove garlic, crushed with salt*
½ *teaspoon sugar*

parsley
basil or marjoram

Cook the tomatoes in the olive oil for 10 minutes.
Add the other ingredients and simmer for 5 minutes.
    This can also be served chilled.

THICK SPINACH SOUP

2 *lb. spinach*
¼ *pint stock*
2 *oz. butter*
4 *oz. grated cheese*
2 *eggs*
nutmeg
salt, pepper

Cook the spinach without water for 30 minutes.
Strain thoroughly, put it into a casserole with the
stock and butter. Stir well, add the beaten eggs
and cheese. Season with salt, pepper and nutmeg.
Cook in a slow oven for 15 minutes. Serve with
croûtons (see p. 166).

DRY SALT COD

5 *large onions*
6 *anchovies (pounded until soft)*
1 *clove garlic*
2 *tablespoons olive oil*
2 *lb. dry salt cod*
a little milk
1 *sprig parsley*
salt, pepper
cinnamon

The fish should be soaked under running water for
24 hours and then steamed for 2 hours. Skin and
bone it and pound it to reduce toughness.
    Cook the onions with the parsley, crushed garlic
and the pounded anchovies in the olive oil until
they are soft. Add the fish and season with salt,
pepper and cinnamon. Cook for 20 minutes, then
cover with a little milk and simmer for 1 hour.

FRIED BREAM

1 *lb. bream*
olive oil for frying
4 *oz. flour*
salt, pepper
1 *lemon*

Cut the bream into slices 1 inch thick. Mix the flour
with the salt and pepper. Dredge the fish slices. Cook
in smoking olive oil. Serve with slices of lemon.

GRILLED MACKEREL

4 *mackerel*
2 *oz. olive oil or butter*
1 *lemon*

Score the fish across in two places and brush with oil or melted butter. Brush the grid with fat to prevent the fish from sticking to it. Place the fish under the grill and cook for about 3 minutes on each side. The fish should be placed very near the grill to start with and be moved further away when the skin is sealed and crisp. Serve with slices of lemon. Herring can be cooked in the same way.

GRILLED RED MULLET

4 *red mullet*
2 *oz. olive oil or butter*
maître d'hotel butter for a garnish

Leave the liver in the fish and make two incisions across it. Brush it with olive oil or melted butter and grill it quickly for about 7 minutes on each side. Serve with maître d'hôtel butter (see p. 163).

RED MULLET WITH TOMATOES

1½ *lb. tomatoes, peeled and sliced*
red mullet (2 or 4 fish according to size)
1 *stick celery, chopped*
salt, pepper
1 *clove garlic, chopped*

1 *tablespoon olive oil*
½ *teaspoon sugar*

Cook the tomatoes, celery and garlic in the olive oil. Sieve and season with salt, pepper and sugar. Put this purée into a fireproof dish, lay the red mullet on it, cover with greaseproof paper and cook in a slow oven for 30 minutes.

RED MULLET IN PAPER CASES

4 *red mullet*
1 *onion*
1 *stick celery*
1 *tablespoon olive oil*
parsley
garlic

Slice the onion finely and chop the celery, fry them until golden in the oil and add chopped parsley and crushed garlic. Make several incisions in the fish and put the onion mixture into them. Wrap each fish separately in greaseproof paper and cook in a moderate oven for about 30 minutes. Serve in the paper so that the juices do not escape.

GRILLED SCALLOPS

4 *scallops*
2 *tablespoons olive oil*
½ *onion, chopped*
1 *tablespoon chopped parsley*
1 *clove garlic*
salt, pepper

Remove the coral and grill the scallops under a hot flame for 5—10 minutes. Slice the coral, mix it with the butter, onion, parsley and crushed garlic. Pour over the scallops. Season with salt and pepper, and re-heat.

SHELLFISH RISOTTO

3 *dozen scampi or prawns*
8 *oz. Patna rice*
1 *onion, sliced*
2 *tablespoons olive oil*
salt
pepper

Cook the shells and claws of the scampi. Drain and keep the water. Dip the shelled scampi in flour and fry in oil. Fry an onion until golden, add the rice, moving it about in the fat with a wooden spoon until each grain is cooked, which will be between 20 and 30 minutes, add the scampi, which should have been kept warm. Season with salt and pepper.

SOLE WITH PARMESAN CHEESE

4 *soles*
4 *oz. grated Parmesan cheese*
2 *oz. butter*
parsley
thyme } *bouquet garni*
bay leaf
salt, pepper

Remove the skins from the fish and put them in a fireproof dish, season with salt and pepper. Dot with butter. Cook in a moderate oven until one side is brown, turn fish over to brown the other side. Simmer the fish in ½ pint water with a *bouquet garni* for 10 minutes. Strain the liquid over the fish. Sprinkle with grated cheese. Cook for another 5 minutes until cheese is melted.

SOLE WITH WHITE WINE SAUCE

4 *small soles*
2 *oz. butter*
4 *tablespoons chopped mint*
2 *tablespoons chopped parsley*
1 *clove crushed garlic*

SAUCE:
1 *oz. butter*
1 *onion, sliced*
1 *glass white wine*
salt, pepper

Skin the soles on both sides, make two crosswise incisions in the top of each fish. Fill these with butter, parsley, mint and garlic well mixed together. Wrap each sole in greaseproof paper and bake in a hot oven for 15 minutes. Serve with the following sauce.

Melt the butter, cook the onion in it until soft and golden. Add the wine and simmer for 10 minutes. Add a little water, season with salt and pepper. Simmer for another 10 minutes.

BROAD BEANS WITH BACON

2 *lb. broad beans, cooked*
2 *oz. bacon*
1 *small onion*
1 *oz. butter*

Chop the onion and bacon finely. Melt the butter, cook the onion and bacon in it for 5 minutes. Add the broad beans and cook gently for 5 minutes more.

NEW CARROTS WITH MARSALA

2 *lb. carrots*
1 *oz. butter*
1 *wine glass Marsala*
salt

Cut the carrots lengthwise, put them in a pan and cook gently in the butter for 2 minutes. Pour in the Marsala, simmer for a minute or two, add $\frac{1}{4}$ pint of water, season with salt. Cover the pan and simmer for 30 minutes.

MUSHROOMS IN BATTER

8 *oz. mushrooms*
olive oil for frying

BATTER:
4 *oz. flour*
1 *white of egg*
salt
3 *tablespoons olive oil*
1 *gill warm water*

Sieve the flour with a pinch of salt, mix in the olive oil, add the water and beat until smooth. Leave to stand for 2 or 3 hours, stir in the beaten egg white immediately before the batter is to be used.

Cut the mushrooms into thickish slices, coat them in the batter and fry quickly in hot olive oil.

GRILLED MUSHROOMS

8 *oz. field mushrooms*
1 *clove garlic*
salt
olive oil

Put olive oil, chopped garlic, and a sprinkling of salt on to the underside of each mushroom. Cook quickly under the grill, in a heat-proof pan in which they can be served.

PEAS WITH HAM

2 *lb. peas*
$\frac{1}{4}$ *pint stock*
1 *oz. lard*
4 *slices of ham*
salt, pepper

Cut the ham into strips. Put all the ingredients into a double saucepan. Cook for 45 minutes.

PIPERONATA (Stewed Tomatoes and Pimentos)

4 *red pimentos*
6 *tomatoes*
1 *onion*
2 *oz. butter*
salt, pepper

Melt the fat, slice the onions and cook until golden. Slice the pimentos and remove the seeds. Add them to the onion and cook slowly for 15 minutes. Peel and quarter the tomatoes. Put them in the pan. Season with salt and pepper, cook for another 30 minutes.

POTATO CROQUETTES

2 *lb. potatoes*
2 *oz. Parmesan cheese*
2 *eggs*
salt, pepper
nutmeg
4 *oz. breadcrumbs*
oil for frying

Cook the potatoes in boiling salted water. Sieve them and beat in the grated cheese and an egg, season with pepper and nutmeg. When the mixture is cool, shape into balls, roll in egg and breadcrumbs and fry quickly in olive oil.

SPAGHETTI

Good spaghetti should be made from durum se-molina (hard wheat).

Put the spaghetti into a large pan of salted boiling water. If the pasta is too long to go in to start with, watch it until the parts under water begin to soften, and then gently push the rest under the water. The pasta is ready when it is soft but still very firm. Drain the water off by pouring the pasta gently into a large sieve. If the sieve is then balanced on top of the pan in which the pasta was cooked and put on to a very low gas, it will stay hot for some time without becoming overcooked. It is very important not to overcook the pasta in the first place: if it has been overcooked the pieces will stick together in a con-gealed mass.

The amount of pasta needed per head will vary according to circumstances: a 1-lb. packet is enough for 4 if it is to be the main course.

All pasta should be cooked in this way.

RICE (for Risotto)

Italian rice is better than Patna for risotto but it is rather more expensive and not always obtainable. Patna rice is a good substitute. Fry a sliced onion gently in olive oil until it becomes soft and golden. Pour in the rice. Stir the rice about in the fat until each grain is covered, gradually add hot chicken stock, about a quarter of a pint at a time; continue adding stock until the rice is cooked.

A pound of rice will absorb about 2 pints of stock and take 20 to 30 minutes to cook. It should be stirred fairly continuously, particularly towards the end when the rice will become soft and likely to stick to the pan.

One chicken bouillon cube makes enough stock for 1 lb. of rice if it is diluted slightly more than is allowed for in the instructions.

BAKED GREEN NOODLES

12 *oz. green noodles*
Bolognaise sauce (see p. 272)
Béchamel sauce (see p. 165)
4 *oz. grated cheese*

Cook the noodles as described on p. 266 until they are nearly soft. Make half the amount of Bolognaise sauce described on p. 272 and the same amount of Béchamel sauce (p. 165).

Cover the bottom of a casserole with Bolognaise sauce, cover this with a layer of Béchamel sauce, and then a layer of green noodles. Repeat these layers until the dish is full. Spread the grated cheese on the top and bake in a moderate oven for 30 minutes.

CHEESE AND ANCHOVIES WITH BAKED BREAD

8 *slices French bread*
2 *oz. butter*
8 *anchovy fillets*
4 *oz. Bel Paese or Gruyère cheese*

Cut the bread into slices ½ inch thick. Lay them in a shallow dish with a slice of cheese between each. Cook in a moderate oven for about 10 minutes until the bread is crisp and the cheese melted. At the same time melt the butter in a frying pan and heat the anchovy fillets in it. Pour them over the baked bread when it is ready.

BABY MARROWS IN BATTER

1 *baby marrow per person*
frying batter (see p. 265, recipe
  for mushrooms)
salt
olive oil for frying

Cut the marrows into thin slices. Sprinkle with salt and leave in a colander for an hour to drain. Coat with batter and fry quickly in olive oil.

CHICKEN RISOTTO

½ *a boiling chicken (the whole*
  chicken should weigh about
  4 lb.)
1 *onion*
3 *tomatoes*
1 *stick of celery*
1 *green pepper*
4 *oz. mushrooms*
1 *glass white wine*
3 *oz. butter*
4 *oz. Parmesan cheese*
salt, pepper
garlic
thyme
1 *thick slice ham*

8 *oz. rice*
basil

Skin the chicken and take the meat off the bones and slice it before cooking. Fry the sliced onion in 2 oz. melted butter until it is golden. Add the chopped vegetables and the chicken and fry together for 2 to 3 minutes. Pour in the wine and cook for 2 minutes. Add thyme and basil or marjoram, season with salt and pepper. Cover with water, put a lid on the pan and cook slowly for 2 hours.

Cook the rice as for plain risotto (p. 267). Just before serving put in the chicken and sauce and stir in the grated cheese and 1 oz. butter. Serve with watercress.

EGGS WITH GRATED CHEESE

4 *eggs*
1 *oz. butter*
1 *tablespoon cream*
1 *oz. grated Parmesan cheese*
salt, pepper

Melt the butter in a saucepan. Beat the eggs. Pour them into the butter, stirring as they cook. Add the cream. Season with salt and pepper. Stir in the grated cheese just before the eggs set.

CHEESE FONDUE

4 *eggs*
12 *oz. Gruyère cheese*
½ *oz. butter*
¼ *pint milk*
salt, pepper

Cut the cheese into small cubes and soak them in the milk for 4 hours. Put the butter, beaten eggs and cheese in a double saucepan. Season with salt and pepper. Cook very slowly until creamy.

Serve with dry toast.

FORCEMEAT BALLS

8 oz. minced veal
1 lb. minced gammon
3 onions, chopped
2 sticks celery, chopped
2 carrots, chopped
butter
parsley
thyme
basil
cinnamon
4 oz. flour

eggs
salt, pepper

Mix the veal and gammon with the finely chopped herbs, cinnamon, salt and pepper. Bind the mixture with egg. Shape into balls. Roll in flour. Melt the butter, brown the vegetables in it. Add ½ pint of water, season with salt and pepper. Bring to the boil. Cook the meat balls in this sauce for 45 minutes. Arrange on a dish with sauce poured round them.

HARICOT BEANS WITH BACON ROLLS

8 oz. haricot beans (red or white)
8 oz. streaky bacon
parsley
garlic
nutmeg
cinnamon
pepper

Soak the beans overnight. Chop the parsley, mix it with the crushed clove of garlic, a little grated nutmeg, cinnamon and pepper. Spread a little of it on each rasher of bacon. Roll the rashers up and line the bottom of an earthenware casserole with them. Put the beans on top. Cover with water. Cook very slowly for 8 hours, adding more water if the beans get too dry.

STUFFED MARROW

1 medium-sized marrow
4 oz. rice
4 oz. chopped bacon
2 oz. mushrooms
parsley
salt, pepper
1 oz. butter

Cook the rice in a lot of boiling salted water until it is cooked but still very firm. Drain it. Melt the butter, cook the sliced mushrooms slowly, add the bacon. Mix with the rice. Cut the top off the marrow, scoop out the inside. Fill with rice mixture. Replace the top. Put into a fireproof dish. Cook with the lid on in a moderate oven for an hour.

MEAT RISOTTO

8 *oz. frying veal or beef*
1 *onion*
1 *carrot*
1 *stick celery*
1 *glass white wine*
cooked rice as for risotto (p. 267)
4 *oz. grated Parmesan cheese*
8 *oz. rice*
4 *oz. butter*
salt, pepper

Melt 2 oz. butter in a pan. Put in the carrot and celery finely chopped. When they are brown add the meat cut up into small pieces. Stir the meat about so that it is sealed on all sides, put the wine into the pan and simmer for 2 minutes. Season with salt and pepper, cover with a little water and cook slowly for an hour.

Mix this with the rice. Stir in grated cheese.

PASTRY PIZZA

DOUGH:
6 *oz. flour*
2 *oz. butter*
1 *egg*
¼ *oz. yeast*
salt, pepper
tomatoes, cheese and anchovies
  prepared as for bread pizza
  (see p. 271)

Dissolve the yeast in a little water. Mix all the ingredients into a dough. Cover the bowl and leave to rise for 2 hours. Spread the dough in a greased shallow dish with the tomatoes and anchovies on top. Cook in a hot oven for 25 minutes. Add the cheese and cook for another 5 minutes.

SAUSAGES WITH TOMATO SAUCE

1 *lb. pork sausages*
8 *oz. tomatoes*
1 *dessertspoon sugar*
sage
salt, pepper
1 *tablespoon olive oil*

Peel and quarter the tomatoes. Season with salt, pepper, sugar and a little sage, and simmer for 10 minutes. Fry the sausages slowly until they are brown. Put them in the tomato sauce, simmer for 5 minutes.

PIZZA

4 *oz. flour*
½ *oz. yeast*
water
salt
4 *tomatoes*
6 *anchovy fillets*
3 *oz. Bel Paese cheese*
basil
1 *tablespoon olive oil*

Fresh yeast can be obtained from many bakers, and keeps for a considerable time (at least a month) in a refrigerator. The dough for pizza, like all bread mixtures, should be kept at room temperature while it is being made. Put the flour in a bowl, add a pinch of salt. Mix the yeast with a little warm water. Put the yeast into the flour and mix well. Add enough warm water (about a gill) to make a stiff dough. Knead it thoroughly, until the dough becomes elastic. Put it in a warm place, covered with a cloth until it has doubled its size. Roll the dough out on a floured board. It should be ¼ inch thick.

Prepare the tomatoes, cheese and anchovies while the dough is rising. Peel the tomatoes, and chop them into small pieces, cut the cheese into thin slices, halve the anchovies.

Put the pizza dough on to a baking tin, cover it with tomatoes, then arrange the anchovies on top. Sprinkle with basil. Pour a little oil over it and a little on to the baking dish. Bake in a hot oven for 25 minutes. Add the cheese and bake for another 5 minutes.

RAVIOLI

PASTE:

6 *oz. flour*
1 *teaspoon salt*
2 *eggs*

FILLING:

8 *oz. minced beef*
4 *oz. minced pork*
1 *onion, sliced*
1 *carrot, sliced*
1 *stick celery, sliced*
½ *glass white wine*
¼ *pint stock*
1 *dessertspoon tomato purée*
1 *oz. butter*
2 *oz. breadcrumbs*
1 *egg*
salt, pepper

Sift the flour and salt on to a board. Pour the beaten eggs into a hole in the middle of the flour. Knead the eggs and flour to a soft dough. Divide the dough into halves.

Brown the carrot, onion and celery in the butter. Add the minced meat and cook for 10 minutes. Put in the wine, tomato purée and stock and cook in a slow oven for 2 hours. Mix with the breadcrumbs and egg. Roll the two pieces of dough very thin. Put teaspoonfuls of the meat mixture on to one of the pieces at 1½-inch intervals. Cover with the other piece of dough. Cut into squares.

Cook in boiling stock until the pieces rise to the top. Serve in a little of the stock or in tomato sauce as for spaghetti (p. 272), with grated cheese.

SPAGHETTI BOLOGNAISE

12 *oz. spaghetti*
1 *onion, sliced*
1 *carrot, sliced*
1 *stick celery, chopped*
1 *dessertspoon concentrated*
  tomato purée
4 *oz. minced beef*
2 *rashers streaky bacon*
2 *oz. chicken liver, chopped*
1 *glass white wine*
½ *pint stock*
1 *clove garlic*
3 *oz. butter*

4 *oz. grated cheese*
salt, pepper

Melt 1 oz. butter, cook the onion in it until soft, add the bacon cut into small pieces, the carrot and the celery. When these are brown put in the meat and stir so that all the pieces are coated with fat. Add the liver, stirring in the same way. Put in the tomato purée, the wine and the stock. Season with salt, pepper and crushed garlic. Simmer for 40 minutes.

Cook the spaghetti as on p. 266. Stir the sauce into it with 2 oz. butter and the grated cheese.

SPAGHETTI WITH OIL AND GARLIC

12 *oz. spaghetti*
2 *tablespoons olive oil*
1 *clove garlic*
4 *oz. Parmesan cheese*
parsley
salt, pepper

Cook the spaghetti as described on p. 266. Put it into a pan with warm olive oil and chopped garlic. Stir it well. Season with salt and pepper and chopped parsley. Serve grated cheese separately.

SPAGHETTI WITH TOMATO SAUCE

12 *oz. spaghetti*
1 *tablespoon olive oil*
1 *onion, sliced*
1 *clove garlic, chopped*
1 *lb. tomatoes, peeled and*
  quartered
4 *oz. Parmesan cheese*
salt, pepper
basil (fresh or dried)

Cook the spaghetti as described on p. 266. Mix with the sauce just before serving, stirring in 2 oz. melted butter and the grated cheese.

THE SAUCE:
Cook the onion with the garlic in the olive oil. When it is soft and transparent, add the tomatoes, a little basil, salt and papper. Simmer for 30 minutes, sieve. Add sugar if the tomatoes are not very ripe.

SPAGHETTI WITH TOMATOES AND ANCHOVIES

12 oz. spaghetti
1 tablespoon olive oil
3 oz. butter
1 lb. tomatoes
6 anchovy fillets
4 oz. Parmesan cheese
parsley
1 onion
1 clove garlic
salt, pepper

Cook the spaghetti as described on p. 266. Mix with the sauce and sprinkle with grated cheese before serving.

THE SAUCE:
Prepare the sauce in the same way as for the tomato sauce (p. 272), adding pounded anchovies and chopped parsley.

SPINACH WITH GRATED CHEESE

2 lb. spinach
4 oz. grated cheese
4 oz. butter
salt

Put the spinach in a big saucepan. Cook without water with the lid on until tender. Sieve. Stir in the grated cheese and the butter cut into small pieces. Season with salt and serve hot.

STUFFED ARTICHOKES

4 artichokes
2 oz. chopped anchovies
1 clove garlic
2 tablespoons olive oil

Make a stuffing by mixing the chopped anchovies and crushed garlic with the breadcrumbs.

Cut outside leaves of the artichokes off, remove as much as possible of the choke or fluffy part which grows in the bottom, and cut off the top part of the remaining leaves.

Put the stuffing into the artichokes. Put them into a pan with the olive oil. Cover the pan and cook slowly for an hour.

STUFFED MUSHROOMS

1 lb. large mushrooms
2 oz. ham or bacon
2 oz. grated Parmesan or
   Gruyère cheese
garlic
parsley
2 oz. breadcrumbs
olive oil
salt, pepper

Make a stuffing by mixing the breadcrumbs with the stalks of the mushrooms finely chopped, the grated cheese, chopped parsley and garlic. Season with salt and pepper.

Spread the mixture on the tops of the mushrooms, place them in a fireproof dish, put a little olive oil on top of each. Cover the dish and cook in a moderate oven for 30 minutes.

TAGLIATELLI WITH BACON AND MUSHROOM SAUCE

12 *oz. tagliatelli (or any other pasta)*
8 *oz. mushrooms*
4 *oz. bacon*
4 *oz. butter*
4 *oz. grated cheese*
salt, pepper

Cook the pasta as described on p. 266. Stir in the sauce just before serving.

SAUCE:
Melt 2 oz. of butter in a saucepan. Add the sliced mushrooms and the bacon finely chopped. Cook slowly until the mushrooms are soft (about 15 minutes). Stir in the cheese and the rest of the butter.

PRAWN RISOTTO

2 *dozen prawns or 1 lobster*
3 *oz. butter*
1 *small onion*
8 *oz. rice*
4 *oz. grated cheese*

Cook the rice as for plain risotto (see p. 267). Melt 1 oz. butter and heat the cooked prawns in it. Add them to the rice. Stir in 2 oz. melted butter and the grated cheese. Season with salt and pepper.

STUFFED CABBAGE

½ *white cabbage*
stuffing (as for marrow — see p. 269)
2 *pints stock*

Blanch the leaves of the white cabbage in boiling salted water for 5 minutes. Fill each leaf with stuffing made of a mixture of meat, rice and onions as for stuffed marrow (p. 269), roll the leaf and tie it with string. Poach them gently in stock for an hour.

STUFFED LETTUCE

4 *small round lettuces*
1 *anchovy fillets*
1 *teaspoon capers*
1 *teaspoon olive oil*
2 *clove garlic*
1 *glass white wine*

STUFFING:
2 *oz. breadcrumbs*
12 *black olives*
6 *anchovy fillets*
1 *oz. sultanas*
1 *teaspoon capers*
1 *clove garlic*
parsley

1 *tablespoon olive oil*
salt
pepper

Stone and chop the olives. Chop 6 anchovy fillets, parsley and garlic. Mix these with the other stuffing ingredients. Moisten with olive oil, season with salt and pepper. Put a little of the stuffing between the leaves of the lettuces, tie the tops up with string. Melt the olive oil in a large pan, chop 2 anchovy fillets and garlic and put them in the pan with the capers. Add a little water, put the lettuces in the pan and cook slowly for 1 hour. Pour in the wine and cook for another 10 minutes.

STUFFED PANCAKES (1)

filling as for ravioli (p. 271)
4 oz. flour
¼ pint milk
¼ pint water
1 oz. butter
1 egg
2 oz. grated cheese
1 oz. butter
¼ pint stock

Put the flour into a bowl. Beat the egg into it and gradually stir in the milk and water. Add the melted butter, season with salt. Beat thoroughly and leave to stand for 2 hours.

Make the pancakes in the usual way. Fill each pancake with the filling, roll them up and arrange them in a shallow fireproof dish. Dot with butter, sprinkle with grated cheese and pour in the stock. Heat the dish in a moderate oven for 20 minutes.

STUFFED PANCAKES (2)

pancake mixture as for stuffed pancakes (1)
8 oz. spinach, sieved
1 egg
2 oz. grated Parmesan cheese
2 oz. cooked chicken liver
2 oz. Bel Paese cheese
1 pint Béchamel sauce (see p. 165)

Make the filling by mixing the spinach, egg, chicken liver and grated cheese. Spread the mixture on the pancakes and roll them up. Pour the Béchamel sauce into a shallow dish, put the stuffed pancakes into it. Cover with slices of Bel Paese cheese, dot with butter. Bake in a moderate oven for 20 minutes.

VEGETABLE SOUFFLÉ

3 lb. peas
3 eggs
1 small onion
2 oz. ham
1 oz. grated cheese
2 oz. butter
1 tablespoon flour
salt
¼ pint milk

This can be made with any green vegetable and should be served alone or with fried meats. The following recipe for green peas can be adapted for other vegetables.

Fry the onion in butter, add the peas. Pour boiling water over them, season with salt and cook until the peas are tender. Pass through a sieve. Melt 1 oz. butter, add flour, stir until the flour is cooked. Add warm milk slowly, stirring all the time. Put the ham, cut into strips and the grated cheese into the sauce. Mix in the sieved peas. Add the egg yolks and the stiffly beaten egg whites.

Pour the mixture into a buttered cake tin, cover top with greaseproof paper and steam it for 1 hour.

STUFFED PIMENTOS

1 *pimento per person*
stuffing as for stuffed marrow
  (see p. 269)
2 *oz. olive oil or butter*

If possible get yellow, red and green pimentos. Cut off the tops, remove the seeds and core. Pour boiling water over them to soften the skins a little.

Fill with the stuffing, put a little butter or olive oil in a fireproof dish, arrange the pimentos in it, cover the dish and cook in a moderate oven for 45 minutes.

FRIED CALVES' LIVER

1 *lb. calves' liver*
1 *or 2 eggs*
8 *oz. breadcrumbs*
4 *oz. butter*
1 *teaspoon lemon juice*
parsley
salt, pepper

Season the liver with salt, pepper and lemon juice. Leave for 1 hour. Roll in egg and breadcrumbs. Fry quickly in butter. Sprinkle with chopped parsley and serve with quarters of lemon.

CALVES' LIVER WITH ONIONS

1 *lb. calves' liver cut in very*
  thin slices
2 *lb. Spanish onions, sliced*
2 *tablespoons olive oil*
salt

Cook the onions in the olive oil until soft. Add the liver and fry quickly on both sides until cooked (about 3 minutes a side).

STEWED KIDNEYS

1 *lb. veal or lambs' kidneys*
1 *glass white wine*
parsley
2 *oz. butter*
½ *teaspoon grated lemon peel*
1 *teaspoon lemon juice*
salt, pepper

Blanch the kidneys in boiling water and lemon juice. Skin and slice them. Season with salt and pepper. Cook slowly in the butter with the lemon peel for 30 minutes. Add the wine. Simmer for 2 minutes.

CHICKEN LIVER CROÛTONS

1 *lb. chicken livers*
2 *oz. bacon or cooked ham, diced*
4 *slices bread, made into croûtons*
4 *oz. butter*
1 *dessertspoon lemon juice*
4 *oz. flour*
¼ *pint stock*
salt, pepper

Brown the ham in the butter. Add the chicken livers, diced and floured. Stir them in the butter until sealed. Put in the stock and lemon juice. Season with salt and pepper and cook slowly for 10 minutes. Pour the mixture over the croûtons (see p. 166).

CHICKEN AND RICE

1 *cold chicken*
12 *oz. rice*
4 *oz. mushrooms*
2 *sticks celery*
salt, pepper
2 *tablespoons olive oil*
½ *dessertspoon lemon juice*

Boil the rice in a lot of salted water for 15 minutes. Drain and while still warm pour the oil over it. Season with nutmeg, pepper and salt. When cold mix in the cold chicken, cut into pieces, and the chopped celery.

CHICKEN STUFFED WITH HAM

1 3—4 *lb. boiling chicken*
6 *oz. cooked ham, minced*
1 *clove garlic*
fennel, chopped
pepper

Mix the ham with fennel, pepper and crushed garlic. Stuff the chicken with the mixture. Cook in ½ pint water in a moderate oven for 3½ hours.

PIGEON WITH WHITE WINE

2 *pigeons*
2 *oz. tongue*
1 *onion*
1 *glass white wine*
¼ *pint stock*
2 *oz. butter*
2 *lb. peas*
pepper
basil

Slice the onion and cook it in the butter. Cut the ham and tongue into small pieces and add to the onion. Put in the pigeons and brown them. Add the wine. Simmer for 2 minutes, add the stock. Season with salt, pepper and nutmeg. Put a cover on the pan and cook slowly for 1½ hours. Add the shelled peas and cook for 20 minutes more.

FRIED BREAST OF CHICKEN

4 *slices of chicken breast*
2 *tablespoons flour*
4 *oz. butter*
salt, pepper

Flour the chicken. Season with salt and pepper. Melt the butter in a frying pan, fry the chicken quickly for 3 minutes on each side. Cover the pan with lid and cook more slowly for about 30 minutes.

RABBIT WITH MARSALA

1 *rabbit*
1 *carrot*
1 *stick celery*
1 *onion*
8 *oz. tomatoes*
1 *aubergine*
1 *pimento*
salt, pepper
marjoram
2 *tablespoons olive oil*
1 *glass Marsala*

Brown the sliced onion, carrot and celery in the olive oil. Cut the rabbit into pieces, flour them and brown them in the pan with the vegetables. Pour in the wine, simmer for 2 minutes. Add the tomatoes, peeled and quartered, and ½ pint of water. Season with salt, pepper and marjoram. Cover the pan and cook slowly for 45 minutes. Cut aubergine into cubes and the pimento into slices. Add them to the pan and cook for another 30 minutes.

ROAST TURKEY (STUFFED)

1 *turkey*
1 *lb. liver*
1 *lb. chestnuts*
8 *oz. prunes*
4 *pears*
1 *glass white wine*
1 *oz. butter*
salt, pepper
nutmeg

Make a stuffing for the turkey as follows:
Soak, cook and stone the prunes. Shell the chestnuts and cook them in water. Peel the pears and cut them into small pieces. Chop the prunes and chestnuts. Cook the chopped liver, prunes, chestnuts and pears for 10 minutes in the butter. Add the white wine, season with salt, pepper and grated nutmeg. Stuff the turkey with the mixture and roast it in the usual way.

BEEF AND PORK STEW

1 *lb. beef, cut into pieces*
4 *oz. lean pork, cut into pieces*
1 *carrot*
1 *onion*
1 *stick celery*
2 *oz. butter*
½ *glass white wine*
1 *tablespoon tomato purée*

½ *pint stock*
salt, pepper

Brown the sliced vegetables in the butter. Add the meats and brown them. Put in the tomato purée and the wine, boil for 1 minute, add the stock. Season with salt and pepper, cook slowly in a covered pan for 2 hours.

BEEF STEW WITH RED WINE

round of beef, weighing 2—3 lb.
1 clove garlic
1 glass red wine
parsley
thyme
bay leaf
salt, pepper
1 onion
4 oz. bacon
1 tablespoon olive oil

Marinate the meat for 2 to 3 hours in the red wine with the herbs, garlic and seasoning. Heat the olive oil in a pan just big enough to hold the meat, brown the onion, add the meat and brown it on both sides. Put in the bacon, cut into medium-sized pieces, and brown it. Strain the marinade into the pan, boil for a minute or two, add a cupful of water and simmer, covered with a lid, for 3 hours.

BEEF STEW WITH WHITE WINE

round of beef weighing 2—3 lb.
2 large onions
2 tomatoes, peeled and quartered
1 stick celery, chopped
1 carrot, sliced
2 oz. butter
1 glass white wine
salt, pepper
basil

Melt the butter in a pan just big enough to hold the beef, fry the onions until golden, put in the beef, brown it on both sides, add the vegetables. Season with salt and pepper, add a little basil and the white wine. If necessary add a little extra stock or water and cook slowly for 3 hours.

FRITTO MISTO (Mixed Grill)

4 very small lamb chops (boned)
8 forcemeat balls (see p. 269)
8 slices chicken liver
8 slices young marrow
breadcrumbs
egg
basil
salt
oil for frying

All the ingredients should be in very small pieces. Small pieces of brain or sweetbreads can be added. Dip the pieces in egg, coat with fine breadcrumbs, season with salt, pepper and chopped basil. Fry quickly in a deep pan of smoking olive oil.

OSSO BUCO

4 *pieces of veal, cut from the leg across the bone about an inch thick*
2 *tablespoons butter*
garlic
1 *chopped clove*
lemon rind
½ *pint stock (a chicken bouillon cube will do)*
½ *glass dry white wine*
2 *oz. flour*
4 *tomatoes*

FOR THE MIREPOIX:
2 *leeks, sliced*
2 *Spanish onions, sliced*
1 *head celery, chopped*

4 *oz. lean bacon, diced*
1 *tablespoon olive oil*
thyme
½ *bay leaf*

THE MIREPOIX:
Fry the onions in the olive oil until there is enough moisture to cook the rest of the vegetables. Add the leeks, celery, garlic, thyme and bay leaf. Season with salt and pepper. Stew slowly for 40 minutes.

Melt the butter in a frying pan, flour the slices of veal and brown on both sides. Put the vegetables into a casserole, add the tomatoes peeled and quartered, the wine, the stock and lastly the meat, and cook slowly for 1½ hours. Before serving, add chopped or finely grated lemon peel.
Serve with rice.

ROAST LAMB

1 *leg of lamb*
garlic
4 *oz. butter or 4 tablespoons olive oil*
rosemary
salt, pepper

Put 1 or 2 cloves of garlic into the meat near the bone at the fillet end. Lay a sprig of rosemary on top of the meat. Sprinkle with salt and pepper. Baste with the butter or olive oil and cook in a hot oven for 30 minutes per lb.

LAMB WITH WHITE WINE

2 *lb. of leg of lamb*
2 *carrots*
2 *tomatoes*
1 *onion*
1 *stick celery*
½ *orange*
1 *wine glass of white wine*
garlic
marjoram
salt, pepper
2 *tablespoons olive oil*

Heat the olive oil in a stewpan. Fry the sliced onion until golden. Rub the meat with garlic, salt, pepper and marjoram, brown it with the onions. Put in the peeled and quartered tomatoes and the chopped carrots and celery. Cook for 10 minutes. Add the white wine and cook for 1 minute. Cover the pan and simmer for 2 hours. Squeeze the juice of half an orange over the meat before serving.

MINCED MEAT BALLS

1 *lb. minced meat (veal or beef)*
2 *eggs*
1 *thick slice of bread*
lemon peel
1 *clove garlic*
milk
2 *oz. butter for frying*
salt, pepper

Mince the garlic, parsley, lemon peel and the meat. Soak the bread in a little milk. Mix it with the meat Stir in the beaten eggs. Season with salt and pepper. Shape into flat cakes on a floured board. Fry the cakes quickly in smoking butter for about 7 minutes on each side.

ROAST LOIN OF PORK

loin of pork weighing 3—4 lb.
garlic
rosemary
salt, pepper

Rub the meat with a cut clove of garlic. Stick more garlic into it under the skin. Strew with rosemary, season with salt and pepper. Fill a roasting pan with water 2 inches deep. Put the pork in the water. Cook in a moderate oven for 45 minutes per lb.

GRILLED PORK CHOPS

4 *pork chops*
garlic
1 *piece of fennel*
12 *juniper berries (optional)*
3 *tablespoons olive oil*
salt, pepper

Stick a clove of garlic into each chop. Chop the fennel and mix it with a crushed clove of garlic and the juniper berries. Put some of the fennel mixture over each chop. Pour olive oil over the chops and leave to marinate for 2 hours.

Grill the chops for 25 minutes, turning them over once or twice. Season with salt and pepper.

PORK WITH RED WINE

loin of pork weighing about 3 lb.
2 *tablespoons olive oil*
salt, pepper
2 *cloves garlic, chopped*
chopped parsley
1 *glass red wine*

Season the pork with salt and pepper. Brown in the olive oil. Add the garlic, parsley and wine. Cook in a moderate oven for 1½ hours. Pour the sauce over the meat.

STEAK WITH TOMATO SAUCE

4 *thick slices of rump steak*
1½ *lb. tomatoes, peeled and*
    quartered
1 *clove garlic*
2 *tablespoons olive oil*
parsley
salt, pepper

THE SAUCE:

Melt 1 tablespoon olive oil, cook the tomatoes in it with the garlic crushed with salt and the parsley.

Melt 1 tablespoon olive oil in a frying pan, season the steaks with salt and pepper, brown on both sides. Add the sauce, simmer for 10 minutes.

STUFFED BEEF

1 *lb. rump steak cut in a thick slice*
2 *oz. good liver sausage or*
    chicken livers
2 *oz. ham*
2 *oz. tongue*
1 *oz. grated Parmesan cheese*
1 *egg*
1 *thick slice of white bread*
1 *onion*
1 *stick celery*
1 *small carrot*
parsley
salt, pepper

Soak the bread in water and squeeze the water out. Mix it with chopped onion, carrot, celery, parsley, liver, ham and tongue, the grated cheese and the beaten egg. Season with salt and pepper and add basil or marjoram to taste.

Spread the stuffing on the meat, roll it up and tie it with string. Cover with dripping and roast in a hot oven for 45 minutes, basting once or twice. This can be made with less good meat and pot roasted in the usual way. Serve cold. If pot roasted it should be allowed to get cold in the pan in which it was cooked.

VEAL OLIVES (1)

8 *thin slices of veal*
8 *slices of ham*
1 *wine glass Marsala*
sage
2 *oz. butter*
salt, pepper

Beat the slices of veal until they are very thin. Lay a slice of ham on each and a very little sage. Roll them and tie with string. Melt 2 oz. butter in a pan, brown the rolls in this. Add the Marsala, cook gently for a minute. Season with salt and pepper. Cover the pan and simmer for 30 minutes.

VEAL OLIVES (2)

8 *thin slices fillet veal*
8 *anchovy fillets*
12 *capers*
4 *oz. flour*
butter or olive oil for frying

Pound the anchovies and capers together. Spread the mixture on each fillet. Roll and tie with string. Flour the rolls. Fry quickly in olive oil.

VEAL CUTLETS (1)

4 *cutlets on the bone*
1 *egg*
4 *oz. breadcrumbs*
butter for frying
lemon
parsley

Trim the fat or gristle from the cutlets. Beat them, coat with egg and breadcrumbs. Fry rather fast in butter. Serve in a heated dish garnished with parsley and slices of lemon.

VEAL CUTLETS (2)

4 *veal cutlets on the bone*
1 *egg*
4 *oz. breadcrumbs*
4 *slices ham*
4 *oz. grated Parmesan cheese*
butter

Prepare and cook the cutlets as for plain veal cutlets. When they are cooked put a slice of ham, 1 oz. grated Parmesan cheese and 1 tablespoon melted butter on each cutlet. Cover the pan and cook until the cheese has melted (about 5 minutes).

VEAL STEW

1½ *lb. stewing veal (preferably from the shin)*
1 *onion*
2 *tomatoes*
2 *pimentos*
1 *glass white wine*
2 *oz. butter*
salt

Fry the sliced onion in butter until it is soft and golden. Cut the meat into fairly small pieces, put them in the pan and brown them. Pour in the wine and let it cook for a minute. Add the tomatoes, peeled and quartered, and the pimentos sliced. Just cover the meat with water. Season with salt. Simmer with a lid on the pan, for about 2 hours.

VEAL WITH TUNNY FISH AND ANCHOVIES

1½ *lb. fillet veal*
4 *whole anchovies*
4 *oz. tunny fish*
1 *onion*
2 *carrots, sliced*
1 *stick celery, chopped*
¼ *pint olive oil*
1 *bay leaf*
2 *cloves*
2 *tablespoons lemon juice*
2 *tablespoons capers*
salt, pepper

Remove all the fat from the meat. Cut 2 anchovies into strips and lay them on the meat. Roll it and tie with string. Put in a saucepan, add the onion stuck with cloves, carrots, celery, bay leaf and salt. Cover with water and simmer for 1½ hours. When cold, drain the meat and slice thinly. Fill a casserole with the slices. Cover with the following sauce: Pound 2 anchovies with the tunny fish, add the olive oil gradually and then the lemon juice. Strew capers over the top. Leave in a cold place for 24 hours.

To serve: Arrange the slices on a flat dish with the sauce poured over them.

SWEET PASTRY

8 *oz. flour*
4 *oz. sugar*
4 *oz. butter*
1 *egg*
1 *teaspoon baking powder*
milk

Put the flour in a bowl. Rub in the fat. Add the other ingredients and work gently until a smooth dough is formed. Leave for at least an hour in a cool place.

APRICOT TART

2 *lb. apricots*
2 *oz. sugar*
vanilla
sweet pastry (see above)

Cook the apricots in a little water with the sugar and a drop of vanilla. Cut them in halves and stone them. Arrange them on the pastry. Cook in a hot oven for 20 minutes and more slowly for another 10 minutes.

CHESTNUT PYRAMID

1 *lb. chestnuts*
4 *oz. sugar*
¼ *pint double cream*

Score the chestnuts and put them in a hot oven for 10 minutes. Peel them and cook in boiling water until soft. Drain off the water. Mix with the sugar. Put through a sieve directly on to the serving dish. Cover the top with whipped cream.

CHOCOLATE MOULD

3 *oz. cocoa*
3 *oz. butter*
3 *oz. sugar*
3 *oz. ground almonds*
3 *oz. petit beurre biscuits*
1 *egg*
1 *egg yolk*

Beat the butter and cocoa, add the ground almonds. Dissolve the sugar in a little hot water. Add it to the butter mixture. Beat the egg and egg yolk and add them. Cut the biscuits into small pieces and stir into the mixture, being careful not to crumble them. Grease a mould, put the mixture into it and leave in a cold place to set.

CREAM CHEESE WITH ALMONDS AND DRIED FRUIT

4 *oz. unsalted cream cheese*
1 *oz. ground almonds*
½ *oz. candied orange peel, thinly sliced*
2 *oz. sugar*
1 *egg yolk*

1 *oz. mixed raisins and sultanas*
1 *teaspoon grated lemon peel*

Put the cream cheese into a bowl. Beat the egg yolk, stir it into the cheese together with the other ingredients. Hand granulated sugar separately.

SOUR CREAM WITH LIQUEUR

1 *pint cream*
1 *small glass liqueur (rum, brandy or kirsch)*
2 *oz. sugar*

Pour the cream into a basin, leave it to thicken and turn slightly sour, or turn it sour with lemon juice. Strain it through muslin and beat in the sugar and liqueur. Serve slightly chilled. Unsalted cream cheese can be used instead of cream.

STUFFED PEACHES

4 *large peaches*
2 *oz. macaroons*
1 *small egg yolk*
1 *tablespoon sugar*
½ *oz. butter*

Halve the peaches, remove the stones and a little of the fruit. Crush the macaroons, mix them with the extra fruit and other ingredients. Fill the holes left in the peaches with this mixture. Cook in buttered fireproof dish for 30 minutes in a moderate oven.

APRICOT ICE CREAM

½ *pint single cream*
4 *egg yolks*
4 *oz. castor sugar*
1 *lb. apricots*

Make the cream as for strawberry ice cream (see below).

Cook the apricots with the sugar and a little water. Sieve. Add to the cream and freeze.

CASSATA

½ *pint single cream*
4 *oz. castor sugar*
2 *oz. mixed glacé cherries, angelica, candied peel and walnuts, finely chopped*
4 *egg yolks*
1 *strip lemon peel*

Make the cream as for strawberry ice cream (see below). Add the chopped lemon peel during the cooking and the other ingredients when it is cool. Freeze.

STRAWBERRY ICE CREAM

½ *pint single cream*
4 *egg yolks*
4 *oz. castor sugar*
1 *lb. strawberries*

Put the beaten egg yolks into a double saucepan with the cream. Cook very slowly, stirring all the time until it thickens. Add the sugar and the crushed strawberries. Freeze in the ice tray of a refrigerator turned to its lowest temperature, stirring every half hour.

COFFEE SORBET

5 *tablespoons coffee*
3 *tablespoons sugar*
1 *pint water*

Put the coffee and sugar into an earthenware jug and pour boiling water over them. Strain through a fine sieve or muslin when cold. Pour into the ice tray of a refrigerator and leave to freeze.

LEMON SORBET

¼ *pint lemon juice*
2 *oz. sugar*
½ *pint water*

Make a syrup by boiling the sugar with the water for 5 minutes. Mix with the lemon juice and freeze in the ice tray of a refrigerator.

Jamaica

COOKING IN JAMAICA

The word Jamaica brings with it pictures of Caribbean splendour, white coral beaches lapped by blue waters — millionaires in super-luxurious hotels on Montego Bay eating chi-chi food prepared by the greatest chefs. Well of course Jamaica is all that, the playground of the international rich, but it also has its own static population and its own traditions in food. As few of us can ever get to those glamorous holiday resorts that Jamaica has to offer the tourist, why not to try to get the taste of their cooking into our palate, as an infinitely cheaper substitution!

I suggest you start your Jamaican holiday in your kitchen with a session of making banana jam — a simple and rich jam, with a completely different taste from any other confection.

The next step could be — I am still keeping it nice and easy — to make a Sour Sweet Salad, which has an extremely well-balanced flavour to it.

If you have by now got the strong urge to go to any length of trouble to cook Jamaican and give a barbecue party, then the moment has arrived to get yourself organised for 'Jerk Pork' You will not only have to organise yourself, but you will have to enlist the help of a local farmer and find out when he next kills a pig, so that you can collect from him ½ pint of pig's blood — essential to Jerk Pork. Given enough drive and ambition, you will overcome all these obstacles — and the result will be something exquisite, but if you are faint-hearted, I suggest you stick to the simpler recipes.

RICE AND RED PEAS

8 *oz. red peas*
½ *pint coconut milk (see p. 253)*
2 *oz. salt pork or bacon*
1 *lb. rice*

The peas are the oval red seeds of large runner or French beans. Boil the peas until tender, drain and set aside. Grate the coconut flesh, add a little water and hang in a muslin bag to drain. Add the liquid to the peas. Fry the salt pork, add the rice, peas, coconut milk and about a pint of water. Cook slowly until all the water is absorbed. Serve with fried bananas.

JERK PORK

1 *side lean pork*
1 *lb. salt*
1 *teaspoon saltpetre*
6 *hot red peppers*
1 *teaspoon pimento grains*
1 *teaspoon cinnamon*
2 *onions*
1 *escallion (green onion)*
½ *pint pig's blood*

A famous speciality of Portland, Jamaica. Scald the pork and remove bones. Grind all the other ingredients together in a mortar and mix with the pig's blood. Marinade the pork in this for 12 hours, turning from time to time. To cook, place a rack made of green sticks over the fire. Lay pimento leaves across it, then arrange pork on top. Cover with more pimento leaves and then a slab or board to keep the meat flat. Leave to roast, turning at intervals until well done.

SOUR SWEET SALAD

12 *oz. shredded cabbage*
2 *oranges*
1 *apple*
2 *tablespoons lime juice*
cucumber and tomato to garnish

Peel the orange and cut finely across the fruit to make very small sections. Grate the apple. Mix cabbage, apple and orange with lime juice. Arrange in a salad bowl, garnish with cucumber and tomato and serve with mayonnaise.

STAMP-AND-GO FRITTERS

1 *lb. dried salt cod*
1 *onion*
1 *tomato*
1 *small chilli*
2 *oz. flour*
fat for frying

Soak the fish for 12 hours. Boil gently in unsalted water until tender. Drain, flake the flesh when cool. Mince the onion, tomato and chilli. Pound with the fish until smooth. Shape into cakes, fry on both sides in hot fat. Serve with yams, sweet potatoes or ockra. The Jamaicans always serve a variety of vegetables with each main dish.

JAMAICAN PIE CRUST PASTRY

8 oz. flour
1 teaspoon salt
4 oz. cooking fat
about 4 tablespoons water to mix

Sift flour and salt into a bowl. Take out 4 tablespoons and blend with water to make a paste. Cut the fat into the rest of the flour in pieces the size of peas. Stir the flour paste into the flour and fat mixture to make a dough that will barely hold together. Form into a ball, place on a floured board and roll out as required. Wrap in waxed paper or foil and chill before using. This pastry will keep for several days in a cold place.

GUAVA PIE

24 ripe guavas
8 oz. brown sugar
1 teaspoon mixed spice
1 oz. butter
pie crust pastry (see recipe above)

Peel guavas, cut in half and scoop out the seeds. Canned guavas may be used. Line pie dish with pastry, fill with alternate layers of guava, sugar and spice until dish is full, then add dots of butter. Cover the pie with the second layer of pie crust, seal the edges with milk, pinch round rim and prick top with a fork to allow steam to escape. Bake in a hot oven for 15 minutes, then lower heat to moderate temperature and cook for 30—40 minutes until brown.

DUMP-AND-STIR CAKE

8 oz. flour
6 oz. sugar
4 oz. butter
2 eggs
2 teaspoons baking powder
¼ pint milk
1 teaspoon vanilla essence
2 teaspoons lemon or lime juice

2 tablespoons orange juice
½ teaspoon salt

Sift flour, baking powder, salt, rind and sugar together over the fat in a bowl. Mix well together. Add the unbeaten eggs, vanilla and milk and beat well together. Add the juices and beat again. Bake in sandwich tins in a moderate oven for 20—30 minutes. Fill with cream if desired.

BANANA JAM

12 ripe bananas
2 teaspoons lime juice
2 lb. sugar
½ pint water

Bring water and sugar to the boil, then add diced bananas and lime juice. Cook for 30 minutes or until thick.

Jewish Cookery

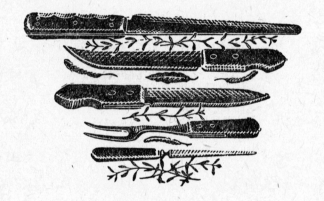

JEWISH COOKERY

Jewish cookery is essentially a friendly family affair performed by Mother for big family gatherings or holy days. It has many traditional dishes, which are slightly altered in different countries and by different mothers — but the *par excellence* Jewish dishes tend to pop up in every Jewish community all over the world.

Chopped Liver can be found as easily in a San Francisco Jewish restaurant as at the table of a Jewish family in Hong Kong. The principle is the same, but there are hundreds of ways of preparing it. Some use calves' liver, some use all sorts of minced offals with 'a taste of liver', but all have the hard-boiled egg, the onion and the chicken fat for flavouring. I think the recipe which is given here with chicken livers is just about the best of the lot — I find it invaluable for sandwich fillings or served as a first course for a dinner party, with thin slices of hot toast.

Kneidlech for clear soups is used in Jewish cookery during Passover, when Jewish people are not allowed to eat anything prepared with ordinary flour. Now this dire necessity has inspired the Jewish cooks to create a dream of a concoction made of matzo meal, light and tasty — an absolute work of art.

Gefillte Fish (Stuffed Fish) has become such an international favourite that you can even buy it in tins — but you don't know what you are missing if you don't take the trouble to make it yourself.

Another delicious Jewish dish, closely connected with religious traditions, is Cholent. The author of *Love and Knishes* (a hilariously funny Jewish cookery book) says that there are as many cholents as there are cooks and her conclusion is that 'a cholent is any food that has the stamina to withstand 24 hours of cooking'. The long cooking is necessary, because cholent is cooked slowly in the oven during the Sabbath, when Jewish cooks are not allowed to work, but the family likes to have a hot meal all the same. I should think it is just as good a solution of the cooking problem for a career woman — the cholent will cook itself, while she is in the office.

CHOPPED LIVER

8 *oz. chicken livers*
1 *small onion*
1 *hard-boiled egg*
1 *tablespoon breadcrumbs*
chicken fat
salt, pepper

Cook livers in chicken fat until tender — about 5 minutes. Then mince very finely with the onion and hard-boiled egg and breadcrumbs. Season with salt and pepper and add a little chicken fat to form a good paste.

KNEIDLECH (for soups)

4 *oz. medium matzo meal*
½ *pint boiling water*
1 *teaspoon chopped parsley*
1 *egg*
2 *tablespoons chicken fat*
salt, pepper
pinch nutmeg
pinch ginger

Pour boiling water over the meal and mix well. Add the beaten egg, fat, salt, pepper, nutmeg and ginger. Mix thoroughly and leave to stand for 2 hours in a very cold place. Then form into small balls and drop into boiling soup. Simmer for 10—15 minutes until cooked.

GEFILLTE FISH

3 *lb. mixed bream, cod, fresh*
  haddock
3 *eggs*
3 *onions*
2 *carrots*
1 *stick celery*
1 *tablespoon chopped parsley*
1 *oz. ground almonds*
2 *tablespoons matzo meal*
salt, pepper

Simmer the skins and bones of the fish in 1½ pints water with 1 sliced carrot, the chopped celery, onion, salt and pepper for 45 minutes. Strain. Mince and chop the fish, mix well with the parsley, ground almonds, beaten eggs and enough matzo meal to bind the mixture. Roll into balls. Simmer these gently in the fish stock with the other sliced carrot for 1 hour. Remove the balls from the stock, arrange a slice of carrot on top of each. Reduce the stock and pour a little over each ball. It should set when cold. Serve cold.

POTATO LATKES

4 *potatoes*
2 *oz. flour*
1 *tablespoon chopped onion*
2 *eggs*
salt, *pepper*
cooking fat

Peel the potatoes and soak them in cold water for 1 hour. Grate them, drain off the liquid, then add the beaten eggs, sifted flour, chopped onion, salt and pepper. Cook tablespoons of the mixture in a little hot fat, first on one side then on the other.

CARROT TZIMMIS

2½ *lb. brisket of beef*
2 *oz. chicken fat*
juice of 1 *lemon*
2 *lb. potatoes*
2 *oz. sugar*
1 *lb. carrots*
2 *onions*
salt, *pepper*

Gently simmer the meat and sliced onions in boiling water seasoned with salt and pepper for 1½ hours. Add sliced carrots and potatoes and continue cooking for 30 minutes further. Transfer meat and vegetables to a casserole. Make a roux of the flour and chicken fat and gradually add 1 pint stock from the saucepan, sugar and lemon juice. Pour over the meat and vegetables and bake in a moderate oven for 30 minutes.

STUFFED CABBAGE LEAVES

1 *large white cabbage*
1 *lb. minced raw beef*
8 *oz. cooked rice*
1 *oz. brown sugar*
¼ *pint tomato purée*
2 *oz. sultanas*
salt, *pepper*
2 *medium onions*
1 *teaspoon lemon juice*

Pull the leaves off the cabbage except for the small ones at the heart. If the biggest have a very large middle stalk, cut the hardest part of it out. Put the leaves in salted boiling water for 5 minutes. Then drain and dry with a cloth. Mix the meat, rice, grated onion, salt and pepper and bind with a little tomato purée. Take each cabbage leaf separately, place 2 tablespoons of the stuffing on it and roll up in a neat parcel with the ends tucked in. If liked fasten with a thread (this must be removed before serving). Line a pan with a few scalded cabbage leaves and lay the parcels side by side on these. Pour over the remaining tomato purée, about ¼ pint water, sugar, sultanas and lemon juice. Cook over a very low heat for 2 hours. If the liquid evaporates add a little more water from time to time.

BARLEY SOUP

1 *quart stock*
½ *glass medium barley*
2 *finely cubed carrots*
1 *onion*
2—3 *small tomatoes*
few celery stalks
1 *oz. mushroom stalks*
salt, pepper

Chop vegetables and simmer all the ingredients together for about 1 hour, seasoning to taste during cooking.

ALMOND PUDDING

4 *oz. ground almonds*
5 *oz. castor sugar*
4 *eggs*
rind of 1 *lemon (grated)*

Beat the egg yolks and sugar until white and creamy. Mix with the almonds and lemon peel. Fold in the stiffly beaten egg whites. Cook in a very slow oven for 40 minutes. Serve cold sprinkled with castor sugar.

HONEY CAKE

1 *lb. flour*
8 *oz. honey*
8 *oz. sugar*
3 *eggs*
1 *teaspoon ground ginger*
1 *teaspoon cinnamon*
½ *teaspoon ground mace*
grated rind of ½ *lemon*
4 *oz. chopped candied peel*
3 *tablespoons oil*

1 *level teaspoon bicarbonate of soda*
2 *oz. shredded almonds*

Warm honey and oil together. Sift the flour, bicarbonate of soda and spices into a bowl, make a hollow in the centre and pour into it the beaten eggs, peel, lemon rind and sugar and lastly the honey mixture. Knead to a firm dough. Turn into a shallow greased tin, sprinkle with shredded almonds and bake in a moderate oven for 1 hour.

CINNAMON BALLS

6 *oz. ground almonds*
1 *tablespoon cinnamon*
8 *oz. castor sugar*
3 *egg whites*
icing sugar to coat

Beat the egg whites stiffly, then mix in the remaining ingredients. Roll into balls and bake on a greased tin in a slow oven for 25—30 minutes. When cooked roll the balls in icing sugar.

CHOLENT

2 *lb. brisket or short rib*
8 *oz. butter beans*
2 *lb. small potatoes*
1 *onion*
1 *tablespoon sugar*
salt, pepper

DUMPLING:
4 *oz. flour*
1 *oz. chopped suet*
1 *oz. grated onion*
2 *teaspoons chopped parsley*
1 *grated potato*
salt, pepper

Place beans in the bottom of a large casserole, then add a layer of chopped onion and potatoes. Mix together all ingredients listed for dumpling, making one large roll, and place this in the centre with the meat. Cover with the rest of the potatoes. Season with salt, pepper and sugar. Cover with boiling water and place greaseproof paper over all. Cover with very tight lid and cook in the middle of a very low oven until the following day if desired. This traditional dish is often served on the Sabbath when a hot meal is required. It can be prepared on Friday and left to cook in a cool oven.

GRIMSLICH

2 *matzot*
2 *oz. fine meal*
2 *oz. ground almonds*
½ *teaspoon cinnamon*
2 *eggs*
4 *oz. dried fruit*
2 *oz. sugar*
2 *oz. fat*

Soak the matzot in cold water until soft, then squeeze dry and beat well. Add the beaten egg yolks and the almonds, meal, cinnamon, dried fruit and sugar and mix thoroughly. Lastly fold in the stiffly beaten egg whites. Drop spoonfuls in hot fat and fry until golden brown on both sides. Sprinkle with more sugar and serve hot.

LOCKSHEN PUDDING

1 *lb. cooked vermicelli*
4 *oz. sultanas*
1 *oz. candied peel*
¼ *teaspoon cinnamon*
2 *oz. sugar*
2 *oz. margarine*
2 *eggs*

Melt the margarine and mix with the vermicelli. Add beaten eggs, sugar, sultanas, chopped peel and cinnamon. Bake in a pie dish for 30—40 minutes in a moderate oven.

Mexico

COOKING IN MEXICO

Mexico abounds in beautiful tropical fauna, exotic flowering trees, orchids of many kinds and a rich array of fruits and vegetables.

Mexican cooking not only uses the country's vast resources, but also has a colourful historical background to supply culinary ideas. You can detect a strong Indian and Spanish influence in their kitchen, and their tortillas and variety of spices are world famous.

Tortillas belong to the staple diet of the Mexicans, just as bread does to the Western Household and rice to the Eastern. For the genuine Mexican tortillas you need maize and a lot of skill in preparing them.

Avocados have become a familiar sight during the last few years all over the world — what a delicious addition they are to our diet too. I find the Mexican way of making Avocado salad very good — the Mexicans ought to know how to use a fruit which grows in such abundance in their country.

Shrimp Polenta will have everybody guessing if you serve it up as a first course for a dinner party — it is an unusual and delicate mixture of flavours and yet needs no outlandish ingredients.

Mexican Chicken is slightly reminiscent of Spanish cooking, but somehow just a shade more exotic — another party favourite with a number of hostesses. Fudge-making is always a beloved kitchen game for families with teenage children — we always make large quantities of fudge just before Christmas. The Mexican Orange Fudge is a very good recipe — it is cheering to produce something which you could not buy in the shop around the corner.

AVOCADO SALAD

1 *large avocado pear*
2 *small onions, chopped*
2 *tomatoes, peeled and chopped*
paprika
salt
lettuce
French dressing (see p. 161)

Peel and mash the avocado. Mix the onion and tomato with it. Season with salt and paprika. Serve chilled with lettuce and French dressing.

BUTTER BEANS IN SAUCE

1 *lb. butter beans*
4 *oz. bacon (any cheap cut)*
1 *onion, sliced*
1 *lb. tomatoes, peeled and*
  quartered
1 *tablespoon black treacle*
1 *tablespoon chilli powder*

1 *teaspoon salt*

Put the beans into an earthenware casserole. Mix the bacon slices with them. Cover with onion and tomato. Sprinkle with chilli powder and salt. Warm the treacle in ½ pint warm water and pour over the beans. Bake covered, in a slow oven, for 2 hours.

SHRIMP POLENTA

1 *pint shrimps*
4 *oz. maize flour or semolina*
2 *onions, minced*
2 *tablespoons concentrated tomato*
  purée
8 *oz. ham, diced*
4 *oz. mushrooms, sliced*
3 *rashers bacon*
salt, pepper

Pour 1 pint boiling water on to the semolina and cook slowly until thick. Chop the bacon and fry lightly. Add the tomato purée, mushrooms, onion and ham. Simmer in ¼ pint water for 10 minutes. Fill a buttered fireproof dish with alternate layers of semolina, tomato mixture and shrimps. Cover the dish, cook in a moderate oven for 30 minutes.

TAMALE PIE

4 *oz. semolina*
1 *lb. minced beef*
4 *tomatoes, peeled and quartered*
6 *stoned green olives*
2 *minced onions*
2 *teaspoons chilli powder*
2 *tablespoons olive oil*
basil
salt, pepper

Cook the semolina in 1 pint boiling water until thick. Fry the onion and the beef in olive oil, add the tomatoes, olives, chilli powder, a pinch of basil, salt and pepper. Simmer for 10 minutes. Put half the semolina in the bottom of a fireproof dish, then the meat mixture and lastly another layer of semolina. Cover and bake in a moderate oven for 30 minutes.

ENCHILLADAS

8 tortillas (*pancakes make
a good substitute*)
2 onions, chopped
1 lb. minced beef
1 clove garlic
4 tomatoes, peeled and quartered
1 tablespoon chilli powder
oregano
salt, pepper

4 oz. grated cheese
fat for frying
2 rashers streaky bacon

Fry the bacon until all the fat is melted. Remove bacon pieces and fry the onion in the fat until golden, add the meat, crushed garlic, tomatoes and seasonings. Simmer for 10 minutes. Spread this mixture on to the pancakes, roll them, arrange in a shallow fireproof dish. Sprinkle with cheese. Bake in a moderate oven for 20 minutes.

MEXICAN CHICKEN (1)

1 boiling chicken, jointed
4 pimentos or 1 tin pimentos
1 onion, sliced
1 clove garlic
2 tomatoes, peeled and quartered
4 oz. butter
1 oz. flour
½ teaspoon chilli powder
salt, pepper

Brown the chicken pieces in 2 oz. butter. Add the pimentos, onion, crushed garlic, tomatoes, chilli powder, salt and pepper. Pour in enough water to cover the chicken. Simmer for 1½—2 hours. Melt the remaining 2 oz. butter, stir in the flour, cook for 1 minute. Gradually add the strained chicken stock, stirring all the time. Arrange the chicken on a flat dish. Pour the sauce over, surround with the vegetables.

MEXICAN CHICKEN (2)

1 chicken, jointed (*roasting is
best, but the dish is good with
a boiling fowl*)
4 small onions
1 clove garlic
1 oz. flour
2 tablespoons concentrated
tomato purée
4 cloves
1 tablespoon tarragon vinega
1 glass white wine
1 green pepper, sliced and seeded

12 stoned green olives
4 oz. seeded raisins
2 oz. butter

Fry the chicken lightly in the butter. Transfer to a large fireproof dish. Toss the onions in the butter, add them to the chicken. Stir the flour into the fat, cook for 1 minute, gradually add the tomato purée and ½ pint water. Pour this over the chicken. Add the cloves, crushed garlic, vinegar, wine and green peppers. Simmer, covered, for 1½ hours, adding the raisins and olives for the last 15 minutes.

BEEF STEW WITH SPLIT PEAS

2 *lb. topside*
2 *tablespoons olive oil*
2 *tablespoons concentrated*
   tomato purée
½ *lemon, sliced*
6 *whole small onions*
4 *oz. split peas*
1 *teaspoon allspice*

parsley
salt, pepper

Brown the meat on all sides in the olive oil. Put all the ingredients in a casserole with enough water to barely cover. Cover the pan. Cook in a moderate oven for 2 hours or until tender.

PORK CHOPS

4 *pork chops*
1 *green pepper*
½ *teaspoon chilli powder*
1 *onion, sliced*
1 *lb. tomatoes, peeled and*
   chopped
2 *oz. rice*
basil
salt, pepper

Put the chops in a fireproof dish. Cover each with onion and a tablespoon of rice. Remove seeds from the pepper, chop it and mix with the tomatoes and chilli powder. Spread this over the chops. Sprinkle with chopped herbs, salt and pepper. Cover the dish. Bake in a moderate oven for 1 hour.

VEAL WITH NOODLES

1 *lb. veal, cut into thin slices*
2 *onions, sliced*
2 *teaspoons chilli powder*
1 *teaspoon paprika*
flour
2 *oz. grated cheese*
salt
2 *oz. lard*

Beat the veal and dredge with flour seasoned with salt and paprika. Fry lightly on both sides in the lard. Add the onions and chilli powder. Fry for 2 or 3 minutes. Pour ½ pint water into the pan and simmer for 20 minutes. Stir in the grated cheese. Serve with noodles (see p. 266; cook as spaghetti).

TORTILLAS

2 *lb. maize*
2 *oz. slaked lime*

Soak the maize in water and the slaked lime for 12 hours. Simmer in the same water until tender. Drain and wash the maize. Pound into a smooth paste. Roll out very thin. Bake on an ungreased griddle.

MEXICAN VEAL CUTLETS

4 *boned veal cutlets*
1 *onion*
1 *green pepper*
½ *teaspoon chopped garlic*
½ *pint stock*
½ *pint milk*
2 *egg yolks*
salt, pepper
fat for frying
4 *oz. cheese*

Fry the cutlets with the sliced onion, sliced pepper and chopped garlic until browned but not completely cooked. Place in an oven dish. Season the milk and stock with salt and pepper to taste, and simmer until the liquid begins to thicken. Remove from heat, stir in the lightly beaten egg yolks and pour over the cutlets. Bake in a moderate oven for 30—40 minutes until the sauce has browned. Sprinkle with grated cheese and place under a hot grill until the cheese is golden. Serve at once.

ORANGE FUDGE

½ *pint evaporated milk*
12 *oz. sugar*
juice and grated rind of 2 large
  oranges
2 *oz. chopped almonds*

Melt 4 oz. sugar in a saucepan; when it has browned, add the orange juice. Stir well and add evaporated milk (previously warmed). Stir the rest of the sugar into the pan and cook slowly until the mixture comes away from the sides. Add the grated orange peel. Beat until the mixture sets when tested in cold water. Stir in the nuts. Pour into greased tins. Mark into squares when cool.

CHILLI SAUCE

3 *large tomatoes, peeled and*
  quartered
2 *tablespoons chilli powder*
2 *teaspoons dry mustard*
2 *teaspoons horseradish sauce*
½ *teaspoon sugar*
pinch of cayenne pepper
1 *teaspoon curry powder*

4 *tablespoons vinegar*
1 *onion, sliced*
1 *clove garlic, chopped*

Simmer all the ingredients together, adding a little water if necessary. Pass through a sieve. Serve with anything needing a hot spicy sauce.

The Middle East

COOKING IN THE MIDDLE EAST

It is only a very narrow strip of sea which divides the Rock of Gibraltar and Europe from Morocco and Africa. Legend has it that the two continents were not divided by the sea in ancient times until Hercules tore them apart with his strong hands and broke them in two. Near Tangier, you can still see the famous rock of Hercules, the excact spot where this feat was accomplished.

I strongly believe that there is a basis of truth to most of these old legends, but I have grave doubts about the particular one. Simply because there is such marked difference between the two sides of that narrow strip of sea that they are obviously two different worlds. Of course, Gibraltar is a highly peculiar place, with its British administration and friendly British policemen — but even on the Spanish side you still feel conscious that you are in Europe. When you set foot on the other side in Africa, you are whisked back to biblical times where burnoused figures walk sedately along with overladen mules. There are colourful and motley markets full of noise and outlandish spices. You enter restaurants where you are seated on very low benches and are served Moroccan Couscous by bowing Arabs. Practically all Middle Eastern dishes have an unusual mixture of the sweet and savoury. Nutmeg and cinnamon are often used in savoury dishes — spices which the Westerner reserves for sweet dishes. It is a matter of tradition, because why should we discard apples stuffed with minced chicken, if we consider it quite in order to eat apple sauce with pork? We serve turkey with cranberry sauce, so why should we not try to roast a chicken the Arabian way with honey and nuts? Once you start looking at Arabian cooking from this angle you will find that it offers plenty of new scope for cooks with imagination.

TUNISIAN ANCHOVIES

18 *fillets of anchovies*
½ *teaspoon ground nutmeg*
1½ *teaspons finely chopped fresh mint*
bread or toast

Drain the anchovies of all oil. Mix the mint with the nutmeg and roll each fillet in the mixture. Serve on small fingers of bread or toast as hors d'ouvre.

MUNKACZINA (Arabian Salad)

3 *oranges, peeled and sliced thinly*
2 *medium onions, sliced thinly*
4 *oz. black olives, stoned*
2 *tablespoons oil*
salt, pepper

Mix all the ingredients together, season with salt and pepper.

ARABIAN MUTTON AND TOMATO SOUP

2 *oz. cooked vermicelli*
1½ *lb. neck and breast of mutton*
8 *oz. tomatoes, peeled and sliced*
12 *oz. onions, sliced*
1 *oz. butter*
1 *tablespoon chopped mint*
1 *teaspoon salt*
¼ *teaspoon pepper*
2½ *pints hot water*

Melt the fat in a large saucapen, add the onion and fry till light brown, add the meat, tomatoes, mint, salt and pepper. Pour in the hot water, bring to the boil and simmer for 3½ hours. Remove the meat and cut up finely. Place in the serving tureen, add the vermicelli, re-heat the soup and pour over.

For European tastes this is more of a stew and can be eaten as such.

SYRIAN LENTIL SOUP

1 *lb. lentils*
2½ *pints water*
2 *medium onions, sliced*
2 *tablespoons olive oil or butter*
1 *teaspoon salt*
8 *oz. spinach, chopped*
1 *teaspoon lemon juice*

Wash the lentils thoroughly. Melt the fat in a large saucepan, add the onions and fry for 3 minutes. Add the lentils and salt, stir well, pour on the water, bring to the boil, skim if necessary, and simmer gently for 1½ hours. Add the spinach and cook 15 minutes longer. Add lemon juice and serve.

ARABIAN EGGS

6 *hard-boiled eggs*
2 *oz. butter*
½ *teaspoon salt*
½ *teaspoon paprika* ⎫ *mixed*
½ *teaspoon pepper* ⎬ *together*
½ *teaspoon cinnamon* ⎭

Melt the butter. Shell the eggs and while still warm prick the whites all over, add the eggs to the butter and turn round and round to enable the butter to soak into the egg and cook until light brown, place on warm serving dish and sprinkle with salt and the spices.

ALGERIAN THETCHOUKA

3 *eggs*
2 *large onions, chopped*
2 *cloves of garlic, chopped*
2 *tablespoons oil or butter*
1 *lb. tomatoes, peeled and chopped*
2 *red or green peppers (pimentos), seeded and thinly sliced*
½ *teaspoon salt*
pinch of pepper

Heat the fat in a shallow fireproof dish with a lid, fry the onions and garlic till transparent, add all the other ingredients, stir well, cover tightly and cook gently till soft and pulpy — about 1 hour.

Before serving put the eggs either whole or beaten on the top of the dish, cover and gently cook for 10 minutes or until set. Chopped mint may be sprinkled over the eggs if wished.

ARABIAN BAKED STUFFED SAVOURY APPLES

4 *large cooking apples*
minced cooked chicken
salt to taste
4 *cloves*
1 *teaspoon sugar*
2 *oz. breadcrumbs*
1 *oz. butter*

Cut the top off each apple, scoop out the core completely without cutting through the fruit. Fill each apple with chicken and 1 clove and salt. Stand all in a fireproof dish. Sprinkle with the sugar, breadcrumbs and a dot of butter on each. Bake in a moderate oven for 1 hour or until the apples are quite soft.

ARABIAN ROAST CHICKEN WITH HONEY AND NUTS

1 *chicken*
2 *tablespoons honey*
1 *oz. melted butter*
1 *teaspoon rose water*
½ *oz. pistachio nuts, finely chopped*
2 *oz. crystallized cherries, cut in quarters*
1 *oz. preserved ginger, chopped*

Melt the butter and add to the honey. Prick the breast and legs of the bird and rub some of the honey and butter well in. Pour more of the honey mixture and the rose water inside the bird and roast in the usual way. When done, cut the bird in half, lay flat on the serving dish and sprinkle with the nuts, cherries and ginger.

ARABIAN STEWED MUTTON WITH PRUNES

1½ lb. neck or breast of mutton
1 large onion, chopped
1 oz. butter or dripping
1 dessertspoon flour
¼ teaspoon saffron
¼ teaspoon cinnamon
4 oz. prunes — soaked in cold
water for 12 hours
1 dessertspoon orange flower
water or 1 teaspoon sugar

salt and pepper to taste
hot water

Cut the meat into pieces about ½ × 2 inches. Fry the onion in the fat till light brown, in a casserole, add the flour, saffron, cinnamon, salt and pepper, mix well, add the meat and cook quickly for 2 minutes, stirring well. Cover with hot water, cover and simmer for 2 hours. Add the prunes and the sugar or orange flower water, re-cover and simmer for 1 hour more.

ARABIAN BOILED MUTTON AND GOOSEBERRY JELLY

Boil the mutton in the ordinary way and cover with a good layer of jelly before serving.

MOROCCAN BEAN COUSCOUS

8 oz. dried beans, soaked
overnight
½ teaspoon salt
1 lb. semolina
1 dessertspoon oil or melted
butter
2 pints cold water

Put the semolina in a basin, moisten with boiling water to make the grains swell and leave for 20 minutes. Stir with a fork. Repeat this once more when the grains should be sufficiently swollen, add the oil and stir well. Put the beans in the pan of a steamer, add salt, cold water. Place a clean cloth in the top of the steamer and put the semolina on this, cover tightly, bring to the boil and simmer for 3 hours. Stir the semolina with a fork 3 times during the cooking. Serve with meat or chicken dishes.

PERSIAN STUFFED QUINCES

4 quinces
minced cooked mutton or chicken
salt, to taste
1 tablespoon honey
1 oz. butter

Core the quinces, cover with boiling water and simmer for 20 minutes. Drain and stuff with the seasoned meat. Place in a shallow fireproof dish, pour on the honey, dot with butter and bake in a moderate oven for 1 hour.

STUFFED GREEN PEPPERS

6 *green peppers*
12 *oz. beef*
1 *small tomato*
1 *tablespoon chopped parsley*
1 *teaspoon salt*
pinch pepper
4 *oz. rice*
4 *tablespoons tomato sauce or*
    ketchup
¼ *pint water*

Cut off the tops of the peppers and remove seeds. Half-cook the rice, and drain well. Mince the beef and onion and peel the tomato and chop small. Mix together all ingredients except tomato sauce and water, and stuff the peppers with this filling. Stand the peppers in the water in an oven dish, top with tomato sauce and bake in a moderate oven for 1¼ hours.

MOROCCAN BANANA FRITTERS

pancake mixture (see p. 183)
bananas
liqueur
sugar
breadcrumbs
fat for frying

Peel bananas and cut in half lengthwise. Cover with the liqueur of your choice and leave to soak for 1 hour. Then dip bananas into the pancake mixture, sprinkle with breadcrumbs and fry in hot fat until golden. Sprinkle with plenty of sugar and serve very hot.

FRUIT DRESSING

¼ *pint sour cream*
1 *teaspoon lemon juice*
1 *teaspoon grated lemon rind*
2 *tablespoons thin honey*
1 *tablespoon pineapple juice*
pinch salt

Whip cream, add the other ingredients and whisk for 5 minutes. Serve with fresh fruit salad.

GOOSEBERRY JELLY

gooseberries
sugar
water

Wash the fruit and add ¼ pint water to each 1 lb. Stew slowly till quite soft. Put in a flannel bag and allow to drip for 12 hours. Do not squeeze the bag. For each 1 pint juice measure 1 lb. sugar. Warm the sugar. Bring the juice to the boil, add the sugar, stir well, bring again to the boil, and boil for 15 to 20 minutes, stirring constantly.

Test and put in warm clean jars. Seal.

Poland

COOKING IN POLAND

The Poles have had the stormiest and most struggling career as a nation and strangely, or naturally enough, this resulted in a very high achievement in all their arts — including the of cookery. They are a gifted and heroic people passionately attached to their national traditions. They have always taken an intelligent and lively interest in good food and the large peasant population had a Slavonic gusto in producing original and tasty dishes from the simplest and cheapest ingredients.

Soups play an important part in the diet of a Polish family. They have adopted the Russian Borshch and transformed it into their own national soup. The basis of Borshch is beetroot, a cheap enough vegetable, but don't be misguided into thinking that it is a flimsy little soup. It is not only a wholesome nourishing soup, it also has fragrance and colour to make it attractive.

Bigos is an excellent one-course meal — I find it most useful and economical when I want to use up left-over meat without spending a long time in the kitchen.

All the Polish cakes and pastries are delightful, but just let me point out my favourite: Cheese Pastries. They take a few minutes to prepare, they are economical and they make the best cheese straws blush with shame.

For a summer dish of salad, or picnics, the Polish way of making a Cream Cheese Spread is slightly unusual, but has the flavour of a bright summer morning.

HERRINGS WITH SOUR CREAM

4 *herrings*
¼ *pint milk*
1 *glass white wine*
2 *tablespoons wine vinegar*
1 *onion, sliced*
1 *clove garlic*
¼ *teaspoon mustard*
2 *egg yolks*
2 *tablespoons sour cream*
1 *teaspoon paprika*
6 *peppercorns*

parsley
thyme
½ *bay leaf*
salt

Soak the herrings in milk for 1 hour. Strain. Cook them for 7 minutes in the vinegar and wine, with the onions, garlic, peppercorns, and salt; add water if necessary. Strain off the juice, cool and mix with the beaten egg yolks, paprika, sour cream and mustard. Cover the herrings with the sauce. Serve chilled.

BEETROOT SOUP

2 *oz. streaky bacon, chopped*
1 *leek, sliced*
1 *onion, sliced*
2 *raw beetroots, cut into strips*
4 *oz. shredded cabbage*
1 *tablespoon tomato purée*

¾ *pint stock*
1 *dessertspoon vinegar*

Fry the bacon with the leek and onion until golden. Add the other ingredients and 2 pints water. Simmer for 1 hour.

BORSHCH

KVAS:
1 *lb. uncooked beetroot, sliced*
crust of rye bread
2 *pints water*

The basis of this soup is Kvas, which is then mixed with meat or vegetable stock.

Put the beetroot in a casserole. Boil the water, allow to cool. Pour over the beetroot, add the crust. Leave covered with a cloth for 3—4 days until the beetroot ferments slightly. The amount of fermentation can vary according to taste. Mix with stock. Serve hot or cold, with a spoonful of sour cream on each plate.

CHRISTMAS EVE BORSHCH

8 *oz. beetroot, sliced*
½ *celeriac, sliced*
1 *small carrot, sliced*
½ *oz. dried mushrooms*
parsley, chopped
½ *oz. butter*
½ *pint Kvas (optional)*

garlic
salt
stock

Simmer all the vegetables and the garlic in 2 pints of water, until the beetroot is cooked. Remove the mushrooms to make mushroom patties (see p. 316). Pour the hot soup over the patties.

UKRAINIAN BORSHCH

8 oz. pork
1 beetroot
½ celeriac
8 oz. tomatoes
½ small cabbage
1 onion
1 small carrot
1 oz. flour
½ oz. butter
¼ pint Kvas (optional)
¾ pint stock

¼ pint cream
salt

Cook and sieve the tomatoes. Cut the other vegetables into thin strips. Simmer half of them with
the meat in water, until the meat is tender. Melt
the butter, cook the rest of the vegetables in it. Add
them to the tomatoes and other vegetables. Stir in
the flour and stock. Add the Kvas. Bring to the boil.
Serve in hot soup plates, with thick cream on top
of each portion. The cream used in Russia is sour,
but this is a question of taste.

DRIED MUSHROOM SOUP

2 oz. dried mushrooms
2 pints stock
1 oz. flour
1 oz. butter
3 tablespoons sour cream

salt, pepper

Blanch the mushrooms. Simmer in the seasoned
stock until tender. Melt the butter, add the flour,
cook for 1 minute. Gradually add the stock and the
mushrooms. Stir in the sour cream before serving.

ONION SOUP

8 oz. onions, sliced
3 slices wholemeal bread
1 gill cream
2 oz. butter
4 egg yolks
salt

Cut the bread into strips. Melt 1 oz. butter in the
oven, put the bread into it, turning it so that all
sides are covered with butter, and bake until crisp.
Melt the rest of the butter, cook the onions in it
until transparent. Put onions and baked bread in
a saucepan, pour 2 pints water over them, simmer
for 40 minutes. Sieve, beat the egg yolks with the
cream, put them in a saucepan, pour the sieved
onion mixture on them and reheat without boiling.
Serve in hot plates.

SAUERKRAUT SOUP

8 *oz. sauerkraut*
4 *oz. pork*
4 *oz. smoked sausage*
8 *oz. lard*
½ *oz. flour*
caraway seeds
1 *pint vegetable stock*

Cut the pork into strips and the sausage into slices. Simmer in the vegetable stock until the meat is cooked. Cook the sauerkraut in ½ pint of water until tender. Strain the stock. Keep the meat separate. Add the sauerkraut stock. Thicken with a roux made of the lard and flour. Add the meat, flavour with caraway seeds.

BAKED POTATOES

4 *medium potatoes*
4 *oz. breadcrumbs*
4 *oz. butter*
salt

Roll the peeled potatoes in the breadcrumbs mixed with salt. Dot with butter and cook in a hot oven for 1 hour, turning them from time to time.

BEETROOT SALAD

1 *lb. cooked beetroots*
1 *horseradish, grated*
1 *teaspoon sugar*
1 *teaspoon salt*

½ *teaspoon caraway seeds*
juice of 3 lemons

Peel and slice the beetroot. Mix the horseradish and other ingredients together. Pour them over the beetroot.

CABBAGE

1 *savoy cabbage*
1 *dessertspoon sugar*
salt
2 *oz. butter*
4 *oz. breadcrumbs*

Shred the cabbage. Cook quickly in boiling water with the sugar for 10 minutes. Strain and put the cabbage into a fireproof dish. Cover with the breadcrumbs, dot with butter. Cook in a moderate oven for 20 minutes. Cauliflower can be cooked in the same way.

POTATO PANCAKES

6 *medium potatoes*
½ *pint milk*
2 *oz. butter*
3 *eggs*
nutmeg
salt

Boil the potatoes in salted water until cooked. Sieve. Mix with the egg yolks, beat in the milk. Flavour with nutmeg. Fold in the stiffly beaten egg whites. Cook as ordinary pancakes.

POLISH PANCAKES

12 oz. flour
¾ pint milk
2 oz. sugar
½ pint water
1 oz. butter
1 tablespoon brandy
4 eggs
½ teaspoon yeast
pinch salt

Beat the egg yolks into the flour, then gradually beat in all the other ingredients except whites of eggs. Leave to stand for 1—2 hours. Beat the egg whites until stiff, and fold into the pancake batter just before using. Fry pancakes in butter, and fill with sour cream or jam. If a savoury pancake is required omit sugar and fill with cheese or minced cooked meat.

MUSHROOMS AND SOUR CREAM

1¾ lb. mushrooms
¾ pint sour cream
3 oz. butter
2 tablespoons milk
1 onion
paprika
salt, pepper
½ tablespoon flour

Chop the onion and brown in the butter. Add the flour, brown and then add the milk little by little. When this is boiling add the sliced mushrooms, salt, pepper, paprika to season and half the sour cream. Stew gently until the mushrooms are tender, and just before serving stir in the rest of the sour cream.

PORK AND SAUERKRAUT

6 pork chops
2 onions
1 oz. butter
2 cloves garlic
salt and pepper
1 bay leaf
1 lb. sauerkraut
1 apple
2 tablespoons pearl barley
1 teaspoon caraway seeds
¾ pint boiling water

Brown the chops, chopped onion and garlic in the melted butter. Add the water, salt, pepper and bay leaf and simmer for 30 minutes. Add sauerkraut, chopped apple, pearl barley and caraway seeds and cook all together for about 1 hour or until meat is tender.

BEEF CAKES

1 *lb. steak*
1 *slice bread*
3 *oz. butter*
2 *onions, chopped*
1 *tablespoon breadcrumbs*
1 *egg*
1 *oz. flour*
½ *bay leaf*
6 *peppercorns*
½ *pint meat stock*
salt

Fry ½ tablespoon chopped onion in 1 oz. butter until soft. Soak the bread, squeeze out the water. Mince the bread, one onion and meat. Mix with the egg, season with salt and pepper. Shape into 8 cakes. Roll in breadcrumbs. Melt the rest of the butter, fry the cakes. Put them on a plate to keep warm. Put the rest of the onions in the fat. Cook until tender. Stir in the flour, cook for 1 minute. Gradually add the stock. Season with salt, peppercorns and bay leaf. Pour the sauce over the meat cakes, simmer for 30 minutes.

BIGOS (Cabbage Stew)

1½ *lb. sauerkraut*
1 *onion, sliced*
1 *oz. flour*
1 *oz. butter*
1 *glass white wine*
1 *lb. left-over meat or poultry*
   (not mutton)
1 *pint stock*
paprika
salt

Simmer the sauerkraut in the stock for 1½ hours. Cook the onion in 1 oz. butter, add the flour, cook for 1 minute. Chop the sauerkraut and add the onion mixture to it. Cut the meat into small pieces. Put the meat and the sauerkraut mixture into a casserole, add the wine, season with salt and paprika, mix well. Cook in a slow oven with the lid on for 1 hour.

HUSSARS ROAST

2 *lb. sirloin*
1 *onion, chopped*
juice of ½ lemon
½ *oz. flour*
3 *oz. butter*
1 *tablespoon brown breadcrumbs*
1 *egg yolk*
salt, pepper

Beat the meat, sprinkle with salt, dredge with flour. Melt 2 oz. butter, brown the meat in it on both sides. Add the lemon juice and a little water. Simmer. Cook half the chopped onion in the rest of the butter until transparent, add the breadcrumbs, season with salt and pepper. Mix with the egg. Make crosswise incisions in the meat. Fill with the stuffing. Fry the rest of the onion in a casserole, add the meat and about ½ pint water. Cook covered, in a moderate oven, for 1 hour or more until the meat is tender. Serve with the sauce on page 316.

MUSHROOM PATTIES

3 *oz. flour*
1 *egg yolk*

FILLING:
1 *onion, chopped*
1 *oz. dried mushrooms*
1 *oz. butter*
1 *tablespoon breadcrumbs*
1 *egg white*
salt, pepper
parsley, chopped

Mix the egg yolk with the flour. Knead until smooth. Roll out and cut into 2-inch squares. Put a little of the following mixture in each square. Pinch the edges together to form a triangle, and cook in boiling water for 5 minutes.

FILLING:
Boil the mushrooms until tender. Melt the butter, add the mushrooms and the onion, stew until the onion is transparent. Mix with the breadcrumbs, beaten egg white, parsley, salt and pepper.

SAUCE FOR ROAST BEEF

2 *onions*
1 *clove garlic*
1 *sliced a carrot*
1 *tomato*
juice of half a lemon
2 *tablespoons grated horseradish*
basil
½ *bay leaf*
2 *oz. ham*
2 *glasses red wine*
1 *oz. butter*
1 *oz. flour*

½ *pint vegetable stock*
1 *teaspoon sugar*
salt
parsley

Melt the butter. Chop the onions, garlic, carrot, parsley. Cook in the butter with the bay leaf and a pinch of basil until browned. Stir in the flour, add the stock. Simmer for 40 minutes and sieve. Return to pan, add wine and lemon juice. Cut ham into strips. Peel tomato, remove seeds, cut flesh into slices. Add ham, tomato and horseradish. Serve hot.

SOUP NOODLES

1 *egg*
1 *oz. flour*
chopped parsley
salt

Beat the egg, mix with the flour and parsley. Season with salt. Pour this batter into boiling thin soup. It should cook quickly and look like ribbon noodles.

STEAK AND MUSHROOMS

4 *slices rump steak (about 6 oz. each)*
4 *oz. butter*
1 *onion, chopped*
4 *oz. mushrooms, sliced*
¼ *pint cream*
½ *pint stock*
1 *oz. flour*
4 *potatoes*
salt, pepper

Fry the onion in half the butter for 5 minutes. Add the mushrooms. Pour in the cream and the stock. Flour the meat. Season with salt and pepper. Fry quickly on both sides in the rest of the butter. Cook in the mushroom sauce in a covered pan for 30 minutes. Add the diced potatoes and cook for another 30 minutes.

FRIED VEAL WITH CAPER SAUCE

4 *slices frying veal*
1 *oz. flour*
¼ *pint cream*
¼ *pint stock*
salt, pepper
½ *lemon*
1 *dessertspoon capers*
¼ *teaspoon sugar*

3 *oz. butter*

Trim and beat veal. Season with salt and pepper. Fry quickly in the butter, put on a plate to keep warm. Stir the flour into the fat, cook for 1 minute. Add the stock, cream, lemon juice, capers and sugar. Pour over the veal and reheat.

ROAST CHICKEN

1 *chicken*
8 *oz. breadcrumbs*
4 *oz. butter*
1 *egg*
parsley
salt

Make a stuffing of the breadcrumbs, egg yolk, parsley and the stiffly beaten egg white; season with salt. Stuff the chicken and sew up the holes. Roast in a hot oven, basting frequently, for about an hour. Serve cut in half with the fat and juices from the pan poured over. This should be accompanied by a green salad.

CHOCOLATE ARKAS

½ *pint double cream*
3 *oz. sugar*
4 *oz. cooking chocolate*
2 *eggs*
2 *egg yolks*
vanilla

Beat the eggs, egg yolks and sugar until white. Add the cream and the melted chocolate. Beat until frothy. Pour into a buttered dish and steam until the mixture is set. Chill and serve with semi-sweet biscuits.

CHERRY DUMPLINGS

8 *oz. Morello cherries*
8 *oz. flour*
1½ *oz. butter*
2 *egg yolks*
2 *oz. breadcrumbs*
1 *gill milk*
2 *oz. melted butter*
2 *oz. castor sugar*

Cream the butter, add the egg yolks, breadcrumbs and milk and mix to a smooth paste. Beat in the flour and a pinch of salt. Shape the dough into small dumplings with 2 cherries in the middle of each. Cook in boiling water for 5 minutes. Drain, arrange in a dish with melted butter and sugar on the top.

RUM BUCKWHEAT

4 *oz. buckwheat or ground rice*
1 *pint cream*
1 *oz. sugar*
1 *small glass rum*
¼ *teaspoon salt*
strip of lemon peel
*icing sugar and cherries to
 decorate*

Put the buckwheat and sugar in a bowl and pound it. Add the other ingredients, pour into a pie dish and cook in a slow oven for 2 hours. Turn out, cover with icing sugar and decorate with cherries.

VANILLA PUDDING

1 *pint cream*
6 *oz. sugar*
4 *eggs*
4 *egg yolks*
vanilla
cherries to decorate

Beat the eggs, egg yolks and sugar until soft and creamy. Add the cream and vanilla and beat until frothy. Pour into a greased dish, cook slowly until custard sets.

APRICOT CAKE

9 *oz. flour*
6 *oz. butter*
3 *oz. sugar*
8 *oz. apricots*
2 *oz. castor sugar*
3 *egg whites*
2 *oz. icing sugar*

Rub butter into flour, add castor sugar. Knead as for shortbread. Divide into five parts, bake in tart tins in a slow oven for 40 minutes. Stew the apricots with the sugar and a little water. Sieve them. Add the purée to the stiffly beaten egg whites. Spread it between the layers of shortbread. Dredge with the icing sugar.

DOUGHNUTS

5 oz. flour
3 egg yolks
1 dessertspoon rum
salt
1 oz. sugar
1½ oz. melted butter
1 teaspoon grated lemon peel
½ oz. yeast
2 tablespoons milk
apricot jam

Beat the egg yolks with the sugar and lemon peel. Dissolve the yeast in a little warm milk. Mix it with the sugar mixture, add the rum, the rest of the milk and a pinch of salt. Mix in the flour. Knead it thoroughly, add the melted butter and knead again. Cover with a cloth, leave to rise; when it has doubled its size, shape in rounds on floured board. Put a little jam into each, fold in the corners. Leave covered in a warm place to rise again. Fry in deep fat with a lid on the pan until golden brown. Strain with a perforated spoon on to absorbent paper. Roll in icing sugar.

FAVORKI-CHRUST

8 oz. flour
2 oz. butter
3 egg yolks
1 whole egg
2 oz. sugar
⅓ teaspoon bicarbonate of soda
¼ pint single cream
salt

Rub the fat into the flour, add the other ingredients and mix to a smooth paste. Roll out thinly, cut into strips 4 inches long and 1 inch wide. Make a slit at one end of each strip and push the other end through it. Fry quickly in deep fat until golden brown.

MOCHA MERINGUE

6 egg whites
12 oz. icing sugar
¼ pint strong Mocha coffee

CREAM:
3 egg yolks
3 tablespoons sugar
2 tablespoons mocha coffee
1 teaspoon flour
¼ pint double cream

Make ¼ pint coffee (see p. 57), dissolve the sugar in it, simmer until it becomes thick syrup. Fold in the stiffly beaten egg whites. Line 2 cake tins with paper, bake the mixture in these for 1 hour in a cool oven. Spread the following cream between the two meringue shells.

THE CREAM:
Beat the egg yolks and sugar, add the flour. Put the bowl over boiling water, bring the cream to the boil, add it to the mixture and beat until thick. Allow to cool, add the coffee and beat until smooth.

POLISH BABA

5 *egg yolks*
4 *oz. castor sugar*
¼ *pint milk*
1½ *oz. yeast*
1 *lb. plain flour*
2½ *oz. melted butter*
vanilla
saffron
½ *teaspoon salt*

Beat the egg yolks and sugar over hot water until white and thick. Dissolve the yeast in a little warm milk. Add it and all the other ingredients except the butter to the eggs. Beat until thoroughly blended. Pour in the butter and beat again. Fill a greased tin with the mixture to one third of its depth. Cover and leave to rise in a warm place. Bake in a hot oven for 1 hour.

YEAST CAKE

1 *lb. flour*
3 *oz. sugar*
3 *oz. butter*
4 *eggs*
2 *oz. sultanas*
½ *pint milk*
2 *oz. yeast*
salt
grated lemon peel
icing sugar

Dissolve the yeast in a little warm milk. Mix the flour, sugar and a good pinch of salt in a bowl. Add 3 beaten eggs, milk and yeast. Knead until smooth. Add softened butter, lemon peel and the sultanas to the dough. Half fill a greased baking tin with the dough, leave in a warm place to rise until double its size. Glaze with a little beaten egg. Bake in a hot oven for 40 minutes. Cover thinly with icing sugar.

CHEESE PASTRIES

2 *oz. flour*
2 *oz. butter, cut into pieces*
2 *oz. Parmesan cheese, grated*
1 *egg*
paprika
salt

Put the flour, butter, cheese, paprika and salt into a bowl. Mix with a spoon until the dough is smooth and firm. Leave for an hour. Roll out thin. Cut into fancy shapes, glaze with the egg, bake in a hot oven for 10 minutes.

CREAM CHEESE SPREAD

4 *oz. cottage cheese*
3 *radishes*
12 *slices cucumber*
chives
1 *tablespoon cream*
salt

Add the cream to the cheese, beat until light. Peel and slice the cucumber, sprinkle with salt, leave to drain. Cut the radishes into thin slices, chop the chives. Mix cucumber, chives and radishes with the cheese. Season with salt.

Russia

COOKING IN RUSSIA

When one thinks about Russian cooking, one usually has in mind the excellent Russian restaurants one has visited in the various capitals of Europe. The aristocracy of old Russia prided itself on very lavish and rich tables, but the large population of peasants in those days lived mainly on rye bread, curd cheese and soups. The emigré chefs carried on their own traditions, while in the U.S.S.R. for many years the meals were more a kind of refuelling than a pleasure to the palate. Although their diet is about 80 per cent starch, there are a number of regional traditional dishes, which are slowly coming back on the menus of Moscow restaurants.

There is one thing in common with both branches of cookery: they make extensive use of sour cream or smetana, which gives a national characteristic to their food.

All the soups in this section are worth noting — they follow the best formula for soup-making: the right mixture of inexpensive ingredients resulting in a rich and nourishing dish. The fish dishes are all much more interesting than our usual ideas on fish and have enough vegetables cooked with them to make a very satisfying main course. Russian Salad is of course an international favourite — nothing could be more perfect for a cold buffet. Piroshki, Bliny and Beef Stroganoff are all classics in Haute Cuisine and every hostess with a reputation to be proud of likes to produce them at times. A less well known but equally superb dish is the Russian Turkey with Cherry Sauce — try it once for a very special occasion.

The richest of all rich cakes is without a doubt Malakoff Cake — and the cunning part of it is that the taste of rum makes it so delicious to eat that you hardly realise that in a few minutes you have consumed more calories than during a whole meal.

BABY BEETROOT SOUP

2 bunches baby beetroot with
    leaves
lemon juice
1½ pints stock
2 tablespoons sour cream
fennel
sugar

salt, pepper

Shred the beetroot and the leaves. Simmer in salted water with ½ teaspoon lemon juice and ¼ teaspoon sugar until tender. Add the stock and the cream. Reheat, sprinkle with chopped fennel.

BORSHCH

1 onion, sliced
1 parsnip or petrouschka, sliced
1 carrot, sliced
1 beetroot, sliced
6 oz. shredded cabbage
2 pints stock
2 tablespoons tomato purée
1 dessertspoon vinegar
½ bay leaf
1 tablespoon sugar

2 oz. lard
salt, pepper
½ pint sour cream

Melt the lard. Fry the onion, carrot, parsnip and beetroot in it for 5 minutes, stirring so that all pieces are covered with fat. Pour on the stock and add the tomato purée and vinegar. Season with salt, pepper and sugar. Simmer for 20 minutes. Serve with a spoonful of sour cream to each plate.

CABBAGE SOUP

2 cooked beetroots
2 carrots
2 onions
1 pint stock
¼ pint sour cream
1 cup shredded cabbage
4 cloves
1 tablespoon lemon juice

marjoram
salt

Mince the beetroot, carrot and onions. Simmer for 30 minutes in the stock. Add the cabbage, cloves, marjoram and salt and simmer again for 20 minutes. Add the lemon juice. Serve with a spoonful of cream on each plate.

MEAT BROTH

1 lb. stewing beef
1 lb. shredded cabbage
1 carrot, sliced
1 parsnip, sliced
1 onion, sliced
1 potato, diced
2 tomatoes, peeled and quartered

1 oz. lard
salt

Simmer the meat in 1½ pints salted water for 2 hours. Remove the meat, simmer the onion, carrot and parsnip in the broth for 30 minutes. Add the tomato, cabbage and potato. Simmer for another 30 minutes.

SORREL SOUP

1 *lb. sorrel*
1½ *pints stock*
fennel
1 *tablespoon cream*
1 *tablespoon cornflour*
2 *hard-boiled eggs, chopped*
salt, pepper

Remove the hard stalks from the sorrel. Cook without water. Sieve. Add the stock and reheat. Mix the cornflour with the cream, add them. Season with salt and pepper. Serve hot or cold, garnished with the chopped hard-boiled egg.

BREAM WITH HORSERADISH AND APPLE

2 *lb. bream*
2 *cooking apples*
4 *tablespoons grated horseradish*
1 *stick celery*
1 *leek*
2 *onions*
½ *bay leaf*
thyme
parsley
lemon
salt, pepper

vinegar
1 *teaspoon sugar*

Chop the celery, onions and leek, simmer in 1 pint water for 15 minutes. Add 1 dessertspoon vinegar, the herbs, salt and pepper. Cut the fish across into pieces 2 inches wide. Poach them in the stock for 20 minutes. Drain and arrange on a dish. Grate the apple, mix with the horseradish, 1 dessertspoon vinegar and the sugar. Garnish with this mixture and slices of lemon.

STUFFED PIKE

1 5-*lb. pike*
6 *oz. white bread*
2 *onions, chopped*
3 *carrots, chopped*
2 *parsnips, chopped*
1 *beetroot, chopped*
1 *teaspoon sugar*
2 *eggs*
1 *tablespoon vegetable oil*
salt, pepper

Cut the fish into thick slices. Remove the flesh without damaging the skin. Take out the bones. Chop the flesh and mix it with the bread, previously soaked in water, the water squeezed out, the onion, the eggs, sugar and oil. Season with salt and pepper. Stuff the fish slices with the mixture. Mix the rest of the vegetables together. Arrange alternate layers of mixed vegetables and fish slices in a fireproof dish, beginning and ending with layer of vegetables. Cover the dish. Simmer for 3 hours. Sieve the vegetables and strain over the fish before serving.

STUFFED HADDOCK

4 *fillets of haddock (2 lb.)*
4 *onions, chopped*
2 *slices bread*
¼ *pint milk*
2 *eggs*
4 *oz. breadcrumbs*
2 *oz. butter*
salt, pepper
flour

Soak the bread in milk. Fry the onions in butter until soft. Squeeze out the bread, mix with the onions and 1 egg. Season with salt and pepper. Spread the mixture on the fish. Roll, dredge with flour, cover with beaten egg and then with breadcrumbs. Fry in butter and serve with the butter poured over.

MUSHROOMS IN SOUR CREAM

¼ *pint sour cream*
8 *oz. mushrooms*
4 *oz. grated cheese*
1 *oz. butter*
1 *teaspoon flour*
salt

Slice the mushrooms. Cook them in the butter. Add the flour, cook for 1 minute, gradually add the cream. Season with salt. Arrange in a flat dish, cover with grated cheese. Cook in a hot oven for 10 minutes.

RUSSIAN SALAD

8 *oz. mixed cold pork and cold*
   chicken
2 *cooked beetroot, diced*
4 *cooked potatoes, diced*
2 *gherkins, diced*
½ *cucumber, diced*
2 *hard-boiled eggs, chopped*
3 *tablespoons olive oil*

1 *tablespoon wine vinegar*
salt, pepper
¼ *teaspoon mustard*

Mix the meat, vegetables, and hard-boiled eggs together. Dress with the oil and vinegar, seasoned with mustard, salt and pepper.

SAUERKRAUT WITH MUSHROOMS

1 *lb. sauerkraut*
1 *oz. dried mushrooms*
¼ *pint sour cream*

Cook the mushrooms. Drain and reserve 4 tablespoons of the water in which they were cooked to add to sauerkraut. Chop the mushrooms and mix with the sauerkraut. Add the cream, cook slowly for 1 hour.

HERRING SALAD

4 oz. cooked mushrooms, sliced
4 new potatoes, diced
1 beetroot, diced
pickled cucumber, sliced
parsley, chopped
4 salt herrings
3 tablespoons olive oil
1 tablespoon wine vinegar

¼ teaspoon mustard
salt, pepper

Mix the olive oil, salt, pepper, vinegar and mustard. Mix the cucumber, mushrooms, potatoes and beetroot together. Arrange these round the herrings, pour the dressing over and sprinkle with chopped parsley. Serve very cold.

BAKED POTATO CAKE

4 medium potatoes
3 pickled herrings
6 oz. salami
¼ pint sour cream
4 oz. breadcrumbs
2 oz. butter
salt, pepper

Bake the potatoes in their skins, peel and cut into thin slices. Chop the herrings, slice the salami. Butter an ovenproof dish. Fill it with alternate layers of herrings, potatoes and sausage, beginning and ending with a layer of potatoes. Spread each layer with sour cream and season with salt and pepper. Cover the top with breadcrumbs and dot with butter. Bake in a moderate oven for 40 minutes.

HAM PASTIES

8 oz. flour
2 eggs
2 egg yolks
salt
4 oz. cooked ham or pork,
    chopped
brown sauce
1½ oz. butter
lemon juice

parsley

Mix the flour with the eggs and egg yolks until a stiff paste is formed. Leave for 2 hours. Roll out and cut into small rounds. Fill with the meat mixed with a little sauce, the lemon juice, ½ oz. butter and parsley. Pinch the edges together. Cook in boiling salted water for 20 minutes. Serve with melted butter mixed with lemon juice and chopped parsley.

GAME PATTIES

12 oz. puff pastry (see p. 205)
8 oz. cooked pheasant
2 chopped hard-boiled eggs
2 oz. rice, cooked
1 oz. butter
salt, pepper

Roll the pastry out and cut into rounds. Put a little of the following mixture between two rounds of pastry. Press the edges together. Melt the butter, cook the chopped game, hard-boiled eggs and rice in it for 5 minutes, mixing it well. Season with salt and pepper. Bake the patties in a hot oven for 15 minutes.

MUSHROOM AND EGG PATTIES

8 *oz. puff pastry (see p. 205)*
2 *hard-boiled eggs*
2 *oz. rice*
2 *oz. dried mushrooms*
1 *onion, sliced*
2 *oz. butter*

Soak the mushrooms. Boil them until tender. Drain, keep the water. Boil the rice in the mushroom stock until cooked. Drain. Melt the butter, fry the onion in it for 10 minutes, add the mushrooms and fry for another 5 minutes. Chop the eggs, mix them and the rice with the onions and mushrooms. Roll out the pastry. Spread the rice mixture on half of it, cover with the other half. Bake in a hot oven for 20 minutes. Cut into slices.

PIROSHKI

choux pastry made with 8 oz. flour
  and no sugar (see p. 92)
¼ *pint Béchamel sauce*
  (see p. 165)
2 *oz. grated cheese*
4 *oz. mushrooms, sliced and*
  cooked
4 *oz. flour*
1 *egg yolk*
4 *oz. breadcrumbs*

Mix 1 oz. grated cheese with the choux pastry. Divide into 2 sections and bake in flat tins in a moderate oven for 20 minutes. Turn out of the tins. Mix the sauce with 1 oz. grated cheese and the mushrooms. Spread this on one sheet pastry, cover with the other sheet. Cut into oblong pieces 3 inches long and 1 inch wide. Cover with breadcrumbs, then with flour, then with beaten egg yolk and lastly, with another layer of breadcrumbs. Cook in deep hot fat.

RICE WITH HARD-BOILED EGGS

8 *oz. Patna rice*
4 *hard-boiled eggs, chopped*
1 *tablespoon chopped parsley*
2 *oz. butter*
salt

Cook the rice in boiling salted water. When cooked but still firm, drain and mix with hard-boiled eggs, parsley and butter.

BLINY (Russian Pancakes)

2 *lb. flour*
1 *pint milk*
1 *oz. butter*
2 *eggs*
1½ *oz. yeast*
1½ *teaspoons malt*
2 *tablespoons sugar*

Dissolve the yeast in half the milk. Mix into a dough with half the flour. Leave in a warm place to rise for an hour. Add the salt, sugar, egg yolk and melted butter. Warm the rest of the milk and stir it in gradually. Add the rest of the flour slowly. Beat well. Leave to rise for an hour. Beat again. Leave to rise for an hour. Beat again, add the stiffly beaten egg whites. Leave to rise for 30 minutes. It should be the consistency of thick cream. Cook in the same way as pancakes. Serve with melted butter and salted herrings or anchovies or smoked salmon.

STUFFED CABBAGE

1 *large savoy cabbage*
1 *lb. stewing beef, minced*
1 *egg*
2 *onions, chopped*
1 *oz. lard*
2 *oz. butter*
1 *oz. flour*
3 *tablespoons sour cream*
salt, pepper

Put the cabbage in cold water. Bring to the boil, drain. Reserve the cabbage water; when cabbage is cold, separate the leaves. Melt the lard, cook the onions for 5 minutes, add the beef, cook for another 5 minutes. Season with salt and pepper. Bind with the egg. Fill the cabbage leaves with the mixture. Roll them, lay them in a fireproof dish, cover the bottom with water; dot with 1 oz. butter. Cook in a slow oven for $1\frac{1}{2}$ hours. Melt the rest of the butter, stir in the flour, cook for 1 minute, add $\frac{1}{2}$ pint cabbage water, stirring all the time. Add the cream. Pour the sauce over the cabbage rolls.

BEEF STROGANOFF

$1\frac{1}{2}$ *lb. fillet steak*
8 *oz. mushrooms*
1 *small onion*
$\frac{1}{2}$ *pint sour cream (Smetana is a possible substitute)*
4 *oz. butter*
nutmeg
salt

Beat the steak, cut into strips about 1 inch wide. Melt 2 oz. of the butter, cook the onion until transparent. Add the beef, cook quickly for about 5 minutes, making sure that all sides are browned. Cook the mushrooms separately in the rest of the butter. Season with salt and a little nutmeg. Add to the beef. Warm the cream, stir it into the meat and mushrooms. Serve with rice.

BEEF STEW

1 *lb. steak*
8 *oz. tomatoes, peeled and quartered*
2 *carrots, sliced*
4 *oz. cooking fat*
$\frac{1}{2}$ *pint stock*
1 *wineglass red wine*
salt, pepper

Flour the meat. Season with salt and pepper. Melt the fat, brown the vegetables and put them in the bottom of a casserole. Brown the meat in the same fat. Put in the casserole on top of the vegetables, cover it with another layer of vegetables. Pour in the stock. Simmer in a moderate oven for 2 hours. Sieve the vegetables, add the wine. Pour this sauce over the meat. Serve with noodles or macaroni.

SOLYANKA (Steak with Gherkin Sauce)

4 *slices fillet steak (about 6 oz.*
each)
2 *onions, chopped*
2 *gherkins, sliced*
1 *tablespoon tomato purée*
¼ *glass white wine*
2 *oz. butter*
salt, pepper

Cut the steaks into 1-inch strips. Fry the onion in half the butter, add the gherkins, tomato purée, wine and stock. Season with salt and pepper. Simmer for 40 minutes. Melt the rest of the butter. Fry the steak on both sides. Arrange in a fireproof dish on top of the tomato mixture. Cook in a moderate oven for 30 minutes.

KIDNEYS WITH GHERKINS

1 *lb. ox kidneys*
1 *onion, sliced*
1 *oz. butter*
1 *oz. flour*
¼ *pint stock*
1 *lb. new potatoes, cooked*
gherkins

salt, pepper

Fry the onion in the butter for 5 minutes. Add the thinly sliced kidney and cook slowly until tender. Season with salt and pepper, stir in the flour. Cook for 1 minute; gradually add the stock. Arrange on a dish, pour the sauce over the kidneys and surround with potatoes and gherkins.

BRAISED LAMB CHOPS

4 *lamb chops*
1 *small cabbage*
2 *carrots*
1 *turnip*
2 *potatoes*
½ *pint stock*
1 *oz. butter*
1 *oz. flour*

salt, pepper

Shred the carrots, cabbage and turnip, dice the potatoes. Brown them in the butter, stir in the flour. Put them in a casserole, arrange the chops on top, season with salt and pepper, pour in the stock. Cover the casserole and cook in a moderate oven for 1 hour. Cool, skim off the fat, and reheat.

CAUCASIAN SHASHLIK

½ *leg lamb (about 1 lb.), boned*
8 *oz. green bacon*
2 *oz. butter*
salt, pepper

Cut the meat into 1-inch cubes. Melt half the butter and brown the cubes on all sides. Cut the bacon into slightly smaller cubes. Put alternate cubes of bacon and meat on to 4 skewers. Season with salt and pepper. Brush with melted butter. Cook under a hot grill, turning the skewers from time to time so that the meat is cooked evenly on all sides. Serve with plain boiled rice.

LIVER IN SOUR CREAM

1 *lb. calves' liver*
¼ *pint milk*
¼ *pint sour cream*
1 *tablespoon flour*
1 *onion, sliced*
1 *oz. butter*
½ *pint stock*
salt, pepper

Melt the butter, lightly fry the onion. Add the liver cut into fairly thin slices, floured and seasoned with salt and pepper. Cook for 10 minutes, turning the liver so that all the pieces are browned on both sides. Pour on the milk, sour cream and stock, and simmer covered with a lid, for 30 minutes in a moderate oven.

BRAISED TONGUE

1 *ox tongue*
1 *dessertspoon sugar*
1 *tablespoon flour*
1 *oz. butter*
1 *small glass red wine*
juice of 1 lemon
strip of lemon peel
2 *oz. sultanas*
2 *oz. almonds, blanched and
    shredded*
1 *carrot, sliced*
1 *turnip, sliced*

½ *bay leaf*
thyme } *bouquet garni*
salt

Simmer the tongue in water with the vegetables, a *bouquet garni* and salt. Skin it and leave to cool. Make sauce as follows:

Melt the butter, cook the flour in it for 1 minute, gradually add wine and enough of the water in which tongue was cooked to make a thick sauce. Add the lemon juice, lemon peel, sugar, sultanas, almonds. Cut the tongue into slices and reheat it in the sauce.

PORK CHOPS WITH BEETROOT

4 *pork chops*
1 *cooked beetroot, thinly sliced*
1 *tablespoon vinegar*
1 *onion, chopped*
2 *tablespoons breadcrumbs*
lard
salt, pepper

Brown the chops in the lard. Put them into a fire-proof dish. Put the onions, beetroot, vinegar and breadcrumbs into the pan, season with salt and pepper and add ½ pint of water. Simmer for 5 minutes and pour over the chops. Cook, covered, in a moderate oven for 40 minutes. Strain the sauce over the chops before serving.

CHICKEN CUTLETS (1)

breast of ½ chicken
1 slice bread
¼ pint cream
2 oz. butter
2 oz. breadcrumbs
salt, pepper

Remove the breast of the chicken and skin it. Bone it. Soak the bread in the cream and squeeze it a little. Mix it with the minced chicken. Season with salt and pepper. Divide into 4 pieces, shape into cutlets, roll in breadcrumbs. Fry slowly in butter until cooked and brown.

CHICKEN CUTLETS (2)

1 small chicken
3 chicken livers
4 oz. mushrooms, finely chopped
2 onions, finely chopped
1 egg
breadcrumbs
2 oz. butter
2 oz. flour
salt, pepper
lard

Remove the skin from the chicken breast and mince and skin the wings and legs. Cut the meat into small pieces. Cook the onions in the butter until golden, add the pieces of chicken, mushrooms, salt and pepper, and fry lightly. Blanch the chicken livers, cut into small pieces and add to the mushroom mixture. Cut the chicken breast into thin slices, beat well and spread the mushroom mixture on them. Roll them up and secure with a wooden stick. Dredge with flour, brush with beaten egg and roll in breadcrumbs. Fry quickly in lard until browned on all sides, and transfer to a casserole and cook in a moderate oven for 20 minutes.

PARTRIDGE WITH CREAM SAUCE

2 partridges
2 oz. butter
1 oz. flour
1 gill double cream
juice of ½ lemon
8 oz. mushrooms

Slice the mushrooms and stuff the birds with them. Put half the butter in the roasting tin and half on the birds, roast in a moderate oven for 15 minutes. Cut in halves. Make a sauce by cooking the flour in the fat in the tin and adding the cream and lemon juice. Put the partridges back in the tin and cook for another 15 minutes.

TURKEY WITH CHERRY SAUCE

sliced breast of turkey
8 oz. cherry jam
cinnamon
ginger
cloves
2 oz. butter
1 glass Madeira

Heat the jam slowly with a little water, a pinch of cinnamon and ginger and 2 cloves. Rub through a sieve. Melt the butter, heat the turkey slices in it, add the Madeira and cook again for 1 minute. Pour the sauce into the middle of a dish and arrange the turkey round it.

APPLE FOOL

6 *cooking apples*
juice of 1 *lemon*
2 *oz. sugar*
1 *tablespoon blackcurrant jelly*
cinnamon
2 *tablespoons breadcrumbs*
1 *glass claret*

Peel and slice the apples. Simmer them with a little water and the breadcrumbs, sugar and cinnamon. Sieve them and, when cold, add the claret, lemon juice and melted blackcurrant jelly. Beat well, serve cold. This is served as a soup in Russia, but would be more acceptable as a sweet in England.

APPLE SOUFFLÉ

4 *large cooking apples*
4 *oz. sugar*
1 *egg*

Peel and slice the apples, cook with a little water and sugar until tender. Sieve, cook again until very thick. Mix in the egg yolk and fold in the stiffly beaten egg white. Put in a greased soufflé dish, cook in a hot oven for 15 minutes.

EASTER PUDDING

8 *oz. dry cream cheese*
2 *eggs*
½ *pint cream*
4 *oz. butter*
8 *oz. sugar*
4 *oz. raisins*
4 *oz. sultanas*

vanilla
lemon peel

Whisk the sugar and eggs until thick, beat in the butter. Mix this with the cream cheese and dried fruit. Flavour with vanilla and grated lemon peel. Put into a muslin bag and leave to drain for 2—3 days. Shape into a pyramid.

KISYELI

1 *lb. red currants*
8 *oz. raspberries*
2 *oz. semolina or ground rice*
   or potato flour
4 *oz. blackcurrants*
4 *oz. sugar*

Stew the fruit with the sugar and just enough water to stop it burning. Strain off the juice. Mix a little of the juice with the semolina, heat the rest and stir it into the semolina. Cook this mixture for 5 minutes, stirring all the time. Chill and serve with whipped cream.

MALAKOFF CAKE

1 *sponge cake made with sugar,
  eggs and flour but no fat*
6 *oz. butter*
6 *oz. sugar*
6 *oz. almonds*
1 *glass rum*
2 *egg yolks*
¼ *pint milk and rum, mixed*
½ *pint double cream*

Chop the almonds finely and roast them by putting a little sugar in a frying pan and tossing the almonds in this until they are slightly brown. Cream the butter and sugar and beat in the almonds, rum and egg yolks.

Cut the cake into 3 flat sections, soak each in a mixture of rum and milk. Put a layer of cake followed by a layer of filling into a cake tin of the same size. Repeat these layers and cover with a final layer of cake. Leave in a very cold place for 12 hours. Turn out before serving and cover with whipped cream.

WALNUT AND ALMOND KASCHA

4 *oz. walnuts*
4 *oz. almonds*
¾ *pint milk*
1 *oz. semolina*
apricot jam
glacé cherries, chopped
8 *oz. short pastry*
4 *oz. icing sugar*

Shell the walnuts, blanch and peel the almonds. Pound them together until smooth. Put the milk in a flat dish in the oven, leave it until a brown skin is formed, then strain the skin off and keep it. Put the dish back in the oven and repeat the process 4 times. Cook the semolina with the milk until quite thick. Line a tart tin with pastry, fill it with alternate layers of semolina, skin from the milk, mixed jam, cherries and nuts. Sprinkle with breadcrumbs over the top, cook in a moderate oven until brown. Cover with icing sugar and brown under a grill.

BUCKWHEAT

2 *cups kasha buckwheat*
3 *cups water*
2 *oz. butter*
salt

Boil the kasha in salted water, stir until thick. Cook in a slow oven for 3 hours. Stir in the butter. Serve with borshch.

CREAM CHEESE TARTS

8 *oz. flour*
2 *oz. butter*
2 *oz. lard*
8 *oz. cream cheese*
1 *teaspoon sugar*
salt

Make short pastry with the flour, butter and lard mixed with a little water. Roll it out and cut into rounds. Arrange in small tart tins, fill with cream cheese mixed with the sugar and seasoned with salt. Serve with borshch or as hors d'oeuvre.

CHERRY PUDDING

1 *lb. cherries (weight after stoning)*
5 *eggs*
4 *oz. flour*
2 *oz. butter*
2 *oz. chopped almonds*
2 *oz. breadcrumbs*
1 *dessertspoon cinnamon*
4 *oz. sugar*

SAUCE:
1 *glass red wine*
4 *oz. cherries*
3 *oz. sugar*

Rub the butter into the flour, then add eggs, sugar, chopped almonds and cinnamon and beat together. Butter a mould which will go into the oven and pour a little of the mixture in. Sprinkle a few breadcrumbs on top. Bake for a few minutes in a hot oven. When cooked add a layer of cherries and cover this with another layer of the mixture and breadcrumbs. Bake again. Repeat the process until the dish is full. Brown the top layer and turn out the pudding on to a dish. To make the sauce, sieve the cherries to make a purée and mix with red wine and sugar. Heat, and pour over the pudding.

RUSSIAN EASTER EGGS

It is the custom in Hungary and Russia to exchange highly decorated hard-boiled eggs at Easter. Here are two characteristic ways of decorating them.
1. Unravel threads from any cotton material the dye of which is not fast. Wind them around the eggs, using as many different colours as possible. Wrap a piece of rag round the whole and cook in boiling water for 10 minutes. Remove the wrappings and there will be a multicoloured pattern of criss-crossing lines on the egg.
2. Lay onion skins round the egg, wrap a piece of rag round to keep them in position. Cook in boiling water for 10 minutes. The eggs will be a beautiful golden colour.

RUSSIAN TEA

Make tea in the usual way. Serve without milk but garnished with slices of lemon and glacé cherries.

Scandinavia

COOKING IN NORWAY, SWEDEN AND DENMARK

All three of these Scandinavian countries have a great many common traits in their kitchen, but they also have a number of national characteristics. The Norwegian and the Swede are both hearty eaters of fish — meat is considered quite a delicacy in some parts of these countries — consequently it is their fish recipes which are well worth following. You will find a number of recipes in this section which are all part of that glorious mixture called Smörgasbord. Smörgasbord is the Swedish way of starting a meal — it consists of dozens of varieties of hors d'oeuvre — you need a lot of will power to leave room for anything else afterwards. However, I find that two or three of the following recipes for hors d'oeuvre are plentiful for the uninitiated. Either of the two Herring Salad recipes is ample for a prelude to a dinner party or for a cold luncheon.

It is difficult to point out favourites among the Scandinavian fish recipes — I find them all excellent. Fish soup is perhaps the most unusual and beautifully easy recipe, which kills two birds with one stone: it is both soup and fish course rolled into one. All the sauces for fish are outstandingly tasty in this section — guaranteed to liven up the dullest fish.

The Danes too, go in for a great number of cold, pickled and smoked specialities which they like to serve on thin slices of rye bread, heaped up in large quantities and artistically decorated. It is in the Danish kitchen that we can find a very good selection of meat recipes — their pork and veal dishes are an absolute treat.

Danish pastries are again one of those national specialities which have swept the whole world. Apart from the basic Danish Pastry, there are the Almond Tarts and Chocolate Almond Cake, both delightful to eat with a cup of coffee. Lastly, let me just draw your attention to a very simple recipe: Walnut Meringues. They are only different from ordinary meringues because you put some chopped walnuts in them, and yet this one thing gives a subtle delicacy to them.

SMÖRGASBORD

The Swedish smörgasbord consists of both hors d'oeuvre dishes of all kinds and a number of light entrées. It is as though the French notion of *hors d'oeuvre variés* had been combined with the grand old-fashioned English breakfast at which the sideboard was covered with delicious hot dishes under silver covers, from which the fortunate guest could take his pick. It is capable of great variation: it can be quite modest or very elaborate. The common factor is attention to decorative and appetising detail. Each dish is quite small, but arranged in such a way as to please the eye and stimulate the appetite. As eaten in Sweden, smörgasbord is not a meal in itself but an overture to the main course. The following is a selection from the many possible dishes for a smörgasbord.

STUFFED EGGS

4 *hard-boiled eggs*
5 *anchovy fillets*
1 *oz. butter*
prawns

Slice the eggs and cut a little off the underneath of the white so that they will stand steadily. Pound the yolks with the anchovies and the butter. Hang prawns by their tails round the egg whites and fill with the yolk mixtures.

CALVES' LIVER TERRINE

1 *lb. calves' liver*
4 *oz. veal*
8 *oz. fat pork*
1 *onion*
8 *anchovy fillets*
2 *oz. flour*
3 *eggs*
½ *pint cream*
4 *truffles*
8 *oz. streaky bacon*

Mince the liver, veal, pork, onion and anchovies several times. Pass through a sieve. Stir the flour into the eggs, blend with the cream. Add the liver mixture with the truffles. Line a shallow fireproof dish with bacon rashers, fill it with the mixture and cook in a *bain-maire* for 1½ hours in a slow oven. Cover with greaseproof paper, put a weight on the top, leave in a cool place for 24 hours.

ANCHOVY EGGS

4 *hard-boiled eggs*
2 *oz. butter*
5 *anchovy fillets or anchovy paste*
lettuce
tomatoes
parsley

Slice the eggs lengthwise. Remove the yolks and beat until very soft with the butter and the sieved anchovies or anchovy paste. Pile this mixture into the egg whites. Arrange each on a lettuce leaf. Surround with sliced tomatoes and garnish with parsley.

SARDINE ROLLS

2 *lb. fresh sardine (smelts can be used instead)*
1 *anchovy fillet to each sardine*
2 *oz. butter*
2 *oz. breadcrumbs*

Fillet the sardines and lay one anchovy on each fillet. Roll them up together. Arrange in a buttered fireproof dish, pour the oil from the anchovies over them. Sprinkle with breadcrumbs, dot with butter. Bake for 20 minutes in a moderate oven.

PICKLED HERRINGS

2 *large salt herrings*
1 *oz. allspice*
2 *bay leaves*
4 *oz. sugar*
6 *black peppercorns*
1 *small onion, chopped*
½ *pint vinegar*

Clean the fish and remove the heads. Soak overnight, skin and fillet the fish. Cut the fillets in ½-inch slices, arrange in a shallow dish. Mix all the other ingredients with the vinegar, pour over the fish. Leave in a cold place for several hours before serving.

This is one of the essential dishes for a smörgasbord.

HERRING SALAD (1)

1 *salt herring*
2 *medium potatoes, cooked and diced*
1 *cooked beetroot, diced*
1 *large apple, peeled and diced*
2 *pickled gherkins, diced*
hard-boiled eggs, cooked beetroot and sour cream to garnish
1 *small onion, chopped*
4 *tablespoons vinegar*

2 *tablespoons sugar*
pepper

Clean the fish and remove the heads. Soak overnight, skin and fillet. Cut the fillets into small pieces and mix well with the potatoes, apples, beetroot, gherkins and onion. Mix the sugar with the vinegar, season with pepper. Pour this over the other ingredients. Leave in a mould in a cool place for several hours. Unmould and serve garnished with hard-boiled eggs, beetroot and sour cream.

HERRING SALAD (2)

4 *salt herrings, soaked overnight*
2 *medium potatoes*
2 *apples*
1 *onion*
2 *hard-boiled eggs*
2 *tablespoons white wine vinegar*
2 *tablespoons olive oil*
salt, pepper
¼ *teaspoon dry mustard*

1 *tablespoon chopped chives*
¼ *pint cream*

Cook the potatoes in their skins, cool, peel and dice. Peel and core the apples and cut into dice. Chop the onion finely. Cut the herrings into small pieces. Separate the whites of the eggs and chop. Sieve the yolks. Arrange all the ingredients in a bowl, mixed or kept separate as you prefer. Pour the following dressing over them:

Mix the oil and vinegar, season with salt, pepper and mustard. Add the chives and work in the cream.

EGGS AND SHRIMPS WITH MAYONNAISE

4 *hard-boiled eggs*
1 *pint shrimps*
½ *pint mayonnaise (see p. 161)*
¼ *pint cream*
chives
pepper

Cut the eggs in half lengthwise. Arrange down the middle of a dish, sprinkle with finely ground black pepper. Surround them with the shrimps (from which the heads and tails have been removed). Stir the cream into the mayonnaise, pour over the eggs. Strew chopped chives over the top.

ANCHOVY EYE

12 *anchovy fillets*
1 *onion*
1 *egg yolk*

The use of a raw egg to be mixed at the table with the other ingredients is a characteristic smörgasbord dish.

Arrange the finely chopped anchovies round the outside of a small dish, with a ring of finely chopped onion inside them. Place a raw egg yolk in the middle.

EGGS IN MUSTARD SAUCE

2 *oz. butter*
2 *oz. flour*
½ *pint milk*
1 *teaspoon dry mustard*
salt, pepper
4 *hard-boiled eggs*

Melt the butter, cook the flour in it for 1 minute, gradually add the hot milk, stirring all the time. Season with salt, pepper and mustard. Cut the eggs in half lengthwise, arrange them in a shallow dish, pour the sauce over them.

SHRIMP AND HARD-BOILED EGG FLAN

*short crust pastry made with
6 oz. flour (see p. 206)*
3 tablespoons olive oil
1 tablespoon wine vinegar
1 dessertspoon vinegar
½ teaspoon dry mustard
1 tablespoon cream
4 hard-boiled eggs
½ pint shrimps
6 anchovy fillets, cut in strips
*2 pickled cucumbers, peeled and
sliced*

Line a greased tart tin with the pastry and bake blind in a moderately hot oven. Mix the oil and vinegar with the sugar and mustard. Beat in the cream, stirring until thick. Remove the whites from the eggs and cut into strips. Mix with the shrimps from which the heads and tails have been removed. Sieve the egg yolks. Pour a little of the dressing over the egg whites and the shrimps, and put them in the middle of the pastry case. Arrange egg yolk and cucumber round the edge. Put the anchovies in a criss-cross pattern on the top. Serve the remaining dressing separately.

JELLIED PORK AND VEAL

2 lb. pork ⎫
2 lb. veal ⎬ *any inexpensive cut*
2 tablespoons salt
14 peppercorns
1 dessertspoon allspice
2 bay leaves
4 cloves
1 onion
1 carrot
2 tablespoons white wine vinegar
gelatine

Simmer the meat for 10 minutes. Skim. Add the herbs, spices, vegetables and seasoning. Simmer until tender (1½—2 hours). Drain the meat, remove from the bones and chop finely. Return bones to the pan and simmer for another 30 minutes. Strain, add the meat to the stock and simmer for 10 minutes. Dissolve the gelatine (using enough to set the liquid according to the instructions on the packet) in a little water, add it to the meat and stock. Add the vinegar, and season lightly with salt and pepper. Leave in a mould to set. Unmould and serve cold.

DANISH CHEESE SALAD

2 oz. Samsoe cheese
1 oz. Danish Blue cheese
1 red pimento
1 green pimento
1 onion
French dressing

Cut the pimentos lengthways, remove grains, and put in boiling salted water for a moment. Allow to cool, then cut into small pieces and soak in dressing. Chop the onion, cut the Samsoe into small strips and the Danish Blue into small dice. Mix all together in French dressing.

POTATO SALAD

4 *medium potatoes*
3 *tablespoons olive oil*
1 *tablespoon white wine vinegar*
1 *tablespoon chopped onion*
1 *tablespoon chopped parsley*
1 *tablespoon chopped chives*
salt, pepper

1 *medium pickled beetroot,*
   finely chopped (see p. 348)

Cook the potatoes in their skins until just tender. Cool, peel and slice them. Stir the vinegar into the olive oil, season with salt and pepper. Put the potatoes into a salad bowl with the onions, parsley, chives and beetroot on the top. Mix all the ingredients gently, leave to stand for several hours. Mix again before serving.

CUCUMBER SALAD

1 *cucumber*
French dressing (see p. 161)
dill or dill seeds

Peel cucumber and cut it into thin slices. Sprinkle with salt and leave for 30 minutes, drain and arrange in a shallow dish, covered with French dressing. Sprinkle with chopped dill or dill seeds.

ONION CASSEROLE

4 *Spanish onions, sliced*
1 *oz. butter*
4 *oz. minced lean pork*
4 *oz. minced veal*
½ *pint milk or* ½ *pint cream*
   and 1½ *gills water*
1 *oz. breadcrumbs*
½ *gill stock*

salt, pepper

Fry the onions in the butter until golden. Mix the meat and the breadcrumbs. Season with salt and pepper. Place half the onions in the bottom of a greased fireproof dish, cover with the meat mixture, then the rest of the onions. Pour in the stock. Bake in a moderate oven for 30 minutes.

ONION AND ANCHOVY RAGOÛT

1 *onion, sliced*
1 *oz. butter*
2 *hard-boiled eggs*
10 *anchovies*
1 *tablespoon cream*
pepper

Cook the onions in the butter until golden. Drain and mince with the eggs and anchovies. Season with pepper. Transfer to a shallow fireproof dish, pour the butter from the pan over, add the cream. Cook in a moderate oven for 20 minutes.

ANCHOVY AND POTATO PIE

2 *small onions, sliced*
2 *oz. butter*
4 *medium potatoes*
1 *large tin anchovies*
¼ *pint cream*

Fry the onions in 1 oz. butter until transparent. Peel and cut the potatoes as for very thin chips. Arrange potatoes, onions and anchovies in layers in a buttered fireproof dish, beginning and ending with a layer of potatoes. Pour a little of the anchovy oil into the dish, dot with butter and cook in a hot oven for 10 minutes. Add the cream and continue baking in a hot oven for 1 hour or until potatoes are soft.

GREEN PEA SOUP

2 *lb. shelled peas*
2 *sprigs parsley*
1 *sprig mint*
2 *pints chicken stock*
1 *oz. butter*
1 *oz. flour*
salt, pepper
20 *very small carrots, cooked*

1 *tablespoon chopped parsley*
¼ *pint cream*

Simmer the peas, with the herbs, in the stock until tender. Strain, reserving the liquid, and pass through a sieve. Melt the butter, cook the flour in it for 1 minute, gradually add the stock and the purée of peas. Season with salt and pepper. Add the carrots, stir in the cream. Heat but do not boil. Serve hot or chilled.

SPLIT PEA SOUP

1 *lb. split peas*
8 *oz. pork*
½ *teaspoon ginger*
salt, pepper

This sustaining dish is widely eaten in Sweden by tradition on Thursdays.

Soak the peas in 4 pints water overnight. Cook in the same water. Skim off the skins as they rise to the surface, add the pork when new skins have stopped appearing. Simmer until tender (about 2 hours). Remove the pork and keep warm. Sieve the soup, season with salt, pepper and ginger. Serve the pork as a side dish with the soup. It should be eaten with mustard. Onion or leek can be substituted for the ginger if preferred, in which case they should be added at the same time as the pork.

FISH SOUP

2 lb. haddock with head, bones
  and skin
1 carrot
2 sticks celery
2 sprigs parsley
1 bay leaf
2 cloves
6 peppercorns
salt
2 oz. butter

1½ oz. flour
1 pint milk

Simmer the fish with the vegetables, herbs and seasoning until tender. Strain, keep the liquor and the best pieces of fish. Make a sauce as follows:

    Melt the butter, cook the flour in it for 1 minute, gradually add the fish stock and the milk. Season lightly with salt and pepper and add the flaked fish pieces.

SPRING SOUP

2 spring onions, sliced
1 small cauliflower
1 stick celery, chopped
8 oz. peas
8 oz. spinach
parsley
2 carrots, sliced
2 pints chicken stock
2 egg yolks
¼ pint cream
salt, pepper

1 oz. flour
½ oz. butter

Put the onion, celery, peas, carrots and cauliflower, broken into flowerets, in a pudding basin and steam them until tender. Cook the spinach separately. Drain and chop the spinach. Melt the butter and cook the flour in it for 1 minute. Gradually add the stock. Add the vegetables. Season with salt and pepper. Beat the egg yolks with the cream. Pour the soup slowly into this mixture. Reheat. Serve garnished with chopped parsley.

TUESDAY SOUP

2 carrots
1 parsnip
1 oz. dripping
1 piece celeriac
1 slice turnip
1 small onion
5 oz. rice or barley
2 pints stock
1 pint milk

salt, pepper

It is customary in Sweden to make soup the main dish on Tuesay. This is a characteristic one, but the root vegetables can be varied according to taste. Slice the vegetables and brown them in the butter. Add the stock and the salt and pepper and simmer for 30 minutes, add the rice and simmer until the rice is tender (about 15 minutes). Stir in the hot milk.

BRUSSELS SPROUTS SOUP

1½ *lb. Brussels sprouts*
4 *rashers streaky bacon*
1 *small onion, sliced*
1 *oz. flour*
2 *pints stock*

salt, peper
nutmeg

Cook the sprouts in boiling salted water until tender, drain, simmer and chop roughly. Fry the bacon rashers lightly, chop them finely, stir in the flour, cook for 1 minute, gradually add the boiling stock. Season with salt, pepper and grating of nutmeg.

CABBAGE SOUP

½ *small cabbage, shredded*
1 *oz. butter*
2 *oz. brown sugar*
2 *pints stock*
4 *black peppercorns*
salt

Fry the shredded cabbage, reserving a few shreds, in the butter until brown, stir in the sugar, add the stock, season with salt and pepper. Simmer for 2 hours. Strain, add the uncooked cabbage shreds and simmer rapidly for another 5 minutes.

FRIED SALMON

4 *salmon steaks*
½ *pint vinegar*
4 *oz. butter*
salt
lemon or Hollandaise sauce
  (see p. 161)

This can be made very well with the frozen salmon imported from the Pacific. Marinate the salmon in the vinegar for an hour. Drain and then dry the fish. Melt the butter and fry the fish on both sides until golden brown. Serve with lemon or with Hollandaise sauce.

NORWEGIAN FISH BALLS

2 *lb. haddock or bream*
3 *oz. butter*
5 *oz. flour*
2 *eggs*
¾ *pint milk*
salt, pepper

Poach the fish in a little very gently boiling salted water, for 15 minutes. Drain, reserving the liquor for the sauce, and flake when cool. Mince the fish, beat in the butter, flour, egg yolks and milk, season with salt and pepper. Shape into balls and cook in briskly boiling salted water, for 15 minutes. Serve with fish sauce (see p. 353).

FISH SOUFFLÉ

2 *lb. fresh haddock or cod*
3 *oz. butter*
3 *oz. flour*
½ *pint milk*
3 *eggs*
salt, pepper

Cook the whole fish if possible in a little gently boiling salted water for 15 minutes, or in a court-bouillon. Drain, reserving the liquid, and allow to cool. Remove the flesh and flake into small pieces. Melt the butter, cook the flour in it for 1 minute, add ½ pint fish stock and the milk. Add the fish, season lightly with salt and pepper, gradually beat in the egg yolk. Fold in the stiffly beaten egg whites and bake in a greased dish for 45 minutes in a moderately hot oven.

DANISH PLAICE

2 *plaice (about 1 lb. each,*
   filleted)
2 *glasses white wine*
4 *oz. flour*
1 *egg*
2 *oz. breadcrumbs*
4 *oz. butter*

FOR THE SAUCE:
1 *oz. butter*
1 *oz. flour*
scant ½ pint milk
1 *bunch small asparagus*
4 *oz. mushrooms, sliced*
juice of ½ lemon
salt, pepper

Cook 4 fillets slowly, just covered by the wine, in a buttered fireproof dish. Keep warm. Cut the remaining fillets into 3 pieces, roll in flour and then in egg and breadcrumbs. Make the sauce as follows:

Melt the butter and cook the flour in it for 1 minute, gradually add the liquor from the fish and the milk. Add the cooked asparagus and the mushrooms, previously cooked in the butter with the lemon juice, and season with salt and pepper. Keep the sauce warm while quickly frying the uncooked fillets in the butter. Arrange the fish cooked in the wine down the middle of a dish, cover with the sauce. Put the fried fillets round the edges. Serve with potato purée.

HADDOCK FILLETS WITH LEMON SAUCE

2 *lb. haddock fillets*
juice of ½ lemon
1 *oz. butter*
½ *pint lemon sauce (see p. 354)*
¼ *pint shrimps*
salt

Roll the fillets (cut into smaller pieces if preferred) and secure with cocktail sticks. Arrange in a fireproof dish, add the lemon juice and enough water to cover the fish. Sprinkle with salt and dot with butter. Bake in a moderate oven for about 30 minutes (the time will vary according to the size of the fillets). Serve with lemon sauce and garnish with prepared shrimps sautéed in the butter. Fish prepared in this way can be garnished with chopped dill or parsley instead of shrimps.

BAKED HALIBUT

4 *slices halibut*
12 *oz. tomatoes, peeled and sliced*
1 *small onion, sliced*
2 *oz. melted butter*
¼ *pint cream*
salt, pepper

Put the fish in a shallow fireproof dish having first removed the skin. Cover with the tomatoes, sprinkle with salt and pepper and pour in the melted butter. Add the onion, bake in a moderate oven for 20 minutes. Remove the onions. Pour the cream over the tomatoes and fish. Bake for another 10 minutes.

GOLDEN COD

1½ *lb. cod fillets*
1 *oz. butter*
¾ *oz. flour*
½ *pint mixed fish stock and milk*
1 *teaspoon dry mustard*
1 *tablespoon vinegar*
½ *teaspoon sugar*
4 *cold boiled potatoes*
salt, pepper

Poach the fillets in a little milk until tender. Drain and reserve the milk for the sauce. Melt the butter and cook the flour in it for 1 minute, gradually add the fish liquid and enough extra milk to make up ½ pint and stir in the dry mustard, vinegar and sugar. Flake the fish and put it in a shallow fireproof dish, surround with slices of potato. Pour the sauce over and bake in a moderate oven for 20 minutes. Serve garnished with croûtons.

BAKED COD

2 *thick slices of cod (about 12 oz.*
  each)
salt
paprika
mushroom sauce (see p. 353)
6 *rashers streaky bacon*
1 *oz. butter*

Sprinkle the fish with salt and paprika. Cut 3 bacon rashers into small pieces and put them in the bottom of a fireproof dish. Put the cod on top of them, cover with the rest of the bacon in small pieces. Sprinkle heavily with paprika. Dot with butter. Bake in a moderate oven for 45 minutes. Strain off the liquid and use for the sauce.

FRIED MACKEREL

4 *small mackerel*
½ *pint vinegar*
6 *oz. breadcrumbs*
fat for frying
lemon
1 *tablespoon salt*

Marinate the mackerel in the vinegar for 1 hour. Dry and roll in breadcrumbs mixed with the salt. Fry on both sides in hot fat. Serve garnished with lemon.

HAM OMELETTE

2 *oz. bacon*
½ *oz. butter*
2 *egg yolks*
1 *egg white*
½ *pint milk*

salt, pepper

Put the diced bacon in the bottom of a greased fire-proof dish. Beat the eggs in the milk, season with salt and pepper, pour over the bacon. Bake in a moderate oven for 45 minutes.

BAKED OMELETTE

4 *eggs*
½ *pint cream or milk*
salt, pepper

FOR THE FILLING:
mushrooms, shrimps, lobster or
  asparagus in thick white sauce

Beat the eggs, add the cream and season with salt and pepper. Pour the mixture into a buttered fireproof dish (a heavy omelette pan is ideal) and bake in a moderate oven for 15 minutes. Transfer to a heated dish, cover half the omelette with the hot filling, fold the other half over it. Serve at once.

STUFFED CABBAGE (Norwegian)

1 *small cabbage*
1 *oz. minced beef*
salt, pepper
1 *pint stock*
1 *pint Béchamel sauce*
  (see p. 165)

Cut the middle leaves out of the cabbage, fill the hole with the meat seasoned with salt and pepper, tie the outside leaves together at the top. Simmer in the stock for 3 hours. Serve with Béchamel sauce and thin slices of toast.

STUFFED POTATO PANCAKES

4 *medium potatoes*
1 *egg yolk*
4 *oz. flour*
1 *small onion*
salt, pepper
2 *oz. ham*
1 *oz. butter*

Boil the potatoes in their skins. Peel and sieve. Mix with the flour and egg yolk until smooth. Season with salt and pepper. Chop the onion and the ham and brown in the butter. Roll out the dough ½ inch thick. Cut into rounds with a pastry cutter. Spread the ham mixture on to half the rounds, cover with the other rounds, pinch the ends together. Poach in boiling water until they rise to the surface. Serve with melted butter.

VEAL HEADCHEESE

3 *lb. leg of veal*
3 *lb. lean pork*
2 *tablespoons salt*
3 *whole allspice*
4 *cloves*
6 *peppercorns*
½ *bay leaf*
1 *small onion, sliced*

Get the butcher to cut the veal into 3 pieces across the bone. Put it in a large pan with the pork and 2 quarts cold water, bring to the boil and skim. Add all the other ingredients, cover the pan and cook slowly, covered, for 3 hours or longer, until the meat is tender. Strain, remove the meat from the bones, return to the pan and cook for another hour. Mince or chop the meat. Strain the liquid, add it to the meat and boil them together for 10 minutes. Pour into moulds and leave in a cold place to set.

This is a modified version of the real headcheese which requires a whole hogshead and is therefore not generally practical.

BROWNED POTATOES

2 *lb. potatoes*
2 *oz. breadcrumbs*
4 *oz. butter*
salt

Wash the potatoes and cook in salted water until tender. Cool and peel and cut into dice. Melt the fat, mix some of the breadcrumbs with enough of the potatoes to cover the bottom of the pan. Fry until crisp and brown, drain and keep hot. Cook the rest of the breadcrumbs and potatoes in same way.

BEETROOT À LA LINDSTROM

2 *medium beetroots*
1 *egg*
2 *oz. breadcrumbs*
fat for frying
fried onion to garnish

Boil the beetroots in water until tender, peel and cut into ¼-inch slices. Dry the slices and dip them into beaten egg, roll in breadcrumbs. Fry in shallow fat until crisp and brown. Serve garnished with fried onions.

PICKLED BEETROOT

10 *small beetroots*
½ *pint vinegar*
salt
4 *oz. sugar*
1 *clove*

Cook the beetroots in boiling salted water until tender. Drain and cut into thin slices when cool. Mix the vinegar with a little water, the sugar and the clove. Season with salt. Pour this over the beetroot and leave in a cool place for several hours.

LIVER TERRINE (Danish)

1 *lb. pig's liver*
1 *small tin anchovy fillets*
4 *oz. fat bacon*
4 *eggs*
12 *rashers streaky bacon*
½ *pint thick white sauce*
1 *clove garlic*
salt, pepper

Mince the liver, fat bacon and anchovies twice. Pass through a sieve. Mix with the beaten eggs, crushed garlic and white sauce. Season with salt and pepper. Line a shallow ovenproof dish with bacon rashers. Fill with the liver mixture. Bake in a slow oven in a *bain-marie* for 2 hours. Cover with greaseproof paper, put weights on the top. Leave for 24 hours in a cold place.

LAMB AND CABBAGE

3 *lb. shoulder of lamb*
1 *small cabbage, shredded coarsely*
1 *oz. fat*
salt pepper
parsley

Prepare and cook the meat as for lamb stew. Melt the fat, brown the meat in it. Set aside. Brown the cabbage. Arrange alternate layers of meat and cabbage in a casserole. Season each layer with salt and pepper. Add enough water to cover the contents of the casserole. Cover with a lid, cook slowly for 1 hour. Serve garnished with chopped parsley.

SHOULDER OF LAMB WITH DILL SAUCE

4 *lb. shoulder of lamb*
1 *tablespoon salt*
4 *sprigs dill*

FOR THE SAUCE:
1 *oz. butter*
1 *oz. flour*
½ *pint stock*
1 *tablespoon vinegar*
1 *dessertspoon sugar*
2 *tablespoons chopped dill*
1 *egg yolk*
salt, pepper

Pour 3 pints boiling water over the lamb, simmer for 10 minutes and skim. Add the salt and the dill. Simmer in a covered pan for 2 hours. Leave to cool, skim off the fat, strain and use the liquid to make the sauce. Reheat the meat in a moderate oven and serve with the following sauce:
Cook the flour in the butter for 1 minute, gradually add the stock, vinegar, sugar and salt. Pour a little of the sauce over the beaten egg yolk, return to the pan and reheat carefully. Stir in the chopped dill.

BRAISED BEEF (Danish)

1 *lb. rump steak*
1 *oz. butter*
1 *oz. flour*
salt
4 *peppercorns*
½ *bay leaf*

Trim the steak, but leave in 1 piece. Sear in the butter, sprinkle with seasoned flour. Transfer to a shallow fireproof dish, add the peppercorns and bay leaf. Just cover with water, put a lid on the dish and cook in a moderate oven for 1 hour or longer if necessary.

SAILORS' STEW

3 lb. stewing steak
2 oz. flour
2 oz. butter
6 medium potatoes, sliced
3 onions, sliced
¼ pint red wine (optional)
salt, pepper
parsley

Cut the meat into 1-inch cubes, roll in seasoned flour. Sear in the fat and set aside. Brown the potatoes in the fat and set aside. Do the same with the onions. Arrange alternate layers of potato, meat and onion in casserole; the first and last layers should be potato. Sprinkle each layer with salt and pepper. Rinse out the frying pan with the wine and ¼ pint water, pour into the casserole. Cover with a lid and cook slowly for 2 hours or longer. Garnish with chopped parsley.

BEEF À LA LINDSTROM

1¼ lb. minced beef
1 medium potato, cooked and
  mashed
2 egg yolks
1 gill cream
2 pickled beetroots, finely sliced
1 small onion
2 tablespoons capers

salt, pepper
fat for frying

Mix the beef and the potato, add the egg yolks, cream, beetroot, onion and capers. Season with salt and pepper. Shape into flat cakes and fry quickly on both sides in hot fat.

ROYAL POT ROAST

4 lb. topside
1 oz. butter
1 onion, sliced
4 anchovies
1 tablespoon vinegar
1 tablespoon whisky or brandy
1 tablespoon brown sugar
10 black peppercorns
salt
2 tablespoons double cream
  (optional)

Sear the meat on both sides in the butter. Fry the onions and anchovies until brown, transfer to a casserole just large enough to hold the meat, and all the other ingredients except the cream, and 2 pints water. Cover with a lid, cook slowly for 3 hours, turning the meat twice during cooking. Remove the meat to a dish and keep hot. Strain the gravy, return to the pan, reduce if necessary and stir in the cream.

POT ROASTED PORK LOIN

pork loin (about 3 lb.)
½ pint stock
8 oz. prunes
1 tablespoon cream (optional)
1 glass wine

Get the butcher to bone the loin for you. Stuff the prunes (previously soaked if necessary) into the flesh on the underside, roll and tie with string. Brown on all sides in its own fat, pour off the fat, add the stock simmer in a covered pan for 2 hours. Remove the meat and keep warm. Reduce the sauce by rapid simmering if it is too thin, stir in the wine and simmer for 2 to 3 minutes. Add the cream. Hand the sauce separately, serve with browned potatoes (see p. 348) and apple sauce.

PORK CHOP WITH PRUNES

2 lb. loin chops, ½ inch thick
8 oz. prunes
½ pint wine (red or white)
flour
salt, pepper
1 oz. butter
1 teaspoon red currant jelly

Soak the prunes in the wine for 12 hours. Simmer them in the wine until tender. Bone and trim the meat. Season the flour with salt and pepper, dust the pork slices with it. Fry on both sides in the butter, until thoroughly cooked. Put on a dish and keep warm. Make the sauce as follows:

Cook the flour in the fat for 1 minute, strain the juice from the prunes into it. Cook until it thickens, add the red currant jelly and the cream. Season with salt and pepper. Arrange the prunes round the pork slices, strain the sauce over the meat. Serve with potato purée.

SAUSAGES WITH APPLE CAKE (Danish)

6 cooking apples
2 oz. butter
2 oz. castor sugar
wine vinegar
salt, pepper
8 rashers streaky bacon
8 chipolata sausages

Peel and core the apples and cut into rings ¼ inch thick. Melt ½ oz. butter and sprinkle in a dessertspoon of sugar and cover the pan with apple slices. Fry quickly on both sides until brown. Drain and arrange in a buttered sandwich tin with their edges slightly overlapping, season with vinegar, salt and pepper.

Fry the rest of the apple rings in the same way, and add them to those in the tin, seasoning each layer. Bake in a hot oven for 20 minutes. Turn out of the tin and surround with bacon rolls and fried sausages.

POT ROASTED VEAL

4 *lb. leg of veal*
1 *oz. butter*
4 *carrots, sliced*
2 *onions, sliced*
¾ *pint stock*
salt, pepper

GRAVY:
1 *oz. butter*
1 *oz. flour*
1 *gill cream*

Sear the meat in the butter on all sides. Add the onions and carrots and cook them a little in the fat. Transfer to a casserole, pour in the stock, season with salt and pepper. Cover the dish and cook slowly for 2 hours. Strain the liquid and leave the meat to keep hot. Melt the butter, cook the flour in it for minute, gradually add the stock and the cream. Adjust the seasoning. Hand the gravy separately and serve the meat with browned potatoes and cranberry sauce or red currant jelly.

VEAL WITH PINEAPPLE (Danish)

8 *thin slices veal*
4 *oz. mushrooms, sliced*
1 *oz. butter*
salt, pepper
4 *slices pineapple, halved*
1 *gill cream*

Beat the veal and sprinkle with salt and pepper. Fry gently on both sides in the butter. Set aside to keep hot. Cook the mushrooms in the butter until tender, set them aside. Heat the pineapple slices in the butter. Arrange the veal on a serving dish with a piece of pineapple on each slice and mushrooms on top. Stir the cream into the juice in the pan, cook gently and pour over the dish.

BRAISED CALVES' LIVER

1 *whole calf's liver (about 2 lb.)*
1 *teaspoon salt*
2 *oz. butter*
6 *whole peppercorns*
½ *bay leaf*
¾ *pint stock*

FOR THE SAUCE:
2 *oz. butter*
1½ *oz. flour*
¼ *pint cream*

salt, pepper

Sprinkle the liver with salt. Fry quickly on all sides in the butter. Add the stock, peppercorns and bay leaf. Simmer with a lid on the pan for about 1 hour. Strain the liquid, cut the liver into thin slices and set aside to keep warm. Melt the butter, cook the flour in it for 1 minute, gradually add the stock and the cream. Season with salt and pepper and pour over the liver.

DILL SAUCE (for Fish)

1 *oz. butter*
1 *oz. flour*
½ *pint fish stock or court-bouillon*
1 *tablespoon white wine vinegar*
1 *dessertspoon sugar*
1 *large tablespoon chopped dill*
  or fennel

salt, pepper
1 *egg yolk*

Melt the butter, cook the flour in it for 1 minute, gradually add the strained fish stock. Stir in the vinegar, sugar and herbs, season with salt and pepper. Add a little sauce to the beaten egg yolk, return in to the pan. Reheat carefully stirring all the time.

FISH SAUCE

2 *oz. butter*
1½ *oz. flour*
½ *pint fish stock*

¼ *teaspoon dry mustard*
salt, pepper

Melt the butter, cook the flour in it for 1 minute, gradually add the hot stock. Season with the mustard, salt and pepper.

MUSHROOM SAUCE (for Fish)

4 *oz. mushrooms, sliced*
2 *oz. butter*
1½ *oz. flour*

½ *pint fish stock*
salt, pepper

Cook the mushrooms gently in the butter until tender. Stir in the flour and cook for 1 minute, add the fish stock gradually. Season with salt and pepper.

LOBSTER SAUCE

1 *boiled lobster*
2 *oz. butter*
1½ *oz. flour*
½ *pint fish stock*
¼ *pint cream*
salt, pepper

Melt the butter, cook the flour in it for 1 minute, gradually add the fish stock and the cream, stirring constantly. Cut the lobster into small pieces, add them to the sauce, simmer sufficiently to heat the lobster. Season with salt and pepper.

BEETROOT SAUCE

raw beetroots
sugar
wine vinegar
red currant jelly

Boil the beetroot until tender, peel and slice finely. Put a layer of beetroot in the bottom of a dish, sprinkle with sugar and vinegar. Repeat the layers until the dish is full. Pour melted red currant jelly over the top. Serve with cold meat.

LEMON SAUCE

2 oz. butter
1½ oz. flour
½ pint fish stock
¼ pint cream
salt, pepper

juice of ½ lemon
1 egg yolk

Melt the butter and cook the flour in it. Gradually add the fish stock and the cream. Simmer for 10 minutes. Add the lemon juice and seasoning. Stir a little sauce into the beaten egg yolk, return to the pan and reheat.

VANILLA SAUCE

½ pint milk
2 egg yolks
1 tablespoon sugar
vanilla
¼ pint double cream

Beat the egg yolks and sugar in a double saucepan, add the hot milk flavoured with vanilla, cook slowly, stirring all the time until mixture thickens. Allow to cool, fold in whipped cream.

GOOSEBERRY SOUFFLÉ (Scandinavian)

1 lb. gooseberries
4 oz. sugar
grated peel of ½ lemon
1 dessertspoon cornflour
½ glass white wine
2 eggs

Cook the gooseberries with a little water, the lemon peel and the sugar until tender. Pass through a sieve. Mix the egg yolks with the cornflour and a little of the purée, add to the rest of the purée and cook slowly for 2 to 3 minutes, stirring all the time. Add the wine, beat the egg whites stiffly, fold into the mixture. Bake in a greased fireproof dish for 30 minutes in a slow oven. Serve with vanilla sauce (see above).

LEMON CREAM

8 *oz. sugar*
1 *glass white wine*
juice and grated rind of 1 *lemon*
6 *egg yolks*

Mix all the ingredients together and cook slowly in the top of a double saucepan until the mixture thickens. Pour into a glass serving dish. Serve cold.

BONDE PIGE

2 *oz. brown breadcrumbs*
1 *oz. butter*
3 *oz. sugar*
1½ *lb. apples*
raspberry jam
¼ *pint cream*

Mix the breadcrumbs with 1 oz. sugar, cook in the butter until crisp. Cook the apples with the sugar until very soft, beat to a purée. Fill a dish with alternate layers of crumbs, hot apple purée and raspberry jam, beginning and ending with a layer of crumbs. Serve cold, topped with whipped cream.

ROYAL BAKED APPLES

4 *apples, peeled and cored*
2 *oz. butter*
2 *oz. breadcrumbs*
2 *oz. sugar*
1 *oz. almonds, grated*

Mix 1 oz. sugar with the breadcrumbs. Roll the apple in 1 oz. melted butter then in this mixture. Fill the hole with a smooth paste made of the almonds mixed with the other 1 oz. of sugar and a little water until very smooth. Dot with butter, bake in a moderate oven for 1 hour or until apples are soft. Serve with vanilla sauce (see p. 354) or whipped cream.

SWEDISH APPLE CAKE

8 *oz. rusk or biscuit crumbs*
1 *oz. butter*
1½ *lb. apples, peeled and sliced*
4 *oz. sugar*
1 *strip lemon peel*

Fry the crumbs in the butter until slightly brown. Stew the apples with the lemon peel, sugar and a little water until very soft, beat to a pulp. Arrange alternate layers of crumbs and apple purée in a greased pie dish. Bake in a moderate oven for 30 minutes. Cool and turn out. Serve with vanilla sauce.

COLD APPLE CHARLOTTE

3—4 *oz. breadcrumbs*
3—4 *oz. butter*
2 *lb. apples*
2 *oz. sugar*

Melt the butter, stir the breadcrumbs about in it until just golden. Cook the apples with the sugar and a very little water until reduced to a pulp, beat to a purée. Fill a greased cake tin with alternate layers of crumbs and apple purée, beginning and ending with one of crumbs, dot with butter. Bake in a moderate oven for 30 minutes. Turn out when cold and serve with vanilla sauce (see p. 354)

SWEDISH RÖD GRÖD (Fruit Fool)

2½ *lb. mixed red currants, black currants and raspberries*
8 *oz. sugar or to taste*
2 *tablespoons cornflour*

Cook the prepared fruit with 2 pints water, and the sugar until tender. Pass through a sieve. Mix a little purée with the cornflour, return to the pan with the rest of the purée and cook gently for 2—3 minutes. Pour into a glass dish, sprinkle with sugar to prevent skin forming and leave to cook. Serve with vanilla sauce (see p. 354) or whipped cream.

DANISH RÖD GRÖD

This is made in the same way as Swedish Röd Gröd (see above) but an ounce or so of sago is used for thickening instead of cornflour, which gives it a more interesting texture.

DANISH PEASANT GIRL WITH VEIL

2 *oz. brown bredcrumbs*
2 *oz. butter*
2 *oz. brown sugar*
1½ *lb. apples*
4 *oz. cooking chocolate, grated*
¼ *pint double cream*

Mix the breadcrumbs and sugar. Fry them in the butter until crisp. Cook the apples with a little water until very soft. Fill a glass dish with alternate layers of crumbs and apple — the first and last should be crumbs — until nearly full. Sprinkle with chocolate. Serve cold, topped with whipped cream.

PRUNE PUDDING

8 oz. prunes
1 teaspoon cinnamon or
  ½ a cinnamon stick
2 oz. sugar
juice of 1 lemon
1 oz. cornflour

Soak the prunes with just enough water to cover. Simmer in the same water until tender. Remove from the water, stone the prunes, return the prunes to the water, simmer for 5 minutes with the sugar, lemon and cinnamon. Mix the cornflour with a little water. Add it to the prunes, stirring all the time. Cook very slowly for 5 minutes. Serve chilled with whipped cream.

WALNUT PUDDING

4 oz. butter
4 oz. flour
2 teaspoons baking powder
½ teaspoon salt
2 eggs
4 oz. soft light brown sugar
small piece vanilla
4 oz. chopped walnuts

1 large cooking apple, peeled and
  chopped

Cream the butter and sugar, beat in the eggs and the flour sifted with the baking powder and salt. Stir in the vanilla, walnuts and apples. Pour into a greased tart tin, bake in a moderate oven for 40 minutes.

SWEDISH WAFFLES

4 oz. flour
2 teaspoons baking powder
2 eggs
½ pint sour cream
1 tablespoon melted butter

Sift the flour and baking powder, gradually add the egg yolks and the cream. Beat well. Fold in the stiffly beaten egg whites and the melted butter just before cooking. Bake in usual way in waffle iron.

SWEDISH PANCAKES

4 oz. flour
1½ oz. sugar
salt
3 eggs
½ pint milk
butter for frying

Sift flour and sugar with a pinch of salt. Gradually add the beaten eggs and the milk. Leave to stand for at least 2 hours. Fry quickly in the usual way, roll and serve with any of the suggested sauces. Traditionally served on Thursday nights.

NORWEGIAN WAFFLES

2 *eggs*
2 *tablespoons sugar*
4 *oz. flour*
½ *pint sour cream*

Sift the sugar with the flour, add the beaten eggs. Gradually beat in the sour cream. Leave to stand for at least an hour. Bake in waffle iron.

ALMOND TARTS

4 *oz. butter*
4 *oz. sugar*
2 *eggs*
8 *oz. flour*
¼ *teaspoon baking powder*

FOR THE FILLING:
6 *oz. ground almonds*
3 *eggs*
6 *oz. sugar*

Cream the butter and sugar, beat in the eggs, gradually add the flour sifted with the baking powder. Grease bun tins and line with the mixture. Fill them with the following almond mixture. Blend the almonds with the sugar and the eggs until a smooth paste is formed. Bake in a moderate oven for 20 minutes.

POLYNÉES

Follow the instructions for almond tarts but reserve a little of the cake dough. Cover the almond filling with strips of this dough in the shape of a cross.

DANISH PASTRY

½ *oz. yeast*
2 *oz. sugar*
12 *oz. flour*
1 *teaspoon salt*
1 *gill milk (room temperature)*
7 *oz. butter (unsalted)*

Cream the yeast with 1 teaspoon sugar. Sift the flour, rest of the sugar and the salt, together. Pour the milk into the yeast, add it to the flour, blend to an elastic dough. Roll out ½ inch thick on a floured board. Cut the butter into small pieces and spread on to the dough. Fold in 3, pinch the sides together and roll towards the pinched edges. Set aside for 15 minutes. Roll and fold in 3 and roll again as before. Set aside for 15 minutes. Repeat this process. Set aside for at least 1 hour in a cool place. Use for almond envelopes (see p. 359), or cut into fancy shapes, bake in a moderate oven, cover with thin glacé icing and chopped almonds.

ALMOND ENVELOPES

Danish Pastry (see p. 358) •
4 oz. ground almonds
4 oz. sugar
1 egg

Blend the almonds with the sugar, work in the egg until a smooth paste is formed. Roll out the dough thinly and cut into 4-inch squares. Fill with 1 tablespoon of the mixture, fold in the corners to meet in the middle. Bake in a moderately hot oven until golden (about 20 minutes), cool and cover with glacé icing. The envelopes can also be filled with vanilla sauce (see p. 354).

LEMON COMBS

Danish pastry (see p. 358)
1 egg
lemon filling (see below)

Roll out ½ inch thick. Cut into rectangles 4 by 2 inches, spread with a spoonful of the filling, fold over and make 4 or 5 cuts in the pastry so that it will splay out when baked. Brush with beaten egg. Bake in a moderately hot oven until golden (about 20 minutes).

LEMON FILLING

2 eggs
juice and rind of 1 lemon
1 oz. flour
8 oz. sugar

Stir the flour into the egg yolks beaten with the sugar. Add the lemon juice and grated lemon peel and cook in the top of a double saucepan, stirring all the time, until the mixture thickens. Cool and fold in the stiffly beaten egg whites.

WALNUT MERINGUES

4 egg whites
8 oz. sugar
4 oz. chopped walnuts
½ pint double cream

Beat the egg whites stiffly, beat in 1 oz. sugar. Fold in the rest of the sugar and the walnuts. Arrange in small moulds on a greased baking sheet. Bake in a very slow oven for 4 hours. When cold seal together in pairs with whipped cream.

SAFFRON BREAD

1 *oz. yeast*
2 *oz. sugar*
1 *teaspoon saffron*
1 *egg*
milk
egg, sugar, chopped almonds
  to garnish
2 *lb. flour*
4 *oz. raisins*
2 *oz. almonds (optional)*

Cream the yeast with 1 teaspoon sugar. Dry the saffron in a cool oven and dissolve it in a little milk. Mix the sugar, 4 oz. flour, egg and the milk. Gradually add the rest of the flour and the raisins. Knead, set aside in a warm place, covered, until it has doubled its size. Knead again. Shape into a plaited loaf or a wreath. Leave on a greased tin to rise for 1 hour. Brush with beaten egg, sprinkle with sugar and chopped nuts. Bake in a moderate oven for 45 minutes.

CHOCOLATE ALMOND CAKE (Danish)

3 *oz. butter*
2 *oz. sugar*
6 *oz. flour*
3 *eggs*
1 *dessertspoon baking powder*
½ *gill milk*
4 *oz. cooking chocolate, chopped*
2 *oz. almonds, chopped*

Cream the butter and sugar until white, beat in alternately beaten egg yolks and flour sifted with baking powder. Add the milk, fold in the chocolate and the nuts. Fold in the stiffly beaten egg whites. Turn into a 6½-inch cake tin lined with greased greaseproof paper. Bake in a moderate oven for 1½ hours.

SWEDISH CROWN PUDDING

5 *oz. potatoes*
6 *oz. ground almonds*
10 *oz. sugar*
3 *oz. butter*
4 *eggs*
brown breadcrumbs

Grate the potatoes finely. Cream butter and sugar and add egg yolks, potatoes, and ground almonds. Beat the egg whites until stiff, then add to the mixture. Line a buttered cake tin with breadcrumbs and pour in the pudding mixture. Bake in a very moderate oven for 45 minutes. Turn out and serve with lemon cream (see page 355).

VANILLA RINGS

4 oz. plain flour
3 oz. butter
3 oz. castor sugar
1 small egg
3 teaspoons vanilla essence
pinch salt

Rub the butter into the flour with finger tips until the mixture is like fine breadcrumbs. Add beaten egg (do not whisk), sugar, vanilla essence and salt. Mix dough with a wooden spoon. Then knead lightly with fingers to make it smooth. Place soft dough in a forcing bag with large nozzle at the end and force out into rings 2 inches in diameter on to a greased baking tray. Bake in a slow oven till light brown.

JYTTE KIRKEGARD'S FINE GINGER BISCUITS

6 oz. plain flour
3 oz. castor sugar
1½ oz. butter
1 tablespoon ginger
1 teaspoon cinnamon
1 small egg
½ teaspoon baking powder

Rub the butter into the flour with the finger tips until it is like fine breadcrumbs. Add the rest of the dry ingredients and mix to a dough with the slightly beaten egg. Roll the mixture into thin sausage shapes ½ inch in diameter and the length of the baking tray. Place these rolls on a greased baking tray about 1½ inches apart. Bake in a medium oven until the mixture turns a darker brown, approximately 8—10 minutes. When cooked, cut the mixture into diamond-shaped pieces. Store in an airtight tin.

DANISH CHRISTMAS BISCUITS

4 oz. plain flour
3 oz. butter
4 oz. castor sugar
1 large egg
1¾ teaspoons cinnamon or
  cardamom
pinch salt
blanched almonds to decorate

Reserve white of egg, 1 oz. of sugar and 1 teaspoon of the cinnamon or cardamom for the glazing. Then rub butter into the flour with the finger tips till mixture is like fine breadcrumbs. Add egg yolk, sugar, salt and the spice. Mix dough with a wooden spoon and then knead lightly with fingers to make it smooth. Roll out dough to ¼ inch thickness. Cut out biscuits with a 1½-inch pastry cutter. Brush the top of the biscuits with the egg white to which 1 oz. sugar and 1 teaspoon of the spice has been added. Place 1 blanched almond on each biscuit. Bake in a slow oven till light brown.

DANISH SMØRREBRØD

Smørrebrød (literally 'buttered bread') or open sandwiches are often served as a meal in themselves in Denmark. Rye bread is used in the main, but wholemeal or white bread is equally satisfying provided it is firm and not too crumbly. Spread with plenty of butter and arrange the ingredients attractively on top. The following recipes give some suggestions for typically Danish smørrebrød.

MIXED SMØRREBRØD

Slices of Samsoe alternated with crisp slices of grilled bacon. Garnish with button mushrooms and watercress.
Tongue slices on a bed of lettuce, garnished with Danish Blue cheese.
Slices of salami with a generous topping of scrambled egg, sprinkled with chopped chives.
Apple rings fried in bacon fat and garnished with bacon rashers.
Small cubes of pork luncheon meat mixed with pickles and choped hard-boiled egg, on a bed of shredded lettuce. Garnish with cucumber. Slices of luncheon meat garnished with lettuce, onion rings and olive.

SMØRREBRØD WITH FISH

Pickled or soused fried herrings, garnished with onion rings and capers.
Smoked cod roe with a slice of lemon.
Sardine on a bed of lettuce and garnished with lemon.
'Shrimps in the rush hour' — a double layer of shrimps.
Smoked salmon.

SMØRREBRØD WITH MEAT

Cold roast lamb with slices of fresh cucumber and piccalilli.
Liver pâté garnished with strips of meat jelly or beetroot.
Thin slices of cold roast pork and salad.
Tongue with sliced hard-boiled egg.
Tongue with Russian salad.

SMØRREBRØD WITH CHEESE

Danish Blue cheese with a cocktail cherry.
Cheese topped with cucumber and radish.
Samsoe cheese with tomato and lettuce.
Cheese with anchovy fillets and tomato.

South Africa

COOKING IN SOUTH AFRICA

South Africa has a unique cookery of its own, closely connected with the social history of the country. The roots of its gastronomic traditions go back to the seventeenth and eighteenth centuries and most typical South African dishes date from those far-away days. The influence of the old-established Malay community in the Cape is also to be noted, and especially in such well-known South African specialities as Bobotie and Sassaties, which have a distinctly oriental flavour.

A popular way of entertaining in the summer months in this country of gloriously reliable weather is the so-called *braaivleis*, which is an alfresco 'meat-and-beer' party: the main ingredients are steak and sausages, and these are grilled over open-air fires, in the style of the American barbecue. 'Mealies', or corn-on-the-cob, are another usual feature of the *braaivleis*.

When you look through these sumptuous South African recipes you will realise that all our labour-saving devices are only substitues compared with what the famous Cape cooks possessed. First of all they had all the foods fresh and home-grown. Secondly they had leisure and servants. To top all this they also took tremendous pride in their home cooking and jealously guarded their special recipes. However, quite a few of these closely guarded recipes have become public property by now, as you will see on the following pages.

Another trait which gives South African cookery its very own characteristic is the imprint made by the Dutch, French, English and German settlers. The homely and substantial eating habits of the Dutch are perhaps the strongest influence in South Africa. All these recipes have a rich and original flavour of their own — a truly interesting and rewarding field for imaginative cooks to explore.

SOUTH AFRICAN ESCALLOPED MEALIES OR SWEET CORN

4 oz. cooked mealies, cut from
  the cob
2 eggs
2 oz. melted butter
1 teaspoon sugar
¼ teaspoon nutmeg

½ pint milk
salt, pepper

Mince or pound the mealies, add the beaten eggs, butter, sugar, salt, pepper, nutmeg and the milk. Mix well together. Butter a shallow fireproof dish and bake in a moderate oven for 20 minutes.

SOUTH AFRICAN MEALIES (Corn on the Cob)

8 mealies (for 4 people or as
  many as liked)
2 teaspoons salt
2 teaspoons sugar
butter to serve

The mealies must be young and the husks green. They must be thrown into enough boiling water to cover, salt and sugar added, brought to the boil and simmered for 20 minutes. The husks and 'silk' may be removed before boiling, or only the 'silk' or both. They are of course served free of husks and 'silk' and eaten with plenty of butter and salt, held in the hand and picked clean with the teeth, as a separate course, generally to start the meal.

SOUTH AFRICAN PICKLED FISH

2½ lb. cod
3 oz. flour
1 teaspoon salt
¼ teaspoon pepper
fat for frying
1½ pints vinegar
2 bay leaves
2 large onions, sliced
1 teaspoon peppercorns
1 oz. flour
1 oz. curry powder
1 tablespoon vinegar

Cut the fish in slices 1½ inches thick. Roll in the 3 oz. flour, salt and pepper. Fry in hot fat till done. Heat the 1½ pints vinegar in a saucepan, add peppercorns, bay leaves, onion slices, bring to the boil and cook until the onions are soft. Mix the 1 oz. flour, and curry powder with the 1 tablespoon vinegar to a paste, add to the boiling vinegar and cook all together for 2 minutes. Arrange the cooked fish in a shallow dish and pour over the vinegar sauce. Keep in a cold place and eat after 48 hours. If kept cold this dish will keep for weeks.

FRICADELS (Mutton Rissoles)

2 *lb. minced raw mutton*
1 *large finely chopped onion*
2 *slices white bread soaked in milk*
2 *tablespoons tomato purée*
1 *beaten egg*
¼ *teaspoon grated nutmeg*
salt, pepper
breadcrumbs

Squeeze the bread dry and mash with a fork. Add the mutton, onion, tomato purée, egg, nutmeg and salt and pepper. Mix all well together, roll into balls the size of an egg, roll in the breadcrumbs, and fry in hot fat till brown.

BOERWORS (South African Sausages)

3 *lb. beef or pork*
2 *lb. bacon fat*
1 *teaspoon pepper*
1 *dessertspoon salt*
½ *teaspoon grated nutmeg*
1 *dessertspoon coriander seed (grated)*
¼ *pint vinegar*

Mince meat and bacon fat and mix all ingredients together. Leave to stand for 3 hours, then mix again and stuff into sausage skins, or form into sausage shapes. To cook, prick and grill for 20—30 minutes under a moderate heat.

MONKEY GLAND STEAK

1 *lb. rump steak*
3 *tablespoons vinegar*
3 *tablespoons tomato sauce*
3 *tablespoons Worcester Sauce*
1 *onion, chopped*
½ *teaspoon mustard*
fat for frying

Beat steak flat. Mix together other ingredients and place the steak in the mixture for 30 minutes. Remove and fry steak in hot fat. Heat the sauce and pour over the steak.

MINCE ON TOAST

12 *oz. cooked meat*
1 *oz. butter*
1 *onion*
1 *teaspoon flour*
pinch curry powder
3 *tablespoons stock*
toast

Mince the meat.
Chop the onion very small and fry in the butter until golden. Add the minced meat, and sprinkle with flour and pinch of curry powder on top. Season with salt and pepper, stir and cook gently for 10 minutes. Add stock and cook for a further 20 minutes. Serve on toast.

SOUTH AFRICAN CHICKEN PIE

1 3½-lb. chicken
2 medium onions, each cut in
   8 pieces
1½ pints water
¼ pint white wine
¼ teaspoon ⎫
   nutmeg ⎬ in a muslin bag
1 bay leaf ⎭
12 peppercorns
1 teaspoon salt
2 oz. butter
1 oz. tapioca
3 tablespoons lemon juice
1 egg yolk, beaten
2 hard-boiled eggs, sliced

4 oz. cooked ham, sliced
short crust pastry (see p. 206)
milk and egg

Cut the chicken in joints. Put these with the water, wine, onion and the bag of spices in a covered stewpan. Bring to the boil and simmer for 30 minutes. Add the salt, butter and tapioca, re-cover and simmer for 20 minutes more or until the chicken is tender. Add lemon juice, egg yolk, hard-boiled eggs and ham. Cool. Put in a pie dish, cover with the pastry, brush the top with a little milk and egg mixed together, and bake in a moderate oven for 45 minutes.

ROAST QUAILS

8 quails
8 green chillies
8 rashers fat bacon
8 fresh vine leaves
4 oz. dripping
pepper

Quails should not be 'hung', as they decompose very quickly.

   Pluck, clean and draw the birds. Put a chilli inside each, wrap a rasher of bacon round each bird, dust with pepper, then wrap the whole in a vine leaf, secure with small wooden skewer. Melt the dripping in a roasting pan, put in the pan and roast in a moderate oven for 30 minutes, basting frequently.

TOMATO BREDIE

4 large or 8 small mutton chops
2 oz. dripping
3 lb. ripe tomatoes
2 large sliced onions
1 teaspoon cinnamon powder
1 bay leaf
1 teaspoon salt
¼ teaspoon pepper
2 oz. brown sugar

Trim surplus fat off the chops. Skin the tomatoes, and cut into quarters. Heat the dripping and fry the chops for 3 minutes each side, remove and put in a large stew pan. Fry the onions till golden brown; add to the chops. Now add the tomatoes, cinnamon, bay leaf, salt and pepper. Turn up the heat and stir gently till the tomatoes dissolve. Taste and if necessary add the sugar. This largely depends on how much sun has ripened the tomatoes: English greenhouse ones are generally not sweet enough. Cook the chops very gently in the tomato purée for 1 hour or until the meat is quite tender and the purée thick and sweet.

BOBOTIE

2 *lb. raw minced mutton*
1 *thick slice white bread, soaked in ½ pint milk*
2 *medium sliced onions*
1 *apple, sliced*
2 *beaten eggs*
2 *oz. curry powder*
½ *oz. sugar*
2 *oz. butter*
12 *blanched chopped almonds*
2 *oz. currants or sultanas*
½ *teaspoon salt, pepper*

Squeeze the bread and mash with a fork. Melt the butter in a stewpan, add the onions and apple, stir, fry for 4 minutes. Add curry powder, sugar, salt, almonds, currants or sultanas, bread and minced mutton. Stir well together and cook gently for 3 minutes. Grease a deep fireproof fish and put in this mixture. Mix the eggs well into the milk, season with salt and pepper, pour over the meat mixture and cook in a very slow oven for 1 hour till the custard is set.

SASSATIES

3 *lb. raw mutton*
2 *oz. dried apricots, soaked overnight*
3 *large onions, sliced*
2 *cloves of garlic, chopped*
2 *oz. dripping*
a *pinch of cayenne pepper*
6 *lemon or orange leaves*
1 *oz. curry powder*
1 *oz. sugar*
½ *teaspoon salt*
3 *tablespoons wine vinegar*

Cut the mutton in small pieces, 1½ inches square. Remove any fat and cut in ½-inch squares. Place on wooden skewers, meat then fat, till each skewer is full.

Cover the apricots with water and boil till soft. Press through a sieve.

Heat the dripping in a saucepan and cook the onions and garlic for 5 minutes till transparent and soft. Add the apricot pulp, leaves, curry powder, sugar, pepper and salt and the vinegar. Stir well, bring to the boil and boil this sauce for 1 minute. Place the skewered meat in a shallow enamel or china dish, not a metal one, cool the sauce, and pour over the meat. Leave to soak overnight, or longer, up to 20 hours, turning the 'sassaties' occasionally. Drain them and grill them under a hot grill on all sides till nicely brown. Heat the sauce, pick out the leaves and pour over the grilled 'sassaties'.

SOUTH AFRICAN BROWN RAISIN RICE

8 *oz. rice*
¾ *pint water*
grated rind of ¼ lemon
½ *teaspoon turmeric*
½ *teaspoon salt*
3 *oz. raisins, seedless*
2 *oz. butter*
2 *oz. sugar*

Wash the rice thoroughly, add lemon rind, cinnamon, turmeric, salt and water. Bring to the boil, cover the pan and simmer for 20 minutes, stirring once or twice, add the raisins and simmer for 20 minutes longer, or until the rice is soft, but not pulpy. Melt the butter, add the sugar and mix lightly into the mixture. This can be eaten with roast mutton or pork, or as a supper sweet dish, with sweetened cream.

SOUTH AFRICAN BANANA FOOL

8 *or* 10 *bananas*
3 *eggs*
2 *tablespoons brandy or rum*
¼ *pint cream, whipped*
2 *oz. castor sugar*
a pinch of nutmeg

Crush the bananas and whip the pulp. Separate the eggs, beat the whites till stiff and the yolks well. Add the yolks to the pulp and half the stiff whites plus the brandy or rum and 1½ oz. sugar. Mix all well together. Mix ½ oz. sugar with the remaining egg whites. Serve, very cold in glasses, with cream on top and the sweetened egg whites on top of the cream. Sprinkle with nutmeg.

GRANADILLA OR PASSION FRUIT FOOL

12 *granadillas*
3 *oz. sugar*
½ *pint whipped cream*

Cut the tops off the granadillas and scoop out the fruit. Mix well with the sugar, add the cream and serve cold in separate glasses.

PAWPAW

pawpaw
sugar
lemon juice

Cut the pawpaw in half. Scoop out all the seeds. Cut in wedges and serve cold with sugar and cut lemons separately as a dessert.

PEACH ISLAND

6 *South African canned peach halves*
2 *eggs*
2 *tablespoons castor sugar*
⅛ *teaspoon salt*
½ *pint hot milk*
¼ *teaspoon vanilla essence*
2 *tablespoons grated coconut*

Separate the eggs. Whip the whites till stiff. Beat the yolks with the sugar and salt. Put in a double boiler and slowly pour on the hot milk, stirring all the time till the mixture thickens to a custard. Add vanilla essence. Cool, then fold in the egg whites. Arrange the peaches in the serving dish, pour on the custard, and sprinkle with the coconut.

PEACH WHIP

4 *ripe peaches, fresh or stewed*
2 *stiffly beaten egg whites*
3 *oz. castor sugar*
4 *oz. cream*
glacé cherries

If fresh peaches are used, peel and stone them. Sieve the fruit. Add half the sugar to the beaten whites, beat again, add the rest of the sugar, and the peach pulp. Continue beating till soft and fluffy. Whip the cream, pile on top and decorate with the cherries.

PINEAPPLE FRITTERS

1 *pineapple*
2 *oz. sugar*
4 *oz. flour*
½ *teaspoon salt*
1 *egg*
¼ *pint milk*

Make the batter by mixing the flour and salt together. Add the beaten egg and one third of the milk, mix thoroughly until smooth, add the rest of the milk, leave for 1 hour. Peel the pineapple, cut in ½ inch rings, sprinkle with sugar. Have a pan of smoking fat, dip each sugared piece in the batter and fry till golden brown outside and soft inside. Dust with sugar and serve.

SOUTH AFRICAN PUMPKIN FRITTERS

8 *oz. cooked pumpkin*
4 *oz. flour*
1 *teaspoon baking powder*
2 *eggs*
¼ *teaspoon salt*
2 *oz. castor sugar*
1 *teaspoon cinnamon*
1 *lemon*
fat for frying

Mix the pumpkin, flour, baking powder and salt thoroughly, add the beaten eggs. Form into flat rounds 3 inches across, 1 inch deep, and fry till brown in deep smoking lard or butter. Mix the cinnamon well with the sugar, sprinkle over the cooked fritters and serve with cut lemon, as a sweet course.

SHREDDED PINEAPPLE

1 *pineapple*
4 *oz. castor sugar*
½ *pint cream*

Peel and grate the pineapple. Stir in the sugar, mix till dissolved, add the cream, whipped till fairly thick, and serve very cold.

STUFFED MONKEY

8 *oz. flour*
6 *oz. butter*
6 *oz. brown sugar*
1 *whole egg, 1 egg white*
½ *teaspoon cinnamon*
¼ *teaspoon salt*

STUFFING:

2 *oz. chopped lemon peel*
4 *oz. ground almonds*
1½ *oz. melted butter*
1 *egg yolk*

Sift the flour, cinnamon and salt, rub in the butter, add the sugar, mix well, add the beaten whole egg and mix to a soft dough. Divide in two pieces and roll ¼ inch thick. Mix all the ingredients of the stuffing well together. Pile on one piece of dough, damp the edges, put the other piece of dough on top and seal the edges. Brush with the egg white and cook in a moderate oven for 30 minutes. Cut in squares and serve.

RICE DUMPLINGS (Kluitjies)

4 *oz. flour*
1 *teaspoon baking powder*
2 *tablespoons fruit juice*
1 *egg*
1 *oz. butter*
4 *oz. rice*

Boil the rice until soft, then drain well. Mix flour, salt and baking powder, then stir in beaten egg, melted butter and fruit juice. Add the cooked rice. Cook the dumplings in boiling fruit juice if possible, simmering with the lid on the saucepan for 10—15 minutes.

MELKTERT

PASTRY:

4 *oz. flour*
2 *teaspoons baking powder*
2 *oz. butter*
2 *egg yolks*
a pinch of salt

FILLING:

1 *pint milk*
8 *oz. sugar*
2 *tablespoons cornflour*
3 *egg whites*
1 *oz. butter*
cinnamon and sugar

Rub butter into sifted flour, baking powder and salt. Add egg yolks and enough milk to make a stiff dough. Roll out thinly and line one large or two small cake tins. To make filling, dissolve cornflour in a little of the milk and boil the rest together with the sugar. Pour on to cornflour mixture and cook for 3 minutes, all stirring the time. Stir the butter. Cool slightly, then fold in the stiffly beaten egg whites. Pour the mixture into the lined cake tins, sprinkle with sugar and cinnamon, and bake in a hot oven for 10 minutes.

MAAS BOLETJIES

½ *pint hot milk*
4 *oz. butter*
4 *oz. sugar*
2 *teaspoons salt*
1 *yeast cake*
6 *tablespoons warm water*
2 *tablespoons caraway seeds*
1 *lb. flour*

Melt the yeast and sugar in the warm water. Sieve the flour and the salt, add the seeds, and the butter, mix lightly with the fingers till the mixture looks like breadcrumbs. Gradually add the milk and yeast water. Knead very thoroughly for 20 minutes. Cover and put in a warm place for 1½ hours. Shape into pieces the size of an egg and pack tightly into a greased straight-sided tin. Brush the top with milk and sugar and bake in a moderate-to-hot oven for 25 minutes.

KOEKSISTERS

12 *oz. flour*
8 *oz. sugar*
4 *eggs*
2 *teaspoons cinnamon*
1 *teaspoon mixed spice*
4 *oz. butter*
½ *teaspoon yeast*
fat for frying

COATING:
1½ *lb. sugar*
1 *pint water*

Mix the yeast with a little sugar, then add to the mixed dry ingredients. Beat the eggs and add these. Knead all together and leave to stand for 1 hour. Roll out and cut into oblong pieces. Fry in deep fat. When cooked dip into a syrup made of 1½ lb. sugar and 1 pint water boiled together with a little cinnamon.

ALMOND CAKES

12 *oz. flour*
12 *oz. butter*
1 *lb. sugar*
12 *oz. ground almonds*
3 *egg yolks*
2 *egg whites*

Mix together flour and salt and rub in butter. Add 12 oz. sugar, 8 oz. almonds, the beaten egg yolks and 1 beaten egg white. Knead well and roll out. Cut into rounds and dip in the second egg white, slightly beaten, and then coat with the remaining almonds and sugar mixed together. Bake for 25—30 minutes in a moderate oven.

KOLOMBYNTJES

8 *oz. butter*
1 *lb. sugar*
5 *eggs*
12 *oz. flour*
2 *teaspoons cream of tartar*
pinch salt
1 *tablespoon milk*
1 *teaspoon bicarbonate of soda*
6 *oz. currants*
1 *teaspoon lemon juice*

Cream together butter and sugar, then add the beaten eggs, flour, cream of tartar and salt. Dissolve the bicarbonate of soda in the milk and beat this in, and finally add the lemon juice and currants. Pour into greased patty pans and bake in a moderate oven for 20—30 minutes.

SOET KOEKIES

2 *lb. flour*
1½ *lb. brown sugar*
1 *tablespoon cinnamon*
8 *oz. chopped almonds*
2 *teaspoons bicarbonate of soda*
8 *oz. butter*
½ *glass wine*
2 *eggs*

Sift flour, cinnamon and bicarbonate of soda and rub in butter. Beat together eggs and sugar and add almonds. Add wine, roll out and cut into shapes. Bake in a hot oven for 15 minutes.

BOER BESKUIT

1 *lb. flour*
4 *oz. butter*
1 *dessertspoon baking powder*
4 *oz. sugar*
1 *teaspoon bicarbonate of soda*
1 *teaspoon cream of tartar*
½ *pint sour milk*
a pinch of salt

Sift flour, baking powder, cream of tartar and salt, rub in butter and add sugar. Then add bicarbonate of soda mixed with a little water, and the sour milk. Knead and form into small balls. Brush with beaten egg and bake in a moderate oven for 1 hour.

PINEAPPLE KONFYT

fresh pineapples
sugar

Wash, peel and core pineapples. Cut into slices ½—¾ inch thick. Weigh the slices, then cover with water and simmer until tender. Drain, keeping the liquid in which they cooked. Now make the syrup, allowing 1 lb. sugar and ½ pint liquid for every lb. of pineapple slices. Make up the liquid with water if necessary. Bring the syrup to the boil, then drop in the pineapple slices and boil until the syrup thickens. Put the slices into jars, fill up with syrup and seal at once.

GROUNDNUT CHOP

boiled rice
2 lb. cooked chicken or lamb, cut
  in ½-inch squares
2 tablespoons olive oil
4 tablespoons peanut butter
  or 6 oz. ground peanuts
1½ pints water
2 teaspoons salt
¼ teaspoon black pepper

mango chutney, fresh grated coco-
  nut, grated green or red peppers
  may be served as accompanying
  dishes

Take a large saucepan and melt the oil in it. Add the peanut butter or peanuts, stir well, add the water, salt and pepper. Cook for 2 minutes. Add the meat, stir into the sauce, cover the pan and simmer gently for 7 minutes. Serve with hot rice and all or any of the accompanying dishes.

SPICED TURKEY

1 10-lb. turkey
1 oz. flour
1 teaspoon sugar
1 teaspoon salt
1 teaspoon pepper
1 teaspoon cinnamon
½ teaspoon ground ginger
½ clove of garlic, crushed
2 oz. butter
2 large onions, chopped
warm water
roast potatoes

Mix the flour, sugar, salt, pepper, garlic and spices together. Rub the turkey well inside and out with this mixture and leave for 12 hours.

Put the bird in a large saucepan, add the onions and cover with warm water. Bring to the boil slowly and simmer for 2½ hours or until tender, but not falling apart. Drain. Put in roasting pan, dot with butter and bake in a hot oven till brown, basting with the stock from time to time. Serve with roast potatoes.

MEALIE MEAL PORRIDGE

4 oz. mealie meal
2½ pints water
1½ teaspoons salt

Boil the water in a thick pot, add the salt, sprinkle in the meal, stirring all the time, cook briskly for 5 minutes, stirring all the time, lower the heat and continue cooking very gently for 1 hour, stirring from time to time to prevent burning and 'lumping'. A milk and water mixture may be used instead of plain water.

South America

COOKING IN SOUTH AMERICA

All the South American countries naturally have their own characteristic dishes, according to their produce and to their climatic conditions. But if you try to discover where their over-all ideas in gastronomy are derived from, you will find a definite Spanish trait.

From Argentina, the land of the beef, come some very interesting and highly flavoured meat dishes like the Puchero. The other fascinating dish from the same country is the Argentine Carbonado, an exotic mixture of sweet and savoury flavours. It seems to me that in the land of plenty of Argentine Beef, they are inordinately fond of mixing fruit and meat in their cookery — probably because 'just steak' is such an everyday occurrence that good cooks hardly give their thoughts to it. I am told that until quite recently the Argentines served steak with every meal, in much the same way as we get the bread on the table without ordering it separately.

From Colombia comes a very filling and satisfying soup called Colombian Cuchuco — very palatable without any sharp or spicy ingredients.

The Bolivians too are very partial to highly seasoned food, but the Bolivian recipe given in this chapter can be served without risk of offending the most sensitive palates. These Stuffed Avocados will lend style and elegance to your dinner table and will start off a dinner party on a high note of gastronomic finesse.

From Venezuela, the land of contrast and exotic unexplored jungles, comes a real work of art in the shape of meat pies: Venezuela Hallacas. In spite of the fact that these meat pies contain no outlandish ingredients, they are a real gourmet's joy. What I like about them is their mundane and ordinary outer appearance coupled with their most luscious filling. It is always fun to watch your guests lift up an ordinary-looking meat pie and go into raputres of praise after the first bite.

PANAMA RADISH SALAD

3 *bunches of radishes, sliced*
½ *teaspoon salt*
¼ *teaspoon black pepper*
1 *small onion, finely chopped*
1 *teaspoon chopped mint*
1 *large tomato, peeled and chopped finely*

2 *tablespoons lemon juice*
2 *tablespoons olive oil*

Mix the oil, lemon juice, salt and pepper well together. Mix all the vegetables together and pour the dressing over.

ARGENTINE VERMICELLI SOUP

2 *oz. vermicelli*
3 *oz. butter or dripping*
1 *lb. tomatoes, peeled and sliced*
1 *large onion, minced*
1½ *tablespoons parsley, chopped*
2 *pints chicken stock*
1½ *oz. grated cheese*
a pinch of saffron
a pinch of chilli powder
salt, pepper

Heat the butter in a stewpan, fry the onions and parsley for 3 minutes, add vermicelli and fry for 2 minutes, till light brown; be careful not to burn it. Add the tomatoes and saffron, cook gently for 5 minutes. Pour on the stock, bring to the boil and simmer till the vermicelli is tender. Add the chilli powder, salt and pepper to taste. Sprinkle with the cheese and serve.

COLOMBIAN CUCHUCO (Barley Soup)

1 *lb. soup bones*
4 *pints water*
1 *bay leaf*
3 *peppercorns*
1 *large onion, chopped*
1 *lb. barley*
water to cover
8 *oz. fresh green peas*
8 *oz. cabbage, finely chopped*
2 *teaspoons salt*
½ *teaspoon pepper*

Place the bones in the 4 pints water, add the onion, bay leaf and peppercorns. Simmer in a covered pot for 2 hours. Wash the barley and place in another pot, cover with water, bring to the boil, strain, re-cover with water and cook for 3 minutes. Strain and add to the strained bone stock when cooked. Bring to the boil, add the vegetables and seasonings and simmer gently until the soup thickens and the barley is cooked.

BOLIVIAN STUFFED AVOCADOS

6 *avocado pears*
4 *oz. cooked chicken, shrimps or fish, finely chopped*
1 *medium lettuce*
¼ *pint mayonnaise sauce (see p. 161)*

1 *hard-boiled egg, sliced*
salt, pepper

Cut the avocados in half and remove the large seed. Mix the lettuce and meat with the mayonnaise, season to taste. Pile on the avocados and garnish with the egg.

SALVADOR SPANISH HADDOCK

1 *3-lb. fresh haddock*
1 *teaspoon salt*
½ *teaspoon pepper*
1 *clove of garlic, crushed*
3 *tablespoons lemon juice*
3 *large onions, sliced*
1½ *lb. tomatoes, peeled and sliced*
2 *tablespoons chopped parsley*
¼ *pint olive oil*

Rub an oval casserole (with a lid) with oil, put the fish in and rub in the garlic, salt, pepper and one-third lemon juice. Leave for 15 minutes. Cover the fish with layers of onions, tomatoes and parsley. Pour over the oil and two-thirds lemon juice. Cover the dish and bake in moderate oven for 30 minutes, basting from time to time. Take the lid off and cook for 20 minutes more till done — basting frequently.

PUCHERO (National dish of Argentina)

2 *lb. beef, cut in pieces* 2 × 3 *inches*
1 *boiling fowl, jointed*
1 *calf's foot, split in 4*
boiling water
1½ *teaspoons salt*
4 *carrots*
4 *sweet potatoes*
2 *tomatoes*
4 *cobs of sweet corn*
4 *potatoes*
2 *onions*

4 *pieces of pumpkin, each 3 inches square*
4 *oz. bacon, cut in 1-inch squares*
8 *slices liver sausage*

This is a substantial dish for several people, 6 or 8.
Take a large pot and half fill it with boiling salted water. Put in the beef, fowl and calf's foot, bring to the boil and skim. Simmer for 1½ hours. Now add everything else, add more water if necessary and simmer till the vegetables are tender. Serve in 3 dishes — one for the meat, one for the vegetables and one for the soup.

CHILLI CON CARNE

1 *lb. beef, cut in ½-inch cubes*
3 *cloves of garlic, finely chopped*
2 *tablespoons chilli powder*
1 *medium onion, finely chopped*
½ *teaspoon salt*
1½ *oz. lard*
2 *oz. flour*

pinch of marjoram
hot water

Heat lard in a saucepan, fry the garlic till brown. Add the meat, rubbed in the flour, salt and chilli powder, fry for 2 minutes. Cover with hot water stir well, add onion and marjoram. Cover and simmer very gently for 1 hour, or until the meat is tender and the sauce thickened.

ARGENTINE CARBONADO

1½ *lb. minced beef*
2 *oz. butter*
4 *medium onions, sliced*
1 *large tomato, peeled and sliced*
1 *teaspoon salt*
¼ *teaspoon pepper*
¼ *pint meat stock*
2 *pears, peeled and sliced*
2 *peaches, peeled and sliced*
4 *plums, peeled and sliced*

4 *medium potatoes, cut in ½-inch dice*
2 *oz. raisins, seedless*

Heat the butter in a casserole, fry the onions till brown, add the tomato, fry for 2 minutes. Add the minced beef, stir well and brown for 2 minutes. Add salt, pepper and stock, cover and cook very gently for 1 hour. Now add the fruit and the potatoes and cook again till tender. Just before serving add the raisins.

COSTA RICAN CASSEROLE OF GUINEA FOWL

1 *4-lb. guinea fowl*
4 *rashers of fat bacon, chopped*
2 *oz. flour*
1 *teaspoon salt*
1 *teaspoon paprika pepper*
1 *large onion, chopped*

½ *pint boiling water*
½ *pint red wine*

Have the bird cut in joints. Chop the liver. Fry the bacon slowly in the casserole, add the pieces of bird and brown. Add the flour, stir well, add everything else. Cover tightly and simmer very gently for 2 hours or until the bird is tender.

ARGENTINE EMPANDAS (Fruit and Meat Turnovers)

FILLING:

1 *large pear* ⎫
2 *large peaches* ⎬ *chopped fine*
1 *tablespoon chives* ⎭
2 *oz. butter*
1 *large onion, chopped fine*
2 *large tomatoes, peeled and chopped*
1 *large green pepper, seeded and chopped fine*
12 *oz. raw minced meat*
2 *tablespoons sugar*
½ *teaspoon salt*
⅛ *pint dry white wine*

CRUST:

8 *oz. flour*
pinch of salt
2 *teaspoons cinnamon*
6 *oz. butter*

2 *egg yolks, beaten*
4 *tablespoons dry white wine*
2 *tablespoons milk*
2 *oz. sugar*

Make the filling first. Heat the butter in a large saucepan and fry the onion till transparent. Add the tomatoes, stir well and simmer gently for 5 minutes. Then add everything else, stir well, cover and cook gently for 15 minutes. Leave to cool.

For the crust, sieve the flour and salt, add a pinch of cinnamon and 1½ teaspoons sugar. Add the butter and mix till the mixture looks like breadcrumbs. Mix half the egg yolk with the wine, add, then add the milk gradually till a soft dough is formed. Roll and cut into rounds the size of a saucer. Put an equal amount of filling on each, moisten the edges and turn the pastry over to form half circles. Seal well. Brush the tops with egg, sprinkle 2 oz. sugar and the rest of the cinnamon. Bake in a hot oven for 15 minutes.

VENEZUELA HALLACAS (Meat Pies)

FILLING:

1 *large onion, sliced*
2 *oz. suet or dripping*
1 *red or green pepper, seeded and finely chopped*
8 *oz. raw beef or veal, minced*
2 *oz. seedless raisins*
2 *oz. stoned green olives*
2 *hard-boiled eggs, chopped*
salt, pepper

CRUST:

4 *oz. flour*
2 *oz. lard*
2 *oz. butter*

2 *small eggs*
pinch of salt

Make the pastry in the usual way. Roll out to the thickness of a penny or thinner and cut into 8 saucer-sized rounds.

For the filling, heat the suet and fry the onion till brown, add the chopped pepper, salt and pepper, fry for 2 minutes. Now add the meat, raisins, olives, chopped eggs. Cook for 4 minutes, gently. Leave to cool.

Put an equal amount of the filling on each round, moisten the edge and put another round of pastry on top. Seal tightly. Bake in a hot oven for 15 minutes.

BRAZILIAN UNCOOKED SAUCE FOR FRIED FISH

1 *teaspoon cummin seed*
3 *cloves of garlic, finely chopped*
1 *teaspoon chopped parsley*
a pinch of saffron
½ *teaspoon salt*
¼ *teaspoon black pepper*
¼ *pint vinegar*

4 *tablespoons water*
2 *tablespoons tomato sauce (optional)*

Pound the cummin seed to a powder, add and pound the garlic, and the other ingredients, stir well.

While the fried fish is still hot, turn for a few seconds in the sauce. Pour the rest of the sauce over the hot fish on the serving dish.

CAZUELA (Chilean Chicken Stew)

1 *stewing fowl (5—6 lb.)*
flour
olive oil
bouquet garni
6—8 *potatoes, peeled but left whole*
8 *oz. French beans*
8 *oz. fresh peas*
1 *small pumpkin*
4 *oz. uncooked rice*
2 *ears corn-on-the-cob, cooked*
salt, pepper
1 *egg*
finely chopped parsley

Cut up the fowl for frying, flour the pieces and sauté in oil. Drain and put in a heavy pot with cold water to cover. Add the *bouquet garni*. Bring to boil, turn down, and simmer, never letting it come to the boil again. Skim from time to time. After an hour add the potatoes and cook until tender, about 40—50 minutes. About 30 minutes after adding the potatoes add the peeled and seeded pumpkin, cut into 3-inch squares, peas, and sliced beans. Cook 10—15 minutes more and add the rice. Cook the rice until tender, about 15 minutes. After about 10 minutes add the corn, salt and pepper. Simmer all together for a few minutes. Remove from the stove, let cool slightly. Break in the raw egg, stir very fast until smooth. The egg should thicken the gravy. Serve in soup bowls and sprinkle with parsley.

PERUVIAN BEAN PURÉE

1 *lb. dried Lima beans*
8 *oz. chopped onion*
2 *oz. butter*
2 *tablespoons chopped parsley*
1 *teaspoon salt*

Soak beans in cold water for 12 hours. Then simmer in salted water for 1 hour. Sieve the beans and mix with 6 oz. onion and the parsley, place in a casserole dish and cover with the remaining onion. Bake in a moderate oven for 20—30 minutes.

SOUTH AMERICAN BLACK BEANS IN GARLIC

1 *lb. dried black beans*
2 *oz. salt pork*
2 *cloves garlic*
1 *teaspoon salt*
1 *teaspoon cummin seed*
1 *oz. butter*

Soak beans in cold water for 12 hours. Simmer in salted water for 2 hours, then drain. Brown the diced pork and thinly sliced garlic in the butter, then mix in the beans and cummin seeds. Serve hot.

CALDO DE QUIMGOMBO (Okra Soup)

1 *lb. okras, with stems removed*
1 *tomato*
1 *onion*
1 *oz. butter*
1 *oz. flour*
1 *bay leaf*
salt, pepper
1 *pint meat stock*

Chop onion small and simmer in the butter for 5 minutes. Stir in flour and a little stock. When the sauce has thickened add sliced okras, chopped tomato, bay leaf, salt and pepper and remaining stock and simmer gently until cooked. Okra or gumbo is a vegetable found in most tropical countries.

CABBAGE WITH CAPERS

2 *oz. dripping*
2 *cloves of garlic, chopped*
1 *large onion, chopped*
1 *clove*
1½ *lb. shredded cabbage*
3 *oz. cooked ham, chopped*
2 *tablespoons capers*
1 *tablespoon vinegar*
1 *teaspoon salt*
½ *teaspoon pepper*

2 *large tomatoes, peeled and chopped finely*
2 *oz. breadcrumbs*

Heat the dripping in a stewpan, add onion and clove, and garlic, fry for 3 minutes. Add cabbage, stir, cover the pan, cook for 3 minutes. Add ham, capers, vinegar, salt and pepper and tomatoes. Stir well, sprinkle the breadcrumbs over, cover the pan and cook gently for 20 minutes, or until the cabbage is tender. A little stock or water may be added if the mixture becomes too dry and apt to burn.

ICED COFFEE (BRAZILIAN)

1½ *pints strong black coffee*
½ *pint drinking chocolate*
1½ *pints milk*
*chocolate ice cream or whipped
  cream*
sugar to taste

Combine all ingredients, adding sugar to taste. Serve in tall glasses topped with chocolate ice cream or whipped cream.

Spain

COOKING IN SPAIN

Spanish cooking is very much like the climate and the landscape of the country — it is brilliant, hot, highly coloured and full of life. The Spaniards give the same hot-blooded treatment to their cookery as they display in their fiery dancing. As in every country with a hot climate, you find the food highly seasoned and rich, full of flavour, and daring in its mixture of unusual ingredients. They use olive oil in their cooking — hardly any butter — and yet their food is never too oily or indigestible. Their famous paella is something of a revelation when you first meet it — the mixture of shellfish, chicken and many other good things may strike you as a very odd medley. It is a masterpiece of a dish, because all those seemingly discordant elements blend together like a top grade philharmonic orchestra. It ought to be served as it is in Spain and in Spanish restaurants, in a paella dish, an outsize frying pan with two small handles. With its vivid and varied colouring, a paella is a pretty enough picture to paint for any artist.

Iced soups are a boon to summer entertaining and the Spanish kitchen provides two very tasty and original ones: Cucumber Soup and Tomato Soup. All the Spanish fish recipes have the same exotic and typically Spanish bravado to them, which has won the hearts of gourmets all over the world. It is quite amazing what a little clove of garlic can do to improve the flavour of any dish — added to all the other tasty bits the Spaniards use.

During the season of green peppers and tomatoes, I often cook a Spanish Piperade for a snatch supper — it is hardly any more trouble than scrambling eggs and is a more substantial dish. Spanish omelette, of course, is an old trusted friend in most households, but less well known are the Spanish sweet dishes. Next time you brood about a sweet course you ought to turn up this Spanish chapter and try Coffee Cream or Chocolate Creams — both sumptuous and easy-to-make desserts.

When you see any quinces at your greengrocer, or if you have them in your own garden, try making Quince Squares — you are bound to go back for more quinces and make some more Quince Squares before you know where you are!

STUFFED COOKING APPLES

4 *large cooking apples*
2 *small potatoes*
2 *sticks celery*
2 *egg yolks*
chervil
parsley
2 *tablespoons lemon juice*
salt, pepper

Wash the potatoes and cook them in their skins. Peel them. Core and halve the apples. Remove as much of the flesh as possible without damaging the skins. Chop the apple flesh, chop the potatoes and mix them together with the beaten egg yolks, the chopped herbs, chopped celery and the lemon juice. Season with salt and pepper. Fill the apple halves with the mixture.

DRIED SALT COD WITH RICE

8 *oz. dried salt cod*
8 *oz. Patna rice*
2 *tomatoes*
1 *onion*
2 *tablespoons olive oil*
salt, pepper

Prepare the fish as for dried salt cod salad (see below). Fry lightly in olive oil. Set the fish aside and fry the sliced and peeled tomato and the sliced onion in the same pan. Remove them from the pan. Pour in the rice, stir it around in the fat, add 1 pint boiling salted water and simmer until water is absorbed and the rice is cooked. Mix the fish, tomato and onion with the rice. Season with salt and pepper. Serve very cold.

DRIED SALT COD SALAD

8 *oz. dried salt cod*
6 *anchovy fillets*
12 *black olives*
1 *onion*
1 *green pepper*
1 *hard-boiled egg*
2 *tablespoons olive oil*
1 *tablespoon vinegar*
salt, pepper

lettuce

Soak the fish for 12 hours. Simmer it in water until soft. Remove the skin and break into fairly small pieces. Slice the onion finely, slice the pepper. Mix the fish with the onion, pepper, anchovy fillets and olives. Dress with the olive oil and vinegar, season with salt and pepper. Arrange on the lettuce leaves and garnish with hard-boiled egg cut lengthwise.

ICED CUCUMBER SOUP

2 *cucumbers*
½ *onion*
1 *dessertspoon lemon juice*
salt, pepper
mint
½ *pint prawns*
½ *pint aspic jelly*

Grate the cucumbers. Mix them with grated onion, the lemon juice and finely chopped mint. Season with salt and pepper. Melt the aspic jelly. Stir it into the cucumber mixture. Serve chilled, garnished with prawns.

SHELLFISH SOUP

1 *lb. onions, sliced*
2 *lb. tomatoes, peeled and*
  chopped
2 *tablespoons olive oil*
1 *clove garlic*
parsley
marjoram
thyme
1 *large cupful prawns or mussels*
4 *oz. vermicelli*
salt, pepper

Cook the fish in 8 pints boiling water. Drain and reserve the water. Heat the olive oil, fry the onions in it until soft. Add the tomatoes, crushed garlic, herbs, salt and pepper; simmer until tomatoes are cooked. Pour in the water in which the fish was cooked, simmer for 15 minutes. Sieve, reheat and add the vermicelli broken into small pieces and the fish. Serve sprinkled with parsley.

SHRIMP SOUP

1 *pint shrimps*
3 *onions*
1 *tomato*
1 *oz. flour*
2 *oz. butter*
1 *glass white wine*
salt, pepper
parsley

If fresh shrimps are used, boil them and keep the water. Take off the heads and tails. Pound the heads with 1 oz. butter. Slice the onions and cook them slowly in the rest of the butter until golden. Stir in the flour and cook for 1 minute. Add the cooking water, if available, the shrimps, the peeled and chopped tomatoes and the wine. Simmer for 5 minutes. Add the shrimps' heads, pass the soup through a sieve. Season with salt and pepper, serve sprinkled with chopped parsley.

TOMATO SOUP

2 *pints chicken stock*
2 *tablespoons concentrated*
  tomato purée
vermicelli
parsley

Bring the stock to the boil, add the tomato purée. Add the vermicelli broken into small pieces and simmer for 15 minutes. Serve garnished with chopped parsley.

ICED TOMATO SOUP

2 *lb. tomatoes*
2 *onions*
salt, pepper
sugar
½ *glass red wine*
2 *cloves garlic*
1 *tablespoon paprika*
2 *tablespoons olive oil*

1 *cucumber*
12 *black olives*
parsley

Mince the tomatoes and onions, season with salt, pepper and sugar, stir in the wine. Crush the garlic, mix it with the paprika, add the olive oil gradually, beating all the time. Mix this with the tomatoes. Chop the cucumber, stone the olives and add them to the mixture. Serve chilled, sprinkled with parsley.

VEGETABLE SOUP

2 *pints chicken or veal stock*
2 *potatoes*
2 *turnips*
4 *oz. haricot beans*
½ *cabbage*
2 *sticks celery*
2 *oz. vermicelli*
2 *oz. rice*

salt, pepper
1 *teaspoon saffron*

Soak the haricot beans overnight and boil them until they are soft. Chop the turnips, potatoes and celery, shred the cabbage. Bring the stock to the boil, put in all the vegetables and simmer until they are almost cooked. Add the vermicelli, rice and saffron. Season with salt and pepper. Simmer for another 20 minutes.

WATERCRESS SOUP

1 *pint stock*
1 *bunch watercress*
3 *potatoes*
¼ *pint milk*
3 *egg yolks*
2 *oz. grated cheese*
salt, pepper

Cut the potatoes into very small pieces, boil them quickly in the stock. Sieve and season with salt and pepper. Chop the watercress and add it to the soup and reheat. Beat the egg yolks with warm milk, pour a little of this mixture into warmed soup bowls, stir the soup directly into the bowls. Serve with grated cheese.

BAKED BREAM

2 *lb. bream fillets*
2 *Spanish onions, sliced*
2 *tablespoons olive oil*
1 *lemon*
salt, pepper
2 *tablespoons breadcrumbs*

Make diagonal incisions in the fish fillets and insert a piece of lemon into each. Put 1 tablespoon of olive oil into a shallow fireproof dish, lay the sliced onions in the bottom, put the fish on top of these, cover with breadcrumbs, sprinkle with salt and pepper. Pour 1 tablespoon olive oil over the top. Bake in a hot oven for 40 minutes.

COD À LA PORTUGAISE

2 *lb. cod on the bone*
2 *onions, chopped*
1½ *lb. tomatoes, peeled and chopped*
4 *oz. rice*
1 *glass white wine*
2 *tablespoons olive oil*
1 *oz. butter*
1 *clove garlic*
parsley

salt, pepper

Cut the fish into 4 thick slices. Fry the onion in the butter until golden. Heat the olive oil in a fireproof dish, lay the cod on the bottom of the dish, cover it with the onion and tomato and chopped garlic. Surround the fish with the cooked rice, season with salt and pepper and finely chopped parsley. Cover the dish and cook in a moderate oven for 30—40 minutes.

FISH WITH RICE

1 *lb. fish (halibut or turbot are best but bream will do well)*
1 *lb. tomatoes*
1 *stick celery*
1 *carrot*
1 *large onion*
1 *piece of fennel (optional)*
basil
thyme
garlic
parsley
salt, pepper
oil for frying

Cut the fish into smallish pieces. Boil the head and bones with the celery, carrot, onion and herbs to make fish stock. Melt the oil, fry the fish in it until golden. Pour off most of the olive oil, put the fish in a fireproof dish in a slow oven with the chopped garlic, the parsley and a little olive oil. Chop the tomatoes and cook them in the pan for a few minutes. Add them to the fish, continue to cook slowly until the fish is tender. Put the rice in the pan, strain 1 pint hot fish stock over it, cook fairly fast until the rice is cooked and the stock absorbed. Arrange the rice in the middle of a dish with the fish and tomatoes round it.

BAKED FRESH HADDOCK

1 *lb. fresh haddock fillet*
1 *tablespoon concentrated tomato*
  purée
1 *clove garlic*
½ *glass white wine*
parsley
breadcrumbs
1 *tablespoon olive oil*

Cut the haddock into slices about 1 inch wide. Put the oil into a fireproof dish, arrange the fish pieces on it. Chop the garlic and sprinkle over the fish, pour the tomato purée and wine over it, cover with breadcrumbs and bake in a moderate oven for 30 minutes. Serve chopped parsley separately.

FRIED HAKE WITH TOMATO SAUCE

2 *lb. hake fillet*
flour
salt
pepper
olive oil for frying

parsley
marjoram
salt, pepper
1 *tablespoon olive oil*

FOR THE SAUCE:
1 *sliced onion*
1 *clove garlic*
1 *pimento*
1 *lb. tomatoes, peeled and*
  quartered
½ *bay leaf*
2 *glasses white wine*

FOR THE SAUCE:
Fry the onion in the olive oil until tender, add the tomatoes, the crushed garlic, the pimento and the flavourings. Simmer gently, add the white wine, continue simmering for 20 minutes, adding water if necessary. Pass through a sieve.

    Cut the fish into pieces about 2 inches wide, roll in seasoned flour. Fry in very hot oil. Serve with slices of lemon and the sauce handed separately.

COLD RED MULLET

½ *pint olive oil*
2 *tablespoons tarragon vinegar*
1 *carrot, chopped*
1 *onion, chopped*
1 *green pepper, seeded and*
  chopped
½ *bay leaf*

1 *sprig parsley*
2 *red mullet*
oil for frying

Dip the fish quickly in very hot olive oil. Make a marinade of the oil, vinegar, vegetables and herbs, simmer the fish in it for 15 minutes. Leave the fish in the marinade for 24 hours. Serve as it is.

SHRIMP ESPAGNOL

1 *pint shrimps*
2 *oz. butter*
1 *onion*
8 *oz. rice*
1 *tablespoon concentrated tomato purée*
½ *pint double cream*

salt, pepper

Fry the chopped onion in the butter until golden. Boil the rice in salted water. Drain and mix it with the onions, add the tomato purée, the prepared shrimps and the cream, season with salt and pepper. Bake in a moderate oven for 30 minutes.

TROUT

4 *small trout*
1 *onion, sliced*
1 *clove garlic*
parsley
1 *oz. butter*
1 *tablespoon olive oil*
1 *dessertspoon wine vinegar*
salt
lemon

Crush the garlic with a little salt, mix it with the well-chopped parsley and ½ oz. butter, add the vinegar and ¼ pint of water. Fillet the trout and fry quickly on both sides in butter. Put the fish into the sauce. Fry the onions in olive oil until golden, add them to the sauce and simmer for 5 minutes. Serve the sauce strained over the fish and garnish with lemon.

EGGS WITH SPINACH

4 *eggs*
½ *red pepper, chopped*
1 *green pepper, chopped*
2 *oz. chopped ham or bacon*
1 *tablespoon olive oil*
salt, pepper
1 *lb. cooked spinach*

chives
parsley

Beat the eggs with a fork, add the peppers, ham and salt and pepper. Melt the olive oil in a frying pan, pour in the egg mixture, cook slowly, stirring fairly often until the mixture becomes like slightly cooked scrambled egg. Pour the mixture on to the spinach, brown under the grill. Garnish with chopped chives and parsley. Serve very hot with thin toast.

HAM AND LENTILS

8 *oz. lentils*
4 *oz. diced cooked ham*
2 *onions*
2 *tomatoes*
1 *clove garlic*
2 *tablespoons olive oil*
salt, pepper

Soak the lentils overnight. Cook in boiling water until tender. Slice the onions and fry in the olive oil until golden, add the tomatoes, peeled and chopped, the ham and the chopped garlic. Cook slowly until the tomatoes are soft. Stir in the lentils, simmer for 5 minutes. Season with salt and pepper. Serve very hot.

PAELLA (1)

8 oz. rice
4 oz. pork fillet
6 scampi
4 oz. cooked chicken
8 oz. peas
8 oz. French beans
6 mussels
½ tin sweet red peppers
2 tomatoes, peeled and quartered
1 onion, chopped
2 cloves garlic, chopped
bouquet garni
1 teaspoon saffron
cayenne pepper
2 pints stock

salt, pepper
2 tablespoons olive oil

This is best made in a deep pan which can be used for frying and also go in the oven. Failing this, the ingredients can be transferred from a frying pan to a casserole.

Cook the peas and beans and heat the red peppers; keep them hot. Melt the olive oil, brown the diced chicken and pork in it. Add the onions and the garlic. Fry until the onions are golden, add the tomatoes, the rice, the *bouquet garni*, the saffron, salt, pepper and stock. Simmer for 10 minutes. Arrange the scampi and the mussels on top. Cook in a hot oven for 10 minutes. Add the peppers, peas and beans and serve directly from the cooking pot.

PAELLA (2)

1 small roasting chicken, cut into
  pieces
4 oz. bacon, diced
2 tablespoons olive oil
1 clove garlic
1 tomato, peeled and quartered
1 teaspoon paprika
8 oz. peas
8 oz. French beans
12 oz. rice

8 crayfish
12 scampi
1 teaspoon saffron

Fry the chicken and the bacon in the oil for 5 minutes. Add the tomato, garlic, beans, peas, paprika and rice. Stir the rice into the fat, pour in 2 pints water, add the saffron when the water comes to the boil. Simmer for 5 minutes, add the shellfish and cook for another 5 minutes, or until the rice is cooked.

PIGS' LIVER TERRINE

1 lb. pig's liver
3 tablespoons olive oil
4 onions
1 sprig mint
parsley
2 red peppers
1 clove
nutmeg
saffron
cinnamon

black pepper
2 oz. breadcrumbs

Chop the liver very fine and blanch in salted water. Chop the onions and the peppers and fry them in the olive oil until soft, add the chopped mint, parsley, the clove, a pinch each of nutmeg, cinnamon, and saffron and a sprinkling of freshly ground black pepper. Stir in the liver. Simmer for 3 minutes. Mix in the breadcrumbs. Pour into a flat dish. Serve chilled.

PIPERADE

1 *green pepper*
1 *small onion*
1 *clove garlic*
8 *oz. tomatoes*
1 *tablespoon olive oil*
4 *eggs*
salt, pepper

Remove the seeds from the pepper and slice it finely. Slice the onion. Cook the onion and the pepper in the olive oil with the crushed garlic until the onion is transparent. Peel and chop the tomatoes. Add them to the onion mixture and simmer for 5 minutes, break in the eggs and cook them slowly, stirring continually. Season with salt and pepper. Serve very hot with dry toast.

CASTILIAN GREEN BEANS

French beans
pimentos
olive oil
1 *clove garlic*
parsley
salt, pepper

Cook the green beans in boiling salt water till tender. Cut up and fry the pimentos in oil, together with a chopped garlic clove and chopped parsley. Drain the beans and mix with the fried pimentos.

PORK WITH BAKED EGGS

4 *oz. fillet pork*
2 *oz. ham*
8 *oz. tomatoes, peeled and*
   chopped
1 *onion, sliced*
1 *oz. flour*
2 *oz. butter*
¼ *pint stock*

salt, pepper
4 *eggs*

Cut the ham and pork into thin strips. Cook them and the onion in the butter until golden, add the tomatoes. Stir in the flour, cook for 1 minute, add the stock. Simmer for 20 minutes. Season with salt and pepper. Turn into a flat fireproof dish, break the eggs into the pork mixture and bake in a moderate oven until the egg is set.

PORK WITH SCRAMBLED EGGS

8 *oz. pork*
2 *onions*
4 *tomatoes*
½ *small marrow*
1 *green pepper*
1 *tablespoon olive oil*
¼ *pint stock*

salt, pepper
scrambled eggs

Melt the olive oil, fry the sliced onions and the pork cut into small pieces in it. Add the marrow cut into 1-inch cubes, the peeled and chopped tomatoes and the sliced green pepper. Pour in ¼ pint stock and simmer for 40 minutes. Season with salt and pepper. Serve with scrambled eggs.

SAUSAGES WITH HARICOT BEANS

1 *lb. sausages*
8 *oz. haricot beans*
1 *onion, sliced*
1 *clove garlic*
1 *oz. butter*
salt, pepper

Soak the beans overnight, cook in salted water until tender; drain. Fry the sausages in the butter, put aside to keep warm. Fry the onion until golden, add the beans and stir about until well mixed with the onion and fat. Season with pepper and garlic crushed with salt. Serve surrounded by sausages.

SAUSAGES WITH LENTILS

4 *oz. lentils*
8 *oz. small pork sausages*
1 *onion*
4 *tomatoes*
1 *clove garlic*
1 *tablespoon olive oil*

salt, pepper

Boil the lentils in salted water; when cooked, drain and put in a frying pan with the olive oil, sliced onion, peeled and chopped tomatoes and crushed garlic. Cook slowly for 30 minutes. Season with salt and pepper. Serve with fried sausages.

SPANISH OMELETTE

4 *eggs*
1 *small onion, chopped*
1 *tablespoon cooked peas*
1 *tablespoon cooked French beans,
    chopped*
1 *tablespoon cooked carrot,
    chopped*
1 *medium cooked potato, diced*
parsley

salt, pepper
½ *teaspoon olive oil*

Beat the eggs lightly, add the vegetables, salt and pepper. Melt the olive oil in a frying pan, pour in the egg mixture, cook quickly for 3 minutes. Cook for another minute under a hot grill.

SPANISH POACHED EGG

4 *eggs*
1 *gill chicken stock*
1 *gill milk*
1 *oz. butter*
1 *oz. flour*
1 *egg yolk*
salt, pepper
nutmeg
2 *oz. grated Gruyère cheese*
ratatouille (see p. 158)

Make the ratatouille (see p. 158) and keep it hot in a fireproof dish in a slow oven. Melt the butter, stir in the flour and cook for 1 minute; gradually add the stock and the milk. Allow to simmer for several minutes. Season with salt and pepper and nutmeg. Stir in the egg yolk. Poach the eggs, drain and arrange on top of the ratatouille. Pour a little sauce on top of each egg, sprinkle with grated cheese. Brown under a hot grill.

BRAISED BEEF

3 *lb. topside*
4 *oz. bacon rashers*
4 *oz. fat bacon*
4 *onions*
4 *oz. mushrooms*
4 *tomatoes*
1 *glass red vine*
2 *carrots, sliced*
1 *clove garlic*
parsley
thyme
basil
½ *bay leaf*
mace
salt, pepper

8 *oz. runner beans*
4 *medium potatoes*
8 *oz. sausages*

Line a casserole with bacon rashers. Put in the beef, covered with the fat bacon. Add the chopped garlic, sliced onions, carrots, a parsley stalk, a little mace, salt and pepper. Fry until the meat is sealed, add the peeled and quartered tomatoes and the wine. Cover with hot water and cook in a moderate oven, with a lid on the pan, for 2 hours. While the meat is cooking, cook the beans and potatoes. Fry the sliced mushrooms in the butter, add the sausages and fry them too. Put in the beans and the potatoes. Arrange the meat on a serving dish, with the vegetables and sausages round it. Serve the strained gravy separately.

RAGOÛT OF BEEF

1 *lb. stewing steak*
4 *oz. pork or ham, diced*
1 *chopped onion*
1 *lettuce*
1 *lb. peas*
8 *oz. runner beans*
½ *small marrow, cubed*
8 *small new potatoes*
2 *oz. lard*

2 *tablespoons concentrated tomato purée*
1 *glass white wine*

Fry the meat quickly on both sides in 1 oz. fat. Add ½ pint water and salt and pepper. Cook slowly for 1 hour. Serve with the following ragoût: sauté all the vegetables in 1 oz. fat, add the tomato purée and white wine, simmer until all the vegetables are tender (about 40 minutes).

CHICKEN WITH PEAS

1 *boiling chicken*
1 *onion, chopped*
1 *glass white wine*
2 *oz. flour*
2 *oz. lard*
1 *pint stock*
1 *teaspoon saffron*
nutmeg
parsley

salt, pepper
2 *lb. peas*

Joint the chicken. Fry in the lard with the onion; when golden, stir in the flour, add the stock and the wine. Season with salt and pepper. Add the parsley. Simmer until tender. Flavour with the saffron and a little nutmeg. Arrange the chicken pieces on a dish, strain the sauce over them and surround with peas.

CHICKEN WITH RICE

2 *spring chickens*
2 *oz. butter*
2 *onions*
4 *oz. lean bacon*
8 *oz. tomatoes, peeled*
2 *green peppers*
8 *oz. cooked peas*
1 *pimento*
parsley
olive oil
salt, pepper

Joint the chickens. Fry in the butter until golden. Slice the onion and fry in the oil until transparent. Cut the bacon into small pieces and slice the tomato, fry them in the olive oil. Add the onion, bacon and tomato to the chicken. Pour in the rice, mix it well with the other ingredients. Pour in the stock, simmer until the rice is cooked and the stock is absorbed. Season with salt and pepper. Slice the peppers and the pimento. Fry them and the peas in a little olive oil. Arrange the chicken and rice on a hot dish, garnish with the fried vegetables ano sprinkle with parsley.

BRAISED LAMB

1 *small leg lamb (about 3½ lb.)*
2 *pimentos*
1 *clove garlic*
1 *glass white wine*
2 *oz. butter*
rosemary
parsley
salt, pepper

Put the lamb in a casserole with the butter and rosemary. Season with salt and pepper. Cover and cook in a moderate oven until tender (about 2½ hours). Serve with the following sauce:

Fry the chopped pimentos, garlic and parsley in a little butter, add the sauce from the casserole and the wine and simmer for 10 minutes. Remove the rosemary and pour the sauce over the meat.

LAMB WITH GARLIC AND TOMATO

1 *thick slice leg of lamb*
6 *cloves garlic*
1 *oz. flour*
1 *oz. lard*
1 *tablespoon concentrated tomato*
 purée
½ *pint stock*

salt, pepper

Put the meat in a roasting pan with the lard, put the garlic round it. Fry the meat on both sides, put in the flour, the tomato purée and the stock. Cook, covered with a lid, in a moderate oven until the meat is tender.

LAMB CUTLETS WITH TOMATOES AND SAUSAGES

4 *lamb cutlets*
8 *chipolata sausages*
1 *slice gammon, diced*
1 *onion, chopped*
1 *lb. tomatoes*
lard
olive oil
salt, pepper

Fry the cutlets in a mixture of lard and olive oil. Season with salt and pepper and put in a casserole. Fry the onion and the gammon in the fat left by the chops. Add the peeled and quartered tomatoes and simmer for 10 minutes. Pour this over the cutlets and reheat in the oven. Serve with sausages fried separately.

LAMB KIDNEYS WITH WHITE WINE

4 *lamb kidneys*
1 *small onion*
1 *lb. peas*
8 *oz. button mushrooms*
4 *slices bacon*
¼ *pint white wine*
parsley
salt, pepper

1 *oz. butter*
espagnole sauce

Skin the kidneys and remove the core. Cut into thin slices. Melt the butter; when hot, put in the kidneys, finely chopped onion and parsley, and the white wine. Season with salt and pepper. Cook fairly fast for 3 minutes. Add the brown sauce, the cooked mushrooms and cooked peas. Simmer for another 10 minutes. Serve with the sauce strained over the kidneys and garnish with fried bacon.

TURKEY

1 *turkey*

FOR THE STUFFING:

8 *oz. pork sausages*
8 *oz. prunes*
8 *oz. dried peaches*
1 *lb. chestnuts*
8 *oz. ham, diced*
4 *oz. mushrooms*
1 *glass sherry*
thyme
marjoram
basil
parsley
salt, pepper

1 *oz. lard*
4 *oz. melted butter*
¼ *pint stock*
1 *glass white wine*

MAKE THE STUFFING AS FOLLOWS:
Brown the ham and the turkey liver (cut into small cubes) in the lard. Add the sausages, the stoned prunes, the peaches, the chestnuts (previously shelled, boiled and roughly chopped), the slices of mushroom and the herbs in a muslin bag. Cook for 10 minutes. Remove the herbs and chop all the ingredients fairly finely, mix with the sherry and stuff the bird. Brush the turkey with melted butter, roast in a hot oven and baste frequently with the stock and wine.

LIVER WITH BRANDY

1½ *lb. calves' liver*
8 *oz. rice*
8 *oz. mushrooms*
2 *tomatoes*
2 *oz. butter*
1 *tablespoon brandy*
salt, pepper

Cook the rice, keep it warm. Melt ½ oz. butter, fry the quartered tomatoes gently in it. Simmer the mushrooms in water for 5 minutes. Chop them and fry them with the liver cut into small squares, in a little butter. Season with salt and pepper. Arrange the tomatoes around the rice. Make a hollow on the top of the rice, put the mushrooms and liver into it. Pour warmed brandy over the liver, set light to it and serve immediately.

BRAISED PORK

2 *lb. loin of pork*
1 *clove garlic*
2 *onions*
2 *tomatoes*
1 *egg plant*
1 *pimento*
2 *oz. butter*
¼ *pint stock*
1 *glass red wine*
sauté potatoes

Rub the pork with the cut clove of garlic. Melt the butter in a casserole, put in the pork and cook in a hot oven until it begins to brown. Add the sliced onions, peeled and quartered tomatoes, sliced egg plant, and sliced pimento. Pour in the wine and cook for a few minutes, add the stock. Cover the pan and cook in a moderate oven for 2½ hours. Season with salt and pepper. Serve with sauté potatoes.

ROAST VEAL

a joint of roasting veal
½ *pint white wine*
1 *clove garlic*
salt, pepper
2 *oz. butter*

Marinate the meat in the wine, with the cut clove of garlic and salt and pepper for 4—5 hours. Brush with melted butter and roast in a hot oven, basting frequently with the wine, allowing 25 minutes cooking time per lb. of meat.

CHOCOLATE CREAMS

8 *oz. sugar*
¼ *pint water*
6 *egg yolks*
4 *oz. plain chocolate*

Melt the sugar in the water, boil it to a thick syrup. Cool and add to the beaten egg yolks. Pour into small greased fireproof dishes, bake in a slow oven until set (about 45 minutes). Cool the dishes and pour the melted chocolate over the creams. Serve chilled.

CHESTNUT CAKES

3 *eggs*
4 *oz. sugar*
3½ *oz. flour*
3 *oz. butter*
4 *oz. almonds*
8 *oz. chestnut purée (see below)*
2 *tablespoons apricot jam*

Beat the eggs and the sugar together over a pan of hot water until they are white, add the sifted flour. Melt 3 oz. butter and fold it into the mixture. Bake in a greased Swiss Roll tin in a moderately hot oven for 25 minutes. Put on a rack and when cool cut into rounds with a pastry cutter. Chop the almonds, put in a frying pan with ½ oz. butter, stir them about over a low flame until browned. Spread the jam over the sponge cake rounds, cover with chopped almonds. Pipe chestnut purée on to the top.

CHESTNUT PURÉE

8 *oz. chestnuts*
3 *oz. sugar*
4 *tablespoons water*

Score the chestnuts and put in a hot oven for 10 minutes. The shells should have become brittle and easy to peel. Put the shelled chestnuts in boiling water and simmer until tender (about 30 minutes). Sieve and mix with a syrup made by boiling the sugar with the water, until a drop sets instantly when put into cold water.

COCONUT CREAM

1 *coconut*
4 *oz. sugar*
4 *egg yolks*
4 *sponge cakes*

Drain the milk from the coconut. Grate the coconut flesh. Cook the milk and the grated coconut in a double saucepan for 30 minutes. Strain through fine muslin. Beat the egg yolks until thick, whisk in the strained coconut. Cook in a double saucepan until the mixture thickens. Pour over the sponge cakes and leave to cool.

COFFEE CREAM

½ *oz. gelatine*
3 *eggs*
1 *pint milk*
2 *oz. sugar*
4 *teaspoons powdered coffee*

Dissolve the gelatine in a little warm water. Beat the eggs lightly, mix with the milk and the sugar. Pour into a saucepan and cook slowly until the custard begins to thicken. Stir in the gelatine and the powdered coffee mixed with a little water. Pour into a glass dish to set.

CREAM VOL-AU-VENT

8 *vol-au-vent cases (see pp. 153,*
  154)
4 *eggs*
2 *oz. flour*
1 *pint milk*
7 *oz. sugar*
vanilla

Whisk the eggs lightly, beat in the flour and sugar until thoroughly blended. Bring the milk to the boil, add a drop of vanilla, gradually beat into the egg mixture. Pour into a double saucepan and cook slowly, beating continuously until custard thickens. When cold, but not set, pour into vol-au-vent cases.

DOUGHNUTS

5 *oz. flour*
2 *oz. butter*
3 *eggs*
vanilla flavouring
salt
sugar
fat for frying

Put ½ pint water into a saucepan with the butter cut into small pieces, and a pinch of salt. Bring to the boil, stir in the flour when the butter melts. Continue to cook slowly until the mixture is smooth and comes away from the sides of the pan. Beat in the eggs gradually. Add the vanilla. Drop small spoonfuls of the mixture into very hot deep fat. When brown and crisp, remove from the fat, drain on absorbent paper. Serve hot and dredged with sugar.

NOUGAT

1 *lb. almonds*
12 *oz. castor sugar*
butter

Blanch, skin and chop the almonds. Melt a little butter in a baking tin, fry the almonds in it until brown. Pound the almonds with half of the sugar, add the rest of the sugar gradually. Cook slowly in a heavy saucepan, stirring all the time until mixture thickens. Pour into shallow tins lined with rice paper. Cut into small rectangular pieces when set.

SPANISH FRITTERS

4 *slices white bread*
1 *pint thin cream*
1 *blade mace*
cinnamon
1 *oz. castor sugar*
butter for frying
apricot jam

Cut the crusts off the bread and cut into fingers 1 inch wide. Soak the fingers in the cream flavoured with mace and cinnamon and sugar for 10 minutes. Drain and fry quickly in the butter. Serve with hot sauce made by heating the jam with a little water and passing it through a sieve.

QUINCE SQUARES

quinces
sugar

Wash the quinces. Cut into pieces and remove the core. Steam them until tender and pass through a sieve. Boil the purée with the same weight of sugar in a preserving pan, stirring continuously until it thickens and comes away from the sides. Pour into shallow tins and leave in a very cool oven to harden. Cut into 1-inch squares and keep in a tin wrapped in greaseproof paper.

WALNUT PUDDING

8 oz. sugar
6 oz. walnuts
5 eggs
cinnamon

Pound the shelled nuts with a pinch of cinnamon until smooth. Beat the eggs and sugar together until smooth and creamy, mix with the walnuts. Pour into a buttered pie dish, cook in a very cool oven until set.

HAZELNUT BISCUITS

8 oz. ground hazelnuts
1 egg
2 oz. flour
1 tablespoon grated lemon rind
juice of ½ lemon
3 oz. castor sugar

Pound the hazelnuts with the sugar in a mortar to a fine paste, add the flour and lemon rind. Beat the egg and lemon juice together and add to the mixture, place teaspoonfuls on a greased baking sheet and bake in a moderate oven until the little biscuits are brown and crisp.

HONEY AND NUT ROLL

PASTRY:
8 oz. flour
4 oz. butter
pinch salt
1 tablespoon castor sugar
1 egg yolk
½ glass sherry
1 tablespoon lemon juice

FILLING:
honey
chopped walnuts and hazelnuts

chopped candied peel
castor sugar

Rub the butter into the flour, add salt and sugar, beaten egg yolk, lemon juice and sherry to make into a stiff paste. If necessary add a little cold water. Roll into a strip. Brush with honey and sprinkle with chopped nuts and chopped candied peel. Roll up and sprinkle with a little castor sugar. Bake in a moderate oven for 20—25 minutes.

Switzerland

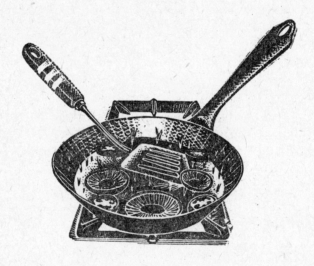

COOKING IN SWITZERLAND

You can spend many a happy holiday in Switzerland and admire the art of the Swiss in looking after you magnificently in all classes of hotels, without realising that there is a typical Swiss kitchen with its own specialities. In the hotels and restaurants you will get an even mixture of French, German and Italian dishes cooked to perfection. Naturally enough, as this lovely little country draws its population from these three language groups. On top of that it draws the tourists from all over the world and caters for them in the most masterly manner.

Behind the international hotels and the large tourist industry there beats the normal rhythm of a home-loving and industrious people. Hard-working families in small villages, isolated farmers on deserted mountain slopes have to cook substantial and down-to-earth meals. Spring Chicken prepared in the Swiss way is just this kind of a meal. Its ingredients are all the kind which every Swiss housewife would find in her larder, once she bought or killed her two chickens. I often have it for a tasty and satisfying Sunday meal for the family — it neither costs more, nor is it more trouble to prepare than a Sunday roast and it makes a simply luscious meal.

As the Swiss are well known for their wonderful cheeses, it is only natural that they also specialise in exquisite cheese dishes and pastries. The best known among these is their Fondue. Fondue in Switzerland is eaten as a communal dish, and I can find no equivalent to it as an 'ice-breaker' for any party. Put a large bowl of Fondue on your dining room table (if possible on a plate warmer) hand out large slices of French bread and let your guests dip into the bowl with them. In less than no time, you will find you need no further stimulants to give the party a swing, especially if you serve a little Kirsch with the Fondue, as the Swiss do.

SPRING CHICKEN

2 *spring chickens*
8 *oz. streaky bacon rashers*
6 *oz. butter*
2 *thick slices bread*
4 *medium potatoes*
salt, pepper

Split the chickens into halves and beat the flesh. Cover with bacon fat and 2 oz. butter and roast in a hot oven until tender (about 15—20 minutes). Cut the potatoes as for chips and fry in the rest of the butter. Fry the rest of the bacon and the bread cut into fingers in the bacon fat. Serve the chicken garnished with the potatoes, bacon and fried bread. Pour surplus bacon fat and butter over the potatoes.

INDIVIDUAL CHEESE SOUFFLÉS

3 *oz. butter*
5 *eggs*
6 *oz. Gruyère cheese (or mixed*
  Gruyère and Parmesan)
salt, pepper

Melt the butter. Beat the egg yolks, add them to the butter, cook for ½ a minute. Add the grated cheese. Cook very slowly until the mixture thickens. Fold in 1 stiffly beaten egg white. Set aside for 30 minutes. Grease small glass dishes. Fold the other beaten egg whites into the mixture. Fill the dishes three-quarters full. Cook in a moderate oven for 30 minutes.

CROÛTE FROMAGE

6 *oz. grated Gruyère cheese*
4 *slices bread*
1 *egg*
½ *pint milk*
juice of ½ lemon
½ *oz. butter*

Beat the egg in the milk. Season with salt and pepper and a little lemon juice. Dip the bread slices in this mixture one at a time. Put alternate layers of soaked bread and grated cheese into a greased pie dish, ending with a layer of cheese. Pour the remaining milk over the dish, dot with butter and bake in a moderate oven for 20 minutes.

FONDUE (1)

4 *eggs*
4 *oz. butter*
8 *oz. grated Gruyère cheese*
½ *glass white wine*
salt, pepper

Pour the beaten eggs into a greased frying pan. Cook very slowly, adding gradually the butter cut into small pieces, the grated cheese and the wine. Season with salt and pepper. Serve immediately the mixture thickens, accompanied by dry toast.

FONDUE (2)

12 *oz. Gruyère cheese*
¼ *pint milk*
2 *oz. butter*
1 *clove garlic, finely chopped*
½ *bottle white wine*

Slice the cheese, melt it in the milk over a low gas, until the mixture begins to thicken. Season with salt and pepper. Add the wine and garlic previously simmered together for 10 minutes. Stir in the butter in small pieces. Serve with French bread.

MEAT LOAF

8 *oz. minced beef*
8 *oz. minced pork*
8 *oz. minced veal*
4 *oz. rolled oats, soaked in milk*
1 *large cooking apple, peeled and chopped*
6 *green olives, stoned*
4 *oz. mushrooms, sliced*

2 *eggs*
salt, pepper

Mix all the ingredients well together. Bind with the beaten eggs. Season lightly with salt and pepper. Bake in a moderate oven in a greased bread tin for 1½ hours.

RUNNER BEAN CASSEROLE

2 *rashers streaky bacon, chopped*
1 *onion, chopped*
1 *clove garlic, crushed with salt*
2 *lb. cooked runner beans*
16 *small new potatoes, cooked*
2 *oz. fat bacon*
salt, pepper

Render the fat bacon and fry the onion in it until golden. Mix in the crushed garlic. Lightly fry the bacon rashers. Fill a casserole with layers of bean, onion, bacon and potatoes, ending with a layer of potatoes. Season with salt and pepper. Bake in a moderate oven for 30 minutes.

SWISS EGGS

4 *oz. Gruyère cheese*
4 *eggs*
1 *gill cream*
salt, pepper
butter

Butter a shallow fireproof dish. Line with slices of cheese. Break the eggs into the dish, keeping them whole. Season the cream with salt and pepper. Pour over the eggs. Sprinkle with grated cheese. Bake in a moderate oven for 10 minutes. Brown the cheese under a grill if necessary.

POTATO CAKE

4 *large potatoes*
2 *oz. butter*
1 *small onion*
salt, pepper

Steam the potatoes without peeling them until just cooked. Peel and roughly grate them. Melt the butter in a frying pan, put in the chopped onion and the potato. Season with salt and pepper. Cover with a lid and fry slowly for 20 minutes. Put a plate over the pan, turn the potatoes on to it. Slide the potatoes back in the pan to fry on the other side.

OVEN-FRIED POTATOES

2 *lb. potatoes*
6 *oz. butter*
salt

Peel and dice the potatoes. Put the butter into a baking tin, melt it in a hot oven, add the potatoes, sprinkle with salt. Cook in a hot oven for 1 hour, turning the potatoes from time to time.

TOMATES FRIBOURGEOISES

1 *lb. tomatoes*
4 *oz. cheese*
4 *oz. diced cooked potatoes*
1 *onion*
1 *tablespoon chopped chives*
salt, pepper

Halve the tomatoes and remove seeds. Sprinkle with salt and leave for a little while. Now mix the grated cheese, cooked potato cubes, finely chopped onion, salt and pepper and fill the tomatoes with this. Cook in a moderate oven for 10—15 minutes. Before serving sprinkle with chopped chives.

BERNER-PLATTE

2 *lb. sauerkraut*
2 *oz. beef*
8 *oz. bacon*
1 *pig's trotter*
1 *Bernese tongue sausage*
1 *onion*
¼ *pint white wine*

Remove the fat from the bacon and cut it into small cubes and fry with the finely chopped onion until they are lightly browned. Slice the meat. Put a layer of sauerkraut in a pan, then a layer of meat, and repeat until you have used all the ingredients, with the pig's trotter, bacon cubes and onion on top. Pour on the wine, and add enough water to cover two-thirds of the ingredients. Simmer with a tight lid on the pan for 1—2 hours. Now add the sliced sausage and cook for a further 20 minutes without the lid. Arrange the sauerkraut in a big dish and garnish nicely with the sliced meat and sausage. Serve with potatoes.

BASLE COOKIES

1½ *lb. honey*
2 *lb. flour*
1 *lb. chopped almonds*
1 *lb. sugar*
4 *oz. chopped candied peel*
juice of ½ *lemon*
6 *tablespoons Kirsch*
1 *oz. cinnamon*
1 *teaspoon baking powder*

GLAZING:

4 *oz. icing sugar*
1 *egg white*
1 *tablespoon lemon juice*

This recipe will make a very large quantity of the cookies — a speciality of Basle. For a smaller quantity halve all ingredients.

Cook the honey and sugar in a very big pan over a low heat. Add the other ingredients little by little until all are blended in. It is important to stir the paste continuously. Now flour a slab or board and put part of the paste on it. Roll out to approximately ½ inch thick and cut into shapes. The paste must remain warm while working with it, otherwise it will get hard and impossible to handle. Leave the cookies overnight and next day put them in a very low oven to dry completely. Take out and paint the glazing over them while they are still warm. To make glazing beat the egg white and combine with icing sugar and lemon juice.

CARROT CAKE

4—6 *eggs*
8 *oz. sugar*
8 *oz. chopped almonds*
6 *oz. raw chopped carrots*
2 *oz. self-raising flour*
grated rind of 1 *lemon*
1 *small glass Kirsch*

LEMON ICING:

12 *oz. icing sugar*
1½ *tablespoons water*
2 *tablespoons lemon juice*
grated rind of 1 *lemon*

Beat the sugar, lemon rind and egg yolks for 15 minutes. Add the almonds, carrots, and flour. Then add the stiffly beaten egg whites and the Kirsch and beat all together. Put the mixture into a well-greased cake tin and bake in a very moderate oven for 1 hour. Ice with lemon icing when cold. This is made by mixing together all ingredients with a palette knife until smooth.

This cake improves with keeping, and is best eaten 2—3 days after baking.

CHEESE CAKE

8 *oz. flour*
6 *oz. butter*
1 *egg yolk*
8 *oz. cream cheese*
1 *oz. candied peel*
1 *oz. currants*
rind and juice of ½ *lemon*
2 *eggs*

2 *oz. sugar*

Make a dough with the flour, butter and egg yolk and roll it out. Line a 10-inch tart tin. Cream the cheese with the egg yolks, grated lemon peel, lemon juice, sugar, currants and peel. Fold in the beaten egg whites. Fill the tart tin with this mixture. Bake in a moderately hot oven for 30 minutes.

COOKING IN THE UNITED STATES OF AMERICA

It is very tricky to generalise or pass judgement on the kitchen of a large country where so many diverse influences have built up the national gastronomy as in the United States of America. The foundation of their kitchen, I believe, is English, but this is really no more than the foundation stone upon which many nationalities have built the skyscraper we call American cooking.

Among the most pleasing features of hospitality in the U. S. A. are the dainty canapés and appetisers which you will find in great variety. Americans serve these lovely little tit-bits every time they offer you a drink too — they made me blush with shame at the thought of the peanuts and cheese biscuits I usually offer at cocktail time. The American housewife or 'homemaker' as she is called, may be a busy career woman, but she takes endless trouble in the prettiness of her food as well as its taste.

The famous Chowders are supposed to have originated in the fishermen's cottages in Newfoundland but have become as American as the Stars and Stripes — rich and tasty soups well worth trying. All the American sea-food recipes are outstandingly good though Lobster Newburg is the best known of all.

You will find many other favourites of American cookery in the following chapter, from Corned Beef Hash to Upside-down Cake. Let me just point out a few winners. During the winter, when lettuces are getting tasteless and insipid, I suggest you turn to the American Cole Slaw for consolation. Cole Slaw is simply a raw cabbage salad which combines freshness with something more solid to bite into than lettuce. For an attractive and substantial cold buffet it is safe to look among the American recipes — they have the most original and delicious ideas on the subject.

Cakes, puddings and pies all will give you an ideal sweet course — the most characteristically American is of course their chiffon pie, for which you will find two very good recipes on the following pages.

AVOCADO COCKTAIL

2 avocado pears
French dressing (see p. 161)
1 tablespoon chopped parsley

Peel and slice the avocados. Pour the dressing over them. Chill. Serve sprinkled with parsley.

BACON AND TOMATO CANAPÉS

8 oz. tomatoes
4 rashers bacon
salt
paprika
1 dessertspoon brown sugar
4 slices buttered toast

Peel and slice the tomatoes. Lay the slices on the buttered toast, cover with the bacon. Season with salt, paprika and brown sugar and cook under a hot grill until the bacon is crisp.

CHEESE BREAD CUBES

4 oz. grated cheese
1 egg
cayenne pepper
salt
2 oz. butter
4 slices bread

Cut the bread into cubes. Melt the butter and mix it with the egg. Roll the bread in this mixture and then in the grated cheese. Sprinkle lightly with cayenne pepper and salt. Grease a baking tray and bake the cubes in a hot oven until the cheese is melted.

CURLED CHEESE CANAPÉS

4 slices white bread
4 oz. grated cheese
butter
Worcester sauce

Spread the butter on the bread, sprinkle with grated cheese and a few drops of sauce. Roll; cook quickly under a hot grill until crisp.

MELON MINT COCKTAIL

2 oz. sugar
3 tablespoons chopped mint
juice of 1 lemon
juice of 1 orange
1 slice water melon
1 slice cantaloupe melon

Boil the sugar with $\frac{1}{4}$ pint water for 5 minutes. Pour over the mint. Mix the orange and lemon juice. Cut small balls out of the melon slices. Chill. Add to the drink just before serving.

SHELLFISH CANAPÉS

1 *lobster or 2 crabs, cooked*
8 *egg yolks, hard-boiled*
4 *oz. melted butter*
¼ *pint double cream*
cayenne pepper
mustard
salt

Cut the meat off the lobster or crabs. Mix with the eggs, pass through a sieve. Beat in the melted butter and cream. Season with salt, cayenne pepper and dry mustard. Spread on slices of toast.

TOASTED CANAPÉS

A great variety of fillings can be used for these. The three following are typical.

TOASTED CREAM CHEESE CANAPÉS

3 *oz. cream cheese*
1 *tablespoon cream*
1 *tablespoon finely chopped celery*
1 *teaspoon chives, chopped*
salt, pepper

Beat the cheese and the cream together until smooth. Add the celery and chives. Season with salt and pepper. Spread this mixture on to thin slices of bread, roll the bread and secure it with a wooden stick. Toast under a hot grill.

TOASTED MUSHROOM CANAPÉS

4 *oz. mushrooms*
¼ *pint thick white sauce*
1 *oz. butter*

Cut the mushrooms into very thin slices, cook them slowly in the butter. Mix into the white sauce. Spread on thin slices of bread, roll them up and fasten with a cocktail stick. Toast under a hot grill.

TOASTED SARDINE CANAPÉS

1 *tin sardines*
½ *teaspoon Worcester sauce*
½ *teaspoon tomato sauce*
1 *tablespoon chopped onion*
4 *green olives, stoned and chopped*
1 *tablespoon French dressing (see p. 161)*

paprika
salt

Skin and bone the sardines. Mix the other ingredients, beating them until they will spread easily. Spread the mixture on slices of bread. Roll them and secure with cocktail sticks. Toast under a hot grill.

TOMATO JUICE COCKTAIL

1 *pint tomato juice*
1 *small onion, finely chopped*
1 *teaspoon lemon juice*
1 *tablespoon wine vinegar*
½ *bay leaf*

celery salt
1 *tablespoon sugar*

Put all the ingredients into a jug. Mix thoroughly, leave to stand for at least 2 hours. Strain, serve very cold.

PINEAPPLE COCKTAIL

1 *pineapple*
3 *oz. sugar*
1 *tablespoon chopped mint*

Peel and dice the pineapple. Boil the sugar with ¼ pint water for 5 minutes. Pour over the pineapple. Chill. Add the mint.

COCKTAIL SHRIMPS

shrimps
white cabbage

Cut enough off the bottom of a large white cabbage to enable it to stand up safely. Put a cocktail stick through each shrimp and stick them in the cabbage.

CLAM CHOWDER

1 *pint clams or mussels*
2 *large potatoes, cubed*
2 *oz. fat salt pork*
1 *sliced onion*
2 *oz. butter*
4 *oz. flour*
1 *pint milk*
4 *dry biscuits*
salt, pepper

Clean the clams and cook in ½ pint of water. Strain, keep the water. Chop the hard clam flesh into dice. Fry the onion in the pork fat. Parboil the potatoes. Put a layer of potatoes followed by a layer of chopped clams into a casserole. Season with salt and pepper. Sprinkle flour on top. Cover with another layer of potatoes and more flour. Pour in ½ pint boiling water, simmer for 20 minutes. Add the milk, the soft part of the clams and the butter. Boil for 3 minutes. Add the biscuits, soaked in milk. Thicken the water the clams were cooked in with a roux. Add this to the chowder just before serving.

CORN CHOWDER

8 *oz. streaky bacon*
1 *sliced onion*
2 *sticks celery, chopped*
2 *green peppers, chopped*
2 *potatoes, diced*
2 *cups sweet corn*
4 *oz. flour*
½ *pint milk*
parsley
bay leaf
paprika
salt

Chop the bacon into small pieces. Fry until lightly brown, add the onion, celery and green pepper and fry them. Put in the potatoes and 2 pints of water. Season with salt, paprika and half a bay leaf. Simmer until the potatoes are cooked. Mix the flour with half the milk, pour the soup into this, stirring all the time. Pour it back into the saucepan and bring to the boil. Add the rest of the milk and the corn, reheat but do not boil. Serve in hot plates sprinkled with parsley.

OYSTER OR CLAM BISQUE

1 *quart oysters or clams (mussels can be used)*
1 *pint milk*
1 *sliced onion*
2 *sticks celery*
2 *oz. butter*
2 *oz. flour*
nutmeg
parsley
bay leaf

salt, pepper

Simmer cleaned shellfish for 20 minutes in water. Drain and sieve the fish. Melt butter, fry chopped onion and celery lightly and add flour. Cook for 1 minute, gradually add the water in which the oysters were cooked. Heat the milk, flavour it with nutmeg, parsley and ½ a bay leaf. Pour the fish sauce and the milk over the sieved oysters, reheat and serve at once.

VEGETABLE CHOWDER

1 *lb. beef bone*
1 *lb. veal bone*
1 *lb. brisket of beef*
1 *large onion*
1 *large tin tomatoes*
1 *head celery, chopped*
1 *lb. carrots, sliced*
8 *oz. runner beans, sliced*
8 *oz. noodles*

parsley
salt, pepper

Simmer the meat, bones and onion in 4 pints water for 2 hours. Add the vegetables, season with salt and pepper. Simmer till vegetables are tender. Remove the bones, sieve the soup. Add the noodles, and extra water if necessary, and cook for another 20 minutes. Serve sprinkled with chopped parsley.

VICHYSSOISE

3 *medium-sized leeks, sliced finely*
1 *medium-sized onion, sliced finely*
4 *medium-sized potatoes, sliced*
  finely
2 *oz. butter*
2 *pints chicken stock*
¼ *pint cream*
4 *oz. watercress, chopped*

salt, pepper

Fry the leeks and onions slowly in the butter until transparent. Add the potatoes and the stock. Season with salt and pepper. Simmer until the potatoes are cooked. Pass through a fine sieve. Stir in the cream and the watercress. This can be served hot, but it is even better chilled.

CRAB STRETCH

2 *dressed crabs*
8 *oz. mushrooms*
½ *pint milk*
1 *oz. butter*
1 *oz. flour*
4 *oz. breadcrumbs*
4 *oz. grated cheese*

salt, pepper

Cook the sliced mushrooms in 1 oz. butter for 15 minutes. Add the flour, cook for 1 minute. Gradually add the milk. Season with salt and pepper. Add the crab to the sauce. Pour into a casserole, cover with breadcrumbs and sprinkle with grated cheese. Cook in a hot oven for 20 minutes.

FISH HASH

1 *lb. cold flaked fish*
1 *lb. cold diced potatoes*
salt, pepper
cooking fat

Mix the fish and potatoes. (Halibut is particularly good for this dish, but less expensive fish will do e. g. fresh haddock.) If haddock is used, season with parsley and lemon juice. Put a little fat in a heavy frying pan, put the potatoes and fish into it and cook until crisp and brown underneath. Fold over like a pancake.

HADDOCK WITH CORN

1 *smoked haddock*
1 *tin sweet corn*
¼ *pint milk*
pepper
4 *oz. grated cheese*
1 *oz. flour*
1 *oz. butter*

Cook the fish gently in the milk. Remove the bones and the skin. Put the fish in a casserole covered with the corn form which the liquid has been drained. Melt the butter, cook the flour in it for 1 minute, stir in the juice from the corn and the milk. Pour this over the fish, season with pepper, cover with grated cheese. Cook in a hot oven for 20 minutes.

LOBSTER À L'AMÉRICAINE

1 *lobster*
1 *small onion, finely chopped*
¼ *pint tomato sauce*
½ *glass sherry*
butter
salt
cayenne pepper

Make tomato sauce by mixing a tin of tomatoes into a roux of flour and butter and passing through a sieve.

Split the lobster, cover each half with onion and a little cayenne pepper. Cook in a little butter for 5 minutes in a large frying pan. Add the tomato sauce and cook for 3 minutes more. Add the sherry and cook for another 7 minutes. Strain the sauce over the lobster before serving.

LOBSTER NEWBURG

2 *lb. lobster, boiled*
4 *oz. butter*
1 *tablespoon sherry*
1 *tablespoon brandy*
2 *egg yolks*
¼ *pint cream*
salt

cayenne pepper
grated nutmeg

Shred the lobster meat and cook it in the butter for 3 minutes. Add the sherry and brandy, mixed with the egg yolks, and cook for 1 minute. Add the cream and seasoning. Put back into the shells before serving.

NEW ORLEANS SHRIMPS

2 *lb. fresh shrimps*
1 *sliced onion*
1 *clove garlic*
1 *bay leaf*
2 *sticks celery*
1 *teaspoon salt*
cayenne pepper
½ *lemon*

MARINADE:

½ *cup finely chopped celery*
1 *spring onion, finely chopped*
1 *tablespoon chopped chives*
5 *tablespoons horseradish*

2 *tablespoons made mustard*
¼ *teaspoon paprika*
6 *tablespoons olive oil*
1 *clove garlic crushed with salt*
3 *tablespoons lemon juice*

Simmer the onion, garlic, bay leaf and celery in 4 pints salted water with a pinch of cayenne pepper for 15 minutes. Add the lemon. Cook the shrimps in this for 15 minutes and allow them to cool in the pan. Shell and clean the shrimps. Leave the shrimps for about 6 hours in the marinade.

Drain the shrimps and serve cold with brown bread and butter.

PLANKED SHAD

4 *herrings (the nearest British equivalent to shad)*
2 *oz. melted butter*
1 *lemon*
parsley
salt
pepper

Split the herrings, put them on a plank (see p. 421) open side upwards. Season with salt and pepper. Brush with melted butter. Cook under a hot grill for 7 minutes. Serve with chopped parsley and slices of lemon.

SCROD

1 *lb. scrod (cod steaks are a good substitute)*
breadcrumbs
melted butter
salt, pepper
parsley butter

Remove the head and tail of the fish and the backbone. Dip in melted butter, then in breadcrumbs. Cook under a hot grill for 15 minutes on one side and 5 on the other. Spread with parsley butter (i. e. parsley beaten up with butter, lemon juice, salt and pepper).

BAKED POTATOES STUFFED WITH MINCED HAM

8 *oz. cooked ham*
¼ *pint milk*
2 *oz. flour*
2 *oz. butter*
parsley, chopped
paprika
4 *oz. grated cheese*
4 *baked potatoes*

Grease the skins of the potatoes and bake in a medium hot oven for 1 hour. Cut them in halves, scoop out the middle and mix with the following mixture.

THE STUFFING:
Melt the butter, add the flour and cook for 1 minute. Add the milk gradually and stir until it thickens. Stir in the ham and the parsley. Season with salt and paprika. Stuff the potatoes with the mixture, sprinkle with grated cheese and bake in a hot oven for 20 minutes.

BAKED POTATOES STUFFED WITH BEEF

1 *oz. butter*
1 *tablespoon cream*
8 *oz. minced beef, cooked*
1 *small onion, minced*
1 *tablespoon parsley, minced*
1 *stick celery, minced*
1 *teaspoon Worcester sauce*
paprika

salt
4 *baked potatoes*
4 *oz. grated cheese*

Prepare the potatoes as for 'Potatoes Stuffed with Ham' (see above). Mix all the other ingredients and fill the potatoes with them. Sprinkle with grated cheese. Bake in a hot oven for 20 minutes.

BOSTON BAKED BEANS

1 *lb. small haricot beans*
8 *oz. fat bacon*
2 *oz. brown sugar*
1 *tablespoon black treacle*
½ *teaspoon made mustard*
salt

Soak the beans for 12 hours in cold water. Drain and cover with fresh water. Simmer until skins are soft (they should burst if blown on). Cut a slice from the bacon, put it in the bottom of a casserole. Cut the rind off the rest of the bacon and cut the bacon into pieces. Put the beans in the casserole, mix them with the bacon, sugar, treacle, mustard and salt. Put the bacon rind on the top. Cover the beans with boiling water and cook in a slow oven with lid on for 8 hours.

CHICKEN À LA KING

1 *lb. cooked diced chicken*
8 *oz. cooked mushrooms*
1 *small tin pimentos*
2 *oz. butter or chicken fat*
3 *oz. flour*
½ *pint chicken stock*
1 *egg yolk*
8 *oz. chopped almonds*
½ *glass sherry*

salt, pepper

Melt the butter in a saucepan, stir in the flour and cook for 1 minute, add the stock gradually. When the sauce has thickened stir in the chicken, pimentos and mushrooms. Cool the mixture and add the egg yolk, stir over a low flame until the sauce is thick. Add the almonds and the sherry. Season with salt and pepper.

CHICKEN TETRAZZI

8 *oz. macaroni*
8 *oz. mushrooms*
3 *oz. butter*
2 *oz. flour*
½ *pint chicken stock*
¼ *pint double cream*
1 *wine-glass sherry*
4 *oz. grated Parmesan cheese*
4 *oz. chopped almonds*
1½ *lb. cold cooked chicken*

Cook the macaroni (see p. 266). Slice the mushrooms and cook gently in 1 oz. butter. Make a sauce with 2 oz. butter, 2 oz. flour and ½ pint stock. Add the wine and simmer for 1 minute, stir in the cream. Mix half the sauce with the chicken, mushrooms and almonds. Put the macaroni in an ovenproof dish, leaving a hole in the middle. Pour the chicken mixture into the hole, sprinkle with grated cheese and bake in a moderate oven until brown.

CHILLI CON CARNE

8 *oz. minced beef*
1 *chopped onion*
1 *clove garlic*
2 *oz. bacon fat*
1 *tablespoon flour*
1 *tablespoon chilli powder*
8 *oz. shelled broad beans*

1 *small tin concentrated tomato*
  purée

Melt the fat, add the onion and garlic and cook until the onion is transparent. Put in the beef and stir until each piece is browned. Add the flour and cook for 1 minute. Add the other ingredients and ½ pint water, cook slowly for 1½ hours.

CORNED BEEF HASH

8 *oz. corned beef*
4 *medium-sized potatoes*
1 *medium-sized onion*
½ *green pepper*
Worcester sauce
2 *oz. butter*
2 *tablespoons flour*
¼ *pint stock*

Boil the potatoes and the onions. Drain. Dice the potatoes and slice the onion. Dice the corned beef. Take the seeds from the pepper and chop it. Make a thick sauce with the butter, flour and stock. Mix the vegetables and meat with the sauce. Fry in a little fat until the underneath is crisp and brown.

FLUFFY EGG NEST

1 *egg per person*
1 *slice toast*
pepper
grated cheese or a slice of ham
salt

Butter the toast and cover it with grated cheese or a slice of ham. Arrange the stiffly beaten egg white on the toast, leave a hole in the middle, slide the egg yolk into the hole. Sprinkle with salt and pepper. Cook in a very hot oven until the white is golden and the yolk is set.

FORT LINCOLN

2 *oz. bacon fat*
2 *oz. flour*
salt
pepper
½ *pint milk*
chopped cold pork (about 1 lb.)
parsley

mashed potatoes

Melt the bacon fat, make a thick white sauce with the flour and milk. Season with salt and pepper, add the pork. Make a border of mashed potatoes, put the pork mixture in the middle of it. Garnish with chopped parsley.

MINCED HAM ON PINEAPPLE SLICES

8 *oz. cooked minced ham*
2 *tablespoons mayonnaise (see*
 p. 161)
1 *teaspoon made mustard*
4 *slices fresh pineapple*

Blend the ham, mayonnaise and mustard. Spread this mixture on slices of pineapple. Bake in a hot oven for 10 minutes.

MUSHROOMS À LA KING

8 *oz. sliced mushrooms*
1 *head celery*
1 *hard-boiled egg*
6 *stuffed olives*
½ *pint thin cream*
2 *oz. butter*
2 *oz. flour*
½ *glass sherry*

paprika
salt

Cook the mushrooms in a little butter. Chop the celery and boil it in salted water. Slice the hard-boiled eggs. Make a sauce with the butter, flour and cream. Add the other ingredients to it. Serve buttered toast.

RICE RING

8 *oz. rice*
2 *oz. melted butter*
nutmeg
salt

Cook the rice in a pan of boiling salted water, strain when it is nearly cooked but still hard in the centre of each grain. Put it in a greased ring mould, pour the melted butter over it and bake in a moderate oven for 20 minutes. Loosen the rice at the sides and turn it out on to a plate. Fill the centre with creamed chicken, creamed mushrooms or any other meat, fish or vegetable in a thick white sauce.

SOUTHERN CORN PUDDING

1 *tin sweet corn or 2 cups corn*
 from the cob
2 *slightly beaten eggs*
1 *teaspoon sugar*
2 *oz. melted butter*
½ *pint hot milk*

salt, pepper

Chop the corn if tinned, grate if raw. Mix with the other ingredients. Season with salt and pepper. Pour into a greased ovenproof dish. Bake in a slow oven for 1 hour.

SPAGHETTI WITH SEA FOOD

8 oz. spaghetti
1 tin concentrated tomato purée
2 oz. butter
1 onion, chopped
1 green pepper, chopped
2 oz. flour
½ pint stock
8 oz. cheese, diced

8 oz. diced cooked lobster, crab or
  shrimps

Melt the butter and cook the chopped onion and green pepper in it for 10 minutes. Add the flour, and when it has cooked, stir in the stock gradually. Heat the tomato purée and add it to the sauce, stir in the cheese and when it has melted add the fish. Serve mixed with spaghetti (see p. 266).

BAKED HAM (1)

a ham weighing 10—14 lb.

The same treatment can be given to small pieces of 'boiling bacon' weighing 2 lb. or so.

Soak the ham for 6—12 hours according to how salty it is.

Put it into a pan, fat side upwards, and bake in a slow oven allowing 52 minutes per lb. for a 10—12 lb. ham. If it is larger it will take less time per lb., if smaller it will take longer.

Remove from the pan 45 minutes before it is cooked, take off the skin and cover with any of the following glazes:
1. Brown sugar mixed with the hot ham fat.
2. 8 oz. brown sugar mixed with 2 oz. bread-crumbs.
3. 8 oz. brown sugar mixed with 2 tablespoons wine vinegar or cider.

BAKED HAM (2)

Cook the ham as for baked ham (1), but baste with one of the following sauces when the skin has been removed:
1. Mix the juice of 2 oranges with ¼ pint pine-apple juice and 4 oz. sugar. Simmer until the sugar has dissolved.
2. Mix ½ pint cider with pineapple juice or any other fruit juice available; simmer together for a few minutes.
3. Mix the juice of 1 orange and 1 lemon with 4 oz. sugar and cook until sugar dissolves.

BARBECUED HAM

2 *lb. slice gammon*
1 *onion, chopped*
2 *tablespoons Worcester sauce*
¼ *pint wine vinegar*
1 *teaspoon mustard*

1 *tablespoon red currant jelly*
1 *teaspoon brown sugar*

Heat the vinegar, add the other ingredients, stir until they are all well mixed. Put the bacon on a grid, pour the sauce over it, bake in a medium hot oven with a lid on the pan for 2 hours, basting frequently.

HAM STEAKS AND CORN FRITTERS

4 *ham steaks weighing 6 oz. each*
  (slices of gammon are a good
  choice)
3 *tablespoons flour*
paprika
1 *oz. butter*
½ *pint milk*
1 *teaspoon Worcester sauce*
2 *tomatoes*
parsley

Melt the butter, fry each slice of ham on both sides to seal juices. Remove ham to an ovenproof dish. Stir the flour into the pan, cook for 1 minute, add the milk gradually, season with Worcester sauce and paprika. Pour the sauce over the ham, cook in a slow oven for 20 minutes. Garnish with slices of tomato and chopped parsley. Serve with Corn Fritters (see p. 427).

HAMBURGERS

1 *lb. beef, minced*
1 *small onion, minced*
salt, pepper
2 *oz. butter*

Mix the meat and onion, season with salt and pepper. Shape into flat cakes an inch thick. Melt the butter, cook the cakes quickly on each side, reduce the heat, cover the pan and cook slowly for 20 minutes.

CREOLE LAMB CHOPS

4 *lamb chops*
1 *sliced onion*
1 *small tin concentrated tomato*
  purée
1 *oz. flour*
2 *oz. dripping*

salt, pepper

Flour the chops and season with salt and pepper. Melt the dripping and brown the chops in it. Cover them with onion, add the tomato purée and 1 pint water. Cover the pan and bake in a slow oven for 1½ hours.

LIVER DUMPLINGS

1 *lb. calves' liver*
2 *eggs*
2 *oz. butter*
1 *small onion, chopped*
2 *oz. flour*
2 *slices white bread*
salt, pepper
parsley

Mince the liver. Soak the bread for 2 minutes, squeeze out the water and mix with the liver. Separate the egg yolks, mix them with the butter, beat into the meat mixture with the flour and the onion.

Season with salt, pepper and parsley. Whisk the egg whites and fold them into the mixture. Shape into balls and cook gently in a saucepan of boiling stock.

PLANKED STEAK

1½ *lb. fillet steak*
mashed potato
butter
parsley

In New England fish and meat are often cooked in this way. A plank is an oak board one inch thick. When new it should be brushed with oil and left in a warm oven for 1 hour. It should be wiped and scraped after use, not washed.

Fry the steak in a little butter for a short time on each side in order to seal the juices. Lay it on the plank, surrounded by mashed potato. Cook in a hot oven until the meat is tender (about 20 minutes). Garnish with melted butter and chopped parsley.

NEW ENGLAND BOILED DINNER

5 *lb. round beef*
3 *parsnips*
6 *carrots*
3 *turnips*
4 *onions*
6 *potatoes*

1 *medium cabbage*
parsley

Simmer the meat for 3 hours in salted water. Add the sliced root vegetables and cook for another 45 minutes. Shred the cabbage and cook again for 15 minutes. Serve with cooked beetroot.

PORK CHOPS WITH PINEAPPLE

4 *pork chops*
1 *oz. butter or bacon fat*
salt, pepper
4 *slices pineapple*

Melt the fat. Fry the chops quickly on both sides. Put them in a casserole, season with salt and pepper. Arrange pineapple on top. Bake in a moderate oven for 45 minutes.

BARBECUED SPARE RIBS

2 lb. pork spare ribs (2 lb. pork
   loin)
1 onion, chopped
1 oz. dripping
2 tablespoons wine vinegar
1 tablespoon Worcester sauce
juice of 2 lemons
1 tablespoon brown sugar
¼ pint chilli sauce
½ teaspoon salt
paprika

Put the meat in a pan, cover with greaseproof paper
and bake in a hot oven for 15 minutes. Make the
sauce described below. Remove the paper and pour
it over the meat. Cook in a medium hot oven for
1 hour, basting frequently.

THE SAUCE:
Melt the dripping and cook the onions until brown,
add ½ pint water and the other ingredients, simmer
for 20 minutes.

STUFFED PORK SPARE RIBS

2 matching spare ribs (2 lb.
   pork loin)
flour
salt, pepper

APPLE STUFFING:
4 oz. fat salt pork, diced
   (substitute streaky bacon)
1 stick celery, chopped
1 onion, chopped
4 oz. breadcrumbs
2 tablespoons parsley
5 cooking apples, peeled and
   chopped
4 oz. sugar

Put one chop (or half the loin) on a rack in a baking
tin, spread the stuffing over it, put the other chop
(or the other half loin) on top. Sprinkle with salt
and pepper, dredge with flour. Cook in a hot oven
for 20 minutes and more slowly for another hour.
Baste with the fat in the pan.

THE STUFFING:
Put the pork fat in a pan and cook until it liquefies.
Remove the hard pieces. Cook the celery and onion
in the fat for 3 minutes. Add the apples, parsley and
sugar. Put a lid on the pan and cook for 20 minutes.
Cook again without lid to reduce liquid. Add the
breadcrumbs, season with salt and pepper.

FRIED CHICKEN

1 roasting chicken weighing
   2½ lb.
4 oz. flour
salt
pepper
1 egg
¼ pint milk
4 oz. breadcrumbs
4 oz. butter

Cut the chicken into small portions. Season the
flour, roll the chicken, first in this, then in the egg,
then in the breadcrumbs. Melt the fat, brown the
chicken pieces in it. Add ¼ pint water, cover the pan
and cook in a slow oven for about 1 hour. Thicken
the gravy with flour, and add more chicken stock
if required.

MARYLAND CHICKEN

1 *roasting chicken (about 3½ lb.)*
4 *oz. flour*
salt
paprika
1 *egg*
4 *oz. breadcrumbs*
4 *oz. butter*
½ *pint milk*

Season the flour with salt and paprika. Roll the chicken in it. Beat the egg with a little water, cover the chicken first with this, then with the breadcrumbs which should first be dried in the oven. Melt the fat, put in the chicken, brown it all over, cover with a lid and cook slowly for 45 minutes.

Make a sauce for it by thickening the fat in which it has cooked with flour and gradually adding milk.

SMOTHERED PIGEONS

4 *small pigeons*
4 *oz. flour*
4 *oz. butter*
1 *chopped onion*
1 *sliced carrot*
2 *sticks celery, sliced*
½ *pint chicken stock*
parsley

salt, pepper

Dredge the pigeons in flour seasoned with salt and pepper. Melt the butter, brown the pigeons on both sides. Add the vegetables, stir them about until well covered with fat. Pour in the stock, cover the pan, cook in a medium hot oven for about an hour. Season if necessary, garnish with chopped parsley.

FRIED SPRING CHICKEN

2 *spring chickens*
salt
paprika
2 *oz. flour*
4 *oz. butter*
¼ *pint thin cream*
parsley

Cut the chickens in half. Season with salt and paprika, dredge with flour. Melt the fat, brown the chickens on each side quickly, leave to cook more slowly in the same pan for 30 minutes. Thicken the fat in the pan with flour, add the cream gradually. Serve garnished with parsley.

ROAST STUFFED TURKEY

1 *turkey weighing 12—14 lb.*

STUFFING:

3 *dozen cooked oysters*
1 *lb. bread*
liver of the turkey
2 *oz. butter*
2 *tablespoons parsley*
1 *teaspoon thyme*
1 *bay leaf*

1 *leaf sage*
salt, pepper

Chop the liver and cook it in the butter until brown. Soak the bread in a little water, squeeze out the water. Mix the bread with the liver, add the chopped herbs. Cook for 1 minute. Add the oysters. Season with salt and pepper, cook for 5 minutes. Stuff the turkey and roast in the usual way. Serve with cranberry sauce.

AVOCADO SALAD

2 *avocado pears, peeled and
  sliced*
1 *oz. gelatine*
juice of 1 lemon
1 *teaspoon chopped onion*
lettuce
mayonnaise (see p. 161)

Make a jelly with the gelatine, lemon juice, chopped onion and ¾ pint water. When it starts to set, add the avocados. Pour into a ring mould. Chill. Serve with lettuce and mayonnaise.

CHICKEN AND CELERY SALAD

8 *slices cooked chicken breast*
4 *sticks celery, chopped*
1 *lettuce*
1 *teaspoon wine vinegar*
mayonnaise (see p. 161)

Mix the chicken and celery. Sprinkle with vinegar. Arrange on the lettuce, cover with mayonnaise. Serve chilled.

CHICKEN AND CHESTNUT SALAD

8 *oz. cold cooked chicken*
8 *oz. shelled cooked chestnuts*
3 *sticks celery, chopped*

1 *red pepper, sliced and seeded*
mayonnaise (see p. 161)

Mix the ingredients carefully together, then mix them with the mayonnaise.

CHICKEN AND OYSTER SALAD

8 *slices cooked chicken breast*
12 *oysters*
1 *lettuce*
mayonnaise (see p. 161)

Mix the chicken and oysters, arrange on the lettuce. Cover with mayonnaise. Serve chilled.

CHICKEN AND WALNUT SALAD

8 *slices cooked chicken breast*
4 *sticks celery, chopped*
12 *walnuts*
1 *oz. butter*

1 *lettuce*
mayonnaise (see p. 161)

Brown the walnuts in the butter, chop them, mix with the chicken and celery. Arrange on the lettuce, cover with mayonnaise. Serve chilled.

COLE SLAW

½ *white cabbage*
French dressing (see p. 161

Cut off the outside leaves of the cabbage, cut out the main stem and the thickest stems in the leaves. Shred and soak in cold water for 1 hour. Drain it and mix with French dressing. This can be varied by the addition of raw chopped apple and sultanas.

KENTUCKY SALAD

1 *pint mixed pineapple and lemon*
  juice
1 *oz. gelatine*
1 *dessertspoon tarragon vinegar*
1 *teaspoon sugar*
½ *cucumber, peeled and sliced*
½ *pineapple, diced*

lettuce
mayonnaise (see p. 161)

Make a jelly with the gelatine, fruit juices, sugar and vinegar. Stir in the cucumber and pineapple as it begins to set. Cut into slices.
   Arrange on lettuce leaves and decorate with the mayonnaise.

MIAMI SALAD

1 *lettuce*
2 *tangerines*
2 *tomatoes*
4 *slices lemon*
1 *tablespoon olive oil*

salt, pepper
sugar

Arrange the tangerine segments, sliced tomato and lemon on lettuce leaves. Dress with olive oil. Season with salt, pepper and sugar.

PINEAPPLE CHEESE SALAD

2 *oz. soft cream cheese*
1 *tablespoon mayonnaise (see*
  p. 161)
2 *slices pineapple, crushed*
1 *tablespoon icing sugar*
1 *gill double cream*
lettuce
pineapple to decorate

Beat the cream cheese until very soft. Beat in the mayonnaise, then the pineapple and icing sugar. Fold in the whipped cream. Freeze in the refrigerator. Cut into slices, serve on lettuce, decorated with pineapple.

SMITH SALAD

1 *cauliflower*
1 *round lettuce*
1 *cos lettuce*
1 *endive*
8 *oz. cooked runner beans*
4 *oz. watercress*
2 *oz. salami*
2 *rashers fried bacon*

6 *ancovy fillets*
4 *oz. Gruyère cheese*
French dressing (see p. 161)

Shred the lettuce and endive, chop the watercress, break the cauliflower into flowerets, slice the beans. Cut the cheese, salami, bacon and anchovy fillets into strips. Mix all ingredients together with French dressing 30 minutes before serving.

THOUSAND ISLAND DRESSING

4 *tablespoons olive oil*
juice of ½ orange
juice of ½ lemon
1 *teaspoon onion juice*
1 *tablespoon chopped parsley*
1 *teaspoon Worcester sauce*
salt

paprika
¼ *teaspoon made mustard*

Mix the olive oil with the fruit juice, add the onion juice, parsley and Worcester sauce. Season with salt, paprika and mustard. Shake thoroughly to blend the ingredients.

TOMATO, PINEAPPLE AND CELERY SALAD

4 *tomatoes*
2 *sticks celery*
2 *rings pineapple*
2 *oz. walnuts, chopped*
mayonnaise (see p. 161)

Cut the tops off the tomatoes, remove the pulp and seeds. Fill with the celery, pineapple and walnuts mixed with the mayonnaise.

WALDORF SALAD

1 *head celery, chopped*
3 *apples, peeled and sliced*
2 *bananas, sliced*
mayonnaise (see p. 161)
4 *oz. walnuts, chopped*

salt, pepper

Mix all the ingredients together, season with salt and pepper. Serve mayonnaise separately.

CORN FRITTERS

1 *tin Indian corn*
2 *beaten eggs*
4 *oz. flour*
½ *teaspoon baking powder*
8 *oz. butter*
salt
nutmeg

Drain and mash the corn, beat until light. Add the eggs, beat again. Stir in the baking powder and flour, season with salt and nutmeg. Melt the butter, drop tablespoons of the mixture into it and cook quickly on both sides.

CREOLE CABBAGE

1 *medium cabbage*
1 *onion*
1 *small tin tomatoes*
1 *green pepper, chopped and*
  seeded
3 *cloves*
½ *bay leaf*
1 *tablespoon brown sugar*

2 *oz. butter*
salt

Shred the cabbage, cook for 8 minutes in boiling salted water. Melt the butter and fry the chopped onion until golden, add the tomatoes, green pepper, cloves, bay leaf and brown sugar. Simmer for 15 minutes. Remove the cloves and bay leaf. Add the cabbage and re-heat.

HARVARD BEETROOT

3 *cooked beetroots*
4 *oz. sugar*
1 *oz. cornflour*
1 *glass wine vinegar*
2 *oz. butter*

Cook the sugar, cornflour and vinegar in a double saucepan, stirring until smooth. Slice the beetroot, mix with the sauce. Leave the beetroot in the hot sauce for 30 minutes. Add the butter just before serving.

HOT SLAW

1 *white cabbage*
½ *pint vinegar*
1 *teaspoon mustard*
1 *teaspoon salt*
1 *oz. butter*

3 *oz. sugar*
2 *egg yolks*

Simmer the vinegar with the mustard, salt, sugar and butter. Shred the cabbage, drain it and pour the hot sauce over it. Stir well, mix in the beaten egg yolks. Serve immediately.

CREAMED POTATO RING

cold mashed potatoes
white sauce (see p. 206)
butter
parsley
chives

salt, pepper

Beat the potatoes until they are soft, mix in the sauce, chopped chives and parsley. Season with salt and pepper. Bake the potato mixture in a ring mould for half an hour in a moderate oven.

BAKED PUMPKIN

1 pumpkin
2 oz. butter

Cut the pumpkin into quarters, remove the seeds. Bake in a moderate oven for 1½ hours. Serve with melted butter.

SPINACH WITH CREAM

2 lb. spinach
salt
nutmeg
1 oz. butter
½ pint double cream
2 tablespoons horseradish sauce
½ tablespoon made mustard

Wash the spinach and remove any hard stems. Cook without water for 30 minutes, drain very thoroughly. Sieve, add the butter. Season with salt, horseradish sauce and mustard. Whip the cream. Put the spinach in a dish, cover with the cream and brown quickly under a hot grill.

TOMATO COB

1½ lb. tomatoes
1 small onion
sugar
salt
pepper
¼ pint double cream

Mince the tomatoes and onion, season with salt and pepper and sugar if the tomatoes are not very ripe. Serve very cold, topped with whipped cream. The tomatoes can be additionally flavoured with mint and garlic.

STUFFED TOMATOES

4 large tomatoes
4 oz. cream cheese
2 oz. chopped walnuts
chives
parsley

Scoop out the flesh and the pips from the tomatoes. Salt them and leave upside down to drain for 15 minutes. Fill with cream cheese and walnuts mixed together. Garnish with chopped chives and parsley.

ANGEL CAKE

4 oz. flour
11 egg whites
10 oz. sugar
1 teaspoon cream of tartar
1 teaspoon vanilla, or a small
   piece of vanilla bean
¼ teaspoon salt

Sift the flour 4 times. Add the cream of tartar. Sift again. Sift the sugar 4 times. Add it to the flour. Beat the egg whites very stiff. Fold in the flour and sugar. Add the vanilla and salt. Bake in an angel cake tin in a moderate oven for 45 minute. Leave in the tin until cold. Turn out and cover with white icing.

DOUGHNUTS

1 egg
4 oz. sugar
¼ pint milk
1½ oz. cooking fat
8 oz. flour
2 tablespoons baking powder
½ teaspoon grated lemon peel
salt

Beat the egg, beat in the sugar and then the milk and melted fat. Sift the dry ingredients into a bowl with a pinch of salt. Beat in the liquids. If the dough is too thin to handle, chill it until it thickens. Roll the dough out until it is ¼ inch thick. Cut it into rounds. Cook in deep fat, turning over to cook on both sides. When cooked, dip into a pan of boiling water, then allow to dry in a moderate oven until crisp. Roll in sugar flavoured with cinnamon if liked.

MUFFINS

4 oz. flour
¾ teaspoon salt
2 oz. sugar
3 teaspoons baking powder
2 eggs
1 oz. melted butter
½ pint milk (scant)

Sift the dry ingredients twice. Beat the eggs, mix them with the flour. Beat in the milk and butter. Pour into small greased tins or paper cases. Cook in a hot oven for 15 minutes. These can be served accompanied by sweet or savoury flavourings: e. g. apple sauce or fried bacon.

APRICOT UPSIDE-DOWN CAKE

1 lb. apricots
4 oz. sugar
2 oz. butter
8 oz. self-raising flour
4 eggs
4 oz. sugar
½ oz. melted butter
salt

Melt the butter, add the sugar, stirring until dissolved, pour into the bottom of a cake tin. Stone the apricots and put them in the tin on top of the sugar. Make a cake mixture as follows and pour it into the tin on top of the fruit.

Beat the egg yolks. Add the melted butter to them. Whip the egg whites, fold in the sugar and then the egg and butter mixture. Fold in the sifted flour very gently. Bake in a moderate oven for 45 minutes. Turn it out.

POPOVERS

4 oz. flour
2 eggs
½ oz. melted butter
½ pint milk (scant)
salt

Sieve the flour with a pinch of salt. Beat in the eggs, and the milk and butter. Stir this mixture slowly into the flour. Grease small ovenproof dishes, fill them one third full. Bake in a hot oven for 10 minutes. Prick the tops to let out the steam.

BAVARIAN CREAM

½ pint milk
2 eggs
2 oz. sugar
2 oz. icing sugar
1 oz. gelatine
½ pint double cream
sponge fingers or macaroons
vanilla

Soak the gelatine in a cup of cold water. Put the egg yolks and 2 oz. sugar into a double saucepan. Gradually add hot milk, stirring until the mixture thickens. Mix with the gelatine. Beat the egg whites until they are stiff. Whip the cream, beat the cream and white of egg into gelatine mixture. Pour carefully into a glass dish and leave until set. Decorate with pieces of sponge fingers or macaroons. These can be used to line dish if preferred.

BROWN BETTY

4 oz. breadcrumbs
4 oz. melted butter
2 lb. apples peeled, cored and sliced
juice and grated rind of ½ lemon
4 oz. brown sugar
1 teaspoon cinnamon

Mix butter and breadcrumbs together. Butter a pie dish. Cover the bottom with one third of the breadcrumb mixture. Mix the apples with the sugar, cinnamon and lemon juice and rind. Put half the apple mixture in the dish, cover with another layer of breadcrumbs, the rest of the apple and lastly the rest of the breadcrumbs. Bake in a moderate oven for 1 hour.

CHILLED FRUIT SALAD

1 egg yolk
2 oz. sugar
juice of 1 lemon
salt
3 slices tinned pineapple, diced
½ small tin cherries
4 oz. grapes, peeled and seeded

2 oz. almonds, blanched and chopped
1 gill single cream

Mix the sugar, cream and egg yolk with a pinch of salt. Cook in a double saucepan until thick. Mix with the other ingredients. Leave in a refrigerator for 24 hours. Serve on lettuce leaves with mayonnaise (see p. 161), or as a sweet with whipped cream.

COFFEE CHIFFON CREAM PIE

pie crust as for apple pie (see below)
1 *tablespoon gelatine*
¾ *pint hot strong coffee*
¼ *pint milk*
8 *oz. sugar*
3 *eggs*

Dissolve th gelatine in a cup of water. Add the hot coffee, 4 oz. sugar and the milk. Beat the egg yolks with the rest of the sugar over hot water. Add the gelatine mixture gradually. Put it into a double saucepan, stirring continually while it thickens. Cool slightly. Fold in the stiffly beaten egg whites. Pour into baked pie crust when cool. Serve very cold with whipped cream.

COFFEE MARSHMALLOW CREAM

1 *lb. marshmallows*
½ *pint strong coffee*
½ *pint double cream, whipped*
4 *oz. chopped walnuts*

Cut the marshmallows into pieces. Melt them in the coffee. Fold in the cream. Pour into a ring mould. Chill. Turn out and decorate with walnuts.

DOUBLE CRUST APPLE PIE

6 *apples peeled, cored and thinly sliced*
1 *oz. sugar*
8 *oz. flour*
salt
1 *teaspoon baking powder*
4 *oz. lard*
2 *oz. butter*

Divide the fat into two parts. Sieve the flour with the baking powder and a pinch of salt. Cut half the fat into the flour until the pieces of fat are very small. Cut in the rest more roughly. Mix with water. Roll on a floured board. Set aside for at least an hour. Divide into two parts. Roll half the pastry and line a tart tin with it. If the apples are very juicy, spread melted butter over the pastry to prevent it from becoming soggy. Cover the pastry with the apples, sugar and dots of butter. Roll the rest of the pastry, cover the apples with it. The top crust should be larger than the dish and slightly folded to allow for shrinking. Prick the top with a fork. Brush with milk or white of egg. Bake in a hot oven for 10 minutes and more slowly for another 35 minutes.

FLOATING ISLAND

3 *eggs*
5 *oz. sugar*
¾ *pint milk*

Make a thin custard with the egg yolks, 2 oz. sugar and the milk. Whip the egg whites, fold in the rest of the sugar. Pour the custard into an ovenproof dish. Put spoonfuls of the egg white on to it. Bake in a hot oven for 5 minutes. The custard can be flavoured with grated lemon peel or vanilla.

FRUIT CHIFFON PIE

pie crust as for apple pie (see p. 431)
1 banana
1 tablespoon lemon juice
2 tablespoons orange juice
2 slices tinned pineapple, crushed
¼ pint double cream

8 oz. sugar
1 tablespoon gelatine

Slice the banana, soak in the fruit juices. Add the pineapple. Dissolve the gelatine in a little cold water. Add the fruit, sugar and enough hot water to make up 1 pint. Fold in the whipped cream when the elly is nearly set. Pour into the baked pie crust. Serve very cold.

MELON WITH PINEAPPLE

1 cantaloupe or honeydew melon
1 small pineapple
1 tablespoon chopped mint
4 oz. sugar

Peel and dice the pineapple. Sprinkle with sugar. Cut the melon into halves, remove the seeds. Fill each half with pineapple. Chill. Sprinkle with mint immediately before serving.

PUMPKIN PIE

pie crust as for apple pie (see p. 431)
1½ cups pumpkin
2 eggs
6 oz. brown sugar
½ teaspoon ginger
juice and grated peel of 1 lemon
½ teaspoon cinnamon
vanilla

½ pint milk
¼ pint cream

Prick the pie crust and bake for 10 minutes. Cut the pumpkin in half and remove the seeds, bake in a moderate oven until tender. Remove the flesh and sieve it. Mix it with the egg yolks, brown sugar, milk and flavourings. Whisk the egg whites and fold them into the pumpkin mixture. Bake in a hot oven for 15 minutes, and more slowly for another 35 minutes.

SNOW PUDDING

2 tablespoons sugar
3 eggs
½ pint milk
1 oz. gelatine
2 tablespoons lemon juice

Soak the gelatine in a little cold water, pour on the lemon juice and enough very hot water to make a pint of jelly. Add the sugar. Fold in the stiffly beaten egg whites. Leave ths to set. Make an egg custard with the egg yolks and the milk. Pour the custard round the jelly before serving.

STRAWBERRY SHORTCAKE

8 *oz. flour*
2 *eggs*
1½ *oz. sugar*
4 *teaspoons baking powder*
1 *oz. butter*
milk
1 *lb. strawberries*
icing sugar

Sieve the baking powder with the flour, add the sugar. Cut the butter in with a knife. Beat the eggs, stir them gently into the mixture. Mix with enough milk to bind. Roll out to fill a tart tin. Bake in a hot oven for 20 minutes. Cut in half. Fill with the strawberries, which should have been hulled and halved. Cover with the other half and sprinkle with icing sugar.

THANKSGIVING PUDDING

4 *oz. suet*
4 *oz. breadcrumbs*
2 *oz. flour*
6 *oz. chopped figs*
8 *oz. brown sugar*
2 *oz. raisins*
8 *oz. walnuts, chopped*

4 *eggs*
cinnamon
nutmeg
2 *teaspoons baking powder*

Mix all the dry ingredients together. Stir in the beaten eggs. Beat for 15 minutes. Steam for 4 hours.

TRANSPARENT PIE

4 *eggs*
4 *oz. butter*
12 *oz. sugar*
3 *tablespoons lemon juice*
1 *teaspoon grated lemon peel*

Make pastry with 8 oz. flour as for double crust apple pie (see p. 431). Bake it blind in a greased tart tin in a hot oven for 10 minutes. Fill with the following mixture:
Cream the butter with 8 oz. sugar until almost white. Stir the beaten egg yolks into the butter and sugar and add the lemon juice and peel. Pour this into the pie shell and bake in a slow oven for 30 minutes. Beat the egg whites stiffly. Fold in the rest of the sugar. Arrange on top of the pie and bake in a cool oven until the meringue is set.

PECAN PIE

5 oz. flour
3 oz. cooking fat
2 oz. butter
pinch salt
3 tablespoons water
3 oz. brown sugar
10 oz. black treacle
3 eggs
1 teaspoon vanilla essence
6 oz. shelled pecan nuts

Sift the flour and salt, and rub in the cooking fat. Add water to make a good dough, roll out and line an 8-inch flan tin. For the filling, cream together the butter and sugar until light and fluffy. Add treacle, beaten eggs and vanilla essence and mix well. Finally add the pecans. Pour the mixture into the pie case and bake in a hot oven for 10 minutes. Lower the heat to moderate and bake for a further 30 minutes. Serve hot or cold with cream.

BAKED ALASKA

1 tin raspberries
1 sponge cake
1 ice cream block
2 egg whites
2 tablespoons sugar

Arrange the sponge cake in a fireproof dish. Pour the tinned raspberries over it and leave to soak for 30 minutes. Whisk the egg whites, fold in the sugar. Cover the cake with the ice cream to within 1 inch of the edges. Pour the meringue mixture over the top, making sure that all the ice cream is covered. Bake in a hot oven for 10 minutes.

BUTTERSCOTCH PARFAIT

2 oz. brown sugar
2 oz. butter
4 egg yolks
¼ pint double cream
½ teaspoon vanilla
¼ teaspoon salt

Melt the butter, add the sugar, cook for 1 minute. Add ¼ pint water, cook until smooth and syrupy. Add the beaten egg yolks, cook slowly, stirring all the time until the mixture thickens. Cool, add to the whipped cream. Flavour with vanilla and salt. Freeze in refrigerator, stirring every hour.

FROZEN EGGNOG

1 ice cream
1 glass brandy or rum

Stir the brandy into the ice cream. Chill again before serving.

Yugoslavia

COOKING IN YUGOSLAVIA

For most people, Yugoslavia evokes the rugged and sunny beauty of the Dalmatian coast, the heavenly bathing in the buoyant Adriatic. The Adriatic along the Dalmatian coast is in fact the only sea I know where one can go for a swim before breakfast *and* enjoy it!

Yugoslav cookery has a slightly Eastern, rich flavour; it uses all the fresh vegetables which you find in such abundance in most parts of Yugoslavia.

The representative Yugoslav dish, which you are bound to taste and like as soon as you get to the country, is Djuvetsch. Village women will be seen balancing big dishes gracefully on their heads in Yugoslavia as they are taking the family Djuvetsch to the bakehouse. The curious thing is that this ancient Yugoslav dish is simply a straightforward casserole and very easy to prepare. It is an excellent one-course meal, because the meat, vegetables and rice are all cooked together in a highly commendable way.

SCRAMBLED EGGS WITH MUSHROOMS

8 oz. mushrooms
1 small onion, sliced
1 tomato, peeled and chopped
1 green pepper, seeded and
    chopped
4 eggs
2 tablespoons olive oil
1 oz. butter

salt, pepper

Fry the onion lightly in the oil, add the other vegetables, mix well, cover and stew slowly until tender. Season with salt and pepper. Transfer to a serving dish. Scramble the eggs in the butter. Serve them on top of the mixed vegetables.

DJUVETSCH: MEAT WITH RICE AND VEGETABLES

1½ lb. mixed pork, veal and beef
4 onions, sliced
4 tomatoes, peeled and quartered
2 carrots, sliced
1 green pepper, seeded and sliced
1 stick celery, chopped
6 oz. uncooked rice
1 teaspoon paprika
2 oz. lard

salt, pepper

Cut the meat into pieces. Brown it in the lard. Transfer to a casserole. Fry the rice in the lard. Add it to the casserole. Fry the onions and add them with the other vegetables. Season with salt, pepper and paprika. Pour in enough hot water to barely cover the contents of the casserole. Cook with a lid on, in a moderate oven for 2 hours.

VEAL WITH MUSHROOMS

1½ lb. veal
4 oz. mushrooms
4 tomatoes, peeled and sliced
2 oz. lard
1 teaspoon paprika
4 oz. cooked rice
4 oz. grated Gruyère cheese
1 oz. butter

Cut the veal into slices. Brown them in the lard, stir in the paprika, add a little water and simmer for 5 minutes. Slice the mushrooms and stew them slowly in the butter for 10 minutes. In a casserole arrange alternate layers of meat, rice, mushrooms and tomatoes, ending with a layer of rice. Sprinkle with grated cheese. Bake in a moderate oven for 15 minutes. Finish under a grill if the cheese is not sufficiently brown.

YUGOSLAVIAN SAUSAGES

1 lb. lean beef
2 oz. fat beef
1 lb. veal
salt and pepper
4 oz. chopped onions

Mince the beef and veal finely and blend all together with salt and pepper. Press into small sausages and cook in a very hot oven or over an open fire until well browned.
Serve with finely chopped raw onions.

A Few Hints

Cream: can be soured by the addition of a few drops of lemon juice. Leaving it to turn sour is not satisfactory if the cream has been pasteurised.

Pastry: any pastry shell which is to be filled with a wet mixture should be brushed with melted butter to prevent sogginess.

Tomatoes: English tomatoes are often slightly under-ripe and should therefore be slightly sweetened. They are improved by a little sugar, and so are new carrots.

Sauces: are less likely to lump if the liquid being added is hot. This is particularly important with milk sauces.

Mayonnaise: must be made in a cool place or it will curdle; if it curdles it can sometimes be restored to the proper consistency by the addition of another egg yolk.

Icing sugar and baked breadcrumbs: if these are put into paper bags before being rolled out they cannot fly all over the place and can easily be poured into a bowl.

Flouring meat, fish, etc.: do this on a sheet of clean paper which can be thrown away. It saves a lot of messy washing up.

Pancakes: keep a small bowl of melted butter beside the stove and brush the pan with it between each pancake.

Deep fat frying: olive oil is the most satisfactory for this as it boils at a higher temperature than animal fat. A pint of olive oil kept especially for the purpose lasts a long time.

Lettuce: never cut lettuce leaves; if they *must* be reduced in size, tear them.

Vinegar: always use wine or tarragon vinegar. Malt vinegar is only suitable for pickling.

Butter: use real butter whenever possible, though the margarines containing ten per cent butter make a good substitute. Margarine, however, is not good for frying.

Stock: keep meat trimmings, vegetable water, etc., for the stock pot if you have one. Concentrated *bouillon* cubes are very good (particularly the ones made by the Swiss firm, Knorr) but do not provide the variety of the home-made kind.

Vanilla: vanilla pods have a flavour different from, and far nicer than, vanilla essence. They keep indefinitely in airtight jars. Keep one in a jar of sugar reserved for cooking cakes, pastries, etc., which demand vanilla flavouring.

Cinnamon: cinnamon, too, is much better bought in the piece than in powder form.

A Note on Wines

Wines are usually known by the places or districts from which they come — the finer wines, often, by the names of individual villages, vineyards, or châteaux, that have become famous. A wine list may look complicated, but it becomes much simpler when you realise that the different types of wine are grouped together — all the Bordeaux wines, red and white ('Claret' is the English name for red Bordeaux); all the Burgundies ('Bourgogne' is the French word); the Rhône wines, the Hocks (Rhine wines), Moselles, Alsatians; the Chiantis and other Italian wines; the Champagnes; and, of course, the Sherries and Ports. Australia, Cyprus, and South Africa, too, provide sound table wines, both red and white, besides Sherries and dessert wines.

Some wines in a wine list will have their years opposite them. Of course there is a vintage every year, but the years when the wine is especially good are called 'vintage years'. The best of the recent vintages for most table wines are 1934, 1937, 1943, 1945, 1947, 1948, 1949, 1952, 1953, 1955, 1957, 1959, and 1961. For Port the best years are 1927, 1934, 1935, 1940, 1942, 1945, 1947, 1948, 1950, and 1955.

The choice of what wine you drink with a particular food is a matter of personal preference. Experience shows that the combinations below go very well together.

Soup, hors d'oeuvre:
  a dry or medium dry Sherry. Dry Madeira is good, too.

Shellfish, oysters, fish, cold chicken, salads:
  a dry white wine, such as Hock, Moselle, White Burgundy, or Graves.
  Champagne.

Roast chicken, game, goose or duck, most meat dishes:
  a red wine, usually a light one like a Claret or a rosé with white meats, and a heavier wine, like a Burgundy, with red meats and the stronger flavours — your opportunity to serve the finest vintage wine.

Sweets, ices:
  a sweet white wine — for example, Sauternes, Champagne.

Nuts, coffee:
  a dessert wine: Vintage port, or the less expensive Ruby Port.

As an *Apéritif* to stimulate the appetite before meals, an alternative to Port, Sherry or Madeira is Vermouth, sweet or dry. Served chilled, Vermouth makes a very pleasant appetiser. For Cups for parties or dances, the most usual base is Claret for a red wine cup, or Hock or Moselle for white. Mulled Wine (heated spiced wine) makes a fine winter drink. The best base is Burgundy, or any full-bodied red wine.

Take care that your wines are served at the proper temperatures. White and Rosé wines should be served cold: if they are dry, 45° to 53° F, if sweet 40° F, but not iced. Red wines should be served at normal room temperature — take the chill off but do not heat — Bordeaux at about 64° F, Burgundy at about 59° or 60° F. Champagne and sparkling wines should be served slightly chilled. Use the refrigerator with discretion; never put ice in the wine itself; never use a swizzle stick for Champagne; never warm or chill wines too much or too quickly. Take the greatest care in handling fine vintage wines. Watch for deposits or sediments. If the wine shows a sediment use a wicker cradle for service, or decant it.

Learn to choose and serve your fine wines correctly so that they blend properly with each course to make a perfect meal.

INDEX